ISLAM IN ASIA

This book was prepared as part of a project
organized by The Asia Society, New York,
on "Islam and Public Life in Asia."

ISLAM IN ASIA

Religion, Politics, and Society

Edited by

JOHN L. ESPOSITO

New York   Oxford
OXFORD UNIVERSITY PRESS
1987

Oxford University Press

Oxford   New York   Toronto
Delhi   Bombay   Calcutta   Madras   Karachi
Petaling Jaya   Singapore   Hong Kong   Tokyo
Nairobi   Dar es Salaam   Cape Town
Melbourne   Auckland

and associated companies in
Beirut   Berlin   Ibadan   Nicosia

Copyright © 1987 by The Asia Society

Published by Oxford University Press, Inc.,
200 Madison Avenue, New York, New York 10016

Oxford is a registered trademark of Oxford University Press

Library of Congress Cataloging-in-Publication Data
Islam in Asia.
Bibliography: p.
1. Islam—Asia. 2. Islamic countries. I. Esposito, John L.
BP63.A1I85 1987   297′.197′095   86-18024
ISBN 0-19-504081-3
ISBN 0-19-504082-1 (pbk.)

1 3 5 7 9 8 6 4 2
Printed in the United States of America

PREFACE

To the extent that Americans are aware of Islam in Asia, their views are strongly conditioned by such dramatic events as the Islamic revolution in Iran, the struggle of the mujahideen in Afghanistan, and the communal violence between Hindus and Muslims in India. To focus solely on these events, however significant, perpetuates several unfortunate misperceptions about Islam. First, Islam is frequently viewed as necessarily violent, anti-Western, and politically and socially reactionary. Second, the sudden spotlight on isolated events distracts observers from an appreciation of the longer-term evolution of the relationship between Islam and society in Asia. Although Islam has provided an underlying unity in fundamental belief and practice, its interaction with diverse cultures and ethnic groups has resulted in Muslim societies with distinctive features and experiences. Third, a focus on dramatic events tends to blind Americans to the varied approaches that the people and governments of Asia are taking in determining the roles Islam plays in their societies today.

Recognizing the need to step beyond the stereotypes and headlines, The Asia Society developed a project in 1983 on Islam and public life in Asia. This project, one of several under the Society's Asian Agenda program, was designed to foster increased American understanding of, and Asian-American dialogue on, the role of Islam in contemporary Asian politics and society. Under the direction of Dr. John L. Esposito, Professor of Religious Studies at Holy Cross College, an interrelated series of conferences, public meetings, and publications was organized by the society. This included a two-day conference in March 1984 that involved fifty Asians and Americans with an interest in Islam in Asia. The conference was followed by public meetings and smaller conferences cosponsored with world affairs councils and universities in fifteen American cities from Boston to Honolulu.

In addition to sponsoring these meetings, The Asia Society commissioned a group of leading American and Asian specialists to write studies on selected aspects of Islam in Asia. Because the vastness of Asia precluded a comprehensive study, it was decided to focus on countries that demonstrate the diversity, complexity, and vitality of Islamic life in Asia. In keeping with the project's public education objectives, it was also decided that the chapters should be written in language accessible to the nonspecialist. The result is a volume that examines the range of issues facing Muslims across Asia today.

This book has been prepared under the auspices of The Asia Society's national public education program on contemporary Asian affairs, America's Asian Agenda. The Asian Agenda program seeks to alert Americans to critical issues in Asian affairs and in U.S.-Asian relations, to illuminate the choices that public and private policymakers face, and to strengthen trans-Pacific dialogue on the issues. Through studies, national and international conferences, regional public programs in the United States, and corporate and media activities, the program involves American and Asian specialists and opinion leaders in a far-reaching educational process.

The Asia Society is indebted to many individuals and organizations for their contributions to the project on Islam and public life in Asia. At the top of the list is John L. Esposito. His knowledge and enthusiasm guided and sustained the project over the past three and one-half years. We are very grateful to all the authors for their thoughtful contributions to this volume, as well as for their participation in the project's earlier activities. We also want to thank the many other Asians and Americans, too numerous to name, who participated in the project's planning and activities.

The Asia Society is grateful to a number of organizations whose support made this project possible. The Andrew W. Mellon Foundation and the U.S. Information Agency provided grants that were critical to the project's success. General program support from the Ford, Rockefeller, and Luce foundations and the Rockefeller Brothers Fund was essential to the Islam project as well as to the parent Asian Agenda program.

Several members of The Asia Society's staff were instrumental in the development and execution of the project leading up to this publication. The greatest credit goes to David G. Timberman, who oversaw the project from conception to completion. His intelligence, good judgment, and perseverance were vital to the project's success. He was ably assisted by Mary Lane, who organized the project's conference and public programs with great skill and aplomb. Eileen D. Chang brought the book manuscript to publication. John Bresnan provided valuable advice and support in the early stages of the project.

Finally, the staff of the Society are grateful to its president, Robert B. Oxnam, who has provided the initial vision and the ongoing support that made possible the project and the parent Asian Agenda program.

December 1986   Marshall M. Bouton
                                                   Director, Contemporary Affairs
                                                   The Asia Society

CONTENTS

Islam in Asia: Ally or Adversary?   3
David D. Newsom

1. Islam in Asia: An Introduction   10
   John L. Esposito

2. Iran: Implementation of an Islamic State   27
   Shahrough Akhavi

3. Pakistan: Islamic Government and Society   53
   Kemal A. Faruki

4. Afghanistan: Islam and Counter-
   revolutionary Movements   79
   Ashraf Ghani

5. The Philippines: Autonomy for the Muslims   97
   Lela Garner Noble

6. Soviet Central Asia and China: Integration
   or Isolation of Muslim Societies   125
   John Obert Voll

7. India: Muslim Minority Politics and Society   152
   Syed Shahabuddin and Theodore Paul Wright, Jr.

8. Malaysia: Islam and Multiethnic Politics   177
   Fred R. von der Mehden

9. Indonesia: Islam and Cultural Pluralism   202
   Anthony H. Johns

10. Asian Islam: International Linkages
    and Their Impact on International Relations   230
    James P. Piscatori

Glossary   262
Selected Bibliography   265
Contributors   269
Index   271

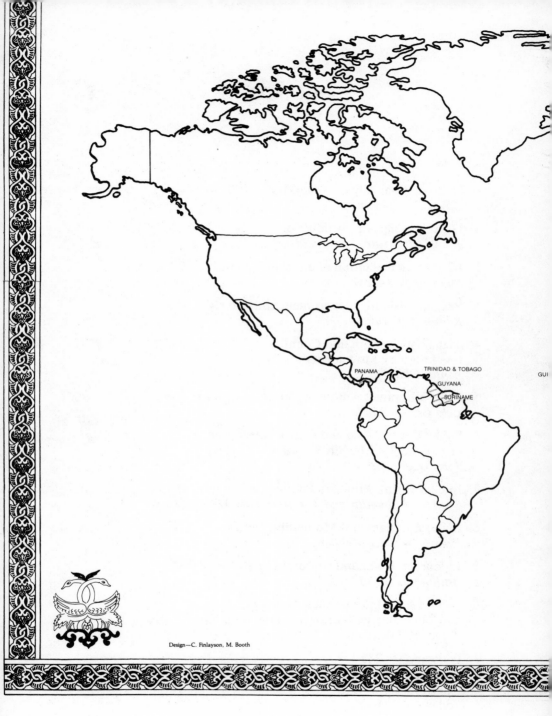

PANAMA

TRINIDAD & TOBAGO

GUI

GUYANA

SURINAME

Design—C. Finlayson, M. Booth

The Peoples of Islam

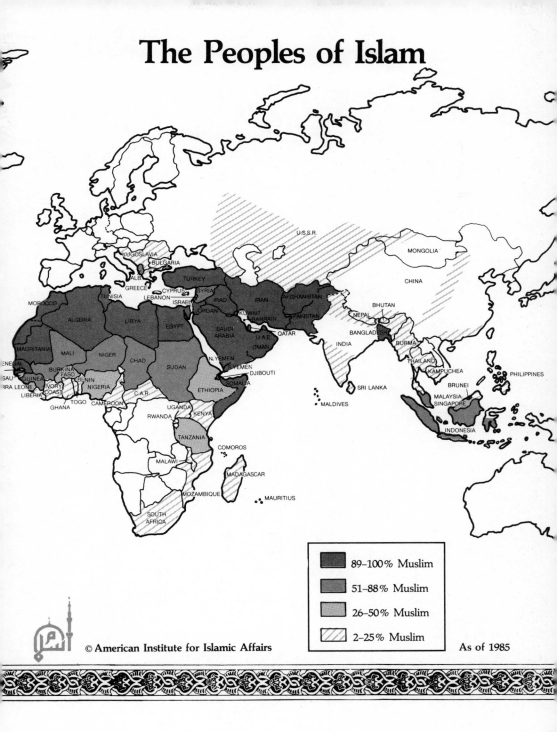

■	89–100% Muslim
▨	51–88% Muslim
▨	26–50% Muslim
▧	2–25% Muslim

© **American Institute for Islamic Affairs**

As of 1985

ISLAM IN ASIA

ISLAM IN ASIA
Ally or Adversary?

DAVID D. NEWSOM

The Need for Understanding

Although Islam is associated in the minds of many Americans with the Arab world, the vast majority of its adherents live in Asia—east of the Persian Gulf. The way in which the United States regards Islam and reacts to events in the Islamic world is no less important a factor in U.S.-Asian relations than it is in U.S.-Middle East relations: Islam creates links and common concerns between these two otherwise quite different regions of the world.

The impression Americans have of another nation or region is inevitably a factor in formulating policy, particularly in a democracy. Policymakers can go only so far in establishing a satisfactory international relationship in the face of negative public perceptions. If the public perceives the people of a country or region as hostile, cruel, greedy, or strange, establishing positive policies toward those people becomes very difficult. American attitudes toward Islam, for example, inevitably affect, in turn, Muslim attitudes toward the United States. Many in the Muslim world look favorably on, and are inclined toward, the United States, but they are inhibited in expressing their views by the strong belief in the Muslim world that the United States is anti-Islam. The image problem is further complicated in the eyes of friends of the United States in Asian Muslim countries because the Western media seem to focus only on the political activities of extremist Muslim movements, not on the more positive aspects of the Muslim community.

The dialogue between the United States and the countries of Islam has not been an easy one. Those who have tried to explain the Islamic world to Americans and vice versa have a sense of the problem. It is often difficult to be a credible interlocutor without being perceived by Muslims as either insensitive by Muslims or an advocate of an unpopular cause by Americans.

American Attitudes Toward Islam

For a variety of reasons, the attitude of many Americans toward the Islamic world tends to be negative. This tendency has now been compounded by a series of recent events in which nations and movements associated with Islam are seen to be striking directly at American interests. The list of anti-American actions is long and includes the policies of Muammar Qaddafi; the postrevolutionary policies of Ruhollah Khomeini; the assassination of America's allies, such as Anwar Sadat; and the taking of innocent American hostages. Some in the United States even blame the increase in world oil prices on Islam: "Racked . . . by powerful sentiment of grievance and resentment against the West, the Arabs see the oil weapon as a gift sent by God to redress the balance between Christendom and Islam."[1]

There is no doubt that the Muslim worldview is fundamentally different than that of the average American and therefore requires an effort to comprehend. In its original form, Islam combined government and religion—a strong contrast to the U.S. secularist tradition of separating church and state. Another area of cultural discrepancy is the notion of the political legitimacy of nation-states—a concept foreign to traditional Islam. Instead, in Islam, the worldwide religious community (ummah) takes precedence. Attitudes toward one's fellow man and non-Muslim states or societies are determined by their perceived relationship to this global religious community. The United States, by contrast, is a multiethnic, multireligious, secular society—albeit with strong Judeo-Christian overtones.

Americans have difficulty identifying with Islam as easily as they do with Judaism or even with some Eastern religions. Islam is recognized as a significant religion, yet those of the Judeo-Christian tradition find much in Islam difficult to comprehend. Americans frequently ask such questions as "Where is the power in Islam?" "Why is it spreading?" and "What is the appeal of so inhumane a religion?" The difficulty of empathizing with Muslims is compounded in the case of church groups in the United States who often see Islam as the primary obstacle to missionaries propagating the Christian faith abroad.

Of course, all Americans do not regard the Islamic world negatively nor do they fail to differentiate between Muslim countries. The American view of Iran is quite different from the attitude of knowledgeable Americans toward Pakistan, Indonesia, Malaysia, or the countries of the Maghreb.

If there is a broadly negative view of Islam in the United States, it springs primarily from two perceptions. One is that Islam, particularly fundamentalist Islam, represents a threat to the interests of the United States. The other is that Islam is basically an inhumane religion. The feeling that Islam in its more militant form represents a threat to the United States is given particular significance because in certain countries, such as Libya and the Philippines, Islam is identified with direct attacks on strategic U.S. interests. Muslim countries are located on important trade routes and hold most of the world's proven oil reserves. Islamic revivalism, therefore, gets more media attention than might similar religious revivals in, say, India or African countries.

The American perception of a threatening Islam is mitigated where the Soviet Union is the target. Islamic fervor in Iran is regarded negatively for causing domestic turmoil and for its threat to political stability in the region, but it is viewed positively in Central Asia and in Afghanistan where it functions to unify resistance to Soviet incursions. In such a case, the perception is that U.S. and Muslim interests are parallel. It is not unnatural that we in the United States should see Islam, even in a militant guise, as a positive factor in those circumstances in which it is used to confront our primary adversary and as a negative factor where it is used to confront the United States and governments friendly to us. Nevertheless, particularly since the revolution in Iran and the events in Lebanon, the tendency seems to be to focus more on the negative aspects and on Islamic movements that confront U.S. interests.

The second source of Americans' negative image of Islam is a distorted view of Islamic social customs. Islam as described by the popular media lends itself to sensationalism, for example, Islamic law penalties, such as flogging, as well as reported acts of fanaticism and terrorism. The fanaticism of Iran has received special attention in connection with events in Lebanon and the Iran-Iraq War:

> Over the centuries, the winds of fanaticism have blown up a merciless throng of killers: the assassins, thugs, kamikazes—and now the suicide bombers. They believe that they are going to a great reward. To die in a jihad, or "holy war," offers a direct passport to Allah and Ali, the revered son-in-law and cousin of the prophet Muhammad. To kill large numbers of infidels in the process is only a greater glory. They may receive a final blessing in a secret ceremony before embarking on their sacred mission. Then they ram their trucks through enemy barricades, detonate their deadly cargo and destroy themselves along with their adversaries—all the while wearing a serene smile of inner peace.[2]

And in a review of contemporary Iran, "Iran: Five Years of Fanaticism," Terence Smith correctly observes that the Iranian revolution grew out of Iranian nationalism, xenophobia, and Islamic fundamentalism. He does, however, take note of the degree to which the strict Islamic code of behavior has had its impact on current Iran:

> Published press reports by the few Western journalists who have been able to visit Khomeini's Iran provide striking glimpses of the new way of life. Women are not to appear in public except in chador, the shapeless black robe that obscures from head to foot. Those who venture out in Western dress risk arrest by Revolutionary Guards, who function as self-appointed keepers of the public morality. Some of the women arrested are held until they sign documents saying they are prostitutes—not the sort of document an Iranian woman wants in the files of the revolutionary administrators.[3]

Because of the close relationship between the United States and Pakistan, considerable attention has been given to the imposition by President Zia ul-Haq of an Islamic code in that country. Press accounts in recent years have focused on the introduction of flogging, greater restrictions on the dress and participation of women in public life, and the conflict between science and Islam.[4] As in the case of Iran, Americans associate Islam with the imposition of restrictive customs. This attention to social customs based on the Islamic legal code reinforces stereotypes common to conventional American wisdom. Islam is identified with polygamy, the seclusion of women, and harsh forms of justice.

There are other obstacles that confound an understanding of Islam in the United States. Some areas of Islam, particularly the Shi'ite areas, are difficult for outsiders to visit and study. The restrictions on travel by non-Muslims to the holy places of Saudi Arabia and Iranian restriction on visits to many of the mosques by outsiders exemplify this inaccessibility.

Understanding Muslim Perspectives

Where accessibility exists, the direct and contentious style of questioning on the part of the Western press makes communication with even friendly, moderate Muslims difficult. Muslims feel obliged to be defensive even though they may personally disapprove of much that goes on. They cannot be totally dispassionate in their comments if they are to be credible to their own people and perhaps to themselves. They may share the non-Muslim's concern over the rise and excesses of fundamentalist Islamic groups, but because they see Western attacks on fundamentalist Islam encompassing all of Islam, they often feel compelled to defend even radical approaches.

It appears to Western observers that Muslims, including Muslim scholars, seem to have difficulty in explaining their religion and society in ways that will be read and understood by outsiders. Muslim writers have a tendency to be theological in their approach and to use extensive Arabic terms and Islamic concepts that bewilder the American reader. It is ironic and unfortunate that there are not many current popular books on Islam written by Muslims.

These communication problems are compounded by basic political differences between Islamic nations and the United States. For years one of the central obstacles to effective relations has been the conflict between the Arab states and Israel. Although the issue has political, territorial, and ethnic contexts, it also has a deep religious element. Muslims from Morocco to Indonesia, both Arabs and non-Arabs, feel sympathetic to the Palestinian cause in varying degrees.

The future and present status of Jerusalem, for example, is an issue that evokes an emotional response throughout the world of Islam. Moving the

U.S. embassy from Tel Aviv to Jerusalem—which has been proposed—
would have repercussions throughout the Islamic world. It is a regrettable
fact that throughout this area the United States is regarded as being on
the wrong side of a very important issue. U.S. identification with Israel
can impede cooperation even in countries far from the Middle East. The
fact that Indonesians and Malaysians feel strongly about aspects of the
Arab-Israeli problem comes as a surprise to many Americans. That reaction is symptomatic of how little Americans understand the thread of solidarity that runs throughout Islam despite differences among Muslim
states.

Cultural encroachments from the West also are seen as a threat to the
stability of Muslim societies. Deep within the traditions of these societies
are lingering feelings regarding the Crusades, which are compounded by
the humiliation that comes from a recollection of the European and
American domination of once-great Islamic societies. Today, this is
aggravated by American publications and films whose attitudes toward
Islam range from patronizing to insulting. Novels, television shows, and
films that express stereotypes of sheikhs as villains arouse particular ire.
Islamic traditions are portrayed without adequate consideration of historic truths or Muslim sensibilities.

Guidelines for Better Understanding

Perhaps the United States is not on a collision course with the Islamic
world, but it is hard to deny that serious problems of understanding and
communication exist. Beyond this lies the concern that if this state of
affairs is not adjusted, substantial interests of both the United States and
Muslim countries can be affected.

There are no easy answers to the differences that exist between Islam
and the West. But are there guidelines for establishing better communication and an effective policy with Islamic nations, including those in
Asia? I think there are.

First, it is important for Americans to realize that, as is true of other
major religions, Islam is diverse. Generalizations are particularly dangerous about a religion that exists in so many different countries and cultures. There are significant differences between a country where Islam
appears in a fundamentalist guise, as in Iran, and where it appears in a
syncretic guise, as in Indonesia. In most countries with Muslim majorities, there is a clear separation between government and religion. In such
cases, these governments share the concern of outsiders over the activities of fundamentalist Islamic movements within their borders.

Second, it is important to recognize that the religious factor is not the
only one. Sensitivity to Western influence in a number of Muslim countries is also based on nationalism, cultural traditions, ethnic pride, economic deprivation, and contests for regional power. The recent history of

the nations of Southeast Asia, each one of which has a Muslim population, is a fortunate one. Successful development has eased economic tensions. The existence of the Association of South East Asian Nations (ASEAN) has minimized the contest for power that might otherwise have erupted in that strategic area of the world. The constant jockeying for political supremacy that exists in the Arab world is fortunately less so in Southeast Asia.

Third, in its approach to the Islamic world, the United States needs to realize that many of our more sensational cultural phenomena are seen as a threat to Islamic society. We cannot stop the flow of rock music, dress styles, movies, and modern mores to other countries. However, if we are to understand the often bitter attitudes in Muslim countries toward us, we must recognize the depth of reactions to the spread of Western social patterns even in the less conservative societies. We should not regard it as a matter of ridicule or a threat to our global political and strategic interests or our basic belief in the dignity of man if there is resistance to the spread of the commercialized popular culture so identified with us abroad.

Expressions of U.S. respect for Islam that are not patronizing and do not disguise the basic problems that exist will evoke a reciprocal reaction from most Muslim states. Such respect can further our relationship with important communities that are under stress, such as those in Afghanistan and in Central Asia. However, in other areas, the Philippines, for example, too direct an American approach to Islamic-related problems can be considered gross interference. These are problems in which the United States cannot play an effective role, and there is very little benefit to be gained by attempting to do so.

In our most trying situation in the Islamic world, namely, Iran, it is difficult to foresee any effective resumption of communications. Although frustrating, it is a fact of life that the United States cannot play a role either in moderating the Iranian revolution or in bringing the Iran-Iraq War to a close. In this treacherous area, only time and patience may bring an opportunity to restore some kind of effective American relationship. It is important meanwhile that we do not apply the Iranian experience to the whole Muslim world or see every impending problem as another Iran.

Is Islam an ally of U.S. interests or a threat? In a sense, this is a false dichotomy. Extreme manifestations of any religion, particularly when combined with deep social and economic inequities, can pose a serious threat to the stability of a country or a region. So it is with Islam. That should not blind Americans to positive relationships with the nations and peoples of the Islamic world. Those relationships, however, are vulnerable to the emotional fervor of fundamentalist belief. That vulnerability can be increased if the United States in the pursuit of its global policies fails to understand and to take into account the issues, the sensitivities, and the desire for respect that are important to Muslim peoples everywhere.

Notes

1. "War Against the West," by J. B. Kelly, *New Republic,* October 11, 1980, pp. 16–19.
2. "The Suicide Bombers," *Newsweek,* November 14, 1983, pp. 69–71.
3. "Iran: Five Years of Fanaticism," Terence Smith, *New York Times Magazine,* February 12, 1984, pp. 21–30.
4. "Trying the Domino Theory on for Size: First Iran, Now Pakistan," *Christianity Today,* April 20, 1979, pp. 46–47; "An Islamic Journey Among the Believers," V. S. Naipul, *Atlantic Monthly,* August 1981, pp. 57–69; "Sectarian Split Thwarts Pakistan's Efforts to Forge Islamic State," *Washington Post,* January 24, 1982, p. A25; "Pakistan Has a Conflict Between Science and Islam," *New York Times,* February 21, 1982, p. E9.

1

ISLAM IN ASIA
An Introduction

JOHN L. ESPOSITO

Islam is the second largest of the world's religions, numbering in excess of 800 million Muslims. The Islamic world includes not only the forty-five Muslim countries that extend from North Africa to South East Asia but also significant Muslim communities in Europe (9 million), the Soviet Union (40 to 60 million), and America (3 million). Yet, it is not the size but the events in the Muslim world throughout the past decade that have focused attention on Islam and Muslim politics in an unprecedented manner: the Arab oil boycott, the Iranian revolution, the Soviet invasion of Afghanistan, Anwar Sadat's assassination, and the Moro independence movement in the southern Philippines.

Increasingly, both Muslim governments and opposition movements appeal to Islam to legitimate their activities and to gain popular support. The rulers of Pakistan and Iran have been overthrown in the name of Islam. Military rulers, ayatollahs, Islamic organizations, and terrorist groups have justified their actions in the name of Islam. The actions and political rhetoric of the day seem to affirm the commitment of many Muslims to a more Islamic political, social, and economic order. Despite the pervasiveness of this phenomenon and its geopolitical significance, our understanding of the contemporary Islamic world has remained astonishingly limited.

Although Islam is truly a world religion, despite the fact that the majority of Muslims live in Asia, for most Americans Islam has tended to be identified primarily as an Arab or Middle Eastern religion. In fact, the Arabs have played a central role in the history of Islam. God's revelation (the Quran) occurred in Arabia to an Arab (the Prophet Muhammad). The language of the Quran and of worship in Islam is Arabic. The historical development of the early Islamic community/state and of Islamic civilization occurred under Arab Muslim rule and patronage. The holiest cities of Islam (Mecca, Medina, Jerusalem) are located in the Arab world.

However, from the ninth century onward, Islamic rule and civilization progressively encompassed Asia and Africa. As a result, the vast majority of Muslims are non-Arab. Indeed, the four most populous Muslim communities are located in Asia: Indonesia, Bangladesh, Pakistan, and India. Their population far exceeds that of the entire Arab Muslim world. More important, Islam in Asia (here defined as extending from Iran to the Philippines) provides the fullest picture of the diverse roles played by Islam in public life today: from Islamic republics (Iran and Pakistan) and Islamic resistance movements (Afghanistan and the Philippines) to the problems of Muslim minorities (India, the Soviet Union, China, the Philippines) and Muslim government accommodation with religious and cultural pluralism (Indonesia and Malaysia).

Despite the richness of the Asian Muslim experience and the proliferation of conferences and publications on Islam during the last few years, a variety of factors, including the geopolitical significance of the major petroleum-producing states, has generally resulted in a disproportionate concentration on the Arab world. The purpose of this volume, like the Asia Society conference that preceded it, is to provide a broader, more balanced perspective of the wide-ranging impact of Islam in the world. Although the vastness of Asia precludes a comprehensive study, we have selected countries that embody the vitality, diversity, and complexity of Islamic life in Asia. Among the central questions addressed in this volume are "How is Islam present in the public life (government, national ideology, law, political parties and actors) of Asian Muslims?" and "In what ways does Islam influence domestic politics as well as the foreign policies of Muslim countries today?"

Islam: Faith and Government

Muslims believe that Islam was revealed by God to guide the personal and public life of all humankind. Its sources are the Quran, the literal and external word of God, and the example of the Prophet. Muhammad (570–632 C.E.) is viewed as the last in a long line of messengers (Adam, Abraham, Moses, and Jesus) sent from God (Allah), first to the Jews and Christians and finally to the Arabs. It is common to date the rise of Islam with the preaching of Muhammad in the early seventh century and the establishment of the first Islamic community/state at Medina in 622.

Islam is a world religion that cuts across tribal, ethnic, and regional/national boundaries. Despite cultural differences, all Muslims share a common set of duties, the Five Pillars of Islam:

1. The profession of faith, that is, witnessing *(shahadah)* that "There is no god but Allah (the God) and Muhammad is his messenger."
2. Prayer *(salat)* performed five times a day.
3. Payment of an alms tax *(zakat).*

4. Fasting during the holy month of Ramadan.
5. The pilgrimage *(hajj)* to Mecca that every adult Muslim, if physically and financially capable, is expected to make.

For Muslims, the divinely mandated duty to submit *(islam)* or to follow God's will is communal as well as individual. All Muslims constitute a community *(ummah),* a brotherhood of believers based upon a shared faith whose identity, unity, and solidarity is supposed to transcend all other loyalties (family, tribal, national). The Islamic community is to be the dynamic vehicle for realization of God's will in history, calling all to worship and serve God.

From its earliest period, Islam bore a distinct difference from its Jewish and Christian sister faiths. The Islamic community was a society in which religion was integral to all areas of life: politics, law, and society. To be a Muslim was to be a member/citizen of a religiopolitical community that was guided by God's revealed will and governed by his messenger, Muhammad, who was both Prophet and head of the community/state in Medina. Islam, then, is a total way of life. For Muslims, belief that religion is not separate from, but rather organically related to, the state, encompassing both private and public life, is rooted in the Quran and the example of the Prophet. This is reflected quite strikingly in the development of Islamic law.

As God's revelation came to be collected and preserved in written form in the Quran, so too Muhammad's words and deeds were collected in narrative reports *(hadith,* traditions) attributed to the Prophet. Both God's revelation and the example of his Prophet reflect the comprehensiveness of Islam. Much of the content of the Quran concerns not only guidelines for worship, but also regulations governing marriage, inheritance, business contracts, criminal punishments, and the conduct of war. Similarly, Muhammad was not only the religious leader, but also the chief executive, judge, and commander-in-chief of the Medinan community/state. As the role model for Muslims, he represented the totality, or all-embracing nature, of Islam. The comprehensiveness of this Islamic vision is articulated and preserved in the formulation of Islamic law, the ideal blueprint or charter for the Islamic state and society.

Islamic law (the *shariah,* path) was developed during the early centuries by jurists who sought to delineate clearly the Islamic way of life. It provides guidelines for private and public life, duties to God and duties to society. Thus, Islamic law encompasses prayer, fasting, and pilgrimage as well as family, criminal, and commercial laws.

Both in Muslim belief and history, religion has occupied an important place in public life: in the ideology of the state and its institutions and in the conduct of politics. Ideologically, the Islamic community *(ummah)* was a religiopolitical state or empire. Muslim rulers (caliphs or sultans), Muhammad's successors as heads of state, were to assure government according to Islam and to spread and defend Islamic rule. The state's official law was the *shariah* (Islamic law) applied by judges *(qadis)* in religious courts.

Given the importance of law, the scholars *(ulama,* learned) who had developed Islamic law became a religious establishment with special status and power in Muslim society. Although there is no official clergy in Islam, the *ulama* functioned as the guardians of religious orthodoxy, the conscience of Islamic society. Because law was a central institution in traditional Islamic society, it was the primary discipline in education. As a result, the *ulama* became a powerful class in Muslim society. They interpreted the law, administered the state's educational system, and controlled religious endowments *(waqf),* that is, property whose income was used to subsidize religious and social services, such as mosques, schools, hospitals, and hostels. They served as advisers and, at times, as critics of Muslim rulers. The importance of law and the *ulama* was further enhanced by the belief in Islamic political thought that a ruler's recognition of Islamic law rather than his moral life was the criterion for establishing the Islamic character and thus the legitimacy of Muslim states and empires.

Islam informed other areas of public life: citizenship, foreign policy, and taxation. Given the ideological orientation of the state, full citizenship was reserved for Muslims. Non-Muslims ("People of the Book," i.e., Christians and Jews) had a protected *(dhimmi)* status. In exchange for payment of a poll tax, they were permitted to practice their religion and to be governed by their own religious leaders, law, and courts. They were also entitled to protection by the Islamic state from external aggression. With exceptions, Christians and Jews generally fared well and made important contributions in government and in commercial and intellectual life.

Religion informed the system of taxation in Islam not only through the poll tax on non-Muslims, but also through a variety of taxes levied on Muslims themselves: an alms tax *(zakat)* on accumulated wealth, an agricultural tax *(ushr),* and a land tax *(kharaj).*

Sunni and Shi'i Islam

The reality of Islamic history often departed from the ideological. Historically, the Muslim community early on divided into two major groups, Sunni and Shi'i. Although sharing a common faith, both differ somewhat in their visions of history, politics, and government. The split occurred over the question of succession after Muhammad's death: Who should lead the Islamic community? The Sunni majority, following the belief that Muhammad had not designated an heir, accepted a process of selection or election of a caliph (successor) as the political authority or head of state. The Shi'i (Party of Ali) believed that Muhammad had designated his cousin and son-in-law, Ali, as his successor and that leadership of the community was restricted to the family of the Prophet. The descendants of Muhammad and Ali, according to the Shi'i, were to be the religiopolitical leaders *(Imams)* of the Islamic community/state. Thus, two forms of Islamic government emerged: the Sunni caliphate and the Shi'i imamate.

Throughout Islamic history, the vast majority of Muslims have remained Sunni. Today, they constitute approximately eighty-five percent of the world's Muslims. With few exceptions, such as Iran, the Shi'i have been citizens in Sunni-governed states. The imamate remained a religiopolitical theory or ideal to be realized at some future date with the coming of a messianic figure, the Mahdi (Guided One). During the interim, Shi'i were to follow the example and leadership of their religious leaders, *ulama* or *mujtahids* (i.e., those who interpret the faith for the community).

Islamic Governments: A Historical Overview

The mission of the Islamic community—to live according to God's law and to extend the rule of Islam throughout the world—influenced the Islamic state's foreign policy. Belief in a universal mission provided the rationale for the expansion of the Pax Islamica through peaceful means and conquest by Muslim traders, mystics *(sufis), ulama,* and soldiers. The world was viewed as consisting of Islamic territory *(dar al-Islam,* the abode of Islam) and non-Islamic territory *(dar al-harb,* the abode of war). Thus both the call to individuals to convert to Islam and the conquest by Muslim armies of non-Muslim empires were legitimated by religion. Within one hundred years of the Prophet's death, the Medinan state had expanded through conquest and peaceful means to become an empire extending from North Africa to South Asia.

> The creation within the space of a single century of a vast Arab Empire stretching from Spain to India is one of the most extraordinary marvels of history. The speed, magnitude, extent and permanence of these conquests excite our wonder and almost affront our reason.[1]

During the Caliphate period (632–1258) an Islamic commonwealth was created with successive capitals at Medina, Damascus, and Baghdad. Stunning political success led to the florescence of law, theology, philosophy, literature, medicine, the sciences, art, and architecture in an Islamic civilization. For Sunni Muslims, these early centuries, when Islam had enormous success, wealth, and power, provided historical validation for the revealed message and universal mission of Islam.

Despite the fall of Baghdad in 1258 and the end of the Islamic caliphate, the expansion of Islam continued as Muslim missionaries, soldiers, traders, and *sufis* carried Islam throughout much of Central and Southeast Asia as well as both West and East Africa. However, unlike the early universal caliphate, the Islamic community and its territory from the thirteenth century consisted of many separate Muslim states or sultanates. Muslim sultanates stretched from Africa to the Indonesian archipelago and included the three imperial sultanates: the Ottoman, the Safavid (Iran-Iraq), and the Moghul (Indian subcontinent). The caliph was replaced by innumerable sultans who continued to rule in the name of Islam.

In understanding contemporary Muslims' sense of their history and its impact upon Muslim aspirations today, it is crucial to note that, despite the breakdown of a central caliphal government, Islam had continued to expand and flourish politically and culturally. The message and rule of Islam were extended throughout much of Asia and Africa, creating new Muslim community/states that professed a loyalty to Islam and whose government and legal, judicial, and educational systems were influenced to varying degrees by Islam. Thus, from Muhammad's seventh-century Arabia to the dawn of European colonialism in the sixteenth century, Islam was an ascendant and expansive religiopolitical movement in which religion was part and parcel of both private and public life.

The expansion of Islam in Asia produced a variety and diversity of Islamically informed societies. All Muslims shared a common faith, confessing their belief in the one God and in his Book and the teaching of his Prophet. However, Islam encountered peoples of vastly different historical backgrounds, languages, ethnic/tribal identities, loyalties, customs, and cultures. In a very real sense an Arab Islam was transformed into Persian, South Asian, and Southeast Asian Islam through the process of assimilation and synthesis. Despite the common core of belief and practice epitomized by the Five Pillars of Islam, Muslim societies differed in the extent and manner to which religion manifested itself in public life—politics, law, and society.

Colonialism

Islamic ascendancy was reversed dramatically from the sixteenth century onward under the impact of European colonialism. The first trade companies proved to be the vanguard of European imperialism. The presence of British, French, Dutch, Russian, and Portuguese trade companies gave way by the nineteenth century to European economic, political, and (often) military dominance in much of the Muslim world.

Independent Muslim states in Africa, the Middle East, and South and Southeast Asia were reduced to European colonies. In Iran and Afghanistan, Great Britain and Russia vied for concessions in tobacco, banking, and railroads. The entire Indian subcontinent (Pakistan, India, and Bangladesh) came under the British raj. Malaysia and Indonesia were governed by the British and Dutch, respectively.

By the late nineteenth and twentieth centuries, European legal codes had replaced much of Islamic and local customary laws. The political, economic, and legal penetration of Muslim societies by the West was further extended as modern Western educational reforms were introduced. Traditional political and religious elites saw their power, prestige, and way of life (customs, values) progressively altered by new "modern," Western-oriented classes of professionals and technocrats. By the twentieth century, the West reigned supreme, dominating much of the Islamic world politically and economically. Its impact on social and cultural life was no less threatening.

Islam and the Modern State

The eclipse of Muslim power and fortunes in a multitude of countries engendered a variety of independence movements during the twentieth century, movements in which Islam reemerged in Muslim public life. In Asia, from Iran to Indonesia, Islam often became a rallying point for anti-colonialism and nationalism. Iranian *ulama* led a successful opposition movement (the Tobacco Protest) in 1891 against the government concessions to the British. The *ulama* then joined with merchants and intellectuals in the Constitutional Revolt (1905–11) that produced both a constitution and a parliament.

In the Indian subcontinent, Islam was used to mobilize Muslims in the Khilafat (Caliphate) Movement to save the Ottoman Empire from dismemberment by the European allies after World War I. Moreover, by the 1930s the Muslim League, which had previously worked closely with the Hindu-dominated Congress Party for an independent, united India, broke with that party and called for a separate Muslim homeland. Islamic ideology, slogans, symbols, and rhetoric were effectively used by the Muslim League in a mass mobilization that culminated in the establishment of Pakistan as a separate state in 1947.

In Southeast Asia the Sarekat Islam (Islamic Union)—established in 1912—gave concrete, organizational expression to a nascent Indonesian nationalism. Islam continued to inform other sociopolitical organizations and parties representing a spectrum of Muslim orientations from conservative to modernist, such as the Muhammadiyah, Masyumi, and Nahdatul Ulama. In the Malay Peninsula, Islam played an important role from its introduction in the mid-fifteenth century by Arab traders and sufi orders. However, unlike Indonesia, religion had not been emphasized in the early development of Malay nationalism. By the mid-1940s, this situation shifted. Malays became increasingly concerned about the British colonial government's proposal to reorganize the traditional Malay states with their sultan-rulers into the Malayan Union. In particular, they feared the reorganization's potential effect on Malay Muslim political dominance and economic well-being vis-à-vis the immigrant, prosperous non-Malay (Chinese and Indian) communities. The Pan-Malayan

Islamic Party, (PMIP, now known as PAS) incorporated conservative religious and militant Malay nationalist concerns. Even the more secular, dominant political party, the United Malay National Organization (UMNO), increasingly devoted more attention to Islamic political rhetoric and Malay Muslim concerns while trying to hold together a multireligious, multiracial society.

Islam in Postindependence Muslim States

Although the experience of Asian Muslims in newly emerging modern states of the post World War II era was quite diverse, for most, Islam became increasingly restricted to private life. The role of religion in public life was either limited or controlled by governments whose elites had little concern for the implementation of religious ideology and who looked to the West for inspiration and models for political and economic development. For countries like Iran and Indonesia, Muslim described the religious background of their population rather than the orientation or practice of their governments. If anything, the Shah of Iran and Sukarno in Indonesia viewed Islam and Islamic activists as forces to be neutralized and controlled. Despite its *raison d'être* as a Muslim homeland, Pakistan's Islamic identity remained politically sensitive but largely unresolved. Afghanistan and Malaysia managed their Islamic identities, like most other Muslim states, through the adoption of a number of constitutional provisions. Such stipulations included acknowledging Islam as the state's religion, requiring that the head of state be a Muslim, and declaring that the *shariah* was a source of the state's law. However, the political, legal, and economic systems of most Muslim countries were otherwise Western in origin and inspiration. In addition, many Asian Muslims faced a new issue that had been a minimal concern in an Islamically autonomous past: life as a minority in non-Muslim-dominated countries, such as India, the Soviet Union, China, and the Philippines.

The Islamic Resurgence

The 1970s represent a new phase in Muslim history. Throughout much of the Islamic world, from the Sudan to the Philippines, religion reasserted itself in Muslim politics in a major and, at times, often volatile manner. The expansion of Islam's role in public life became a key issue in many Muslim societies. Although the Arab oil embargo and the 1973 Arab-Israeli War are often viewed as primary catalysts, the contemporary Islamic revival predates these events and is far more complex in its origins. It is rooted not only in common Muslim concerns and attitudes, but also in specific national experiences.

In many Arab societies, the 1967 Israeli rout of the Arabs led to an identity crisis, a greater concern for authenticity and indigenization, and a desire to link the present with historical and traditional values. This was accomplished by the growth of Islamic organizations; escalating disenchantment with, and criticism of, the West; a "return to the mosque," and a greater emphasis on religious observance. At the same time, events in Asia fostered a climate in which Islam reemerged as a factor, in some situations as *the* factor, in Muslim politics. For example, in Iran the conflict between the Pahlavi monarchy and opposition forces escalated from a reform movement to a clergy-led revolution.

In South Asia, a civil war in 1971 resulted in the secession of Bangladesh from Pakistan and an increasing appeal by the government of Zulfikar Ali Bhutto to Islam in Pakistani politics. The Soviet invasion of Afghanistan in 1978 made that country's liberation an Islamic issue for both Afghan resistance movements and for the international Islamic community. Hindu-Muslim riots brought into focus again the issue of Muslim minority rights in India.

In Southeast Asia, the Malaysian government's attempts to redress conditions that had led to Muslim-Malay-Chinese rioting in 1969 progressively witnessed a reassertion of Malay Muslim identity, the growth of Islamic activism, and the expansion of Islamic institutions in public life. Throughout much of Muslim Asia, the role of Islam in public life has become an important political issue. Whether in Muslim-majority or in Muslim-minority areas (e.g., the Philippines and Thailand), Islam has been appropriated by incumbent governments and opposition movements alike.

The studies that follow investigate the contemporary role of Islam in Asia, addressing such questions as "In what ways has Islam reasserted itself in the public life of Muslim societies from Iran to the Philippines?" "What are the international dimensions of a politicized Islam?" "What does all of this mean for American foreign policy?"

A key factor in U.S. foreign policy and a common criticism of Muslim activists is America's attitude toward Islam in general and Muslim countries in particular. During the past decade, Muslim criticism of America's Arab-Israeli policy has focused on a pervasive bias toward Islam and Muslims, as evidenced by media coverage and the official reaction to events in the Muslim world. In his foreward, David D. Newsom, former under secretary of state, analyzes American attitudes toward Islam and their implications for U.S. foreign policy vis-à-vis Asian Muslim countries. Problems of miscommunication, misperception, and ignorance have planted the seeds of a basically negative attitude toward the Islamic world. "This . . . has now been compounded by a series of recent events in which nations and movements associated with Islam are seen as striking directly at American interests." OPEC, Qaddafi, Khomeini, and Muslim terrorist attacks against U.S. embassies and citizens have reinforced a sense among many that the revival of Islam poses a threat to American global, political, and strategic interests. Newsom discusses a number of guidelines for U.S. policymakers in managing a potentially volatile situation.

American perceptions of Islam and concerns about its potential threat to U.S. interests are often grounded in a very limited awareness of the religiopolitical realities in Muslim countries. As the case studies in this volume demonstrate, although the role of Islam in public life has dramatically increased during the past decade, this is not a monolithic phenomenon. Islamic belief includes a diversity of interpretations, attitudes, and movements. Although many Muslim activists speak of implementing an Islamic alternative to Western secularism, the forms that such attempts take are quite varied. Iran and Pakistan illustrate this fact vividly. Both the Ayatollah Khomeini and General Zia ul-Haq have declared their commitment to implement an Islamic system of government in the Islamic Republic of Iran and the Islamic Republic of Pakistan, respectively. Yet their systems differ markedly. Iran is a clergy-run state, a clericocracy, that functions under the guidance of the Ayatollah Khomeini and his interpretation of Islamic government as rule by the jurisconsult *(vilayat-i-faqih)*. In Pakistan, the process of Islamization of state and society has occurred under martial law. These implementations of Islam reflect the contrasting leadership styles of an ayatollah and a general. Shahrough Akhavi, in chapter 2, analyzes the variety of ways in which Islam permeates Iranian society. He demonstrates Islam's role in political mobilization and ideological militance as well as the extent to which clericalism controls Iran's state institutions and influences political, social, and economic life.

In contrast to Iran, General Zia ul-Haq did not come to power in 1977 through a popular revolution but by a sudden and relatively quiet coup d'état. As Kemal A. Faruki demonstrates in chapter 3, Pakistan's Islamization has been controlled (some would say imposed) not by a religious but by a military leader who exercises final and complete authority over the executive, legislative, and judicial functions of the state. On the one hand, Islamic laws, measures, and institutions that affect political, social (education and the status of women), and economic (taxes and banking) affairs have been introduced. On the other hand, Islam has been used as an excuse for postponing elections, dissolving federal and provincial legislative bodies, and banning all political parties. Although both the Islamic republics of Pakistan and Iran differ in many ways, the impact of Islam on public life has had a similar negative effect on freedom of the press, the status and rights of women and non-Muslim minorities, and on political opposition.

Recent experiments in Pakistan and Iran demonstrate some of the difficulties attending contemporary attempts to establish Islamically oriented states and societies. At issue is the question of pluralism in an ideological state. What limits should Islam place on the activity of political parties, trade unions, political dissent, the media, minorities? Older self-proclaimed Islamic states, such as Saudi Arabia, do not permit political parties or trade unions, nor do they grant citizenship to non-Muslims. More recently implemented Islamic systems have also used the Islamic ideology of the state to restrict political activities. Pakistan has banned political parties; Iran has suppressed opposition parties. Political dissent is rigidly controlled and censorship imposed in the name of Islam. Non-Muslim citizens in a number of Muslim states increasingly fear that Islamic law will be imposed on them and that their full rights as citizens will be reduced to that of protected people *(dhimmi)*. This issue raises the question of tradition and change in Islam. What aspects of Islamic belief and practice are immutable and what areas are open to reconstruction or reinterpretation in responding to new social and historical conditions.

Criticism of Iran and Pakistan's Islamization programs may be summarized in questions that epitomize two of the fundamental issues accompanying the reassertion of Islam in public life. "Whose Islam?"— Is the nature of the state to be determined by military officers (Zia ul-Haq, Muammar Qaddafi), clergy (Ayatollah Khomeini), or an elected council or assembly of Muslims? "What Islam?"—is the classical interpretation of Islam as preserved in legal manuals to be reinstituted or is substantive change possible? Many Muslim critics of current Islamic measures ask, "Why a negative Islam?" Even those who desire Islamic reforms question the seeming equation of an Islamic order with implementation of Islamic penal laws, taxes, banking restrictions, limitations on political participation, and dissent. They ask, "If Islam is a total way of life, where is the emphasis on Islamic political rights, social justice, human rights?" Recent attempts to implement Islamic republics in Iran and Pakistan have often underscored rather than resolved questions about the nature of a modern Islamic state.

The political resurgence of Islam has also taken the form of armed conflict by Islamic resistance movements in countries like Afghanistan and the Philippines. In the former, a Muslim majority wages its struggle *(jihad,* holy war) against Soviet occupation. In the latter, a Muslim minority in the southern Philippines challenged the regime of Ferdinand Marcos and now that of Corazon Aquino in Asia's largest Christian society. Many know of the appeal to Islam by Afghan resistance groups who call their struggle a *jihad* and are referred to as *mujahideen* (holy warriors). Most are not aware of the extent to which the current Soviet-backed regime in Afghanistan also employs Islam in its attempt to gain legitimacy. As Ashraf Ghani's study in chapter 4 illustrates, given Islam's long history in Afghan life and its continued strength and presence among the people, an appeal to Islam by the Soviet-backed government for political legitimacy and popular support was almost inevitable. At the same time, the regime's Muslim opposition denounces it as an atheist state and wages its *jihad.* Yet, despite its common enemy, the Afghan resistance movement remains plagued by divisions into what Professor Ghani calls Islamic fundamentalists and moderates: "All these groups speak in the name of Islam, but their conceptions of Islam are radically opposed" (p. 92).

In contrast to Afghanistan, the Moro National Liberation Front (MNLF) represents a Muslim minority in the predominantly Christian society of the Philippines. The Muslim sultanates in the southern Philippines had successfully resisted the Spanish Christian conquest from the north. However, under American colonial rule and since Philippine independence in 1946, the south has been integrated into a single government. In chapter 5, "The Philippines: Autonomy for the Muslims," Lela G. Nobel examines the political and economic factors that combined with increased Muslim consciousness and led to the emergence of a Muslim protest movement. Appealing to a common Islamic identity, the MNLF sought to transcend traditional linguistic, territorial, and clan differences and thus unite otherwise disparate Muslim communities. With support from Libya and the Organization of the Islamic Conference (OIC), the MNLF negotiated the Tripoli Agreement with the Marcos government in 1977. It proved to be a Pyrrhic victory. Noble analyzes the ideological and organizational problems that weakened the MNLF's effectiveness and the skillful maneuvering of the former Marcos government in thwarting Moro aspirations. However, Muslim separatism became an issue for the Aquino government in 1986. A three-day protest in April by twenty-thousand Filipino Muslims in Catabato City, coupled with kidnaping of ten Catholic nuns and a Protestant missionary dramatically drew attention to Manila's failure to address Muslim grievances. As Muslims become more politically assertive and more active in developing their communal institutions, the Philippine government feels the pressure for greater political autonomy.

The Philippines are but one example of an increasingly important Islamic issue—the status and rights of Muslim minorities. Historically, the vast majority of Muslims have lived in Islamic societies. To be a Muslim meant living in an Islamic community/state committed to the implementation of Islamic law. Where Muslims faced non-Muslim political control, tradition called for emigration or *jihad*. In Asia, the issue of Muslim minority life is important, given the significant Muslim minority communities in countries like China (50 million), the Soviet Union (40 to 60 million), and India (80 million). The comparative significance of these populations becomes clearer when we remember that Egypt, the largest Arab Muslim country, has a Muslim population of approximately 40 million. Contrary to expectations, the experiences of Muslims in China, the Soviet Union, and India reveal quite different modes of behavior.

In chapter 6, "Soviet Central Asia and China: Integration or Isolation of Muslim Societies," John O. Voll raises the question of whether, contrary to traditional norms and expectations, the experience of China and the Soviet Union may support a new definition of Islam's obligations for Muslims who are minorities in their societies. Despite government suppression of traditional Islamic organizations and institutions and severe restrictions on Islamic life and practice, Islam has survived and, more than that, remains a vital factor in Muslim life in these two countries. Professor Voll asks whether this is simply due to a successful coping with oppression or to a more radical process of reconceptualization in Islam. Contrary to the traditional Islamic responses to non-Muslim rule (i.e., *jihad* or emigration), the modern history of Islam in China and the Soviet Union provides an example of adaptation. Muslim minorities have reordered their Islamic way of life in light of the contemporary social and political realities in their Communist states.

For those Muslims who remained in India after the partitioning of the subcontinent in 1947, a new and different stage in Indian Muslim history began. Gone was the centuries-long tradition of Muslim rule: from the early Delhi sultanate to the Moghul empire. Gone, too, was a majority of the Indian Muslims who, after independence, constituted the population of their new Muslim homeland, Pakistan, with its western and eastern (now Bangladesh) wings. Moreover, the relationship of Muslims to Hindus in the new India was severely strained by the mutual distrust that resulted from the slaughter of hundreds of thousands and the subsequent mass migrations. For the first time in their history, the Muslim-Hindu relationship of ruler to ruled seemed reversed as Indian Muslims adjusted to life in a Hindu-majority (approximately eighty-five percent) secular state.

Syed Shahabuddin and Theodore P. Wright, Jr., in chapter 7, "India: Muslim Minority Politics and Society," illustrate the struggle of Muslim Indians to preserve their religious and cultural heritage, their group identity and autonomous social institutions in order to avoid the threat of absorption and assimilation in a society in which they constitute only twelve percent of the total population. Increasingly, Indian Muslims have looked less to the international Islamic community and more toward the organization and solidarity of the local Indian Muslim community for their strength and development. The ability of the Muslim minority community to maintain both Muslim communal identity and Indian national loyalty has become a greater issue in recent years as Muslim grievances about discrimination in education, employment, and government have been exacerbated by the escalation of Hindu-Muslim communal riots.

The struggle of Muslim minorities to safeguard their identities and status has its opposite counterpart in Malaysia and Indonesia where dominant Muslim governments have addressed the issue of pluralism in differing ways. The concerns of non-Muslims must be viewed against the background of Islamic history and law. As discussed earlier, during the Islamic caliphate and sultanate period, non-Muslim citizens were classified as protected peoples who, in exchange for payment of a poll tax, could practice their religion and could practice limited self-government in internal communal affairs. Although such a legal status was relatively advanced when compared to the policy of Western Christendom, today, non-Muslim minorities would consider such a status as second-class citizenship, unacceptable when judged by Western democratic notions of a modern state.

Malaysia is a pluralist state: A multiracial, multiethnic society that consists primarily of Malays (forty-five percent), Chinese (thirty-five percent), and Indians (ten percent). Although not a majority, Malay Muslims have maintained political dominance, and Islam is the established religion. Islam and Malay identity are intertwined. To be Malay is to be Muslim. However, the majority of Malaysia's citizens are non-Muslim. Commercial and economic life in general have been the primary domain of the Chinese and Indians. Malay Muslim-dominated governments have sought to maintain a pluralistic society in which the rights of non-Muslims are safeguarded.

However, as Fred R. von der Mehden demonstrates in chapter 8, "Malaysia: Islam and Multiethnic Politics," the government's attempt to respond to communal riots between Malays and Chinese—by introducing an affirmative actionlike policy to improve the economic status of Malays—has been accompanied by a politicization of Islam that has intensified non-Muslim minorities' apprehensiveness. Increased attention to strengthening the Malay Muslim community through education and jobs has resulted in a reaffirmation of Malay cultural identity and in a greater emphasis on religion and ethnicity in Malay politics. Greater community solidarity has also threatened the fragile communal balance and equilibrium between Malay Muslims and non-Malays (the Chinese and Indians) and among Muslims themselves, from fundamentalists to accommodationists. The expanded role of Islam in public life has extended from party politics to new Islamic banks, pawnshops, university faculties, and activist organizations.

Without a new, revised Islamic position on the status of non-Muslims in a Muslim state, non-Muslim minorities may well wonder what the increased sense of Islamic identity and community may hold in store for them. If Islam is to become more a part of public life, does it not mean the inevitable reinstitution of Islamic public laws? If the greater Islamization of state and society in Iran and Pakistan has tended to move away from the acceptance of minorities as citizens with full rights to that of viewing them as protected *(dhimmi)* citizens, what may Malaysia's future be?

With some 140 million Muslims, Indonesia is the largest Muslim country in the world. Given the linguistic and cultural diversity of the islands that constitute the Indonesian archipelago, Islam might be perceived as a basis for national consciousness. Yet, the division of Indonesian society along religious and cultural lines is, in fact, exceedingly varied, ranging from staunchly Islamic to nominal and even non-Islamic orientations. Although statistically overwhelmingly Muslim, Indonesian culture reflects the strong influences of pre-Islamic Hindu, Buddhist, and animist traditions as well as more recent European (Dutch) values. The Muslim community can be divided into a minority of the Islamically observant (Santri) and a majority of nominal Muslims (Abangan) who dominate the ruling elite as political leaders and government bureaucrats. As Anthony

H. Johns in chapter 9, "Indonesia: Islam and Cultural Pluralism," illustrates, Indonesian Islam is, in a very real sense, sui generis. The role of Islam in Indonesian public life differs as much from Arab and South Asian Islam as it does from its neighbor, Malaysia. Although it constitutes the largest Muslim population in the world, Indonesia is not an Islamic state, nor is it a secular state. The role of Islam in Indonesia's modern political development has been particularly affected by two factors: a religiously based ideology—Pancasila, or the five principles, and the leadership styles of its two postindependence regimes—the leftist government of Sukarno's Guided Democracy and the rightist regime of General Suharto's New Order. Because political Islam is viewed as a threat to the regime, Islamic activists have often been on the defensive.

Although Pancasila has provided the basis for a national unity that embraces all of Indonesia's religious and cultural groups, the delicate balance is threatened by the dichotomy between the religious and the secular in law, education, and politics and, more recently, by the government's attempt to require all community organizations to accept Pancasila as their sole ideological basis. For some Muslim leaders, accepting Pancasila as the basis for all political, social, and educational organizations is tantamount to banishing Islam from public life and restricting it to private practice. Thus, the attempt to make Pancasila the dominant ideology has brought it in direct conflict with Islam in defining both national and individual identity.

If Islam has been reasserted in domestic politics throughout much of the Muslim world, what of its impact on international relations? The renewed emphasis on Islamic identity and solidarity and the international contact and communications now possible owing to modern technology raise many questions about international linkages between Muslim countries. However, as James P. Piscatori observes in chapter 10, "Asian Islam: International Linkages and Their Impact on International Relations," the question is not so much whether there are international relations among the Asian states but whether Islam has anything to do with them.

Despite Muslim activists' ideology and rhetoric and the all-too-common popular image of Islam as monolithic, the realities of Asian Muslims' international relations demonstrate a diversity of practice. Although a shared Islamic identity has not translated into transnational unity, important changes have occurred in institutional development and cooperation both at the nongovernment and government levels.

Throughout Asia, as in most of the Muslim world, the past decade has seen the growth and vitality of youth movements committed to producing generations of Islamically committed and informed citizen/activists. Similarly, missionary (dawah) organizations have multiplied, emphasizing not only the conversion of non-Muslims, but also the religious reawakening of nominal Muslims. Although some organizations are avowedly apolitical, others espouse a holistic view of Islam as an ideo-

logical alternative and guide for state and society. In addition, there are
more violent organizations, such as the al-Jihad groups, that have been
active in countries like Indonesia and the Philippines.

At the government level, Islam has played a mixed role. It is not *the*
determinant of foreign policy but rather a factor that is either appealed
to or circumvented, depending on perceived national interests. Thus,
while Libya and Saudi Arabia have supported the MNLF, Indonesia and
Malaysia have subordinated support for fellow Muslims for the sake of
mutual cooperation with their non-Muslim Association of South East
Asian Nations allies, the (ASEAN). Compromise and pragmatism have
also led Iran's Islamic government to trade with the Soviet bloc when
needed.

Although Islamization of public life has increased in many Muslim
countries during the past decade, this has not been translated into significant government institutional or pan-Islamic linkages. Thus, political
and economic integration between Asian and non-Asian Muslim states
has been quite limited. Here, too, national interest has continued to be
the principal criterion in policy formulation.

The restricted and often diverse use of Islam has been accompanied by
increased contacts between Asian and non-Asian Muslim states in terms
of financial aid, labor exchange, support for missionary activities, and the
transfer of ideas. The Gulf oil states provide substantial development aid
and support for religious activities (conferences, propagation of the faith,
translation and distribution of religious texts, etc.). At the same time,
these states employ large numbers of immigrants from Asian Muslim
countries.

Contacts between Muslims at the international level are further
enhanced by the annual pilgrimage to Mecca, the proliferation of international Islamic conferences and symposia, and the availability of inex-
pensive translations of the writings of leading Islamic ideologues and of
their sermons on audiotape. Such activities increase the sense of an international, or transnational, dimension of Muslim identity, membership
simultaneously in a nation-state and a transnational community of
believers *(ummah)*. International Islamic organizations and institutions,
such as the OIC, the World Muslim League, the World Assembly of Muslim Youth, the Islamic Solidarity Fund, and the Islamic Development
Bank contribute as well to an awareness of a broader Islamic identity and
solidarity. Where these tendencies will lead remains uncertain. Will they
result in increased cooperation and coordination or will they fail to move
beyond the realm of ideological slogans and symbols? Only time will tell.

As the studies in this work illustrate, Asian Islam represents a diversity
of experience and government that is as varied as Asian languages, customs, and terrains. Common to this vast pluriformity is a unity of faith
grounded in a common revelation and sacred history. The dialectic of
unity of faith and diversity of cultural experience is reflected both in private religious practice and in public life. As shall be seen, the roles of

Islam vary widely and are conditioned by the specific sociopolitical situations of individual countries. For many Muslims, Islam is at a critical
crossroads. After centuries of colonial dominance and the postindependence pursuit of a predominantly Western secular path, Islamic activists
wish to chart a more independent and indigenously rooted future in
which Islam will govern not only worship, but socio-political development. The extent to which this will prove feasible remains to be seen.

Notes

1. J. J. Saunders, *A History of Medieval Islam* (London: Routledge and Kegan Paul, 1965),
   p. 39.

2

IRAN
Implementation of an Islamic State

SHAHROUGH AKHAVI

Islam, perhaps, permeates Iranian society in a more intensive and extensive way than it does elsewhere. To investigate the nature and consequences of this phenomenon chapter 2 will address: (1) the historical response of Iranian society to Western impact; (2) the relationship of the religious institution to the state since 1979; (3) political mobilization and ideological militance in revolutionary Iran; (4) Islamic law and its implementation in the revolutionary period; (5) the social, economic, and political impact of clericalism on Iranian society, and the clergy's image of the outside world.

Iranian Reaction to Western Impact

Iranian society prior to the establishment of the Pahlavi dynasty in 1925 can best be examined through a series of historical sketches of the structure of society, the underlying cultural features of that society, and the nature of the state. In a discussion of these factors, it will be important to chart the patterns of Western impact as well as the reactions to such impact by Iran's social classes and state officials.

The structure of Iranian society, although not unchanging, featured a greater degree of continuity from the sixteenth to the nineteenth centuries than has been the case in the twentieth century. At the risk of being somewhat ahistorical, pre-1900 Iran was basically an agrarian society with minimal commercialization of market systems and with correspondingly localized relationships among the key social forces to one another and to the state. Geographical and topographical features, such as broken terrain, impassable mountains, vast stretches of desert, and few and unnavigable rivers, combined to isolate villages and towns from one another.[1]

Iranian historians have themselves tended to see their society in historical terms as composed of a table of ranks, or classes. The terms for these classes may roughly be translated as follows: (1) the nobles and grandees, (2) tribal chiefs, (3) the clergy, (4) merchants, (5) village and town headmen, (6) artisans, (7) villagers, and (8) tribals.[2] Relationships within and among these groups reflected extreme communal diversity: ethnic, religious, linguistic, tribal, and ecumenical. Social historians argue that, taken collectively, the combination of physical barriers, communal cleavages, and the absense of market development reduced significant social solidarity across national territory.

Viewed from the political perspective with regard to the nature of the state and legitimate authority, it becomes even clearer that class political autonomy simply did not evolve at the national level.[3] Under patrimonial rule, the shah could resist demands for charters and rights that would have allowed independence of intermediate groups from the state. Thus, in pre–twentieth-century Iran, even though organizations, such as guilds, brotherhoods, and leagues (e.g., those affiliated with local gymnasia) did flourish, they had no corporate political autonomy or personality. There was no civil society in Hegel's terms: Meaning that local corporations of the type just cited provided a sense of identity to the members but could not accrue political autonomy from the state.[4]

Yet, paradoxically, the state, led by the shah, was also feeble. Although the shah had the legal authority to consume the human and material resources of the empire as though these were his personal property, in reality, during the Qajar period (1785–1925) he seldom was able to extend his power beyond the capital. Many instances could be cited from the social history of Iran to show that regional or local grandees or clergymen obstructed the policies of ruling monarchs.[5]

Western impact may be seen in terms of military conflict, economic challenges, political innovations, and cultural threats. Examples of military confrontations include the series of wars fought against the Russians in previous centuries, which normally ended in substantial losses of territory. Although armed hostilities with Britain were less frequent, they did occur, as for example in the series of engagements collectively known as the Afghan Wars (in the 1830s and 1850s). Also, Iran faced dismemberment, as in 1907 when Russian and British policymakers agreed on an occupation and division of the country into spheres of influence.

Iran was also an arena of great power economic competition and commercial penetration. Grants of concessions to foreign nationals became standard practice in the late Qajar period, and the financial return to the government and the society as a whole was insignificant relative to what the state conceded. Among the most important economic deals was the famous Reuter Concession of 1872, which granted a vast monopoly to a British subject in the areas of railway construction, mining, and banking. It is true that the shah was forced to renege on the Reuter Concession owing to internal opposition, as he was also later to do in the case of the tobacco concession of 1891 (also to a British subject). However, a series of other arrangements were more or less imposed on a craven monarch and an unwilling nation by opportunistic Western businesspersons backed by their governments. The country had become a semicolony in which "Belgians administer[ed] the customs service . . . Swedish officers command[ed] the state police . . . Russian officers staff[ed] and command[ed] the [gendarmerie] . . . Hungarians . . . administer[ed] the Treasury. . . . The Dutch own[ed] and operate[d] the only telegraph line . . . and large industrial operations (textiles)."[6]

By 1919 things had become so bad that the British nearly succeeded in formalizing Iran's de facto semicolonial status by striving to impose a virtual protectorate over the country in the guise of an alliance. The plan failed because of internal opposition and lack of British resolve, but this episode is noteworthy in the sense that it shows how routine it was among great power policymakers to believe that the country was fair game for penetration.

In the Pahlavi period (1925–79), the government itself initiated dramatic economic changes that were vast in their scope and consequences:[7]

1. A national market system was developed so that by the time of the revolution of 1979 it could be argued that despite the continued existence of a dual economy, with its modern enclaves and a separate traditional sector, such a market was significantly in place by the 1970s.
2. The country's economy became integrated into the international market, and this generally meant its transformation from a self-sufficient agricultural nation to a net importer of food commodities.
3. The growth of a predominantly rentier economy evolved, based on oil revenues and the general failure to evolve a healthy balance between agriculture and industry. The stress on oil output led to a serious inability to engage the factors of production in the industrialization effort, as such factors are almost totally uninvolved in the extraction and marketing of oil for profits that come in the form of pure economic rent. In the late Pahlavi period, rentierism was so advanced that the economy was faced with the classic threat of hypertrophy in such situations.[8]
4. High rates of economic growth prevailed from the mid-1960s to the mid-1970s. This may be seen in terms of increases in Gross National Product per year. A very large service sector came into being and some areas, such as transport and construction, grew significantly. However, a problem, which became especially acute with the aborted Fifth Development Plan (1973–78), was that the irrational pursuit of bilateral deals with Western states for nuclear plants and huge industrial projects featured the assembly of manufactured products rather than their domestic creation. The irrelevance of such schemes to the development of an industrial base in

the country has been often noted by economists and consultants who have written on the economic problems of the Pahlavi state.[9] Among the well-known collateral effects of this pattern was the penetration of the economy by multinational corporations. Although it is difficult to generalize, it would seem that at least part of the problem in regard to their operation in Iran was that of monopolizing production and decapitalizing the economy.

As to the political and cultural impact of the West, again only the briefest sketches may be drawn. In the late nineteenth century, constitutionalist ideas politicized an unlikely coalition of modernizing and traditionalist groups who were offended by the Qajar shahs' repeated capitulations to Western demands.[10] Although such constitutionalist pressures led to the promulgation of a constitution and the establishment of a parliament in the early part of this century, the Pahlavi shahs interfered with the functioning of the legislature and violated the provisions of the organic law on a routine and ongoing basis. This led to a continuing crisis between state and society that occasionally boiled over into widespread collective protest, as in 1948–53 and again in 1960–63.[11] Although the second shah gave lip service to the idea of pluralism and political party competition, in reality the politics of the entire Pahlavi period can best be described as growing autocracy and bureaucratization of power.[12]

Adding to the relative deprivation felt by politically conscious Iranians under Shah Mohammad Reza Pahlavi (1941–79) was the perception that his throne was secured by the British and American governments. The nadir of the shah's dependence seemed to come in 1953 when a nationalist movement was denied in its bid to limit the shah to a symbolic role and place effective power in the hands of an elected prime minister. During and after this episode, American support for the shah, which up to then had been relatively moderate, increased dramatically. The CIA's role in the 1953 incidents thus became a sort of primal event, etched into the national consciousness, and never forgotten.

Culturally, major problems of adjustment to foreign penetration arose in the nineteenth century as debate proceeded over the best means of response. Shi'ite religious leaders, although not united, did play a key role in the struggles of the late nineteenth century against the West and the shah's court. It must be noted that historically clerics were not the only social force to rebel against foreign inroads: certain bureaucrats, secular intellectuals (modernists), national minorities, merchants, and some provincial influentials also participated in protest movements.[13]

The historical position of Shi'ites on the question of authority is that only the imam (religious leader) can legitimately rule because of his greater knowledge, piety, and sense of justice. These qualities are his by virture of his blood relationship to the Prophet through the latter's daughter, Fatimah. According to Shi'ite beliefs, historically there were twelve imams, but the last, who disappeared long ago, is to reappear at the Day of Judgment. Therefore, the doctrinal position is taken that only one of these special religious leaders can claim ultimate legitimacy of rule. Beyond this, it is important to stress that clergymen generally are not entitled to executive authority in the Shi'ite doctrine. However, Ayatollah Khomeini has argued strongly, and heterodoxically, that the imams did, indeed, make *ex ante* appointment of the ordinary clergy as trustees in the Hidden Imam's absence.[14]

In the absence of the Hidden Imam, Shi'ites believe that secular rulers may be obeyed but that their rule is based on sufferance rather than doctrinally validated right. Rulers judged to be derelict in carrying out their religious duties, therefore, can be opposed for violating the justice of the Hidden Imam. However, no unanimously agreed upon formula has been generated to test the rule of a secular sovereign,[15] even though it was generally considered that a ruler's deliberate violation of one or more of the Five Pillars of Islam (the credo and its certification of monotheism, prayer, fasting, alms giving and pilgrimage) would constitute grounds for justifiable rebellion. Yet, only a stupid ruler would make such an unequivocal attack on the central provisions of the faith. Hence, the dilemma remained as to whether abuses associated with such things as taxation, the declaration of war, distribution of alms, implementation of certain provisions of the law relating to interest on loans—in short, the stuff and essence of day-to-day governing—were sufficient grounds for rebellion. Most of the Shi'ite jurists over the centuries have tended to be very cautious in these areas and have generally tended to give wide discretionary authority to the ruler in the absence of clear-cut guidelines.

Even so, the Pahlavi shahs in particular moved severely against the clergy and sought forcibly to disestablish the church, as it were. They sought to deprive the clergy of their key resources, so that, by the time of the 1979 revolution, the religious leaders had lost their jobs, shrines, endowments, schools, mosques, and the revenues associated with control of these institutions. Ultimately, the clergy were even challenged concerning their role as the interpreters of the faith.[16] The royal court's tactics in dealing with the clergy in the context of arrant secularizing policies varied from time to time. But they included virtually the entire range from harrassment and administrative obstructionism to imprisonment, torture, and even execution. The Pahlavis therefore achieved what the Qajar shahs had not: the alienation of the religious leadership to the point where they advocated the overthrow of the system and seizure of power and rule by the clerics themselves.

The Relationship of Shi'ism to the State
Since 1979

Since 1979, politics in Iran have been cast in the framework of the fusion of religious and political spheres. It is best to refer to the authoritative formula and practice under which this fusion has been achieved as clericalism, that is, executive rule by the clergy. This development is a natural outgrowth of the doctrinal line argued by Ayatollah Khomeini since the early 1970s that, in the absence of the Hidden Imam, the most learned, pious, and just clergyman of the age should exercise sovereign rule.

It is possible to be quite specific as to the institutional milestones that have served to ratify clericalism in the Islamic Republic of Iran. The first step was taken in March 1979 when a large majority of the population went to the polls and voted in favor of transforming the political system from a monarchy to an Islamic republic. In August of that year, elections were held for a Council of Experts whose job was to be the drafting of a constitution. The majority of this council succeeded in securing a victory for clericalism against a minority that warned of the authoritarian provisions stressed in Khomeini's ideological line *(maktabi)*. In November 1979, the nation ratified a constitution that enshrines the principal of *vilayat-i-faqih* (rule by the jurisconsult) and refers several times to Khomeini by name. The constitution also specifies the creation of an active role for a Council of Guardians of the Revolution. This body—half of whose members were chosen by Khomeini, the remainder by the Supreme Judicial Council (the highest judicial body in the land) was meant to be dominated by clerics. In a word this constitution[17] is radically different from its predecessor, which was promulgated in 1906–7 and, though systematically violated by the Pahlavi shahs, was never formally abolished by them.

Almost simultaneously, the provisional government of Mehdi Bazargan resigned as a result of the American admission of the shah into the United States, the taking of American diplomats hostage in the U.S. embassy in Tehran, and Bazargan's meeting with U.S. National Security Advisor, Zbigniew Brzezinski. The fifth milestone occurred in January 1980 with the Iranian presidential elections. Although Abolhasan Bani Sadr ended up as a rival of the clerics, at first their positions were similar on a range of issues. To the Khomeini clergy, it was more important to conduct the elections than it was to have a clergyman serve as president.

The sixth step came in the March and May 1980 parliamentary elections, which returned a large majority of Islamic Republican Party (IRP) MPs. Emboldened by having passed through these stages, the regime could now afford to dissolve the Revolutionary Council—the dominant execution organ—and proceed with the formation of a clergy-dominated cabinet. After the bazaar strike in October 1980 and a confrontation between Bani Sadr and his enemies on the campus of Tehran University in the spring of 1981, the clergy mounted a campaign to isolate, discredit and, finally, impeach him (June 1981). Although an explosion at the IRP headquarters killed many of its leaders—including its general secretary, Ayatollah Muhammad Beheshti—it was only a temporary setback to clerical consolidation of rule. And it served to unleash a reign of terror that eliminated the regime's rivals from the scene. In December 1982, elections for a council of eighty-three experts were conducted in order to appoint Ayatollah Khomeini's successor(s). The council met simply to adopt procedural ground rules and adjourned with the notion of reconvening only after Khomeini's death. The anticommunist show trials of the fall of 1983 marked the regime's feeling strong enough to break with its tactical leftist allies. Further steps in consolidating clericalism came in the spring of 1984, with the second parliamentary elections, and in the summer of 1985, with the reelection of the incumbent president. Most recently, in November 1985, it was disclosed that the Council of Experts had, in fact, selected Ayatollah Husayn 'Ali Muntaziri to succeed Khomeini. Although he lacks the qualifications of supreme knowledge, piety, and justice, the regime has been trying to burnish his image among the masses.

The picture just drawn should be compared to the Pahlavi era, when secular elites managed to "dis-embed"[18] religion from the state. Today, the power of the clergy is centered mainly in the judicial institutions, with the executive (the cabinet and especially the military) and the legislative branches providing support functions for the legal bodies. Of course, it should be noted that clerics also serve in cabinet and legislative posts. The secular incumbents are the "commissioners" of the clergy. This has given much greater power to the Islamic judges in the Islamic Republic.

Clericalism did not emerge without a struggle on the part of a variety of groups, now defeated, who opposed it for different reasons.[19] The guerrilla organizations felt that the clerics were too conservative on social and economic issues, even though a number of *maktabi* policies are quite radical in the context of Iranian politics. The non*maktabi* clergy rejected Khomeini's clericalism both on doctrinal grounds and out of fear that the Khomeini policies would violate Islamic sanctions for private property and ultimately adversely affect their vested interests in land, commerce, and so on. Some national minorities (including the Sunni tribal forces in the west and north) perceived in clericalism a victory for the forces of ideological conformity and denial of autonomy for their groups.

If one applies Mosca's concepts of the ruling class and the second stratum[20] to Iranian politics, then Khomeini (the *faqih,* supreme legal expert), the members of the Supreme Judicial Council, the members of the Council of Guardians, and those serving as Friday mosque prayer leaders in the major cities (which collectively are represented in a loose corporate body that may be termed the *imam jum'ah* network) constitute the ruling class. The second stratum, which serves as a reservoir for the recruitment of future members of the ruling class, consists of clerical cabinet members, clerical members of parliament, clerical members of the revolutionary committees, and theological seminary teachers and their most promising students. It will be noted that the commanders of the army and the revolutionary guards are not considered members of the ruling class/second stratum because they are essentially the implementers of policy and may more usefully be seen as administrators. The above categorization is less neat than it appears, however, because clerical incumbents in the executive and legislative branches are currently so politically influential that they are, in fact, members of the ruling class. Certainly this must be said to apply to the speaker of the Parliament* and the president of the republic.

The political elite in Iran, today, lest it be forgotten, has been as explicit as it is possible to be about the need to apply the law of Islam in society. As legalists, this elite (ruling class/second stratum) would naturally give priority to the judicial institutions of the state in matters of setting goals, allocating values, extracting resources, and the like. Through 1982, revolutionary courts were semiautonomous institutions of the power structure; but most of these have since merged into the court system under the control of the Ministry of Justice.

If the power structure is represented by the office of *faqih,* the Supreme Judicial Council, the *imam jum'ah* network, and the Council of Guardians of the Revolution, day-to-day decision making occurs in the cabinet. Officials in the judicial institutions are seconded to the cabinet, where they play a key role in the formulation of public policy. The president of the republic, who is also a cleric and commander-in-chief of the armed forces by delegation from Ayatollah Khomeini, attends cabinet meetings.

Apart from the cabinet, with its line of command to the several ministries, the country's parliament represents a forum that sometimes features lively debate over social issues.[21] Most MPs are members of the IRP, which is under the control of the close supporters of Ayatollah Khomeini. But the IRP, like the cabinet, the militia (Pasdaran), the revolutionary committees, and the various agencies—such as the Foundation for the Deprived and the Reconstruction Crusade—are institutions that respond to the lead of the judicial organs and networks.

Membership in these institutions is not as good a predictor of who has power in the country as is participation in the judicial organs and networks. In the second stratum, the most talented of the theological seminary students are recruited by the ruling elite for important political posts. Of course, there may be alternative channels of recruitment. For example, there were several appointments made to the Foreign Ministry from among the so-called Students of the Imam's Line, those who captured the American embassy diplomats. Their patron was Hujjat al-Islam Muhammad Musavi Kho'ayniha, who has close ties to Ayatollah Khomeini and later became deputy speaker of Parliament. In the main, though, it can be expected that the Qum theological colleges will furnish future elites in high political positions. In the past, talented students in Qum were identified in terms of both their scholarship—especially in their skill at dialectical and discursive logic—as well as their knowledge of the substantive material of Islamic jurisprudence. In the current period, the stan-

*Currently also Imam Jum'ah of Tehran.

dards no doubt downplay analytical and synthetic ability—which in the past was sometimes criticized for producing students with purely theoretical and abstract skills—in favor of ideological commitment to *vilayat-i-faqih.*[22]

In this section, our discussion has focused on the clergy's purposive integration of the religious community and the state. It has shown that the organizational power of the clergy rests on the judicial institutions created by the revolutionaries and sanctioned by the Iranian Constitution. Figure 2.1 depicts the major institutions of the Iranian state and their relative power, including political party organs. The justification for including these as state structures is that in the revolutionary system the party becomes an important means of administration because implementation of decisions and policies includes IRP involvement. At the same time, it bears reiterating that the party acts more as a watchdog than as an initiator of ideas and positions. The reference to *hizbullahis* (literally, those of the Party of God) is to street thugs who seek to censor behavior, ideas, and even the clothing of those they disapprove of.

Political Mobilization and Ideological Militance

Ideologies consist of interrelated ideas that are used as weapons to stake out, defend, and promote interests in society. The ideology of Khomeini's regime, *vilayat-i-faqih,* has all the earmarks of revolutionary militance. Its use in the mobilization of people and resources on behalf of revolutionary commitments and policies has been frequently noted by observers. The central concepts are rather clearly laid out and relatively well integrated. It bases its authority on classical Shi'ite legal and political doctrine. Its adepts show passionate commitment to its principles and furnish it with the distinctive social force with which it is strongly identified, namely, that of the urban petite bourgeoisie and the urban poor.[23] Espousers are under strong obligation both to demonstrate their dedication to its ideals and to unify their ranks behind its tenets. It is particularly immune to alternative explanations of the world and is, in that sense, a self-contained system of thought.

Ever since Lenin viewed the Communist party as the general staff of the revolution, revolutionary parties have tended to model themselves after the Bolshevik standard. The IRP, although formally patterned after the Communist Party of the Soviet Union (CPSU), is really not a membership/cadre party. Created after the revolution (although some hold that it existed in elemental form in the 1970s), the IRP is meant to maintain the dynamism of the revolutionary movement, that is, promote permanent revolution. One of its chief allies in this effort is the media, all of which are under the regime's direction and control. The IRP leadership probably would like to control the media through an Iranian equivalent to the CPSU's Central Committee's Agitprop Department. But for now,

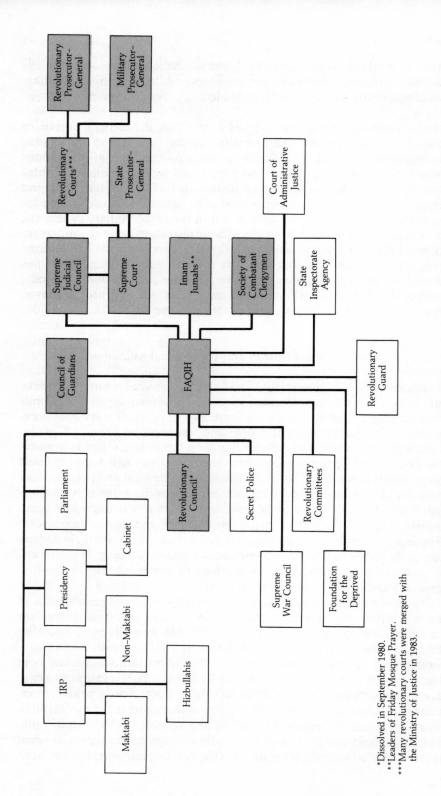

Figure 2.1 State structures of the Islamic Republic of Iran (shaded areas denote more powerful institutions).

*Dissolved in September 1980.
**Leaders of Friday Mosque Prayer.
***Many revolutionary courts were merged with the Ministry of Justice in 1983.

direction and control of the media is more directly in the hands of judicial institutions. The IRP is more of a facilitator, in this connection, than a control mechanism. The most authoritative media organ is *Jumhuri-yi Islami,* a daily newspaper founded by the current Prime Minister, Mir Husayn Musavi. The National Iranian Radio and Television (NIRT) operates, in Lenin's terms, as a transmission belt communicating regime data and values to the people. Formally speaking, the Ministry of Islamic Guidance has legal supervision over the nation's press, radio, and television, and is charged with implementing the press/media law. But given the revolutionary setting, it remains unclear what the chain of command is that links these institutions to the ministry, as opposed, say, to the Society of Combatant Clergymen or the *imam jum'ah* network.

Part of the process of political mobilization through militant ideology is the purge. Those institutions most affected by the purges have been the military (most particularly those elements of the military closely associated with the intelligence services),[24] the judiciary, and the educational organs. In fact, the country's schools and universities have only just recently reopened their doors, as the government has systematically removed un-Islamic teachers, administrators, and students. Initially, Ayatollah Khomeini mocked the idea that he wanted to advocate an Islamic science and an Islamic medicine, and so on. However, the closure of the universities between 1980–83 leaves no doubt that if the regime does not insist on physics and chemistry being taught from an Islamic point of view, this certainly is not the case when it comes to law, economics, history, and the humanities.[25]

But it is not just the military, the judiciary, and the educational institutions that have experienced purges. Rather, purges have extended to all the great departments of the state, from the Ministry of Foreign Affairs to the Ministry of Commerce.[26] The purges have been extensive enough either in their application or their potential to have exceeded the limits of their usefulness.[27] Officials of the regime often lament the shortage of skilled personnel—from the admonition made by current President Hujjat al-Islam 'Ali Khamanah'i to regime zealots, "Do not be more revolutionary than Imam Khomeini,"[28] to the confession by the director of the Plan and Budget Organization that "the biggest difficulty of the Islamic Republic is the question of [insufficient numbers of] skilled and competent people."[29] Ayatollah Husayn 'Ali Muntaziri, Khomeini's own candidate to succeed him, routinely meets with delegations about to be sent abroad to try to induce Iranian expatriates to return.

Purges, of course, became the order of the day after the revolution as prominent figures of the old regime were executed on various charges. But purges directed at the clerics themselves have taken place, too. In a statement made three years after the revolution, the *imam jum'ah* of Qum, Ayatollah 'Ali Mishkini, advocated an identity card system for the mullahs as a means of eliminating undersirables.[30] Ayatollah Khomeini has often threatened purges against recalcitrant clerics whose ranks have even included some of his relatives, such as his grandson, Hujjat al-Islam Husayn Khomeini, and his brother, Ayatollah Murtaza Pasandidah.[31] The most famous episode of a purge against a clergyman is no doubt the "defrocking" of Ayatollah Muhammad Kazim Shari'atmadari in the spring of 1982 for challenging the regime on a wide variety of matters.[32] Other distinguished clerics have been coerced, sometimes through physical intimidation by demonstrators who call themselves "Those of the Party of God" (as in the case of the roughing up of Ayatollah Hasan Taba'taba'i Qummi in the city of Mashhad in 1983)[33] or by indirect innuendoes made by Ayatollah Khomini (as in the case of his oblique attack on the *marja'-i-taqlid,* Ayatollah Muhammad Riza Gulpaygani, for his alleged advice to his followers not to pay taxes to the state).[34]

Another mechanism to maintain high levels of ideological militance and political mobilization is the war with Iraq, which broke out in September 1980. This conflict clearly has had negative economic effects, including inflation, unemployment, shortages of goods and spare parts, low productivity, idle plant capacity, a drain of foreign exchange reserves, a negative balance of trade, poor performance in domestic fixed capital formation, rationing accompanied by corruption, disruptions in the marketing of goods, and so on.[35]

In view of these negative economic consequences, there must be some perceived political benefits to prosecuting the war. From the IRP clerical point of view, the party was able to use the war issue to defeat former President Bani Sadr and his supporters in an internal power struggle. Also, the IRP has exploited the opportunity provided by the war to unite the population against the foreign threat. It is true, of course, that by now every family has had at least one of its members become a war casualty. The people cannot continue to bear such losses indefinitely. But, evidently, the turning point has not yet been reached and the regime is reaping at least some short-run benefits of the wartime mobilization of its populations.

The war also provides justification for the Khomeini clergy's efforts to export their revolution by arguing that Iraq's leaders—and, by implication, their allies in Jordan, Saudi Arabia, and Egypt—are anti-Islamic. Beyond that, the clerics judge it important to keep the army as far away from Qum and Tehran as possible to ensure that professional-minded officers do not begin to question the regime's mishandling of public policies.

It is not that support for the war effort is open-ended even among IRP clerics. To be sure, dissident mullahs have to be very careful how they phrase their words because Ayatollah Khomeini has been so emphatic in stating that the war will continue until Saddam Husayn's Ba'thist government in Iraq falls. Yet, it is possible to discern divergent opinions among the clergymen on the war. For example, during Friday prayers in early spring 1984, Ayatollah Muhammad Riza Mahdavi Kani, then a powerful member of the Council of Guardians went out of his way to hold out the olive branch to the Iraqis by saying that if Iraq were attacked by non-Islamic forces, the Iranians would immediately come to their aid; and he denied that the Islamic republic sought any revenge against Iraq. On the other hand, Hujjat al-Islam 'Ali Akbar Hashimi Rafsanjani, Speaker of Parliament, countered Kani's satement with, "War, war until victory" and "He who makes light of the war shall be considered a plotter, and we must struggle against him." President Khamanah'i put it even more bluntly when he stated, "We shall exact revenge from the blood-thirsty enemy for the bloodletting against the martyrs of Andimashk and Dezfūl [cities damaged extensively by Iraqi rockets]. Peace shall only come by beating the oppressors [into the ground]."[36]

The image projected by the regime of foreigners as enemies of Islam also serves the interests of ideological militance and political mobilization. This view is based on the Islamic perception of a world divided into the abode of Islam and the abode of the infidels. Ayatollah Khomeini's speeches have consistently portrayed outsiders as bent on destroying Islam out of fear. The regime's image of the superpowers, in particular, shows how deeply hostile the government is. In the fall of 1964, during a speech bitterly denouncing a parliamentary act granting U.S. citizens capitulatory rights in Iran, Khomeini declared, "America is worse than Britain; Britain is worse than America. The Soviet Union is worse than both of them. They are all worse and more unclean than each other."[37]

Hostility to the United States is rooted in the belief that the shah's regime not only could not have endured without American support, but was ever and always the willing tool of the United States in all matters of internal and foreign policy. This perception earned the Untied States the sobriquet of the Great Satan. As most people are aware, British and American support for the shah in the face of an extensive anti-shah nationalist movement in the early 1950s enabled the monarch to return to power. It is widely believed in Iran that, in the ensuing years, American multinational corporations and Washington's training and assistance programs, especially in military and intelligence matters, were the backbone of the shah's repression.

In the early weeks of the revolution, anti-American sentiment was not high, but things began to change some time in the summer of 1979—probably because it became useful to the dominant clerical faction to discredit its rivals with charges of links to the United States. The assassination of Ayatollah Murtaza Mutahhari in April 1979 was a key event in the anti-American turn of the regime. Without question, Mutahhari had been the most creative social thinker among the clergy in the prerevolutionary period.[38] He evidently had been one of Khomeini's outstanding students and was the first chairman of the Revolutionary Council. His assassination was blamed on groups allegedly funded by the United States.

Another problem the regime faced was how to deal with the national minorities, especially the Kurds. Kurdish autonomy demands were viewed by the IRP clerics in effect as demands for secession; again the United States was seen to be the hidden hand directing the Kurdish movement. As is well known, the admission of the shah to the United States for medical reasons in October 1979 led to Khomeini's fiery denunciation in a series of speeches that directly preceded the takeover of the American embassy in November. Since that time, despite the release of the Americans in January 1981, revolutionary militance has rested on a perception of the United States as the chief enemy of Islam. In the meantime, the June 1982 invasion of Lebanon by America's ally, Israel, and its aftermath have provided the regime with greater reason to continue to view the United States with deep hostility.

The Soviet Union, too, is considered a dread enemy of Islam. The Iranian regime has never shied away from denouncing the Soviet invasion of Afghanistan in December 1979 and its continued occupation of that country.[39] The 1983 show trials of members of the Iranian Tudah (Communist) party have angered the Soviets, who thinly disguise their ire by attacking unnamed reactionaries in the regime. The Iranian government has also refused to restore the flow of natural gas to the Soviet Union as a result of a price dispute that arose at the start of the Iranian Revolution. The clerical regime has permitted demonstrators to march to the Soviet embassy in Tehran and even to seize and burn the Soviet flag. It has, however, stopped short of allowing them to seize the embassy or to capture its diplomats. The regime probably fears that Soviet retaliation would be far more severe and immediate than was the case with America. The Soviets are seen in the rhetoric as a lesser satan, but satanical for all that. An interesting divergence appears, however, in the regime's image of the clients of the superpowers. As already noted, it criticizes the governments of Saudi Arabia, Jordan, Egypt, Morocco and, of course, Israel (but not Turkey or Pakistan); on the other hand, it speaks approvingly of such regimes as those of North Korea, Cuba, Angola, South Yemen, and others.[40]

In any case the regime's image of outsiders will continue to be shaped by Ayatollah Khomeini's deeply held views about foreign enmity toward Islam. Khomeini believes that "monarchy will never return, but they are trying to bring about an American Islamic Republic."[41] Therefore, confrontation with outside powers will continue to command the long-run attention of the regime's leaders.

Implementation of Islamic Law

Public life in Iran is pervaded by the influence of Islamic law. But a paradox exists. On the one hand, public discourse is replete with the symbols of Islamic law; but in implementing the law's provisions, there has been less headway than one might expect. That this should be so under an Islamic republic is somewhat embarrassing for the regime. The internal press carries stories of punishments meted out to hoarders, drug peddlers, smugglers, those caught drinking alcoholic beverages, sex offenders, not to say political deviants. But even in the ordinary courts, as compared to the revolutionary ones, it is difficult to know how consistently strict Islamic standards are being followed for detaining persons, presenting indictments, issuing arrest warrants, incarceration, gathering evidence, testifying at trials, arriving at appropriate verdicts, and so on. It would be remarkable if strict standards were being applied throughout in view of the revolutionary ferment in society. Revealingly, the state prosecutor general, with jurisdiction over non-revolutinary courts, decreed in March 1982 that persons accused of "warring with God" and "corruption on earth" would henceforth be entitled to a defense attorney; but he ruled that such attorneys had to believe in their clients' guilt as charged (even before a verdict was given). They would be "defense" attorneys, then, only in the sense that they could argue lesser degrees of guilt, and not the innocence, of their clients.[42]

One sign of normalization is the merger of the revolutionary courts with those of the Ministry of Justice. It should be noted that when the chief justice of the Supreme Court, Ayatollah 'Abd al-Karim Ardabili, advocated such a merger in 1982, Ayatollah Khomeini rejected the idea. But ultimately the Ardabili view prevailed, probably because Khomeini was persuaded that the efficiency of the court system was more important than the possible advantages for ideological militance that a separate system of revolutionary courts might bring.[43]

Revolutionary courts, in any case, require the suspension of normal rules. For example, summary trials are prohibited by Islamic law, but it is possible to invoke secondary principles (the collective interests of the community) to argue that temporarily strict Islamic standards should be set aside in order to safeguard the Islamic community from its enemies. The trouble that arises is that the sayings and traditions associated with Imam 'Ali, the most revered of the Shi'ite imams, do not show him having deviated from the strictest standards of the law. And his rule was certainly beset by the kinds of challenges and turmoil characteristic of the revolutionary period. Thus, for contemporary jurists to stray from strict standards when Imam 'Ali had not done so leaves invidious distinctions in people's minds.

At another level, implementation has run into problems in the Islamic republic because of fundamental disagreement over the law's provisions on private property. This complex matter cannot be pursued in detail here, but it is worth noting that a comprehensive land law still has not been implemented. At this point, Khomeini has not taken an unequivocal position on the matter of expropriation and/or confiscation of property. This has meant that factional conflict has continued, with those advocating the principle of expropriation enacting laws in the Parliament only to have them vetoed by the Council of Guardians. In fact, the council at one point was vetoing so much legislation that Ayatollah Khomeini demanded that MPs not promulgate enactments without serious discussion and extensive deliberations to preempt any possible veto by the council.[44] In the fall of 1981, Khomeini seemingly acquiesced to an unusual maneuver by the Speaker of Parliament, who requested the *faqih* delegate some of his powers to the legislature by invoking secondary principles. Although this was done, presumably giving the Parliament powers of overriding the veto of the Council of Guardians, the issue was never put to the test.[45] Evidently, Khomeini must also have had second thoughts on this issue, since in early 1983, he admonished the MPs, "If the Council of Guardians says something is against Islam, then it is against Islam."[46]

Other problem areas in the implementation of Islamic law include internal trade, housing, and labor. As a result of flight by their owners, many apartments and houses stand empty. A housing crisis exists because of the significant rural-to-urban migration in the 1960s and 1970s that was exacerbated during the revolution. The desire by some urban poor to sequester themselves in these abandoned dwellings has brought the conflict to a head. Some of the clerics have supported these property seizures, but legislation enacted to confiscate such residences has been canceled by the Council of Guardians. Nevertheless, serious breaches of the law have taken place in local cases.

Perhaps the most famous case involving an official deliberately violating the council's rulings has been that of Hujjat al-Islam 'Ali Akbar Natiq Natiq Nuri, the minister of the interior. He was called to account by a parliamentary commission for engaging, *inter alia,* in the illegal distribution of "thousands of parcels of property through the Tehran municipality office" in violation of the Law of Municipalities. Nevertheless, Natiq Nuri survived a censure motion brought against him in the legislature, which indicates that the adherents of confiscation are strong in the Iranian Parliament.[47]

The state has nationalized certain industries and all external trade and banking is currently under state control as well. In undertaking these actions, the government alienated merchants in the traditional bazaar and those industrialists the Shah had tried to make into a class supporting his system. Although antagonizing the latter has not hurt the regime very much, the merchants' disaffection poses some serious problems. Historically, they have, after all, been a major source of funds for the clergy, and they controlled the distribution and marketing of commodities inside the country. In October 1980 the bazaars in both Tehran and Qum struck, and similar action has been threatened since then from time to time.

Ayatollah Khomeini declared in December 1982 that in his opinion the country was no longer in a revolutionary situation. He thus issued an eight-point manifesto demanding a total restoration of Islamic norms of legality.[48] Among the document's principles were that regime officials must abandon indiscriminate phone taps, house searches, detentions, and confiscation of property. However, allegations of dereliction continue to be made against Islamic judges by the opposition to the regime. The most active of the opposition groups, the Mujahidin-i Khalq, have declared that the number of political prisoners in Iran has reached the levels they claim used to exist under the shah. Ironically, they have also declared that those numbers were exaggerated in their previous claims and in the pamphlets of the late 1970s. Amnesty International continues to list Iran as one of the world's worst offenders of human rights.[49]

Inevitably, some confusion has prevailed in the revolutionary period in regard to the implementation of Islamic law. After all, a revolution involves a radical break—or an attempt at a radical break—with the past and an as yet incomplete transition to a new system. Because parliamentary enactments had not yet encompassed certain spheres of life, judges were faced with applying the legal standards of the old regime. In March 1982, concerned about the danger of contaminating Islamic implementation with discredited principles, State Prosecutor-General Ayatollah Rabani Amlashi authorized judges to use their discretion and either not apply un-Islamic law or get a ruling on the matter from a more distinguished Islamic judge.[50]

A final area of implementation of great interest pertains to banks. A new piece of legislation has apparently been enacted with provisions for abolishing interest. However, the law has not been given publicity, and it is not possible at this point to determine if these provisions are being observed or not. At a recent meeting between the Speaker of Parliament, Hashimi Rafsanjani, and the governors of the country's leading banks, the Speaker ruled out profit seeking as a basis for the nation's financial institutions.[51] Interest-free loans would be extended, it was alleged, but because the new system went into effect on 1 Bahman 1362/21 January 1984, it is still too soon to tell how effective implementation will be.

There is nothing in Islamic law that categorically prohibits charging interest, but usury is proscribed. Previous efforts, as in Pakistan, have not been successful in dealing with the question of interest. Sometimes, a change of terminology is made so that interest is termed a service charge. Probably the most that can be said about progress in implementing a ban on interest is that although the rates have been reduced considerably, they have not been abolished. To Ayatollah Khomeini's way of thinking the sole function of a parliament is to set an agenda and draft enabling legislation for the strict application of Islamic law.[52] But the interpretation of what constitutes such law has been varied; again, this is an area in which Khomeini has made no categorical statements.

Impact of Clericalism on Society

Clerical rule since February 1979 has had a dramatic impact on the economic, social, and political life of Iranian society. Economic life in Iran during these years has undergone many reversals. Although the regime has greatly reduced the public expenditures of the shah's government, poor economic performance has hampered development programs in the revolutionary period. Weak economies are difficult for revolutionary regimes to avoid. Indeed, regime officials often relate the poor economic performance of the country to the chaotic conditions that exist.

In addition to the unfavorable economic factors already discussed, two additional ones need to be highlighted as particularly significant: The regime is virtually ignoring policy planning for the countryside and, despite its promise to break with the shah's economic model, the Islamic republic is following the same path to a rentier economy. Even worse, in terms of the promises of the government, the country continues to import large quantities of wheat, food products, and consumer goods. Although autarchy is the watchword, the reality is continued dependence on the international market. Bani Sadr, who regarded himself as something of an economic theorist, pushed the concept of severing Iran's ties to international capitalism. But neither in his term of office nor since his fall has it taken place.

Under the monarchy oil production reached a maximum production of 5 to 5.5 million barrels per day. In the revolution, it fell to as low as 0.6 million, and even less in October 1985. The danger for the regime is that it has no coherent industrial and investment policy—not to mention an agricultural one—so that the temptation is to rely excessively on oil revenues to import necessities to service the needs of the people. The standard of living has probably declined in comparison to that of the previous regime, but the distribution of wealth is more equal today than it was under the Pahlavis. Of course, overall income has declined for everyone as well. For the deprived, services are better than before. But problems exist as local clerics experience opportunities for engaging in favoritism and self-enrichment, or both, in connection with the rationing system or other types of patronage. Ayatollah Husayn 'Ali Muntaziri told told a group of Friday Mosque preachers of the Central Province (Tehran) in December 1983 to beware of living apart from the masses and indulging in luxuries. He blamed the gap that had grown between the people and the clergy on the "circumstances of the revolution."[53]

The extensive social impact of clericalism can be seen in matters of education and the role of women in society. Elementary education has been the least disrupted of all education levels in the revolution. But regime officials are mindful that even grammar-school students took part in antimonarchical demonstrations in 1978–79 and, thus, could be mobilized against themselves as well. Informers have thus been posted in various elementary schools to alert authorities of dissident activities. High schools and universities represent a greater challenge to the regime. Purges, as noted before, have hit these institutions, and a similar network of informers keeps tabs on political activity. Moreover, current policy is to repatriate students studying abroad and to deny permission to those seeking to study abroad. Consequently, the capacity of Iran's colleges and universities is strained, as there is a shortage of qualified instructors. One estimate put the shortage of professors at fifty percent.

The Islamic republic is also anxious to have expatriate professionals return to Iran. This is particularly the case for doctors, engineers, and teachers. The regime has even taken a page from the shah's book by establishing a special school in Tehran for the children of Iranian expatriates who have inadequate knowledge of their native tongue.[54]

After being closed for months, the government announced the universities' reopening in the spring of 1983. Admission examinations were taken in the summer, but it was late December before a list was released of those who were successful. Of the more than 60,000 students who sat for the exams, about half (29,371) were accepted. The need to "study the political and moral soundness" of the students was cited as the reason for the six-month delay. Students who were already enrolled when the universities were closed in 1980 came under investigation for ideological deviation.[55] One cannot help but be struck by the greatly reduced number of students compared to prerevolutionary times. What the effect of lower numbers may be is unclear. Large student bodies in the earlier period did not mean the country's needs were being met. But if the allocation of resources for educational needs is inadequate, and the war with Iraq continues, and the country experiences other difficulties, a major educational crisis will soon face the leaders.

Several studies have been published showing that clericalism has significantly advanced its goals with regard to the status of women.[56] Initially, the government was faced with a strong women's rights movement that had participated widely in the anti-shah protests. Determined to apply Islamic standards in connection with the role of women in society, the regime, nevertheless, yielded temporarily in the face of a resurgent movement. The point of conflict was over Ayatollah Khomeini's order that women be veiled in public. On International Women's Day, March 8, 1979, Iranian women demonstrated massively. Although the veiling order was very much on their minds, so, too, was the government's abrogation of the Family Protection Law of 1967—a law that meant married women could initiate divorce proceedings and that made it virtually impossible for men to marry more than one woman. Although many women who participated were not expressing support of the monarchy that had enacted this law, they did oppose its repeal.

The regime was put on the defensive originally, but it adopted the tactic of indirect pressure against the women's movement. For example, it encouraged women who were more proclerical to veil themselves and to petition in the workplace for regulations requiring other women to do the same.

Women televison broadcasters were sacked for refusing to adopt "proper" Islamic headcoverings. Many women workers in government departments were declared redundant, on the pretext of reducing the government bureaucracy. Women judges were dismissed wholesale, barred from practice, and told to look for "clerical and administrative posts" in the judiciary. Many firms and banks began politely to reject women applicants. The ban on abortion, introduced in September 1978 by Sharif-Emami's cabinet as a "concession" to the clergy, was re-affirmed.[57]

There are many verses from the Quran that, if taken literally, reduce women to being helpmates for men at best and, at worst, men's instruments. The inferior status of women in Islamic law is demonstrated from their value in giving legal evidence and to the amount they can inherit. Despite this, there can be little doubt that most women who actively participated in the revolution support the regime's implementation of Islamic law on matters pertaining to them. This probably has to do with the fact that most activist women hail from lower class or petit bourgeois backgrounds. This being the case, their families' values are closer to traditional beliefs, as espoused by the clerics, than those of middle class and professional women.

A final social issue that needs to be examined in the realm of social life is that of the minorities. Historically, the country has contained a wide range of ethnic, linguistic, tribal, and religious minorities. Some of these groups—espeically ethnic, linguistic, and tribal minorities—have challenged the state over questions of power, legitimacy, and autonomy. In the late Pahlavi period, the Kurds and the Azari, Turkish minorities in the west and northwest of Iran, were most active in seeking autonomy.

Kurdish restiveness focused on the regime's refusal to permit Kurds cultural autonomy and, just as important, the regime's deliberately ignoring of the Kurds socio-economic needs. Although the Shi'ite Kurds have entered into a coalition with the clerical government, the Sunnis have been engaged in a bitter conflict with Tehran since late 1979. The regime originally appeared to want to negotiate with the Kurds, and its highly respected emissary, Ayatullah Mahmud Taliqani, shuttled back and forth between the tribes and the government. But Ayatollah Khomeini eventually rejected the proposals of his emissary and blamed the Kurds for wanting nothing less than secession.[58] According to the Dutch scholar Martin van Bruinnissen, revolutionary committees in areas friendly to Tehran (such as Urmia), dispatched revolutionary guards to suppress Kurdish uprisings, even in areas where the Kurds seized land from wealthy individuals who had been ideological supporters of the old regime.[59]

Part of the problem for the regime is that the Kurds became allies of Mujahidin-i Khalq, which is presumed to be responsible for the assassination of many regime leaders. Yet, this is not so compelling an argument when it is noted that the alliance did not exist in the first year of the revolution. But when the Kurdish Democratic party (KDP) agreed in December 1981 to join with ex-President Bani Sadr and the Mujahidin leader-in-exile, Mas'ud Rajavi, in the National Resistance Council,* it placed itself squarely in the main opposition camp.

> [The clergy's retaliation came] in September and October 1982, when the regime launched its biggest offensive yet in conjunction with an attack on Iraq. An estimated 12,000 *peshmargas* [Kurdish fighters] faced human wave attacks by young *Basijis,* long range artillery shells and phosphorous bombs. There were some 25,000 refugees within the Kurdish area, and in the villages and towns under government control there were massacres, forced deportations to other parts of Iran, Shi'i religious propaganda.[60]

Complicating the picture is the fact that at least two Kurdish organizations have been active in recent times. The first is the KDP which is led by 'Abdal-Rahman Qassemlu, a Marxist who probably would prefer full independence but is prepared to settle for full autonomy. The more radical Marxist, Komela (Maoist), sees liberation in the context of a Communist revolution throughout the area. The temptation for regime officials to view all Kurdish opposition factions as inveterate advocates of permanent Communist revolution has been too great for them to resist. Thus, Kurds are viewed as implacable enemies of the Islamic revolution who must be defeated at all costs.

Other minority groups have been less active recently. The ethnic Arabs of the southwest, under Shaykh Muhammad Khaqani, have been silent since 1980. The Azaris may have been intimidated by the Shari'atmadari affair, that cleric being probably the senior mullah from Azarbaijan. Khomeini has many followers in Azarbaijan himself, however. It is important to bear this in mind when contemplating the leanings of the religious university students in Qum. In the past, the student body of the city's theological schools has been thirty-three percent Azarbaijani.[61] If Shari'atmadari could be said to command their loyalties, then the regime would have to move far more cautiously. But this is not the case, because, as noted, Khomeini is the *marja'-i-taqlid*† for many Azaris.

The fortunes of less active minorities, in this case religious ones, may also be noted. The Iranian Jewish community has halved since the revolution. Many Jews have left the country in the wake of the hostility the government has shown to Israel. The government's position on Iranian Jews is that they represent a fifth column and that their activities must be strictly circumscribed. Although a legally constituted religious minority from the Islamic point of view, Iranian Jews are faced with an implementation of Islamic law that has led to the execution of some prominent leaders of their community.[62]

The Baha'is, on the other hand, are in a more precarious situation because they are considered heretical to Islam. Formed in the mid-nine-

---

*The Kurds, Bani Sadr, and Rajavi have since parted ways.
†A title denoting the five or six most distinguished clergymen.

teenth century, the Baha'i faith not only "deviated" from the "true path" when it broke with Islam, but it also placed itself in an untenable situation as far as the clerics are concerned because of its claim to a more authoritative scripture and prophet. In the Pahlavi period, the Baha'is underwent a wave of persecution in 1954–55, but their situation under the Islamic republic is far worse. Baha'ism has been proscribed by the government and its members have been dismissed from jobs, their properties have been sequestered, some have been arrested and others have been executed. Membership in the Baha'i faith is considered in itself to be sufficient evidence of support for Israel and the West.

Conclusions

It has been seen that Islam in Iranian public life is pervasive but that its consequences have not yet been fully measured. Whatever one thinks of the motives and intentions of the Shi'ite clergy in Iran, no one can doubt that it has gone further in the short period of its rule than most people thought would be possible. This discussion has analyzed Iranian Islam on a number of levels, including clergy-state relations, mobilization and ideology, the application of Islamic law, and the socioeconomic impact of clericalism.

Despite many obstacles, the Islamic republic's government has entered its fifth year. The revolution has forced social scientists to reformulate their models to give major consideration to the impact of ideas in the explanation of large-scale social transformations. Max Weber, a pioneer of modern political sociology, argued that great social transformations must be analyzed in the context of the autonomy of cultural factors. Most social science models of revolution have resisted this approach but, unless it is argued that the Iranian phenomenon is not a revolution, clearly this resistance must be abandoned.

Of course, social and economic causes have been tremendously important. But the ideological factors not only were significant in preparing the groundwork for this revolution, but they also continue to be crucial today. For example, the regime has made enemies of the governments of virtually every surrounding country. How else may this be explained except by reference to militant ideology? Again, in earlier periods of Iranian history, the governments tried to avoid being on bad terms simultaneously with both major foreign powers seeking to expand their influence in Iran. But the clerics have thrown caution to the winds and regard both superpowers as satanical. This, too, is a question of ideological imagery.

But ideology is not all with this regime, either. A good deal has been done pragmatically. For example, initial tactical alliances with groups have been discarded later in the struggle for power. In any case, concrete policies have been formulated by the clerics that have had deep-seated real effects in public life. No one can know what the future holds in store, but many are convinced that clericalism will not easily be replaced. Shi'-ism, after all, is a historical fact of Iranian life, and one interpretation of it or another will likely influence Iranian politics in the time to come, whether it be Khomeini's *vilayat-i-faqih* or some alternative variant.

Notes

1. Ervand Abrahamian, "Oriental Despotism: The Case of Qajar Iran," *International Journal of Middle East Studies* [*IJMES*], 5:1 (January 1974), 3–31.
2. For more details, see Ervand Abrahamian, "The Causes of the Constitutional Revolution in Iran," *IJMES*, 10:3 (August 1979), 388.
3. Ahmad Ashraf, "Historical Obstacles to the Development of a Bourgeoisie in Iran," in *Studies in the Economic History of the Middle East*, ed. Michael Cook (London: Oxford University Press, 1970), 308–32.
4. Serif Mardin, "Power, Civil Society and Culture in the Ottoman Empire," *Comparative Studies in Society and History*, 11:3 (June 1969), esp. 258–70.
5. See, for example, Hamid Algar, *Religion and State in Iran* (Berkeley and Los Angeles: University of California Press, 1969), *passim*.
6. Joseph Upton, *The History of Modern Iran* (Harvard Middle Eastern Monograph Series No. 2), Center for Middle Eastern Studies (Cambridge, Mass., 1961), p. 32.
7. Homa Katouzian, *The Political Economy of Modern Iran, 1926–1979* (New York: New York University Press, 1981); Robert E. Looney, *Economic Origins of the Iranian Revolution* (New York: Pergamon, 1982); Julian Bharier, *Economic Development in Iran, 1900–1970* (London: Oxford University Press, 1971).
8. Hossein Mahdavy, "Patterns and Problems of Economic Development in Rentier States: The Case of Iran," in *Studies in the Economic History of the Middle East*, ed. M. Cook, pp. 428–67; Theda Skocpol, "Rentier State and Shi'a Islam in the Iranian Revolution," *Theory and Society*, 11:3 (May 1982), 265–83.
9. Keith McLachlan, "The Iranian Economy, 1960–1976," in *Twentieth Century Iran*, ed. Hossein Amirsadeghi and R. W. Ferrier (London: Heinemann, 1977), esp. 156–68.
10. Nikki Keddie, "Religion and Irreligion in Early Iranian Nationalism," *Comparative Studies in Society and History*, 4:3 (June 1962), 265–95; N. Keddie, *Religion and Rebellion in Iran* (London: Frank Cass, 1966); N. Keddie, "The Origins of the Religious-Radical Alliance," *Past and Present*, 34 (July 1966), 70–80; A. K. S. Lambton, "Secret Societies and the Persian Revolution of 1905–1906" (Middle Eastern Studies), St. Antony's Papers, Vol. 4 (London: Oxford University Press, 1958); Edward G. Browne, *The Persian Revolution of 1905–1909* (London: Cambridge University Press, 1910); Algar, *Religion and State*, pp. 205–256; Ervand Abrahamian, "Causes of the Constitutional Revolution," 399–414 (see n. 1).
11. Richard Cottam, *Nationalism in Iran* (University of Pittsburgh Press, 1979); Willem Floor, "The Revolutionary Character of the Iranian Ulama: Wishful Thinking or Reality?" *IJMES*, 12:4 (December 1980), 481–99.
12. James Bill, *The Politics of Iran* (Columbus, Ohio: Charles Merrill, 1972); Marvin Zonis, *The Political Elite of Iran* (Princeton University Press, 1971).
13. Guity Nashat, *The Origins of Modern Reform in Iran, 1870–1880* (Urbana: University of Illinois Press, 1982); Hamid Algar, *Mirza Malkum Khan* (Berkeley: University of California Press, 1973); Hafiz Farmanfarmayan, "The Forces of Modernization in Nineteenth Century Iran," in *Beginnings of Modernization in the Middle East*, ed. W. R. Polk and Richard Chambers (University of Chicago Press, 1968), 119–51; Shaul Bakhash, *Iran: Monarchy, Bureaucracy and Reform* (London: Ithaca Press, 1978).

14. A. K. S. Lambton, "Quis Custodiet Custodes?" *Studia Islamica,* 5:2 (1956) and 6:1 (1956), 125–48 and 125–46, respectively; Nikki Keddie, "The Roots of the Ulama's Power in Modern Iran," *Studia Islamica,* 29 (1969), 31–53; H. Algar, *Religion and State* (see n. 5); H. Algar, "The Oppositional Role of the Ulama in Twentieth Century Iran," in *Scholars, Saints and Sufis,* ed. Nikki Keddie (Berkeley: University of California Press, 1972), 231–55; Leonard Binder, "The Proofs of Islam," in *Studies in Honor of H. A. R. Gibb,* ed. George Makdisi (Leiden: E. J. Brill, 1965), 118–40; Joseph Eliash, "The Ithna' 'ashari Shi'i Juiristic Theory of Political and Legal Authority," *Studia Islamica,* 29 (1969), 17–30; Eliash, "Some Misconceptions Concerning Shi'i Political Theory," *IJMES* 9:1 (February 1979), 9–25; Said Amir Arjomand, "Religion, Political Action and Legitimate Domination in Shi'ite Iran: Fourteenth to Eighteenth Centuries A.D." *Archives européenes de sociologie,* 20:1 (1979), 59–109; Mangol Bayat, "Islam in Pahlavi and Post-Pahlavi Iran: A Cultural Revolution?" in *Islam and Development: Religion and Sociopolitical Change,* ed. John L. Esposito (Syracuse, N.Y.: Syracuse University Press, 1980), 89–94.

15. Bernard Lewis, "Islamic Concepts of Revolution," in *Revolution in the Middle East,* ed. P. J. Vatikiotis (London: Allen & Unwin, 1972), 33; Hamid Enayat, "Revolution in Iran 1979: Religion as Political Ideology," in *Revolutionary Theory and Political Reality,* ed. Noel K. O'Sullivan (New York: St. Martin's Press, 1983), 200: "In its classical version, Islamic political thought, whether of Sunni or Shi'ite persuasion, does not have a theory of revolution."

16. Shahrough Akhavi, *Religion and Politics in Contemporary Iran: Clergy-State Relations in the Pahlavi Period* (Albany: State University of New York Press, 1980); Michael M. J. Fischer, *Iran: From Religious Dispute to Revolution* (Cambridge: Harvard University Press, 1980).

17. "Constitution of the Islamic Republic of Iran," *Middle East Journal,* 34:2 (Spring 1980), 184–204. Also notable is its specific reference to Ayatollah Khomeini in a variety of places.

18. Said Arjomand, "Shi'ite Islam and Revolution in Iran," *Government and Opposition,* 16:2 (Summer 1981), 293–316.

19. Shahrough Akhavi, "the Ideology and Praxis of Shi'ism in the Iranian Revolution," *Comparative Studies in Society and History,* 25:2 (April 1983), 195–221; S. Akhavi, "The Structure and Foundation of Clergy Social Action in the Iranian Revolution," paper presented to the Persian Gulf Seminar, Center for Strategic and International Studies, Georgetown University, March 10, 1982.

20. Taking the lead offered by Leonard Binder in his book, *In a Moment of Enthusiasm* (University of Chicago Press, 1978), which discusses the Egyptian rural middle holders.

21. Apparently the level of independent-mindedness of certain MPs irritated Ayatollah Khomeini, who attacked MPs for criticizing the government because he views it as weakening Islam. See *Iran Times* (Washington, D.C.), 25 Azar 1362 H. Sh./16 December 1983. All references to articles in *Iran Times* (hereafter *IT*) are to Persian language articles (two of the paper's sixteen pages are in English). For an example of parliamentary criticism of the government, see the same issue of *IT,* which carries an article on the speech of Muhammad Riza 'Abbasi, MP from Kuhdasht and Chagini. In his statement, 'Abbasi sharply attacked the minister of agriculture for his continued references to self-sufficiency at a time when wheat imports had quadrupled.

22. Ayatollah Khomeini has bemoaned the decline in educational standards in the theological seminaries although he said it could not be helped because students were needed for political and military struggle to save Islam. He argued that later educational standards will be restored. *IT,* 18 Shahrivar 1362/9 September 1983. See also the comments by Khomeini's chosen successor, Ayatollah Husayn 'Ali Muntaziri, on the need for the *imam jum'ah*s to return to their books "to the limits of possibility to engage in scholarship ... rather than administrative and trivial matters." *IT,* 2 Day 1362 H. Sh./23 December 1983.

23. The elements of ideology summarized are found in Edward Shils, "The Concept and Function of Ideology," *International Encyclopaedia of the Social Sciences,* Vol. 7, 2nd ed., (New York: Macmillan, 1968), 66–76.

24. For a very detailed investigation, see Gregory Rose, "The Post-Revolutionary Purge of Iran's Armed Forces," *Iranian Studies,* 17:2–3 (Spring–Summer 1984), 153–94.

25. In fact, the president of the republic, Hujjat al-Islam 'Ali Khamanah'i, has urged the further politicization of the universities by introducing the *hizbullahis*—basically ruffians grouped into what they term The Party of God—into them. See *IT,* 6 Aban 1362/ 29 October 1983.

26. *IT,* 6 Shahrivar 1360/28 August 1981.

27. *IT,* 12 Shahrivar 1361/3 September 1982. Minister of Interior Natiq Nuri advocated a purge of even the revolutionary committees.

28. *IT,* 9 Bahman 1360/29 January 1982.

29. *IT,* 2 Day 1362/23 December 1983.

30. *IT,* 31 Urdibihisht 1361/21 May 1982.

31. *IT,* 15 Farvardin 1359/4 April 1980; also *IT,* 14 Farvardin 1360/3 April 1981 and *IT,* 4 Urdibihisht 1360/24 April 1981.

32. S. Akhavi, *Religion and Politics,* 172–80; (see n. 16) S. Akhavi, "The Ideology and Praxis of Shi'ism," 211–14 (see n. 19); David Menashri, "Shi'ite Leadership: In the Shadow of Conflicting Ideologies," in *Iranian Revolution in Perspective,* ed. Farhad Kazemi (Boston: Bosworth, 1981), 119–45. This is volume 13:1–4 of the journal, *Iranian Studies* (1980).

33. Since his early attack on the IRP and the draft constitution, Taba'taba'i Qummi has been under virtual house arrest. *IT,* 1 Farvardin 1360/21 March 1981.

34. *IT,* 2 Day 1362/23 December 1983.

35. Patrick Clawson, "Iran's Economy Between Crisis and Collapse," *MERIP Reports,* 11:6 (July–August 1981), 11–15.

36. *Jumhuri-yi Islami,* 2 Urdibihisht 1362; *Kayhan,* 2 Urdibihisht 1362; *Jumhuri-yi Islami,* 5 Khurdad 1362, and *Ittilia'at,* 24 Urdibisht 1362; all cited in *Nihzat,* 12–26 Khurdad 1362/2 June 1983.

37. Ruhollah Khomeini, *Islam and Revolution,* ed. Hamid Algar (Berkeley: Mizan Press, 1981), 185.

38. S. Akhavi, *Religion and Politics,* 117–29 (see n. 16).

39. Zalmay Khalilzad, "Soviet Dilemmas Strategy in Khomeini's Iran," in *Iran Since the Revolution,* ed. Barry Rosen, (Boulder, Colo.: Social Science Monographs, 1985) pp. 113–32.

40. Richard Cottam, "Iran's Perception of the Global Strategies of Big Powers," in *Iran Since the Revolution,* pp. 133–47.

41. *IT,* 18 Shahrivar 1362/9 September 1983.

42. *IT,* 29 Isfand 1360/19 March 1982.

43. *IT,* 7 Khurdad 1361/28 May 1982. The merger occurred in 1983.

44. *IT,* 8, 15 Bahman 1361/28 January, 4 February 1983.

45. *IT,* 1 Aban 1360/23 October 1981.

46. *IT,* 15 Bahman 1361/4 February 1983.

47. *IT,* 20 Aban 1362/11 November 1983.

48. *IT,* 3 Day 1361/24 December 1982.

49. Amnesty International has charged that the regime in the fall of 1982 was responsible for the execution of eighty percent of all executions by governments worldwide. And the next year, it alleged that the number of individuals the regime officially announced to have been executed was more than the acknowledged 5,000. See *IT,* 7 Aban 1361/29 October 1982, and *IT,* 8 Mehr 1362/30 September 1983.

50. *IT,* 28 Isfand 1360/19 March 1982.

51. *IT,* 2 Day 1362/23 December 1983.

52. Ruhollah Khomeini, *Hukumat-i Islami,* 3rd ed. (Najaf: 1391 H.Q./1971), 53.

53. *IT,* 2 Day 1362/23 December 1983.
54. *Ibid.*
55. *Ibid.*
56. Eliz Sansarian, *The Women's Rights Movement in Iran* (New York: Praeger, 1982); Guity Nashat, ed. *Women and Revolution in Iran* (Boulder: Westview, 1983).
57. Azar Tabari, "The Enigma of the Veiled Iranian Woman," *MERIP Reports* 12:2 (February 1982), 26.
58. *IT,* 16 Shahrivar 1358/7 September 1979.
59. Martin van Bruinissen, "Kurdish Nationalism and Sunni-Shi'i Conflict," paper presented to the Workshop on the History and Politics of Religious Movements in Iran, Institute of Comparative Social Research, Free University of Berlin, West Berlin, FRG, 5–7 September 1980.
60. Fred Halliday, "Year IV of the Islamic Republic," *MERIP Reports,* 13:3 (March–April 1983), 7.
61. S. Akhavi, *Religion and Politics,* 196–97 (see n. 16); *Fischer,* Iran, 79.
62. Farhad Kazemi, "Iran, Israel and the Arab-Israeli Balance," in *Iran Since the Revolution,* pp. 83–95 (see n. 39).

3

PAKISTAN
Islamic Government and Society

KEMAL A. FARUKI

The Spread of Islam and Muslim Rule
in the Subcontinent

Islam came to southern Asia in two main movements. The first, beginning in 712 C.E., came from what is now Iraq, entering the subcontinent at the Indus Delta in the southwest. The second, beginning about 1000 C.E., came from Central Asia through the Khyber Pass in the northwest. Until about 1750, the major part of the subcontinent was under Muslim control. In fact, the last, if only nominal, Moghul emperor remained on the Delhi throne until 1857.

During this long period, the proportion of Muslims in the subcontinent steadily increased, partly by immigration, but much more by conversion, until by about 1500 Muslims became the majority in what are now Pakistan and Bangladesh. At the time of partition and independence in 1947, Muslims constituted roughly one quarter of the total population of the subcontinent, including a significant minority around Delhi, in the upper Ganges Valley, and in the Deccan plain. Muslims and Hindus constituted two separate sociocultural systems living side by side in each town and village; sometimes in peaceful coexistence, sometimes in a state of violent confrontation.

There are two significant matters with regard to the period of Muslim rule that are essential to any understanding of the genesis of Pakistan and the place of Islam within it. First, during Muslim rule, in the search for stability, there was a recurring oscillation between a virtually secular policy and an assertion of Islam as the proper basis for the state and a means for ensuring the loyalty of its Muslim citizens. An attempt at establishing a syncretic state religion was made by the Moghul emperor, Akbar (d. 1605), and the reaction it engendered was toward an uncompromising Muslim politicolegal system in the fixed, traditional form of Sunni Islam of the Hanafi school variety, under the last major Moghul emperor,

Aurangzeb (d. 1707). The effect of this rigid policy was to alienate the feudatory Shi'i principalities in the south and, indeed, Shi'as in general. There followed (Hindu) Mahratta and Rajput revolts followed by Sikh uprisings in which the Sikhs became the highly militant community that they have remained ever since. These internal fissures coupled with the static nature of traditional Muslim thought and practice are largely responsible for the decline of the Moghul Empire after 1707.[1]

Second, when the Moghul decline began, there arose a new school of reformist Muslim thought under Shah Wali Allah of Delhi (d. 1762). He was motivated by the acute realization that nothing short of a drastic rethinking of some Muslim ideas would save the Muslim community. There were three main points in the Shah Wali Allah reforms: (1) an emphasis on a revival of moderate interpretation *(ijtihad)* instead of imitation *(taqlid)*;[2] (2) reconciliation *(tatbiq)* between theology and mysticism and, more significantly, between the Sunni and Shi'i sects; (3) an emphasis on the theoretically nonclerical, priestly (even populist), nature of Islam compared to Hinduism with its Brahminical monopoly of religious knowledge and exposition. This last point found expression through translations, for the benefit of ordinary Muslims, of the Quran into Persian by Shah Wali Allah and into Urdu by his sons.

This reformist trend continued in the nineteenth century with Syed Ahmad Khan's (d. 1898) Aligarh Muslim University. It was designed to produce a new generation of Muslims who were educated in a cosmopolitan manner, fluent in English, and thus able to understand and deal with the realities of the outside world and the modern age. Almost simultaneously there was established in Deoband, a small town also near Delhi, a new *ulama* institution designed to produce theologians and a clerical leadership who would reassert the traditional understanding of Islamic thought and practice. By the twentieth century, therefore, two distinct trends in the Muslim movement existed, the one, modernist, the other, traditionalist. The first led by Jinnah and the Muslim League, the second led by the majority of the Indian Muslim *ulama.*

The movement for Pakistan was led by the modernist, essentially Aligarhian, element, although there were a few traditionalists who supported it. But there were a great variety of motives among the supporters of the Pakistan movement. Some were afraid of Hindu economic domination or majoritarian political power in a united India; others foresaw increasing attempts by militant Hindu organizations to exterminate or forcibly reconvert Muslims into Hindus or even untouchables; yet another group thought a Muslim state was a necessity for preserving Urdu (the language of the urban Muslims in Delhi, the upper Ganges valley, and in Hyderabad [Deccan]). Urdu was an important factor in Muslim identity vis-à-vis Hindus who attempted to impose the Hindi language in northern India. There was a significant amount of literature, largely poetry, in the Urdu language that expressed the cultural distinctiveness of Muslims compared to the Hindus. It did not, however, necessarily have any constructure Islamic or religious content. However, there can be little doubt that among the many motives that led Muslims to support the Pakistan movement, the crucial one was the desire of a significant number to express Islam in political and social terms in a separate state, whether this expression was modern or traditional.

Pakistan, 1947–71

After the establishment of Pakistan in 1947, considerable energy was devoted to restoring a place in public life for Islam, which had been largely eliminated during British rule (except for family law and the law of charitable endowments). During the first year, the new state was primarily concerned with the problems of sheer survival—absorbing refugees from India, setting up the apparatus of the new government from virtually nothing, and contending with the question of Kashmir.

By 1949, the Constituent Assembly had adopted the Objectives Resolution, which has survived to this day as the preamble to Pakistan's three constitutions. This was followed by the Basic Principles Committee Report in 1952 and the first Constitution of the Islamic Republic of Pakistan in 1956. The latter document was framed and passed by a democratically elected assembly but abrogated, before coming properly into effect, by the declaration of martial law in 1958. The word *Islamic* was omitted in the 1962 Constitution of the Republic of Pakistan of Field Marshal Muhammad Ayub Khan. However, it was hastily reinserted with the first constitutional amendment in 1963. Finally, the 1973 Constitution of the Islamic Republic of Pakistan was passed by the government of Zulfikar Ali Bhutto in the National Assembly. All three constitutions contained common Islamic elements:

1. Recognition of the sovereignty of Almighty God over the entire universe, followed by the conviction that temporal sovereignty in Pakistan had been delegated in Pakistan to its people as a sacred trust within the limits prescribed by God's law.
2. The people's intention to implement the principles of democracy, freedom, equality, tolerance, and social justice as enunciated by Islam.
3. Muslim's should be "enabled" to order their individual and collective lives in accordance with Islamic principles.
4. Facilities should be provided for Muslims to understand the meaning of life in accordance with these Islamic principles.
5. The teaching of Islamiyyat (a course on Islam) to Muslims.
6. The observance of Islamic moral standards.
7. The proper organization of taxes *(zakat)*, religious endowments *(awqaf)*,[3] and mosques.
8. The prevention of prostitution, gambling, and the taking of injurious drugs.

  9. The prevention of consumption of alcoholic liquors.
 10. The elimination of *riba*.[4]
 11. The elimination of laws repugnant to the injunctions of Islam.

There were variations of the foregoing elements in each of the three constitutions. For instance, with regard to alcohol, one constitution refers to "discouraging" its consumption, another to its "prevention," whereas the third refers to its "prohibition." Variation also exists with regard to Muslim rules: At times the emphasis is on "providing facilities," at other times on "enabling," and at still other times on "compulsion." Nevertheless, there is a substantial amount of continuity in these documents.

In practice, however, the pre-1947 modernist/traditionalist conflicts were at work from the beginning. The leadership of Pakistan was essentially in modern Aligarhian hands. But the traditionalists and neotraditionalists, Deobandi and non-Deobandi, who found themselves living within the new state or who reluctantly moved there from India once it became clear that partition was inevitable, these anti-Aligarh groups soon reasserted their views. When Jinnah's sister appeared with him immediately after independence, unveiled, clerics were quick to criticize this allegedly un-Islamic behavior.

The difference in views was also in constitutional matters. During the debate on the Report of the Basic Principles Committee of 1952, *ulama* of different schools of thought united to propose an amendment that a committee of *ulama* should have power to veto any government measure or proposed legislation that they considered un-Islamic.[5]

A deadlock occurred in the *Zakat* Committee set up in 1951. Modernists wanted a reformulation of *zakat* that would be more suitable to, and workable in, a contemporary state. For example, classical *zakat* is levied on camels and horses among other items. Modernists, regarding this as a tax on means of transportation, held the view that *zakat* is equally applied to lorries, buses, cars, and taxis. Traditionalists strongly objected on the grounds that if the principle of new interpretation was accepted with regard to *zakat* (one of the Five Pillars [*arkan*] of the Faith),[6] it might be used as a precedent to change the rules regarding other *arkan,* such as prayer, fasting, or the pilgrimage. The result was that the majority recommendations of the *Zakat* Committee were never implemented.

A similar split of opinion between traditionalists and modernists developed in the Commission on Marriage and Family Laws, in which the modernists advocated raising the age of marriage from fourteen to sixteen; placing checks on the arbitrary use of unilateral divorce by the husband; introducing similar checks on plural marriages; and enabling orphaned grandchildren to share by right in their grandfather's estate (they had been excluded by their living uncles according to traditional interpretations of Islamic law).

Matters came to a head in 1953 when agitation led by the traditionalist *ulama* and neotraditionalist elements demanded (unsuccessfully) that the government declare the Ahmadiyya community to be a non-Muslim minority. Members of this sect are followers of Mirza Ghulam Ahmad (d. 1908) who proclaimed himself the Promised Messiah. He came from Qadian, a small town in what is now Indian Punjab. After partition his followers, known as Ahmadis, Mirzais, or Qadianis, moved their headquarters to Rabwah in Pakistan, although a breakaway group maintains its offices in Lahore. Many Shi'a and Sunni Muslims maintain that Ahmadi claims regarding their founder's status and revelations are heretical because they imply a denial of the finality of the Prophethood of Muhammad (o.w.b.p.).* As a result, in 1953 widespread anti-Ahmadi riots took place in the Punjab, followed by dismissal of the Punjab provincial cabinet and the imposition of martial law in that province.

The combined effect of these events during Pakistan's first seven years led to a virtual suspension of further attempts at Islamization. However, during the Ayub era, the recommendations of the Commission on Marriage and Family Laws were given partial effect in the Muslim Family Laws Ordinance of 1961. Matters stayed thus until the breakaway of East Pakistan in 1971, which caused much soul searching as to the causes of this disaster.

Pakistan, 1971–77

The establishment of an independent Bangladesh meant residual Pakistan need no longer concern itself with an eastward commitment and could look westward toward the Muslim heartlands of the Middle East, even if perforce it continued to be concerned about relations with its eastern neighbor, India.

As far as Pakistan's future integrity was concerned, many considered that by neglecting its Islamic commitment for twenty-four years, Pakistan had weakened ties between its two wings. There was one significant addition of an Islamic nature in Bhutto's 1973 Constitution, namely, the promotion of the Arabic language in Pakistan. Although the Pakistan People's Party of Zulfikar Ali Bhutto was considered socialist rather than Islamic in its program, the fact remained that immediately after coming to power Bhutto made a tour of different Muslim countries to enlist their support; Pakistan also hosted the 1974 Islamic Summit at Lahore.

Indeed, Islamic sentiments became more noticeable as the years went by. The growth of such sentiments was only partly explained by the growing importance of Saudi Arabia, Libya, and other Muslim oil-producing states after the 1973 Arab-Israeli War and the international oil crisis. Opposition parties found that accusing the Bhutto regime of indifference

---

*The letters in parentheses stand for "on whom be peace" and are traditionally used after the mention of the Prophet's proper name as an English-language equivalent of the Arabic phrase.

to Islam was a convenient and increasingly effective rallying point. As a result, the Bhutto government gave in to demands for declaring the Ahmadiyya a non-Muslim minority in 1975 and, in its last year or so, the Bhutto government endeavored to establish its Muslim credentials by declaring gambling, horseracing, and nightclubs illegal and by prohibiting the consumption of alcohol.

This, however, was not enough to counter growing opposition. In fact, each of the regime's new concessions to opposition demands on Islamic matters strengthened the opposition's conviction that the government was in retreat and that charging it with being un-Islamic was their strongest weapon. A coalition of nine parties, the Pakistan National Alliance (PNA), brought together two traditionalist *ulama* parties, one neotraditionalist politicoreligious party, and six other parties that, though nonclerical, were of varying degrees of Muslim persuasion on more modernist lines. When general elections were held in early 1977, the PNA was able to put up a convincing performance. Although the demand for an Islamic order played an important part, the widespread disturbances that ultimately led to Bhutto's downfall were based on charges that the Bhutto government had rigged the general elections. An additional factor was the alliance between the *ulama* and the small-scale entrepreneurs who had been adversely affected by Bhutto's nationalization measures and consequently provided funds and organizational structure for the anti-Bhutto movement.

Pakistan After July 5, 1977

Before evaluating the Islamization process of General Zia-ul-Haq's martial law regime, which came to power on July 5, 1977, the regime's method of decision making deserves mention. Those involved included the bureaucracy; judiciary, including the *Shariat* (*sic*) Courts; the Council of Islamic Ideology (CII); the Law Commission; and the Majlis-i-Shura, a national consultative assembly nominated by the martial law government and advertised as a transitional parliament. In addition, committees have been formed from time to time for specific issues. Membership has included bureaucrats, bankers, financiers, economists, industrialists, lawyers, *ulama,* and academics. At the early stage of martial law, the process also included members of the Jamaat-i-Islami party, when it collaborated with the regime and accepted cabinet posts.

With rare exceptions, deliberations have been taking place in virtual secrecy, with an occasional leak to the press. In the early stages, both traditionalists and modernists participated in the creative side of making recommendations; but as time went on, the recommendatory aspect became increasingly dominated by traditionalists. This was reflected, for instance, in the changing composition of the CII until it was entirely traditional and *ulama* dominated as well as in the induction of members of the *ulama* on the *shariah* courts and benches. The administrators as such and the others whose opinions were sought *ex officio* tended increasingly to restrict themselves merely to an examination of the workability of any proposal and to the formulation of laws and regulations for implementation. Only recently have modernists of the Aligarh spirit shown renewed vigor in responding to the effects of the traditionalist legislation.

To attempt a detailed analysis of Islamization in Pakistan under Zia-ul-Haq would be a lengthy task and, in many cases, the trend is far from clear. It is proposed, instead, to deal with a limited number of the more significant or more revealing issues.

Immediately after coming to power, General Mohammad Zia-ul-Haq issued a series of martial law regulations. One made reference to the punishment of theft by amputation of the right hand from the wrist. Although no such sentence had been carried out by the end of 1984, it was clear that Islamization in Pakistan had entered a phase beyond those measures passed by the Bhutto government.

Where the Five Pillars *(arkan)* of the Faith were concerned, greater emphasis was laid on observing the noonday prayer in government-controlled offices. Senior officers were advised to lead or, at least, attend these prayers. During the month of fasting (Ramadan), restrictions on eating in public places became more stringent; and in hotels, travelers and the sick (absolved from fasting by Islamic law) found it difficult to obtain food even in their rooms. Much government fanfare surrounded the annual pilgrimage to Mecca, with high officials photographed and filmed while sending off and welcoming home pilgrims at the docks and airports. Publicity was given to the new regime for allowing more pilgrims. (Government sanction is required for obtaining Saudi currency and booking passage.) The fourth pillar, alms giving *(zakat),* is dealt with later.

Television and film censorship was increased and the dress worn by women participants and a purity view were increasingly applied regarding entertainment at schools and colleges. The walls of offices, calendars, and even billboards were adorned with quotations from the Holy Quran and with sayings of the Prophet Muhammad. In due course, lounge suits, safari suits, and ties were frowned on as un-Islamic. When Zia-ul-Haq's personal example failed to have much effect in 1981, a "national" dress of *shalwar,* or *churidar,* or *pajama*[7] worn with *kamiz* or *kurta* (types of shirts) and with or without a long coat (*sherwani* or *achkan*) was prescribed as obligatory for government employees. Conferences and seminars on Islamic themes proliferated, with and without delegates from other Muslim countries, and were welcomed with banners and extensive publicity. Speeches, usually platitudinous and noncontroversial, were reported very briefly in the press, with greater emphasis given to visual coverage.

But in early 1984, six and one-half years after Zia-ul-Haq came to power, the Central Committee of the Jamaat-i-Islami (Islamic Party)—renamed the Tehrik-i-Islami (Islamic movement) after political parties were officially banned—commented on the state of public morality:

> Open violation of Islamic ethics, rebellion from Islamic teachings has now reached an alarming point in our society. The public media organizations, with the connivance of certain corrupt officers, are bent upon converting our society into a mixed and shameless one. Vulgar songs, semi-nude and immoral advertisements, programs of dance and music, encouragement of mixed gatherings on television, particularly unreserved [sic] dialogue delivered by boys and girls, the color editions of newspapers full of huge colored pictures of women and feminine beauty are only a few examples of this condemnable conspiracy. This dangerous wave of vulgarity has now gripped the country. Performances by foreign troupes attended by certain very important government officials, fancy dress shows, vulgar stage plays in the name of art, mixed gatherings, country-wide virus of VCR, dancing and musical programs, printing of girls' pictures in the newspapers in the name of sports, mixed education, employment of women in certain government departments to make them attractive and the day-by-day rising process of seating men and women under one roof in government and business offices and even in local councils are all "red" signs of dangers against the society and Islamic ethics. This meeting condemns all these things very strongly and demands to the government that it should take immediate steps to stop such shameless, vulgar, and obscene activities and fulfill its promised safety of *chaddar* and *chardiwari*.[8]

Apart from showing how little the Islamization process had impressed the traditionalists and their political parties, the Jamaat-i-Islami resolution gives some idea of their concept of an Islamic society.

That the Jamaat's resolution cannot be dismissed as merely the carping criticism of a party no longer exercising some subordinate political power is shown by the fact that the government-appointed Council of Islamic Ideology proposed even more stringent measures at about the same time. By doing so it seemed to acknowledge that traditional Islamization had not achieved the desired results in enforcing the personal aspects of faith. The CII was reported as advocating the reintroduction of the classical Hanafi punishment *(hadd)* for apostasy from Islam: death for a Muslim man, life imprisonment for a Muslim woman unless she recants. It is reported that in the same set of recommendations to the government, the council asked for the death penalty for "showing disrespect" to the Prophet and for fines to be levied on Muslims who failed to attend the Friday congregational prayers.[9]

Not to be outdone, those *ulama* invited by the government to attend a conference in Islamabad embarrassed their hosts at the end of the conference by voicing disappointment with the Islamization process. They claimed that only five percent of accounts had been rendered interest free in the economy and that even they were not genuinely interest free. They also advocated "severe punishment" for anyone doubting the finality of the Prophethood of Muhammad.[10] What this would mean for the beleaguered Ahmadiyya community was not clear, apart from its implications for non-Muslims who might hold sentiments more in keeping with their own religious convictions.

Would public morality have been worse if there had not been this type of Islamization process? Does the lack of desired results mean, as traditionalists assert more and more, that parallelism between *ulama* and non-*ulama* Islamic understanding must be ended, Islamization must be intensified on purely traditional lines, and enforcement be handled by more competent people? Or is the moral of all this that the current traditional Islamization itself is faulty in implementation and, indeed, conception?

In any case, the question of prayer was taken a step further seven months later in President Zia-ul-Haq's nationwide address on independence day (August 14, 1984). Although important announcements were expected regarding both the elections promised for early 1985 and some of the unanswered constitutional issues, the main feature of the address concerned prayer. The president announced that an organizer of prayer *(nazim-i-galat)* was to be immediately appointed in every village and urban precinct. These organizers were to concern themselves not only with the Friday congregational prayers, but also the five-times daily prayers. Zia-ul-Haq went on to state, according to the full official text printed in the daily *Dawn* of Karachi on August 16, 1984:

> Only those persons are being appointed for this service of religion who have sound moral character and their piety is so exemplary that their words will have deep effect on the hearts of people. The procedure for this exercise *for the time being* [italics added] is based on persuasion and motivation and not on compulsion. But we are determined to succeed in establishing the system of prayer at all cost.

In the field of penal laws, *hudood*[11] (Ar. *hudud*) ordinances were promulgated on the Prophet's birthday (12 Rabi; al-Awwal, A.H. 1399; February 10, 1979, C.E.). These relate to the offenses of theft, highway dacoity, adultery, false accusation of adultery, and consumption of intoxicants. The sixth so-called *hadd* offense of apostasy was not dealt with, although the CII later recommended the reintroduction of the classical death penalty (which is not, however, to be found in the Quran). For the other five, the punishments are more or less in line with the classical rules: (1) amputation of the right hand from the wrist for theft; (2) thirty stripes for highway robbery (dacoity)[12] without violence and imprisonment "until the Court is satisfied of [the prisoner's] being sincerely penitent"—if theft is also committed in the course of the dacoity, then amputation is also applicable, and if murder is committed in the course of the dacoity, then the death penalty is to be imposed; (3) for adultery *(zina),* stoning to death[13] in a public place if the adulterer or adulteress is married, otherwise one hundred stripes; (4) for a false accusation of adultery *(qadhf),* eighty stripes has been prescribed; and (5) for consumption of intoxicants (defined to also include both soft and hard drugs in any form), the punishment prescribed is eighty stripes.

Reliable crime statistics are hard to come by, but the situation appears to have worsened. The Federal *Shariat* [*sic*] Court has failed to authorize the *hadd* punishment for theft in the many cases that have come before it, on the grounds that an Islamic law of evidence must first be in place. For reasons mentioned later, this has still not happened; but clearly a decision cannot be indefinitely postponed. Meanwhile, there is an intense debate on the many dimensions of the subject in the press and elsewhere. For example, is it wrong to punish a thief with amputation before an Islamic system of social welfare is functional? What about real and spectacular types of contructive theft—such as embezzlement, corruption, smuggling, and misuse of public office—that are outside the purview of the classical law on theft, which falls almost entirely on the poor.[14]

On another *hadd* offense, *zina,* the situation is equally complex. Like the classical death penalty for apostasy, the punishment of stoning to death for a married adulterer or adulteress is not derived from the Quran but rests on *hadith* (traditions of the Prophet's practice—compiled some two centuries after his death—some of which are not accepted by many as authentic). On an appeal by the central government to the *Shariah* bench of the Supreme Court, in a referral made originally to the Federal *Shariat* [*sic*] Court, the Federal *Shariat* Court reversed itself and upheld the punishment of stoning to death for a married adulterer or adulteress. No such punishment has so far been carried out, pending the finalization of the new Islamized law of evidence. It should be mentioned that the argument has also been advanced that the evidentiary requirements of Islamic law have not been complied with in any of the cases that have come before the *shariat* courts in the seven years that have elapsed since the *hudud* ordinances came into effect.

On flogging for adultery *(zina)* as applicable to unmarried persons or in cases where (apparently) the strict Islamic evidentiary requirements have not been complied with, there have been anomalies and contradictions. Apart from the case of the blind girl convicted of *zina* who was sentenced to flogging (the sentence was later reversed),[15] there are strange, inequitable discrepancies in the number of lashes awarded in relation to the nature of the offense. There are also conflicting reports about the manner in which the whipping is to be administered. It appears that the provisions of the British Whipping Act of 1909 are still sometimes observed by prison officials rather than the Execution of the Punishment of Whipping Ordinance of 1979. In an undated booklet published by the government, *The Federal Shariat Court,* the then chief justice of the court, Aftab Hussain, distinguished between the old (British) law and the present law: "While the emphasis of the old law was on physical torture as a punishment, the present law modelled according to *shari'a* lays stress on the humiliation of the convict rather than on causing to him physical injuries."

The charge is also made that theft and *zina* provisions are only applied to the poor and ignorant, not to the more privileged classes. In its October 1983 issue, the Herald, a Karachi English-language monthly, interviewed career women. Among others, an actress stated: "I've been in love and had affairs." She then went on to discuss her "current relationship with a man that cannot culminate in marriage. This was something I knew from day one. He made it clear from the very beginning. It did not stop me from entering into or proceeding with the relationship." (pp. 36–37). No attempt was made to invoke the *zina* provisions in this or similar cases.

In economic matters, Islamization has dealt with *zakat, ushr, riba,* and alternative methods of financing and conducting business.[16] A *zakat* ordinance came into effect on June 20, 1980, levying a two and one-half percent compulsory *zakat* tax, at source, on savings and similar accounts, time deposit receipts and certificates, government securities and shares, life insurance policies, and provident funds. Other items were listed on which the individual Muslim was expected to voluntarily make payment, such as gold and silver and manufactures thereof, cash, prize bonds, current accounts, loans receivable, securities other than those subject to compulsory levy, stock-in-trade of commercial and industrial undertakings (including dealers in real estate), precious metals and stones, fish and agricultural produce, animals of various kinds, and wealth and financial assets other than those listed. On October 22, 1983, the federal finance minister, Ghulam Ishaq Khan, stated during the question hour in the Majlis-e-Shura that by August 10, 1983, Rs 3,222 million ($238.7 million) had been collected in *zakat,* whereas the total amount distributed "so far" was Rs 2,375 million ($176 million).

The amount raised in the compulsory *zakat* levy in 1984 was, therefore, about Rs 1 billion ($75 million) compared to the state's secular revenues of Rs 60 billion ($4.5 billion). State *zakat* revenues, therefore, amount to about two percent of the total. Yet, as the above list of items on which voluntary *zakat* is payable shows, the potential of voluntary *zakat* revenue is far greater. Some voluntary payment is still being given directly by donor to donee. But it has not eliminated poverty in the past and the amount being collected by government is unlikely to do so, let alone serve as a substitute for secular taxes for administration and development.

Four different opinions may be noted regarding *zakat:*

1. All *zakat* should be a voluntary act of charity for the sake of God, like the other *arkan.*
2. The items on which *zakat* is leviable and the manner in which it is used to remove, not merely alleviate, poverty and to provide an alternative to secular taxes must be revised so that mere handouts

can be replaced by income-generating and work-generating projects. Further, if *zakat* or a *zakat*like system is to replace all non-Islamic forms of taxation, it should be understood that the principle behind *zakat* is a tax on capital assets not on income.

3. Only when there is a revolutionary or radical change in government and society can *zakat* be effective. In other words, the present regime is not authentically Islamic and not an *ulama*-run state or one run by the Jamaat-i-Islami can bring about true change.

4. Funds for removing poverty and funds for administration and development must be distinguished.

The object of *zakat* is only to remove poverty; there is no Islamic objection of the state raising secular or Western-type taxes for administrative or developmental purposes, such as for the bureaucracy, defense, and education as well as the building of roads, hospitals, and the like. Although this fourth opinion implies that an Islamic economic system is not self-sufficient, it appears to be the one the present regime is pursuing.

The *zakat* distribution system consists of a pyramid with a central committee at the apex and counterparts at the provincial, district, and local levels. Locally elected committees consist of seven men, nonofficial and nonparty. Evidence suggests that at the local level a relative degree of honesty prevails in maintaining accounts and disbursement of funds. One major criticism has been that, because women are totally absent from local *zakat* committies, there is a moral risk in having only men determine and distribute *zakat* to illiterate and often hapless widows, orphaned girls, and young women.

The basic souce of government *zakat* has been deductions from Sunni Muslims only from savings accounts in banks and such schemes as the *khass* deposit certificates (KCDs). These were originally three-year government savings certificates that paid twelve percent interest per annum at six monthly intervals. After *zakat* began to be deducted therefrom, at two and one-half percent, the rate of return was raised to fifteen percent per annum, so that the certificate holder now received twelve and one-half percent *after* the *zakat* deduction was made. In other words, the sums at the disposal of the government from compulsory *zakat* deductions were, in effect, being paid for by the government itself.

As to the significance of this distribution, it has been estimated that an average distribution is made of about Rs 1000 ($75) per annum, or Rs 83 ($12) per month, to each of the *mustahiqeen* (deserving). It was stated by the federal finance minister, during question hour in the Majlis-i-Shura in October 1983, that during the previous two fiscal years Rs 60,772,240 had been spent to rehabilitate 196,949 deserving, which amounts to Rs 308.50 ($22.85) per head. This apparently being sufficient to rehabilitate. Clearly these were simple cases that did not touch the real problems of poverty. The amounts being distributed as handouts do not even meet subsistence requirements and seem to perpetuate beggary. The amounts paid to theological schools and their deserving students are negligible. Basic *ijtihad* (reinterpretation of Islamic legal sources) on the sources and uses of *zakat* is needed. *Zakat* in its traditional form cannot hope to meet the expectations of those who regard it as an essential part of Islam's solution to the economic challenge facing Muslim countries and, indeed, humanity today.

Ushr (literally, a tenth or tithe), an agricultural subsidiary to *zakat,* came into effect much later as a compulsory five percent tax on agricultural produce, with the remaining five percent regarded as voluntary. First-year actual receipts were about Rs 22.5 million ($1.66 million).

There has been no understanding of *riba* (which is prohibited by the Quran) as referring only to usury and excluding bank interest. Instead, official policy (in line with traditional doctrine) has been to eliminate "the curse of interest" interpreted as any fixed, predetermined increase in the capital sum lent. As an initial step, parallel counters were set up in banks (nationalized during the Bhutto regime). These accepted deposits under a Profit-and-Loss Sharing (PLS) scheme. The theory behind this was that the banks would invest their customers' monies in businesses in which the return to the banks' customers would depend on the profits or losses made in these investments.

In early 1981, this PLS scheme was launched. In the first five years, the percentage share of PLS to total deposits has risen to over twenty percent. This is partly due to switching state or state-controlled corporate accounts from interest-bearing accounts to PLS and partly to the attraction of profit that is higher than interest, without any loss so far.[17]

The PLS exercise seems to be artificially controlled by a conclave of various financial and banking officials because the profit announced each year by all the scheduled, government-owned banks is curiously about one or one and one-half percent higher than the interest returns of savings accounts. The profits of the banks' PLS schemes are within one percent of each other, and no bank shows a loss. This extra amount of profit compared to interest has been enough to move increasing sums to the PLS scheme, but the real test of the PLS scheme is when the profit drops below the interest rate in an equivalent interest-bearing deposit or when a PLS account actually shows a loss.

The second crisis point lies in the use to which banks put PLS deposits. In contrast to interest-bearing time deposits and current account deposits on which loans can be made to any responsible borrower, a bank's PLS sums can only be invested in *musharaka* companies (where the banks enter into so-called partnerships with borrowers); in participation term certificates with companies (with a fixed return on profit); or two types of price markup: (1) Instead of borrowing money, the borrower agrees to purchase the item from the bank at an agreed markup, after which he can claim ownership. There is no policy about what happens if there is a failure or delay in payment by the borrower. Markup upon markup is unacceptable to traditionalists as being too transparent a substitute for compound interest; but a flat penalty still does not eliminate the unjust average gained by the one who delays payment. (2) This markup is the major utilization (sixty-five percent) of PLS monies by banks, but this time it is in the commodity-trading operations of the government.

The banks now find they have PLS monies increasingly in excess of what they can handle, even in these so-called interest-free operations. Various solutions are offered. One is to end parallelism and switch over to an entirely interest-free economy, thereby leaving depositors with no option but the PLS scheme and other noninterest-bearing outlets for their savings. Private trade and industry would be forced to resort to noninterest bearing facilities, with banks interfering in day-to-day management of companies. If any attempt was made to do this in haste, it would have totally unforeseen consequences both in terms of savings generated and confidence in the economy of the country. Such a shift could only be safely made, if at all, over a period of decades.

Irrespective of whether it is truly Islamic or not, the present type of Islamization of the economy is unlikely to succeed unless it is done in a stage-by-stage manner, examining the consequences of each step before proceeding to the next one. Unfortunately, time is the one thing the present regime cannot afford. The sincerity of its Islamic professions (in contrast to that of its predecessors, as it frequently proclaims) requires it to accelerate the process of Islamization. Similar political motives are behind the charges by a growing number of traditionalist critics and *ulama* that the slowness of current Islamization (apart from the transparently fictitious nature of some of the interest-free schemes) shows that the regime is *not* sincere.

Notwithstanding the risks, the government appears to have opted for a rapid and complete changeover to Islamic modes of financing by a three-stage process that went into effect on June 30, 1985 (it excludes international transactions). After that date, banks could no longer accept deposits based on interest: All savings must be based on profit and loss. However, the State Bank would be given the power to regulate the maximum or minimum rate of profit or return chargeable by the banks.[18] The *riba* aspect of Islamization dramatically illustrates the dilemma facing the regime and, as with *zakat,* it appears that the pseudotraditional approach has exhausted its possibilities.

Current measures at eliminating "the curse of interest" are advertised as evidence of the concern of government to achieve social justice, but nothing has been done to eliminate from Pakistan the curse of the professional moneylenders. These *soodkhuris* (literally, devourers of usury) are officially registered under the old Moneylenders Act of the British era and are permitted to lend at not more than one percent below the state bank rate. In fact, the *soodkuris* show loans on their books at double the sums actually lent and charge interest at rates as high as sixty percent per annum on the face value of the loan. Operating in Mafia-style gangs, they use force and intimidation to extract payment of what is incontestable usury. Cases have been reported in which families have been forced into selling their children to these moneylenders; the children are then maimed and employed as professional beggars. This whole gruesome business would seem to be the first place at which to tackle a genuine curse on society and a true case of *riba*.

In judicial matters, the Federal *Shariat* Court, based in the capital of Islamabad, also goes on circuit to the provincial capitals. Consisting originally only of judges from the existing judiciary, it has added members of the *ulama* in the ratio of four judges to three *ulama*. Appeals from a *Shariat* Court (in some cases on a mandatory basis) are made to a *shariat* bench of the Supreme Court of Pakistan, composed on similar lines. For the time being, certain fiscal, family, and martial law orders are excluded from the court's jurisdiction. Otherwise, the *shariat* courts are intended to adjudge cases of an Islamic nature or where it is alleged that a particular provision of an existing law is un-Islamic. It acts as an appeal court also on its own volition and against sentences passed under the *hudud* ordinances.

It is proposed that the separation of the judiciary into *shariah* and non-*shariah* courts be extended all the way down to *qazi (qadi)* courts at various subdistrict and district levels. Although some believe that the adversary system of law is un-Islamic, President Zia-ul-Haq has given assurance on more than one occasion that lawyers would still be allowed to appear before these *qazi* courts. Delay in setting up the *qazi* court system was due, it was stated, to the delay in finalizing the Islamic law of evidence. The *qazi* courts are to be introduced on an experimental basis in selected areas.

Finally in the quasi-judicial sphere, mention should be made of the Wafaqi Mohtasib (Ombudsman) Order of 1983. This institution has so far been confined to examination of complaints of overbilling for electricity and the like, and, it appears to resemble the Western institution of ombudsman far more than the classical Islamic institition of *muhtasib*.

In the realm of law, the Council of Islamic Ideology has been examining the Central and Provincial Laws of Pakistan going back to 1834. Brief CII press releases from time to time inform the public that certain laws have been examined and recommendations made to the government, but few, if any, details are given. Various life and other insurance laws are claimed to be basically un-Islamic, and a new approach has been suggested for an Islamic form of insurance.[19]

In classical Islamic law, murder and injuries to the person were regarded basically as matters of private rather than public law. In the case of murder, it was for the tribal relatives *(aqila)* of the deceased to seek retaliation *(qisas)* or compensation *(diya);* the same applied for injuries. After four years of deliberations, the CII submitted a draft ordinance that virtually restated the classical law on the subject, with all its inequalities between men and women and its application to life in a tribal society. The draft gave rise to bitter controversy when it was examined by a select committee of the Majlis-i-Shura. So far nothing has been done to implement the ordinance.[20]

A crucial part of Islamization of law concerns the law of evidence for which a new evidence act (Qanun-e-Shahadat Order) was promulgated in October 1984. The new order differs very little from the 1872 evidence act. Sections were rearranged and renumbered but remained unchanged textually. In less than half a dozen places, out of 166 sections, Islamic references are to be found. In sections 3 and 17 of the order they virtually state that these matters shall be decided in accordance with the Quran and *sunna* (i.e., the practice of the Prophet) without spelling out what are precisely the Quranic and *sunna* provisions. Lawyers and judges trained in the common law system have taken the view, by and large, that the existing law of evidence, based on common law, is satisfactory and requires only a few changes to conform to enduring Islamic principles. The *ulama,* both those newly inducted into the establishment and outside it, want to replace existing law with pre-British traditional Muslim law as set out in the Emperor Aurangzeb's seventeenth-century *Fatawa-i-Alamgiri,* with possibly a few changes.

One major point that remains unresolved concerns the evidence of women. In classical Islamic law, the evidence of one woman was regarded as equal to half that of one man, with the exception of midwifes attesting to the maternity of a child and wives denying adultery on oath, which prevailed over the oath of accusing husbands. Reformist Islamic legal thinking and the increasingly strong women's lobby are insisting on the value of the testimony of a man and a woman as equal.

On educational matters, an Islamic university has been established at the capital in the hope that it will fuse secular and Muslim educations. Funded largely by Saudi Arabia, some senior staff members are from the Middle East, chosen from among those acceptable to Saudi authorities and the *ulama.* It is hoped that this university will also train those who will man the *qazi* court system. A *shariah* training institute was also set up for judges and others dealing with Islamic law. Islamiyyat (Islamic studies) courses were made compulsory at higher levels, including the BA and the BSc degrees. It was intended that only those students who could recite the Holy Quran would be allowed to take the matriculation examination.

Degrees from traditional theological schools and colleges *(deeni madaris)* are recognized on a par with those from universities, but their standards of education were officially admitted to need improvement. The government intends to establish its own theological schools to serve as centers of excellence and models for existing institutions. Finally, Arabic has already been made compulsory in classes six to eight and will be expanded to include both lower and higher classes.

The nature of Islamization in the judiciary and education is far from clear. Sooner or later, traditionalists will assert that existing courts and universities are un-Islamic and this parallelism must be abolished. Once again, a critical point will be reached.

There has been considerable confusion with respect to the education of women and their role in public life. The government has promised conservatives that it will establish separate women's universities. However, it seems that, if carried out, this will be no more than adding postgraduate courses to one or two existing women's colleges and renaming them as universities. There have been moves to ban women from participating in sports, and the law of evidence, as noted above, has been a focal point of confrontation between modernists and conservatives. The Ansari Commission has recommended that henceforth only women over fifty years of age should be permitted to stand for election and then only with the permission of their husbands or other male relatives. The dispute about the place of women has also extended to whether, in view of a woman's evidence being valued as half that of a man, a woman should be permitted to act as a *qazi*. Women's groups have been agitating against proposed measures aimed at reducing their status and rights. On some occasions, women's demonstrations have triggered tear gas and baton-charging on the part of the police, an unprecedented development that has only increased the dispute about the place of women in an Islamic social order.

There are, however, fitful signs that the government is retreating from the traditional position on this matter. Speaking at a women's conference in Islamabad on January 2, 1984, Zia-ul-Haq asserted that according to Islam, women have the right to work outside their home. This may have been prompted by the increasing organization of women to protect their rights and by a recognition of the near impossibility of replacing already employed women. For example, over one quarter of working mothers in the province of Sindh are the sole earning members for their families.[21] The curious blindness of traditionalists toward the problems of the underprivileged is again revealed with regard to women. Early in 1983, the Federal *Shariat* Court also ruled that women can be appointed *qazis*.

On constitutional and political matters, a *Majlis-i-Shura* (consultative assembly) was set up admittedly as a transitional measure and local bodies were set up through elections of screened nonparty candidates. A great deal of debate continues on the implications of the Quranic injunctions to believers to consult among themselves on their mutual affairs and how this affects the relationship between the executive head and the assembly in an Islamic state. Debate also continues about whether Islam permits parties or not. It is maintained by some who argue against parties that Islam does not refer to them anywhere; others argue that neither is there a reference to martial law.

A great deal of the confusion surrounding Islamization has been caused by the failure to resolve the constitutional issue. The regime had hoped to establish its legitimacy or, at the very least, obtain sufficient acceptance from the people by carrying out sweeping Islamization measures. It con-

stantly reiterates that it has already done more in this regard than had
been done by all the governments of the previous thirty years of Pakistan's existence. The net effect seems to be increasing alienation on the
part of the modernists and a failure to satisfy the traditionalists. In
response, General Zia has talked with increasing emphasis about accel-
erating the pace of Islamization. Yet true Islamization, whether fast or
slow, can only be legitimate when it rests in a constitutional form on the
consensus of the community that decides who is competent and when it
accepts the results of its unavoidable *ijtihad.*[22]

There are two major matters, from the Islamic point of view, that have
been raised, as stated, with regard to the constitution. First, should there
be political parties or not? There have been attempts by some traditionalists and the government to try and prove that political parties are un-
Islamic, but these attempts have been regarded by the opposition as a
device by the regime to control the political process and elections, having
no Islamic basis. Here again, the decisive moment cannot be long
delayed. There was also an attempt by the regime to interpret the Quranic
references to *shura* (consultation) into authorizing the executive power to
merely consult but not defer to the views of a people's assembly. The
relevant Quranic verse (42:38) defines believers as, *inter alia,* those who
settle their affairs by *shura.* The opposition has taken the view that this
consultation is mutual and that decisions must be consensual and cannot
be taken to imply that an executive has overriding authority.[23]

These constitutional questions are, in fact, more a screen behind which
are issues regarding regionalism and the risks that an elected government
may institute accountability proceedings against the military regime.

Finally, mention should be made of those measures that are undertaken with the apparent aim of making a consolidated state out of Pakistan, measures in which there is frequently confusion about what is
Islamic and what is merely ethnic tradition or sentiment that has little or
no connection with Islam, such as dress reform and language.

Referendum, Lifting of Martial Law, and Partyless Elections

President Zia-ul-Haq's rule entered a new phase in late 1984 with the
holding of a statewide referendum under which voters were asked
whether they approved of General Zia's Islamization program. If they
answered in the affirmative, voters were advised that he would be
"deemed" to be president for the next five years. This novel juxtaposition
of propositions resulted in an affirmative vote among Pakistan's very
Muslim-conscious populace. Estimates of the turnout vary from official
assertions of fifty percent to more widespread estimates both at home and
abroad of about fifteen to twenty percent.

In February 1985 partyless elections were held, with a significantly larger turnout for a new bicameral central parliament of senate and national assembly and for four provincial assemblies. Indeed, political parties remained dissolved and their offices sealed. In December 1985 martial law was lifted, after a series of sweeping amendments were made to the 1973 constitution which ensured that ultimate power remained with the president.

In early 1986 the previous purely nominated government was replaced by a government from the new members of Parliament. This was necessarily nonparty and the Prime Minister, Mr. Mohammed Khan Junejo, was selected by President Zia. Significantly, the new Prime Minister came from Sind. In spite of President Zia's aversion to political parties, which he asserted were un-Islamic in his view, events moved toward a party-based political system. In the new Parliament, there was a tendency for two rather blurred groups to operate; the OPG, or official parliamentary group, and the IPG, or independent parliamentary group. However, when crucial issues came up, the regime had little difficulty in securing unanimous votes on most occasions. There was a low tolerance level of dissent within Parliament (except on rhetoric) and the speakers (presiding officers) of both the National Assembly and the Sind Assembly were voted out of office when they innocently regarded their proper function to be referees upholding the law among differing viewpoints.

By April 1986 an act came into force reviving political parties under certain restrictions, which most found unacceptable. But none of these post-martial law measures were sufficient to bring political parties into a constitutional relationship with President Zia or his nonparty government. There were two main issues. While the regime insisted that elections be held in 1990, the political parties demanded fresh elections within a few months to take into account the new legalization of political parties. Where Zia-ul-Haq continuing as president was concerned, it was considered by practically all political parties that he must first sever his decisive operational control of the army as chief of staff before he could be considered as a civilian president.

Although most major political parties had come together in a loose MRD (movement for the restoration of democracy) alliance, they had important differences on whether the 1973 constitution required amendment, the degree of provincial autonomy, and on the Islamization measures, which continued under President Zia's newly selected Prime Minister. Undoubtedly there was a far greater measure of freedom of expression and association at the time of writing, but this could easily be withdrawn or the attempt made to withdraw it if political rallies turned into massive antiregime agitation along violent lines. Indeed, there have been hints at the possibility of a reimposition of martial law if necessary.

If Pakistan's past is anything to go by, events often suddenly move very fast, and in unexpected directions.

Summary

Islamization in Pakistan came about by a combination of international and domestic factors; this is certainly true in the country's current phase, which began in the 1970s. Included among the factors that seem to have affected Muslims everywhere are a reaction to the permissiveness of the West, the erosion of family life, and the failure of Muslim societies to meet contemporary challenges by following Western or Communist prescriptions. It is doubtful whether the current version of Islamization in Pakistan has brought about any significant improvements in these matters. There has been too much reliance on traditionalist legalism and compulsion as well as neglect of the essential basis for a moral order (namely *taqwa*) that arouses the conscience to a voluntary and willing compliance with what the moral order demands.

The influx of oil wealth after 1973 in states like conservative Saudi Arabia and revolutionary Libya provided ample money for Islamic movements and causes everywhere. This was done as much for political reasons as any religious impulse. The Iranian revolution of 1979 created a third Islamic model of society. A worldwide drop in oil revenues will have an effect on Islamic resurgence. But it is an oversimplification to assert that "current waves of Islamic activism will die along with the OPEC boom. More than any other single factor, the oil market will determine how long the Islamic resurgence lasts."[24] Islamic resurgence has many other motivating factors besides encouragement from oil-wealthy states.

Yet the quasi-traditional approach of Zia-ul-Haq seems clearly to have exhausted its possibilities after several years, whether considered in terms of the *hudud* ordinances, *zakat, riba,* the position of women, or any of the other areas considered earlier. The greatest gain out of this lengthy exercise may well be that it has exposed the total inadequacy of the traditional approach and has forced Pakistanis of all varieties of belief to face up to the real implications of calling for Islam in public life. One likes to think that it may even have caused some of the *ulama* to ponder these questions.

There is one point at which the current Islamization must prove successful or fail completely: that is, its effect on the unity and integrity of Pakistan. In the long centuries of Muslim rule in the subcontinent, there has been an increasingly wide oscillation between policies that emphasized panreligiousness and those that emphasized the Islamic state. In Pakistan, this indecision has continued in another form. On the one hand, an emotive emphasis on Islam in public life led to religious and sectarian riots, such as those against the Ahmadiyya in 1953. A neglect of Islam in public life, on the other hand, led to interprovincial and ethnic tensions, such as the Bengal language riots in the early 1950s and the eventual separation of the eastern wing of Pakistan in 1971 to form Bangladesh.

The present regime has tried to pursue a traditional Islamization course while emphasizing a Pakistani "nationalism." The two themes have proved to be contradictory. The problem seems to arise because of a failure to distinguish between state and nation. An Islamic state understood in modern terms can embrace many nations or ethnic groups. A nation-state, on the other hand, attempts to subordinate lesser ethnic groups into the dominant ethnic group. Such attempts almost invariably fail.[25] The only viable course for Pakistan would seem to be (in view of the Bangladesh experience and the ethnic discontent that has since arisen in residual Pakistan, notably among Sindhis and Baluchis) to build Pakistan as an Islamic *state* embracing and tolerating diverse ethnic cultures. But in using the Islamic emphasis as the positive bond between ethnic groups, one must beware of repeating the mistakes of the past where Islamization is concerned.

The revival of a traditional, virtually Aurangzeb-style of Islam has once again caused a revival of sectarian tension and conflict between Sunni and Shi'a. To cite but one example, where only the modernist approach could hope to evolve a common approach to *zakat,* by implementing the traditional (Sunni) Hanafi view of a compulsory levy of *zakat,* the Shi'a community was successful in insisting on exemption.[26] A crisis was averted, but the episode left bad feelings between the Sunni and Shi'a that have been further exacerbated by the interest of some Middle Eastern states in some Pakistani sect questions.

This arousal of sect feeling has also extended to the longstanding division among traditionalist Sunnis between Deobandis and Barelvis.[27] The continued attempts of traditionalists to establish their Islamic credentials and ardor by outbidding others in anti-Ahmadiyya proposals and demands for their further penalization is doubtless having incalculable effects on the sentiments of the Ahmadiyya toward a state where they are now being pushed from second-class to third-class status. If these are the feelings of smaller Muslim and ex-Muslim groups, the sentiments of non-Muslims are hardly likely to be better. It would be foolish to presume that between sects and religions there remains even the minimum degree of harmony that the security and well-being of the state requires, particularly in times of external crisis.

One would have thought that the rising tide of religious sentiment might overcome provincial and ethnic feelings, but this has not been the case. In early 1983, there were Shi'a-Sunni disturbances in Karachi apart from the growing annual troubles during the month of Muharram. By the middle of the year, there were widespread disturbances in Sind among the Sindhi-speaking people. According to subsequent government admissions, they caused extensive damage to banks and railway property and a considerable loss of life, for which acceptable figures are not so easy to obtain.[28] This is perhaps not the place to examine all the causes for Sindhi resentment, which has now gone underground. Suffice it to observe that the degree of alienation among Sindhis also might prove extremely dangerous to Pakistan's integrity. What is relevant here is that this most serious development has two aspects that are of Islamic significance.

The first is that the present establishment, both military and civil, persistently confuses Islamization with indigenization. The establishment is overwhelmingly composed of Punjabis and Urdu-speaking migrants from the Indian urban centers of Delhi, Uttar Pradesh, and Hyderbad (Deccan). The establishment—or rather Zia-ul-Haq—has prescribed "national" dress for officials that merely accentuates provincial and ethnic differences. This hostility to contemporary clothing of international design is also symptomatic of an unhealthy xenophobia that has infected the country to the detriment of culture and even knowledge. Similarly, English was at least a neutral language. Accelerated attempts to oust English in favor of Urdu have also adversely affected provincial languages, notably Sindhi. This has resulted in making those who are not native speakers of Urdu or fluent in it increasingly convinced they are second-class citizens, besides penalizing them in the educational system and in official employment opportunities. Attempting to accelerate integration (as defined by the establishment) at a pace far beyond what can be assimilated has widened the gulf between fellow Muslims of different ethnic groups.

The second aspect of Islamic significance is the demonstration effect of the creation of Bangladesh. While Islam requires recognition of Pakistan's public life, given the nature of the origin of the state itself, it does not follow, as the ruling group seems to imply, that if some ethnic group has rejected Pakistan, as did the Bengalis, they cease to be "good" Muslims. This curious illusion continues to affect much of Islamabad establishment thinking: a threat of a sort of hellfire for those who reject Islamabad's version of Islamization-cum-indigenization.

A miscalculation of a different order is the belief that the approval of the *ulama,* the Jamaat-i-Islami, or traditionalist parties can be irrevocably procured by making the right noises: giving them the illusion of participating in the wielding of the pomp and panoply of power by offering them jobs (e.g., on the *shariat* courts, the impending *qazi* courts, and the *zakat* committees at various levels) and by inviting them to seminars and conferences at which they receive flattering hospitality. Although these carrots are often accepted, they are unlikely to alter growing disillusionment with the current version of Islamization. For one thing, the *ulama* and other traditionalists, seeing increasing signs of failure or hollowness in the process, are bound to distance themselves by asserting that the regime failed to correctly understand and apply Islamic precepts, that parallelism must be ended, and that only (for example) the *ulama* can be relied on (once they have unfettered political power) to successfully carry through Islamization. This prospect unfortunately faces any regime as long as there is a clerical element more concerned with public and political power than with the personal uplift of the believer.

A negative but valuable lesson from the present attempt at Islamization may lie in the futility of trying to forestall clerical hostility by appearing to be on their side or even by actually being so: being *with them* does not make a person *of them*. A modernist immediately ceases to be authentic in his ideals and objectives once he tries this ploy, and most others merely appear to be devoid of any ideals or objectives at all. They move from day to day in *ad hoc* fashion, pursuing very short-term gains for which there will inevitably be very heavy long-term bills to pay.

The question arises as to what the next stage is likely to be (barring the influence of outside factors). The first possibility is the capitulation of the regime to *ulama* and Jamaat-i-Islami demands for ending the present parallelism and adopting an uncompromising traditionalism. This could have unforeseen, catastrophic effects. There can be no comparison with Iran or Libya, countries that can afford sweeping atavistic experiments economically as long as they can be rescued by their oil wealth whenever things go wrong. Such a course is not possible in Pakistan where economic viability and stability are not sustained by oil.

Before such an escapade got under way there would probably be a backlash. It is unlikely to be socialism. The gallant struggle of the Afghans to recover their independence should not obscure the fact that for many decades a pro-Soviet socialist element there regarded Soviet assistance as the only way to overcome the clerically dominated conservative religious establishment. The fundamentalist element among the Afghan Mujahideen probably conceive of a liberated Afghanistan as being a reversion to an Afghanistan of, for example, unliberated women. A reaction against traditionalism in Pakistan is unlikely to take the Afghan pattern unless the situation is complicated by internal ethnic conflicts and external factors. Even a secular reaction on an extreme pattern is unlikely because it may well generate not some indefinable Pakistani nationalism but a crop of ethnic nationalisms instead, that are no longer bound by Islamic sentiments in public (and political) life.

The future of Pakistan, therefore, seems almost inescapably linked to a reassertion of the Aligarh spirit and the reformist Islamic movement that can be traced from Shah Wali Allah to Syed Ahmad Khan to Iqbal to Jinnah. Pakistan's problems require *ijtihad* (disciplined judgment or reinterpretation) of a convincing and wide-ranging nature. This, in turn, raises the question of the structural requirements for *ijtihad. Ijtihad,* doubtless, has to be undertaken by those who are "competent." This cannot be a self-proclaimed competence. In Hanafi law, it is only when the *ijtihad* of the competent reaches consensus and this consensus, in turn, is accepted by a consensus of the community that an authoritative understanding of Islam is reached. This is the basis of the doctrine of *ijma* (consensus) that gives authority, legitimacy, and stability to the efforts of those seeking to find answers to problems.

In the past, this process worked retrospectively, rather like judicial precedent; but when the principle is accepted, as it clearly has to be, that fresh *ijtihad* is required on the verdicts of the classical period and decisions have to be made on immediate pressing problems, a structure is required that can take such decisions and relate the competent and the community in the *ijtihad* process.[29] To establish this essential nexus between the competent and the community in the matter of Islamic understanding requires representative institutions within what probably has to be a democratic constitutional structure. That alone can give legitimacy to the results of purported *ijtihad*.

Notes

1. The dilemma that faced Muslim rulers in the subcontinent is set out in some detail in Kemal A. Faruki, *The Evolution of Islamic Constitutional Theory and Practice* (Karachi: National Publishing House, 1971) pp. 81–93; pp. 107–11 (on Shah Wali Allah); pp. 123–29, 177–200 (on Aligarh and Deoband); and pp. 203–37 *passim* for later developments.

2. *Ijtihad:* exerting oneself to the utmost degree to understand the Quran and *sunna* (practice of the Prophet) through disciplined judgment. The interpretation of one considered competent to understand the Quran and *sunna.* Its opposite is *taqlid:* blind imitation, that is, the following of, and acquiescence in, the opinion of another without investigating that other's reasons.

   By about the end of the tenth century C.E., *ijtihad* ceased on foundational questions and approximately three centuries later it ceased on all but novel situations. Thereafter, the "gate of *ijtihad*" was considered "closed." In recent centuries an increasing number of Muslim thinkers have reasserted the right to *ijtihad* of each generation.

3. *Zakat:* literally purification or growth. One of the Five Pillars of Islam. The giving of a portion of one's wealth in charity to purify the remainder that one keeps.

   Awqaf (pl. of *waqf*): literally stopping. Religious endowments. The settlement in perpetuity of the usufruct of any property for the benefit of individuals or for a religious or charitable purpose.

4. *Riba:* literally increase or exceeding. *Riba* is prohibited by the Quran. Traditionalists understand this to mean any increase in a capital sum lent. Some have gone so far as to interpret it to mean any advantage gained from the borrower by the lender (monetary or otherwise) other than repayment of the capital sum originally lent. Modernists tend to regard the *riba* prohibition as directed against usury as distinct from interest. Phrases such as "guaranteed profits" or "commission," and so on have been used in different countries instead of "interest," with varying degrees of apparent acceptance so far.

5. The role of the *ulama* in the early years of Pakistan, their views and their struggle for acquiring power is well set out in Leonard Binder, *Religion and Politics in Pakistan* (Berkeley and Los Angeles: University of California Press, 1963), particularly pp. 152–232, 314–34.

6. The Five Pillars (*rukn,* pl. *arkan*) of the Faith are the *shahada* (bearing witness to the Oneness of God and the Prophethood of Muhammad); prayer as prescribed *(salat);* almsgiving in a prescribed manner *(zakat);* fasting *(saum)* for one month in a lunar calendar year from sunrise to sunset; and the pilgrimage *(hajj)* to Mecca, once in a lifetime for those able to do so.

7. Although the *shalwar* (long baggy trousers also found in parts of Central Asia and the Middle East with variations) are worn by Punjabis, Pathans, Sindhis, and Baluchis (albeit with noticeable ethnic variations), the *churidar* (tight-fitting trousers) and *pajamas* (looser-fitting straight trousers) are characteristic of migrants from India.

8. *Chaddar* and *chardiwari:* literally shawl and four walls. An alliterative allusion to the concept of women's seclusion originally given currency soon after the promulgation of martial law by General Zia-ul-Haq himself.

The *Tehrik-i-Islami* (i.e., Jamaat-i-Islami) statement was issued by the information section of its Central Shura on 2 January 1984 and published in the press the following day.

9. Reported in the press on 6 January 1984.

10. In a statement issued at the conclusion of the National Ulema Conference at Islamabad and reported in the press on 8 and 9 January 1984.

11. *Hudood* (Ar. hudud) (pl. of *hadd*): the primary meaning is limit with a very secondary meaning of fixed. Classical Islamic law regarded the six offenses mentioned as *hadd* offenses for which a fixed punishment was prescribed. All other offenses according to classical Islamic law are liable only to *ta'zir*, that is, discretionary punishments of the *qadi*.

12. Dacoity; highway robbery with the threat or use of violence.

13. *Zina:* illegal sexual intercourse. The punishment in classical law varies according to whether it constitutes adultery by a married person (stoning to death) or fornication by an unmarried person (flogging).

14. Edward Mortimer, *Faith and Power* (New York: Random House, 1982) p. 405 summarizes part of the situation:

> Even if, in many places, traditionalist interpretations are now dominant, they are certainly not unchallenged. Nor is there in any country an *effective* [italics added] consensus on what the authentic Islamic tradition consists of, or how much of it can be restored in practice, or how fast, or in what order. (For instance, are the traditional Islamic punishments a means of recreating a genuine Islamic society, or are they only applicable once it has been recreated?).

15. This despicable episode took place in mid-1983 and was widely reported in the world press.

16. These alternative Islamically permissible methods are stated to be: shares quoted on the stock exchange, *musharaka* (partnerships between lender and borrower), government-issued investment certificates, hire-purchase arrangements, leasing and *mudaraba* companies (joint ventures).

17. At the end of fiscal year 1983, the position was as follows: stock exchange shares Rs. 14.750 billion (16.90 percent); government investment schemes and mutual funds Rs. 2.046 billion (2.34 percent); PLS Deposits Rs.14.203 billion (16.27 percent). The amounts in interest-bearing methods were: government saving schemes Rs.19.084 billion (21.87 percent) and time deposits in banks Rs.37.197 billion (42.62 percent). The applicable rate of exchange was approximately 13½ Pakistan rupees to US$1.

18. On 24 December 1983 the *Morning News* (Karachi) reported that the government was considering completely eliminating interest from the banking system by 1 January 1984 [*sic*]. Three days later on 27 December 1983 *Dawn* (Karachi) carried what appeared to be a leaked report that a high-level meeting in Islamabad was examining a report by "leading financial experts" aimed at eliminating interest from the economy by mid-1985. On 2 January 1984 while inaugurating the "first-ever" Women's Seerat conference in Islamabad, president Zia-ul-Haq stated that Pakistan would establish an interest-free economy by the end of 1984. The *ulama* invited to the National Ulema Conference, in their statement on 9 January 1984, demanded that the country's economy "should be cleansed of interest" by June 1984.

However, see *Dawn* (Karachi) for 15, 24 June 1984 for the Finance Minister's statement and the State Bank of Pakistan's circular to all banks, respectively, on the revised timetable, which proposed to "end interest';' by 30 June 1985. An analysis of this situation may be found in the Economic and Business Review in *Dawn* on 17 June 1984 in "Islamic Banking: Island in Capitalist Ocean" by Babar Ayaz.

19. The objections raised by the Council of Islamic Ideology and other conservatives to insurance are that it contains elements of uncertainty, gambling, and usury. The objection of uncertainty vis-à-vis insurance is an interesting contrast to the CII's objection to bank interest on the grounds of its (predetermined) certainty. The CII's objections to insurance are reported in *Dawn* (Karachi) on 28 December 1983.

20. See *Dawn* (Karachi) 14, 15 April 1984 for an excellent account by Syra Rashid on the current *qisas* and *diya* controversy entitled, "Is the Draft Ordinance Workable?"
21. Reported in *Dawn* (Karachi) 13 January 1984, p. 16.
22. Regarding the theoretical basis and structural requirements for an *ijtihad*-machinery, see Kemal A. Faruki, *Islamic Jurisprudence,* (ed. 2nd) Karachi: National Book Foundation, 1974), pp. 152–65, 187–94; for the relationship with non-Muslims in an Islamic state, see pp. 195 ff. The problems of *ijma* and *ijtihad* are also dealt with in Kemal A. Faruki, *Islam: Today and Tomorrow* (Karachi: Pakistan Publishing House, 1974) in chap. 8, *"Ijma'* and the Gate of *Ijtihad"*; chap. 15, "The Three-fold Question of *Ijtihad"*; chap. 20, "The Role of Analogy in Islamic Law"; chap. 34, *"Ijma'* and *Ijtihad* for Modern Conditions"; and chap. 37, "The *Shari'a* and Individual Liberty." The question of non-Muslims in Pakistan is also considered by Faruki in chap. 45, "Minorities in Pakistan."
23. An examination of the contemporary debate in the Muslim world regarding *shura* is contained in an article by Dr. Fazlur Rahman in the University of Chicago's *History of Religion,* Vol. 20, No. 4, May 1981, pp. 291–301, entitled "A Recent Controversy Over the Intepretation of *Shura.*"
24. Daniel Pipes on "Oil Wealth and Islamic Resurgence," p. 51 in *Islamic Resurgence in the Arab World,* ed. Ali E. Hillal Dessouki (New York: Praeger, 1982). However, the article is a useful account of how oil wealth has been used for Islamic or ostensibly Islamic cause.
25. There is a considerable amount of current literature on the question of ethnicity (which persists even in the original nation-states of Western Europe). The literature shows that the wisest course is to recognize and not fight ethnic diversity in a state whether it is the Basques and Catalans in Spain, the Bretons and Corsicans in France, or the Welsh and Scots in Britain.
26. Traditional Shi'a law regards the *zakat* obligation to be only payable to the *ulama* of one's own school or to the nominees of the *ulama,* as in Iran.
27. These two subsects (as distinct from schools of law) within the Sunnis of the subcontinent have their origins in the late nineteenth century C.E. Deoband was the subcontinental "orthodox" Sunni, the Hanafi equivalent of, say, al-Azhar in Cairo, whereas the Barelvis, who also began originally in what is now the Indian province of Uttar Pradesh, approve of worship at saints' tombs to seek their intercession and place greater emphasis on Sufi mysticism.
28. In a statement reported in *Dawn* (Karachi) on 23 December 1983, the Federal Minister for Railways, Abdul Ghafoor Khan Hoti, said that about thirty-five railway stations in Sind's Sukkur division alone were totally or partially destroyed at an estimated property loss of a little over Rs.1,500 million ($111 million).
29. See n. 22.

4

AFGHANISTAN
Islam and Counterrevolutionary Movements

ASHRAF GHANI

"The Muslim people have become very ignorant. It seems that the Islamic State is daily on the decline and the Mullahian* who are sellers of Religion, prefer ready cash to Religion."[1] So wrote King Abdur Rahman of Afghanistan (1880–1901) in his autobiography published in 1886. On July 1, 1980, Babrak Karmal, president of the Soviet-backed regime in Afghanistan, stated in a speech to the religious leaders, "You, esteemed scholars and clerics are the true heirs of the great prophets. On the one hand, sincere respect for you is incumbent on the people and the state, especially on me. But, on the other hand, on the basis of your sacred duty, you, too, have the obligation to guide the people towards peace, happiness, brotherhood, good deeds, and search for knowledge.[2]

The harshness of Abdur Rahman's pronouncement is surely as surprising as the conciliatory tone of Karmal's utterance. Abdur Rahman was no westernizer and Karmal's unswerving loyalty to Soviet-style Marxism has been public knowledge for at least two decades. The issue posed by both remarks is that of clothing political power with cultural legitimacy. Since the founding of Afghanistan in 1747, that has meant coming to terms with Islam. The relationship of Islam to the state has varied from period to period, but the crucial issue has always been the authoritative locus of interpretation of Islamic discourse.

Who talks to whom about what and under what circumstances are the elements that compose the notion of discourse. When actors phrase or justify their differing social interests in a common cultural idiom, the resultant discourse can be characterized as dominant. In a society where there are a number of prevalent ways of talking and reflecting about rela-

*Mullahian is the plural of *mullah,* a religious specialist.

tionships, the degree of dominance of a discourse can be best investigated in periods of crisis.

Examination of Afghan society and state in terms of these criteria will allow us to grasp the significance of Islam in the public life of the Afghans. But to do so, we must first delineate the ethnolinguistic characteristics of the country.

Sociocultural Diversity

Thirty-two languages belonging to four linguistic families are spoken in Afghanistan. This heterogeneity is, however, tempered by three factors: (1) Pashtu and Persian are clearly the two dominant languages, followed by the Turkic languages; (2) in addition to their mother tongue, a large number of the people understand one of these dominant languages; (3) for hundreds of years, Persian has been the dominant language of bureaucracy, commerce, scholarship, and the media, and an increasing portion of the population comprehends it.

As a result, language and ethnicity are not identical. Ethnic identity, however, has been a salient element in the self-conceptualization of the Afghans. The four dominant ethnic groups are: (1) the Pashtuns, who speak Pashtu and who have been the dominant political and, probably, the most populous group in the country since 1747; (2) the Tajiks, who speak Persian; (3) the Hazaras, who speak a Persian dialect; and (4) the Uzbecks, Turcomans, and others who speak Turkic languages. In addition to these major groups there are, of course, numerous smaller groups in the country.

All members of all major ethnic groups of Afghanistan are Muslims, even though they may differ in their adherence to different interpretations of Islam. In fact, except for the small number of Hindus, Sikhs, and Jews, close to 99.5 percent of the inhabitants of Afghanistan are Muslims. This is a potentially important unifying factor, and situations of crisis have shown that Islam has often emerged as the dominant discourse in such situations.

Islamic Institutions and Arenas

The entrenchment of Islam in Afghan society as a set of beliefs, practices, and institutions that have been enacted in public arenas precedes the 1747 founding of the state. Three broad categories of actors have been speaking in the name of Islam and concentrating their activities in four arenas. The actors are the *sufi* (mystic) brotherhoods, the *ulama* (scholars), and the various hereditary groups who derived their legitimacy from their alleged descent from the Prophet of Islam or other famous figures of Islamic and/or local history. The arenas are the shrines, mosques, schools, and law courts. The relationship among actors and arenas needs to be briefly described.

The primary relationship in a Sufi order, premised on the unequal capacity for knowledge among people, is the relationship between a spiritual guide, or master, and his followers. When an order is small, the community is face to face and all the disciples of a master know each other. But, with expansion, a chain of individuals emerges who mediate between the master and the dispersed disciples. The shrine of the original founder and those of his major disciples in various localities provide organizational centers and arenas for the ritual enactment of adherents' beliefs. *Sufi* orders are politically important as networks that unite people from very different social and geographical groups into one organizational structure with an interconnected leadership.

The *ulama* also constitute their own network. Their training, in theory, differs significantly from that of *sufi* adepts who search for charismatic guides. It consists of a well-defined curriculum in an Islamic school *(madrasa)*. The *ulama* are considered to be the repositories of Islamic legal and ethical knowledge and norms. The schools, courts, and mosques are the arenas of their actions.

The third category of actor is more complex and includes a wide diversity of groups. Those who claim to be descendants of the Prophet of Islam and are accepted as such by their communities are called *Sayyids*. They enjoy overwhelming local prestige, if not wealth or influence. At the other end of the social scale are those who derive prestige as descendants of a figure whose reputation was confined to a limited locality. Depending on circumstances and individual inclinations and aptitudes, the actions of actors in this category may or may not be confined to one arena, such as a shrine. *Mullahs,* the religious specialists in charge of the village mosque(s), form a distinct group within this category.

The financial support for these actors, arenas, and institutions is provided by voluntary contributions from the faithful, private wealth of the leaders, and endowments (awqafsing, *waqf*).[3] The endowments are probably the most significant. Through the centuries, rulers, wealthy and powerful individuals, and multitudes of ordinary people donated property to shrines, mosques, and schools. The trusteeship of these properties remained within the same families for decades and sometimes centuries. To supervise their economic holdings and cater to their social networks, these families had their own administrative, financial, and, at times, military bureaucracies and retainers. Their power, though initially derived from the charisma of their ancestors, was thus routinized and diversified.

A community of any significance, therefore, had its religious elite who, through elaborate webs, were linked to each other across the Muslim lands as well as to other strata of the society. Political decision makers extended recognition of the importance of the religious elite through ties of personal allegiance between rulers and religious figures, tax exemptions on their holdings, and/or assignment of state revenues for their upkeep. It was in such a cultural milieu that the Afghan state was founded.

Islam and the Origin of the Afghan State

Two broad patterns of transition to statehood can be identified in this area of the world. States have either resulted from the transformation of *sufi* brotherhoods and/or other religious movements or have been the outcome of tribal politics. The Safavid dynasty in Iran (1501–1732) exemplifies the former trend, whereas the founding of the Afghan state in 1747 illustrates the latter.

The Safavid empire was an ideological state in which the ruler, as the perfect guide of the *sufi* order, was committed to forcibly establishing the Shi'a interpretation of Islam as the dominant form of religious worship in his dominions. Under these conditions the *ulama* consolidated their political position in the form of a distinctively hierarchical organization that retained an active role in the politics of Iran in subsequent centuries. In contrast, the rulers of Afghanistan's Durani empire (1747–1818), deriving their power from their tribes, were not committed to enforcing a particular form of religious interpretation through the power of the state. The initial difference in the pattern of state formation has had profound consequences for the position of the religious establishment and the ideological place of Islam in the two polities.

The distinctive feature of the Durani empire was the existence of a strong tribal aristocracy that, at the level of the central government, was ethnically Pashtun and religiously of the Sunni interpretation of Islam. The *khans* (tribal aristocrats who were officially recognized by the state as the leaders of their clans) were the major political and economic powers in their communities. They were also the major figures in the process of conflict resolution within their communities. Tribal law and not Islamic law *(shariah)* provided the body of norms and practices used in the adjudicative process. In certain crucial matters, such as inheritance, the tribal code radically departed from the injunctions of Islamic law. During the Durani perod, Islamic law had to adjust to the tribal code, not the other way around.

As individuals, the *khans* showed considerable piety, but, as a group, they were not keen on yielding their privileged place in the institutions of the state to members of the religious establishment. In their capacity as landlords and leaders of their clans, they saw to it that, like other groups of specialists, such as carpenters, barbers, and musicians, ordinary religious practitioners *(mullahs)* remained subordinate to them. This pattern of relationship between local landlords and *mullahs* remained in force until 1978.

Four aspects of the religious policy of the Durani rulers are worthy of notice: (1) They confirmed the trustees of endowments *(awqaf)* in their positions as well as created new endowments and made contributions to the old ones. The financial underpinning of the Islamic institutions was thus buttressed by the government. (2) Drawing on the models of other Muslim empires, crucial elements of the religious establishment—such as the chief *qadi* (judge), the royal *Imam* (religious leader) and so on,— were officially incorporated within the organizational structure of the state. (3) To check the power of the *khans,* the monarchs delegated considerable power to individual members of the religious establishment who served as their advisors and confidents. As part of the same policy, the rulers relied on members of the Shi'a community, who were a minority in the country, for bureaucratic and military service. (4) In their foreign conquests—especially that of India, which provided the bulk of their revenue—the Durani rulers relied on Islamic justification. They posed as champions of faith against Hindu expansion, which they succeeded in checking militarily but not politically. In these activities, they had the support of some of the leading *ulama* of India.

Although Islam was very much part of the daily life of the Afghans in this period, it was not the key element in the legitimation of the state. Indeed, during the crises of succession among contenders to the throne, alignments were based on tribal rather than Islamic factors. It was taken for granted that the state was Islamic, but there was no attempt to rely on Islam as the dominant cultural strategy for the acquisition of legitimacy at home. With the breakdown of the empire in 1818, the global political context underwent such change that the attention of all the actors was turned to Islam.

Uses of Islam by the Afghan State, 1818–1978

Three aspects of the global change in political conditions need to be underlined: the territorial expansion of European imperial powers into areas that until then had been under Muslim domination; the increased weakening of the hitherto Islamic interstate system, symbolized by the epithet, "sick man of Europe" for the Ottoman Empire; and the rise of movements of resistance against European expansion in which Islam provided the dominant terms of reference. Christian was the broadest category under which all Europeans could be subsumed and Islam was the logical term for the opposition.

In India and Central Asia, opposition movements failed to check British and Russian imperialism; in Afghanistan, the story was quite different. After twice invading the country (1839–42 and 1878–80), Britain failed to annex the area and came to terms with her Russian imperial rival in declaring Afghanistan a buffer state. The British government controlled the foreign relations of the country between 1880 and 1919 but, even during this period, had little direct impact on the shaping of the events inside the country. The Afghans, therefore, had considerable autonomy in the choice of cultural strategies through which political relations could be justified.

Islam, in this context, emerged as the dominant discourse.[4] The new symbolic ascendancy of Islam, however, entailed neither a corresponding increase in the power of the religious actors nor constancy in the realm of meaning of Islam. The reasons for this seeming paradox are not difficult to fathom, but, for the sake of clarity, the issues of power and meaning have to be addressed separately.

That the increasing frequency of Islamic discourse did not involve an expansion of the power of the religious establishment was mainly due to the fact that, from 1818 to 1978, political power remained within the Muhammadzai lineage, a branch of the Durani clan of the Pashtun ethnic group. As the rulers began to use Islam to legitimize their power, they retained a keen interest in retaining control of that discourse. In addition to this central fact, there were four other reasons why the religious establishment did not become politically dominant: (1) the *khans,* as the embodiment of the landed tribal elite, managed to maintain a position superior to most members of the religious establishment and one of relative equality with the religious elite. (2) Between 1880 and 1929, the rulers of the country attempted to change the organizational structure of the religious establishment, including the management of endowments *(awqaf),* which resulted in curtailing religious establishment's financial autonomy. Although the religious groups were allowed considerable autonomy in the management of their affairs in subsequent decades, they never regained the type of financial autonomy that control of endowments had given them prior to the 1880s. (3) With the emergence of India and Pakistan as independent states after the withdrawal of British forces from the subcontinent in 1947, the global political context changed again. The dominant discourse of the intellectuals after 1947 was Afghan nationalism, not Islam. (4) Starting with the first decade of the twentieth century, the Afghan intelligentsia was forging its control of two new arenas: modern schools and the press. The expanding government bureaucracy was increasingly staffed by graduates of these schools, not those of the religious schools. Thus, although the role of nationalist intellectuals in the institutions of the state was increasing, that of religious intellectuals was declining.

In their first appearance on the political scene, intellectuals emerged as Islamic modernists rather than Afghan nationalists. Their efforts, therefore, were concentrated on changing the content of the dominant (Islamic) discourse rather than introducing a novel (nationalist) discourse. In this regard, they were following in the footsteps of the Afghan rulers, especially Abdur Rahman, whose negative pronouncement on religious figures we quoted earlier. Whereas the Islamic discourse propagated under Abdur Rahman's supervision stressed loyalty to the ruler (even if he were unjust), payment of taxes, *jihad* (holy war) under the banner of the ruler, service on the borders of Islam, and hard work, the modernists, on the other hand, interpreted Islam as the way to scientific and technological development, equality of the citizens before the law, wholesale reform of the state institutions, and anti-imperialism.[5] The control of the press and the schools allowed the modernists' views to appear to represent that of the entire society.

With the ascent of one of their members to the Afghan throne in 1919, the program of the modernists became state policy. The pursuit of these goals, however, soon brought the reforming king, Amanullah, into a head-on clash with various sectors of society, and he was eventually overthrown in 1929. "Islam in danger" was the dominant slogan of the opposition in this period. Indeed, from 1818 onward, a number of movements that arose in armed resistance to the policies of the state stressed Islam as their dominant symbol. The military defeat of these movements during the nineteenth century allowed the Afghan rulers to reshape the religious establishment. The opposition's success in overthrowing the reformist king in 1929 resulted only in more formal stress on the Islamic character of the state. Owing to circumstances outlined earlier, social relations did not change and the Afghan intellectuals spoke in secular political terms. After 1929, the rulers of the state did not attempt to formulate and enforce an all-embracing religious policy. Islam increasingly became one element within a symbolic repertoire that could be called on situationally by the rulers of the state for their legitimation.

A central factor that affected the relations between rulers and the social forces in society was the change in the financial basis of the state. From 1955 on, foreign aid provided the bulk of the funds for government expenditures, with five major consequences: (1) the state became the most important economic power in the country and the major source of employment; (2) the expansion of the size of the bureaucracy gave the intellectuals who were staffing it considerable power in affecting other segments of society; (3) military officer training became increasingly concentrated in the Soviet Union; (4) socialism emerged as the slogan of a vocal group of the intellectuals; this tendency was countered by an equally insistent demand for the formation of an Islamic government; (5) the rulers of the state failed to forge organic ties with members of the landed, merchant, and religious elites in the country.

By 1973, changes in the national economy, decreased foreign aid, increased unemployment among high school and university graduates, debates on uneven regional development, and charges of ethnolinguistic favoritism on the part of the state pointed to sociopolitical crisis.

It was in this context that Prince Daud—the strongman of the country between 1953 and 1963 who masterminded closer ties with the Soviet Union and attracted the large-scale foreign aid—seized power in 1973 and declared Afghanistan a republic. He failed, however, to check the crisis. And when he moved against his erstwhile leftist allies in April 1978, he was overthrown by his Soviet-trained officers. The officers passed political power to the Khalq (masses), a self-styled Marxist party.

The Khalq Party and Islam

After coming to political power on April 27, 1978, the Khalq party swiftly moved to monopolize its power by attempting to subordinate all social forces in the country to a one-party system. A speech by Hafizullah Amin, the strongman of the regime, is typical. He declared:

> The democratic Republic of Afghanistan, as a proletarian regime, has been founded on the basis of the epoch-making ideology of the working classes and is moving forward. On this basis, we are building in Afghanistan a society free of exploitation of man by man, that is a classless society. . . . The friendship between the peoples of Afghanistan and the Soviet Union is an essential element of our proletarian internationalism and patriotism. Whoever stands in the way of friendship between Afghanistan and the Soviet Union is an enemy of our homeland, our system, and our revolution.[6]

A few days later, however, Nur Muhammad Taraki and Hafizullah Amin, the two top leaders of the party and the state, were utilizing a different set of symbols. In adherence to the custom of the Afghan monarch, they inaugurated the reading of the Holy Quran to mark the beginning of the month of fast (Ramadan), one of the Five Pillars of Islam. The photographs taken on this occasion were displayed on the front pages of the official press.

How was a commitment to the "epoch-making ideology of the working classes" squared with the obligations of being powerholders in a Muslim society? To answer this question, we must look at how those who spoke in the name of Islam were treated, how the status of Islam was defined, how the key events in the Muslim calendar were observed, and how Islam was used ideologically to justify the party's policies and give the regime legitimacy.

The offensive posture of the regime and its flaunting of Marxist slogans quickly brought the party, composed of a small number of intellectuals without a strong social basis, into conflict with all the elements that saw the assumption of political power by the party as a danger to Islam and Afghanistan. The response of the regime to religiously inspired opposition as well as to any other form of opposition was brutal. Hundreds of religious figures, intellectuals, *khans,* and merchants were imprisoned and executed. Terror prevailed.

Meanwhile, the official policy insisted that Islam would be respected as long as it remained separate from politics. Taraki, in one of his speeches, went clearly to the heart of the matter by declaring,

Some people mix politics and religion and make use of the True Religion of Islam as a political tool. After the Saur [April] Revolution there is absolutely no room for such practices. We respect our *mullahs* and other religious figures. As repeatedly emphasized, when they do not dabble in politics and do not stand opposed to the Saur Revolution, we will honor and respect them. But should they engage in demagoguery, deceive the masses, and don the veil of religion to rise against the Saur Revolution, we will not permit it. Every class has its own theoreticians.... We the theoreticians of the working class will not permit the theoreticians of other classes to make the slightest move against the interests of the workers and the peasants.[7]

Taraki's insistence on the separation of religion and politics stands opposed to the entire Islamic tradition of political thought that has insisted on the unity of these two elements. The implications of his implicitly equating Islam with the ideology of exploiters was, of course, not lost on his listeners.

Nevertheless, on at least three occasions, prominent members of the party in the course of their participation in key Muslim events attempted to redefine the meaning of Islamic symbols. On the occasion of the birthday of the Prophet of Islam, in the former royal palace, Bareq Shafie, then minister of information, argued that "for the first time, the millions of Muslim toilers in Afghanistan have acquired complete freedom of determination and action and have thrown away the chains of non-white Muslim exploiters from their hands and feet." On the occasion of raising the banner at the alleged tomb of Ali, the fourth caliph of Islam, in the northern city of Mazār-i-Sharīf, the Khalqi governor claimed that Ali "was among those individuals who struggled for the realization of Islamic ideals against oppressive class relations and fought against monarchs and despots."[8] On the day commemorating the martyrdom of Hussain, son of Ali and grandson of the Prophet, another Khalqi minister argued that "Islam has always defended the cause of truth, justice and equality. The sacrifice of the great leaders of Islam in this path stands as a model worthy of emulation by all mankind."[9] These examples show that the religious calendar in a Muslim society is such that its rulers are forced to reaffirm the Islamic nature of the polity on ritual occasions throughout the year. Under the Khalqi Marxist regime, the number of such symbolic occasions is kept to the strict minimum.

The strength of the nonsecular opposition, however, soon forced the regime to seek legitimacy on the basis of Islam. The regime had no choice but to forge its own interpretation of the meaning of Islam. Taraki's speech of May 24, 1979, was an attempt at redefinition of terms. "The yardstick of Islam," he argued, "is service to the masses. On the basis of this criterion, we, compared to anyone else, are the true servants of the masses."[10] But on June 14, 1979, he was forced to claim that "our every single step and action is according to Islam and *Shari'a*."[11]

By August 1979, the regime was forced to seek legitimacy through the established religious agency of the *ulama.* Two manifestos—issued by a special "general council of the Muslim scholars of Afghanistan" and by *Jamiat-ul-Ulama,* the latter an appointed body since 1929—attempted to bestow legitimacy on the Khalqi state and the person of Taraki. The declaration issued by the "general council" stated,

> Our Khalqi state is the servant of the creatures of God and the protector of the religion of Islam and the *Shari'a* of Muhammed. . . . All the policies of this regime have been in accordance with *shari'a* and all the edicts issued have been according to Islam.[12]

The personal background and qualifications of Taraki became the focus of the declaration of *Jamiat-ul-Ulama.* It stated that Taraki

> was born in a poor Muslim household in a village far away from the capital. . . . The story of his life is that of struggle against injustice and oppression. Therefore, we unanimously declare that such a person of high determination is the leader and *Ulil-amr* [legitimate authority] of the Muslim people of the Democratic Republic of Afghanistan. On the basis of the verse of the Holy Quran ["Obey your God, your Prophet, and those who have authority on you"], we consider it obligatory on all the people of the Islamic society of Afghanistan to render him obedience.[13]

The verse on the basis of which Taraki was seeking legitimacy was the same as that used by Abdur Rahman. But, whereas Abdur Rahman was one of the few kings of Afghans to pass his crown peacefully to his successor, Taraki's end was violent. In September 1979, he was eliminated by his trusted lieutenant, Hafizullah Amin. *Jamiat-ul-Ulama* immediately issued a statement of support, urging obedience on the plea that Amin was already in power. Amin formally acknowledged the continual political role of the religious establishment by appointing a number of religious figures to the commission entrusted with drafting a constitution. The Soviets, however, had lost their trust in him. On December 24, 1979, Soviet troops invaded Afghanistan and, after overthrowing Amin, installed Babrak Karmal, head of the Parcham (banner) faction of the Khalq, as leader of the party and the state.

Islam and the Soviet-Supported Parcham

During its two years of publication (1968–69), only once had the Parcham newspaper acknowledged the existence of an Islamic symbol: that of the martyrdom of Hussain, the grandson of the Prophet. Only in its last issue, devoted to the life and thought of Lenin, was the place of religion in society touched on. An anonymous author argued that "believing in a religion is a matter that depends on the conscience of a human being and conscience has to be free. . . . Progressive elements never interfere in the religious affairs of the believers."[14]

In power, the Karmal regime has not attempted to treat Islam as an issue of individual conscience but as a potential political discourse. The symbolic shift in emphasis from the Taraki-Amin period has been clear from the beginning. In its first declaration, the revolutionary council addressed itself to the "Muslim people of Afghanistan and the world," not to the socialist community. Karmal, himself, affirmed that "the Holy Religion of Islam and our national heritage are inseparable aspects of our national system and national culture."[15] He even went so far as to call the Soviet intervention an "act of God."[16]

These have not been isolated utterances. The regime has undertaken a major publicity campaign to assure the Afghan people that Islam has a secure place in the Soviet Union. Its propagandists have argued that the advent of the October Revolution gave the Muslims of the Soviet Union rights that had been previously denied to them. Statistics on the number of mosques in the Soviet Union and the celebration of major Muslim events—such as the ceremony in Moscow commemorating the birthday of the Prophet—are given wide publicity. Muslim religious figures from the Soviet Union have been invited to Afghanistan, and delegations composed of members of the Afghan religious establishment are sent for visits to the Asiatic republics of the Soviet Union.

Inside the country, all the major events of the Muslim calendar are celebrated by the state and the media has given prominent coverage to the visits of high-ranking Khalq party officials to religious shrines. Attempts at finding Islamic justification for policies have been numerous. Karmal has frequently argued that "Islam is the religion of peace, brotherhood, equality, economic organization, and social justice."[17] The editor of a provincial newspaper, after acknowledging that mistakes in the enforcement of land reform were the cause of popular anger, wants the "honorable and hardworking peasant to know that land reform and water distribution are implemented on the basis of the holy religion of Islam which is the guarantor of social justice."[18] The prevalent discourse on Islam issuing from Kabul now has an unmistakable resemblance to the ideas of the modernists of the 1910s and 1920s.

The religious policy of the regime has not been confined to the propagation of a modernist discourse alone. The regime's aim has been to win over the religious establishment and to give it an institutional niche within the machinery of the state.

To assure the religious establishment of a regular financial base, the regime has embarked on a number of measures. Properties in land attached to religious institutions in the form of *awqaf* as well as the private properties of the members of the religious establishment have been exempted from the provisions of land reform. Payment of allowances to poor *mullahs* and of expenses incurred by mosques for electricity have also been announced. The regime has given institutional recognition to the religious establishment by founding a department of religious affairs. In July 1980, this department convened the first conference of Muslim scholars and clerics in Afghanistan. To facilitate better communication between the religious figures and party functionaries, special clerics' rooms in the offices of the party have been established. In the Fundamental Principles, a document that is supposed to serve as the basic law of the land, until the promulgation of a constitution, not only has the party undertaken to "uphold and respect the principles of the Holy Religion of Islam,"[19] but has also declared itself bound in implementing the principles of the sacred *shari'ah* in its law courts.

The connection between these measures and the search for legitimacy is revealed in the address of Karmal to the first congress of Muslim scholars and clerics, quoted at the beginning of this discussion. The reason for Karmal's meek tone, in contrast to the harsh rhetoric of Abdur Rahman, is that his listeners doubt his sincerity and the actions of the regime daily contradict his words.

The brutal use of force by the Red Army has caused the loss of life of tens of thousands of Afghans, the migration of millions, and the destruction of hundreds of villages. The majority of the Afghan people are still not convinced that they have irreversibly become part of the Soviet sphere of influence, and the use of Islamic discourse by Parcham has done little to convince them of the legitimacy of the Karmal regime. How has Islam fared among the opponents of the Khalq, Parcham, and the Soviet army?

Islam in Opposition to Afghan Marxism and the Soviet Army

The sudden assumption of political power by the Khalq party in April 1978 took the Afghan people and the international community by surprise. Initially, a wait-and-see attitude was the dominant domestic and international reaction. Yet, Islamically inclined groups who had openly and frequently clashed with Khalq since its inception in the 1960s had no hesitation in actively opposing the new regime. To dislodge the party from power, they called on the faithful to raise the banners of *jihad* (holy war) and become *mujahedin* (freedom fighters for the path of Islam). Understanding the character and aims of these groups requires that we briefly take account of their orientation in the 1960s and 1970s. Besides the traditional arenas of Islamic discourse that have already been described, the Muslim activists during this period made use of three new arenas: the university, the press, and the Parliament.

In Kabul University, which had become one of the important political arenas in the country, a group calling itself the Muslim Youth emerged into prominence. The members of the group were noteworthy for their simultaneous attack on the left, the state, and the traditional religious leadership. The views of Saif-ul-Din Nasratyar, who represented the group in the student council of the university, are typical. In an interview he proclaimed that the "present culture has no links to the true Islamic culture. Therefore, we consider an all-sided struggle for its overthrow essential and believe that the shaping of a progressive and humane society is only possible under Islamic culture."[20] Gulbudin Hikmatyar, who is now leader of the fundamentalist Hizb-i-Islami group in Peshawar, was also a representative of the group in the student council.

The newspaper Gahez (Dawn), at the time when a free press was tolerated, emerged as the organ of the Islamically inclined intelligentsia. Mawlavi Yonus Khalis, now the leader of another fundamentalist group in Peshawar, was a frequent contributor to the paper. At the time, he represented a more reformist orientation in comparison to the Muslim Youth, as the following quote from one of his articles reveals:

> Acquisition of [state] power by the force of capital or by the sword is against Islam. Islam is opposed to the practice of giving jobs to the unfit people on the basis of kinship, connections or corruption and urges its followers to actively struggle against such injustices. The faithful should not allow that the prevalence of such practices bring about the destruction of the Islamic society.[21]

In order to guarantee the Islamic character of Afghan society, a large number of *mullahs* entered into the most political of all arenas, the Afghan Parliament. In a marked departure from the past, they openly challenged *khans* and other influential individuals for seats in the bicameral Parliament; elections were held twice in the 1960s. Muhammed Nabi Muhammedi, who now heads the Harakat (movement) group in Peshawar, was typical of those who won. He gained prominence as a result of his confrontation with Babrak during a nationally broadcast debate on a vote of confidence. Karmal had asserted that there was no contradiction between Marxism and religion and that he and his comrades were good Muslims. It fell to Mawlavi Muhammedi to recite detailed passages from Marx, Engels, Lenin, and Stalin to demonstrate the opposition of Marxist ideologues to religious belief.

Given such a history of confrontation between Muslim activists and the Khalq party, it was not surprising that after the takeover by the latter, the former fled the country in large numbers and donned their battle uniforms. The conduct of armed opposition against a communist party in power that was backed by the military might of the Soviet Union, however, was dependent on favorable international conditions. The internal problems faced by the Shah of Iran left him with little opportunity to play an active part in shaping events in Afghanistan. But the situation in Pakistan was uniquely favorable to Islamically inclined groups.

The Pakistani army, after the populist interlude of Zulfikar Ali Bhutto (1971–77), had, once again, seized power in July 1977. General Zia-ul-Haq has adopted the slogan, "Islamization of Pakistan," and seems to have no intention of yielding power. The advent of his regime has, therefore, given the fundamentalist Jamaat-i-Islami and other Pakistani religiously oriented groups a relatively more significant role in the shaping of some government policies. Afghan resistance has been a beneficiary of these policies. As the activist Islamic groups in Afghanistan had a long history of relations with their Pakistani counterparts, it was not surprising that the latter used their ties with the government of Pakistan to assure support for their clients.

Jamaat and some other religious elements have had a significant mediating role in the choice of the Afghan groups that were to be given official organizational recognition by Pakistani authorities and, thereby, become the recipients from international sources of financial and military aid funneled through official channels in Pakistan. Despite the existence of a plethora of organizations that represent different ideological hues of Afghan society, the Pakistani authorities have elected to deal with only six religiously oriented groups. These can be regrouped along two lines and, in fact, are now allied in two opposed, loose coalitions.

The moderates are composed of the National Salvation Front (headed by Sibghatullah Mujadidi, whose family has been the hereditary leaders of the Naqshbandi *sufi* order), The National Islamic Front (headed by Sayyid Ahmed Gilani, whose ancestors have been the hereditary leaders of the Qadiriya *sufi* order), and the Islamic Revolutionary Movement (led by Mawlavi Muhammed Nabi Muhammedi and representing the stratum of rural and urban activist *mullahs*).

The alliance of fundamentalists is composed of Jamiat-i-Islami (led by Burhanudin Rabani, a former lecturer at the school of theology of Kabul University and a founding member of the Muslim Youth), Hizb-i-Islami (led by Gulbudin Hikmatyar, a former student of engineering at Kabul University and founding member of the Muslim Youth), and yet another Hizb-i-Islami (led by Mawlavi Yonus Khalis, a *mullah* who had minor posts in the government). Since the Soviet intervention in December 1979, the fundamentalist alliance has been joined by Abdu Rab Abdur Rasul Sayyaf, a former lecturer at the school of theology of Kabul University and another founding member of the Muslim Youth. Also, two groups led by *mullahs* have seceded from the Islamic Revolutionary Movement and have joined the ranks of the fundamentalists.

All these groups speak in the name of Islam, but their conceptions of Islam are radically opposed. The moderates, in theory, seem to be committed to finding a political solution to the present crisis but have no clearly defined program of what the restoration of an Islamic state, to which they are committed, will mean in practice. In the spring of 1983, the leaders of the three moderate groups openly welcomed an initiative by the former king of Afghanistan in seeking a political solution. The fundamentalists, however, have threatened to kill the former king should he set foot in Pehsawar. The fundamentalists, in theory, see their task to be that of bringing about an Islamic revolution in the Muslim world. In this vision, the struggle against the Soviets in Afghanistan is an important but subordinate aspect of the larger task of restructuring society. They are not only opposed to those who have exercised political domination in the past in Afghanistan, but are equally vehement in their denunciations of the traditional religious elite, who, in their view, are to be blamed for the moral degeneration that has brought about the present tragedy.

Division among resistance groups is also reflected on the battlefield inside Afghanistan. Instead of coordinating their activities against the Soviet and Afghan army, their followers have often turned their guns against each other and engaged in major conflicts over control of turf. Furthermore, despite the overwhelming symbolic stress on Islam, all have had to make allowances to the ethnolinguistic and religious particularities of their respective followings. It is notable that, although the rank and file of the fighters is drawn from all the groups composing the population of Afghanistan, most leaders belong to the Pashtun ethnic group or have significant ties to it—the latter is true of Mujadidi and Gilani. The only major Tajik leader is Burhanudin Rabani, whose group, Jamiat-i-Islami, is viewed to be predominantly Tajik. The people of Panjshir are also Tajik, and under the charismatic leadership of Ahmed Shah Masud of this organization, they have produced one of the few unified internal resistance organizations and have defied repeated Soviet attempts to subdue them.

In marked departure from the past history of Afghanistan, the class of *khans* has been completely bypassed in the leadership of the Peshawar-based resistance. So have the Shi'a and members of the Hazara ethnic group. This, despite the fact that the Hazara people, the majority of whom are Shi'a, have managed to maintain considerable autonomy from the government in their mountainous central region of the country. Various groups that represent the more secular trends of Afghan nationalism have also been completely excluded from consideration for leadership.

The relationship between Pakistani decision makers and the leaders of the Pakistani-based Afghan resistance seems to be quite symbiotic. The Pakistanis, through their control of money and arms, have allowed a small number of groups a prominent role. These groups, in turn, have placed all their confidence in the government of General Zia and the religiously based Pakistani parties and have excluded themselves from establishing any relationships with other shades of opinion in the Pakistani political spectrum.

On the surface, the nexus seems to have worked well for both sides. Pakistan generals, who, as military advisers to King Hussein learned from their experience of Jordan's problems with the Palestinian resistance in the 1960s, can compliment themselves on having prevented the formation of a state within a state. While, despite their bickerings, the Pakistani-selected Afghan groups in Peshawar have contributed to preventing the consolidation of Soviet power in Afghanistan. The leaders of the Afghan resistance, in turn, can claim credit for the conduct of the war and the simultaneous struggle for the Islamization of society. Such optimistic outlooks, however, gloss over the deep sense of gloom in the refugee camps and the increasingly negative reaction against these organizations inside Afghanistan.

The refugee community has become vocally critical of the high style of

life of most of the leaders and their lack of attention to the welfare of
ordinary refugees. Charges of corruption against top leaders of both moderate and fundamentalist groups are commonly heard. The reliance of
most leaders on members of their families to run the affairs of their organizations and their lack of financial accountability to their followers are
resented. The high-handed manner in which some of the leaders have
dealt with those critical of their policies (charges have included kidnap-
ping, torture, and executions) both in Pakistan and inside Afghanistan
have aroused strong discontent.[22] There are reliable reports that in some
parts of Afghanistan, individuals have been so incensed by the conduct
of the resistance fighters that they have willingly led the Russian troops
to their hiding places.

With some major exceptions, such as in the Panjshir Valley, the main
shortcoming of the resistance has been its inability to pay attention to the
local needs of the communities or attempt to win over the confidence of
the local people. In a large number of cases, local populations have borne
the brunt of Soviet reprisals invited by actions of the resistance undertaken without prior consultation. Similarly, a number of refugees in Peshawar who find their conditions unsatisfactory are increasingly blaming
the resistance for their plight. Furthermore, the class of *khans* and tribal
elders, who have seen their authority eroded by the emergence of local
mullahs and young fundamentalists, are being increasingly wooed by the
government in Kabul. In sum, the self-appointed leadership of the resistance has kept aloof of the Afghan population inside and outside Afghanistan, relying on the religious discourse to ensure a following. But speaking in the name of Islam has neither brought unity of ranks nor
unconditional popular support.

Islam, Revolutionary, and
Counterrevolutionary Imagery

Regardless of who wins the war, Islam will constitute an important element in the ensuing strategies of gaining legitimacy. The way power was
seized and the symbols with which the antagonists have faced each other
in the battlefield has made this all but inevitable.

The Khalq takeover was a coup d'état and not a revolution. Mass struggle did not precede but succeed their mastery of the state. Their claim to
being revolutionaries is, therefore, more in the realm of rhetoric than
practice. The first year of the regime did involve a radical departure from
established cultural practices. But the party had no popular mandate for
such experimentation and was quickly isolated.

Whatever ambiguity may have existed regarding the nature and direction of the party was sealed by the Soviet invasion. Following that fateful
intervention, foreign intervention and not the revolution was at stake.
The opposition groups have had no need to don the mantle of counter-

revolution. They have simply been putting themselves forth as the defenders of the most sacred cultural symbol of the Afghans, Islam.

The intensity of the opposition, however, has left the Soviet-backed regime with no choice but to confront their antagonists at the level of the dominant cultural discourse. Should the Soviet-backed regime consolidate its power, it will not easily drift into defining itself in overt opposition to Islam. This, in turn, will mean that Islam would serve as a symbolic reservoir of opposition to such a regime, whether in a covert or overt form.

Yet, Islam has not brought unity to the opposition ranks. The diversity within the opposition movements is such that, in the unlikely event of a Soviet withdrawal, a full-scale civil war among the groups speaking in the name of Islam is highly probable. At issue will be the control of the state and the establishment of the winner's brand of Islam as the dominant discourse in the country.

Since the war in Afghanistan is no longer a local but a regional and international issue, no quick end is in sight. Is the average Afghan feeling war weary or is he willing to wage the battle until death or victory? The answer is anyone's guess. But the response of the majority of Afghans still living inside the country will determine the shape of the cultural and political order to emerge.

Notes

This discussion is based on field research carried out between 1973 and 1977 in Afghanistan and field trips in 1980, 1982, and 1983–84 in Pakistan. I am grateful to the Wenner-Gren Foundation for financing my research on Islamic discourse and institutions in urban Pakistan. This chapter draws on that research. I am also happy to acknowledge the comments of Richard Bulliet, John L. Esposito, William Roff, Rula Saadeh-Ghani, and the members of the Asia Society conference on Islam on an earlier version of this chapter.

1. *Pand Nama-i-Dunia Wa Din* (Advice on the World and Religion). Kabul, 1886:107.
2. *Anis* (a daily), July 2, 1980:1
3. For an excellent analysis of the origin and subsequent history of one *waqf,* see Robert Duncan McChesney, "Waqf at Balkh: A Study of the Endowments at the Shrine of Ali Ibn Ali Talib," Ph.D. diss. Princeton University, 1973.
4. For a major example see Barbara Daly Metcalf *Islamic Revival in India: Deoband, 1860–1900,* Princeton University Press, 1982.
5. For details, see my "Islam and State Building in a Tribal Society: Afghanistan 1880–1901," *Modern Asian Studies,* 1978, 12, 2:269–34; and "Literature as Politics; the Case of Mahmud Tarzi," *Afghanistan* 1977, 29, 4:62–71.
6. *Anis,* July 21, 1979:2.
7. *Ibid,* March 11, 1979:3.
8. *Ibid,* February 11, 1971:1, 7; and March 24, 1979:3.
9. *Ibid,* December 1, 1971:1.
10. *Ibid,* May 24, 1971:1.
11. *Ibid,* June 14, 1979:3.
12. *Ibid,* August 11, 1979:1, 7.
13. *Ibid,* August 15, 1979:1.

14. *Parcham* (Banner), no. 3, April 6, 1979:1, 3.
15. *Anis,* January 26, 1980:1.
16. See Karmal's June 18, 1980, speech as reported in translation in "Foreign Broadcast Information Service [FBIS] Daily Report: South Asia" (Washington, D.C.), June 20, 1980:c/1–5.
17. *Anis,* June 2, 1980:1.
18. *Ithhad* (Unity), August 27, 1982:2.
19. The full text is printed in FBIS (see n. 16).
20. Interview with *Karwan* (newspaper), August 8, 1971:4.
21. *Gahez* (Dawn), no. 40, December 1969:1.
22. Aziz ur-Rahman Ulfat, a nationalist intellectual was assassinated for his vocal opposition in Peshawar in September 1983. He was the author of *Jihad wa Dastha-i Pusht-i-Purdah* (Jihad and Hidden Hands) 1358/1979; *Buhran-i-Afghanistan* (The Crisis of Afghanistan) 1359–1980; *Afghanistan ya Sarzamin Mardha, Jamqha, wa Kuha* (Afghanistan, the Country of Men, Wars, and Mountains) 1360–1982; *Siyasi Lubi* (Political Games) 1361–1983. The newspaper *Afghan Mujahid* also contains a large number of critical articles.

5

THE PHILIPPINES
Autonomy for the Muslims

LELA GARNER NOBLE

For well over a decade, a debate over appropriate political structures and policies for Muslims was a central feature of Philippine public life. The primary participants in the debate were the Moro National Liberation Front (MNLF)—a militant separatist movement officially recognized as representative of Philippine Muslims by the Islamic Foreign Ministers' Conference—and the Marcos government, which denied the MNLF's representativeness and opposed its assumptions and goals. This study attempts to describe the positions taken by the participants during two periods: (1) the years from 1972 through 1976 when the MNLF successfully challenged existing government structures and policies and negotiated a tentative agreement outlining the institutions for its own agenda and (2) the years from 1977 to approximately 1984 when the government "implemented" the tentative agreement in ways that institutionalized its dominance.

Because the debate included divergent interpretations of history and of the current status of Philippine Muslims, it is difficult to describe its context without using information that is itself controversial. Hence, in this study, where assumptions are presented, they describe the perspectives on history and current status held by Muslims and the Marcos government, respectively. These assumptions, in turn, shaped the goals and tactics of the protagonists and must be evaluated in assessing their successes and failures.

Some basic information can, however, be stated at the outset. Islam came to the islands that now constitute the Republic of the Philippines in the fourteenth century; by the time the Spaniards arrived in the sixteenth century, Islam had affected socioeconomic and political structures in the southern islands and was spreading northward. Because the Muslim sultanates in the south were better organized than the more localized structures in the north, the Muslims were successful in staving off Spanish conquest and, hence, Christianization. The Spaniards, however, persisted in their effort to subjugate the sultanates, with help from Filipino converts.

Weakened by centuries of warfare, the Muslims finally succumbed to the Americans' superior military strength. The Americans then attempted to consolidate control over the Muslim region in the south and integrate it into the governmental system of the Philippines. After independence in 1946, integration continued (at least superficially). Muslim politicians participated in government processes; Muslim students attended government-provided schools in both the south and the north; Christians, with government encouragement, migrated south to Muslim areas.

Meanwhile, most Muslims remained divided among themselves and alienated from Christian Filipinos. The most obvious division among Muslims was linguistic, but language differences were reenforced by differences in territorial identifications, economic activities, social and political structures, art forms, and hierarchies of values. On these bases, thirteen different Muslim groups were identified, though four predominated: in Mindanao, the Maguindanaon of the Cotabato region and the Maranao-Ilanun of the Lanao region; in Sulu, the Tausug and the Samal. Internally, these groups were further divided by clans and by status within clans.

Although the Islamic resurgence increased Muslim consciousness in ways that to some extent transcended the traditional identifications among Muslims, it and other factors—primarily the political and economic consequences of migration—exacerbated relations between Muslims and Christians.[1] These developments, moreover, coincided with a general deterioration in the capabilities of Philippine political structures to meet the demands of the entire population. Thus the stage was set for the emergence of a protest movement among Muslims; particular circumstances determined the timing of its emergence and the nature of its leadership.

The Moro National Liberation Front, 1972–76

Origins

The MNLF dates its beginning from a massacre that occurred on Corregidor island in 1968. Here is the account given by MNLF Chairman Nur Misuari on the fifteenth anniversary of the massacre:

> That event occurred on the black night of 18th of March 1968. Over two-hundred of our innocent youths, mostly unlettered ones, were lured into a clandestine politico-military organization known as "Operation Merdeka" and its military arm "the Jabidah" with the sinister intention of infiltrating the brotherly state of Sabah so as to create internal commotion preparatory

to the launching of full-scale military invasion by the armed forces of the Philippines for the seizure of the territory from Malaysian rule. Two naval boats with some helicopters were readied at Corregidor island to be used to transport the supposed saboteurs to Sabah.

This evil scheme, however, boomeranged against Marcos and his regime owing to the cold-blooded execution of our brothers who, upon knowing the ulterior motives behind their highly secretive recruitment and training, refused to embark on their mission. They demanded their enlistment papers into the armed forces of the Philippines as promised and their monthly pay or salary as well. The Chief of the Operation Major Eduardo Martelino, reportedly tried to sort out those demands, particularly the matter of payment of salary, but to give in to the demand for official enlistment was contrary to the credo of the Operation, for obvious reasons. . . .

So tense and explosive the outlook had became so much so that Marcos, the blood-thirsty evil-incarnate, summarily ordered that all evidences of the sinister plan be suppressed and destroyed, with the obvious implication that all those who had potential to expose the treacherous scheme be done away with.

But Allah in His infinite wisdom did not allow the criminals to pursue their conspiracy successfully. And so one wounded survivor, after going through the ordeal of floating in a driftwood for several hours in the shark-infested channel of Corregidor, following his miraculous escape from the scene of the execution, was rescued from the sea by some fishermen and the lid of secrecy imposed on the invasion plan was exposed most glaringly to the peoples of world.

And in the ensuing crisis and the series of demonstrations by the youths from various parts of our homeland, the MNLF and the Bangsamoro Revolution came to life, rising as it were from the womb of our colonial society. With the birth of the MNLF and the Bangsamoro Revolution, the decision to form the Bangsamoro Republik, as an independent and sovereign political entity, distinct and separate from the nations of the world including the Philippines, was unanimously reached.[2]

Some of Misauri's information is presented with a certitude not characteristic of other accounts, but he has not overstated either the intensity of Muslims' emotional reactions or the pivotal role the massacre played in Muslim political mobilization. Whoever authorized the Jabidah force, or whatever its real purpose, it was clear that the force had been secretly organized, that the recruits had been told they were being trained for a mission in Sabah, that at least twenty-eight of them were killed, and that the Marcos administration did everything it could to cover up the incident, including some things that made it look foolish. Muslim historian Cesar Majul recounts how "platoons of young army recruits from Luzon were organized to march through the hall of Congress, avowing they were the trainees who had been at Corregidor, and, lo, here they were, very much alive." The ploy failed when Muslim university students queried the recruits in Muslim dialects, which, of course, they could not speak, so the government tried again, herding truckloads of Muslims from reg-

ular army units into a Manila mosque for prayers. The purpose, according to Majul, was to "prove to the faithful that Muslims in the armed
forces were not only alive but also encouraged to keep their faith strong
and to attend congregational prayers." The soldiers were embarrassed,
however, and admitted that the army was using them to deflect attention
from the massacre.[3]

The government did succeed ultimately in controlling both congres-
sional investigations and military trials and in securing acquittal of all
the accused. The cost of this success was high because the verdict
increased the outcry among Philippine Muslims and encouraged them
toward further political organization. The cover-up also confirmed the
conviction of Malaysian officials that Marcos had, indeed, intended to
take Sabah by force. The result was a recognized congruence of interests
between young Muslims in Manila—who had heretofore directed their
political energies toward radical student organizations and/or subsumed
them in the entourages of traditional Muslim leaders—and Muslims in
Malaysia, particularly in Sabah—who felt Marcos had betrayed them
after they had made significant compromises to restore good relations
with the Philippines. Malayan confidence in the goodwill of Philippine
officialdom had been shaken badly by President Macapagal's announcement of a Philippine claim to Sabah in 1962 and by his subsequent efforts
to mediate between Malaya and Indonesia during their confrontation
over the formation of Malaysia. Marcos's actions—in the perception of
the Malaysian leadership—were simply further examples of Philippine
perfidy.

Among the Muslim students, the cooperation that had begun during
the Corregidor protests in Manila was given informal structure later in
1968 in Zamboanga City. There was further consolidation in 1969 when
groups of young Muslims began going to Malaysia for military training.
A central committee of seven members was constituted. They named Nur
Misuari—an instructor from Sulu at the University of the Philippines—
as chairman and agreed to call their organization the Moro National Liberation Front.[4]

The trainees' return from Malaysia coincided with other developments. Also reacting to the Corregidor massacre, an old Muslim political
leader in Cotobato, Datu Udtog Matalam, had formed the Muslim Independence Movement (MIM) with the goal of gaining independence for
Mindanao and Sulu, the areas in the southern Philippines that Muslims
had traditionally dominated. Mindanao, however, and specifically Cotabato, had had a large Christian migration in recent decades that had
caused endless disputes between Christians and Muslims over land ownership and that threatened Muslim political control. Matalam's MIM
appealed to Muslims but frightened Christians; both reactions resulted in
the creation of armed bands, outbreaks of violence, and a buildup of government armed forces.

The situation deteriorated further as politicians began to mobilize for the 1971 elections.

> Because of escalated fighting by the end of 1970—Ilagas and Christian armed groups against Blackshirts, Barracudas, and other minor Muslim armed groups—there were other signs of discord everywhere. Schools in many towns had closed; farms were left abandoned; commerce had stagnated; the number of refugees was increasing. One report has given a very conservative estimate that at least 30,000 Muslims, Christians, and Tirurays [a tribal group] had left their homes for safer areas.[5]

June 1971 brought another massacre. Armed "Christians" entered Manili, a barrio in North Cotabato, when most of the men were out working their fields; they summoned the remaining residents—old men, women, and children—into a mosque for a "peace conference" and killed at least seventy of them with grenades, guns, and knives.

Again, the massacre had both internal and international ramifications. It convinced Muslim leaders that "there was collusion among Christian politicians, settlers, and some commanding officers of the Philippine constabulary in Cotabato and Lanao" and that the plight of Muslims was likely to worsen because many of these Christians had strong connections with the Nacionalistas (Marcos's party). Hence, Muslim leaders—"a senator, a former senator, congressman, high government officials, heads of Muslim associations, religious and academic scholars and intellectuals, professionals and businessmen, and student leaders"—met in Manila and drew up a manifesto in which "they pledged before God that if justice could not be brought by legal or peaceful means, they would do their best to preserve their community and lands,regardless of their personal ambitions or political differences."[6] The manifesto reassured Muslims, irritated the government.

Of equal importance was the effect of Manili on Libyan leader Colonel Muammar Qaddafi, who heard of the massacre, expressed his concern to the Philippine government, and began a program of aid for Muslim refugees and religious activities that subsequently expanded to military and diplomatic support for the Muslim cause.

The conclusions of the 1971 elections did not resolve the escalating unrest in the south or elsewhere. Most of the critical Muslim-Christian contests resulted in Christian victories; the violence continued, though apparently at a lower level. In other areas of the Philippines, election results were interpreted as a major loss for Marcos. Debates in the Constitutional Convention—called in an effort to secure order and justice through institutional changes—were bitter and had pro- or anti- Marcos implications. Bombings and shootouts occurred in the Manila area. Marcos attributed them to Communists; his opponents charged his own men with having started them. Floods deluged areas of Luzon and threatened a nationwide rice crisis.

Finally, under seige on every front, unable to maintain control through traditional mechanisms, and unwilling to trust democratic processes to produce new ones, Marcos declared martial law in September 1972. The declaration cited the revolutionary goals and activities of lawless elements motivated by "Marxist-Leninist-Maoist techniques and beliefs" supported by a foreign government, and the "equally serious disorder in Mindanao and Sulu."[7] Martial law, he said, would allow him both to remove anarchy and maintain peace and order and to reform the country's institutions.

In the south, however, martial law had effects contrary to Marcos's intentions. Violence escalated from sporadic local conflict with specific economic and political causes to intense and widespread fighting that was, from the Muslim perspective, explicitly antigovernment in its objectives. Muslims saw martial law as excluding them from decision making by centralizing power in Christian hands and as leaving them only two options: accepting the regime and its promises or resorting to armed rebellion. In this context, the regime's immediate moves to collect guns from civilians were incendiary. Having already identified collusion between local Christian adversaries and government forces and officials, Muslims had no intention of giving up the weapons they regarded as essential for self-protection, and they fought to keep them. The government sent in additional troops, thereby increasing both the Muslims' feeling of vulnerability and their determination to defend themselves. In 1973, fighting spread through Cotabato, Zamboanga, Basilan, Sulu, and Tawi Tawi, and armed Muslim bands and Philippine armed forces maintained an uneasy equilibrium in Lanao.

At this stage the MNLF emerged. Its dominance over both spontaneously formed partisan groups and the private armies of Muslim politicians was secured by the fact that its ideology and organization provided the basis for cooperation among Muslims divided by language, culture, and clan. Equally important, it established connections with Libya and Malaysia that provided it with funds for guns and ammunition and a refuge. In 1974, the MNLF leadership made a further move, an effort to gain recognition and support for its cause from the Islamic foreign Ministers' Conference.

Assumptions and Goals

The cause, as articulated in the position papers prepared for the Foreign Ministers' meeting in Kuala Lumpur, is essentially a nationalist struggle against colonial domination.[8] According to the account given, the Moros (the term is Spanish, transferred from a familiar Muslim enemy—the Moors of Spain and North Africa—to the new enemy in the Philippines in the sixteenth century) constitute a distinct people, a nation, with a traditional homeland—Mindanao, Sulu, Basilan, and Palawan. They had "among the first independently organized communities in the Malay world," even before the coming of Islam at the end of the thirteenth century. Thereafter, the migration of a series of "Muslin princes" introduced "a new awareness in their spiritual life," "a new direction in their ethical outlook," and "innovations in social and political relationships."[9] Islam and its concomitant social and political structures had spread as far as Manila when the Spaniards arrived in the sixteenth century, conquered the isolated settlements in the north and central islands, and co-opted the inhabitants into what they intended to be a final, triumphant struggle against the infidel Moros to the south.

For three hundred years, the Moros resisted Spanish domination, determined (the account continues) "to defend not only the integrity of their national homeland, but also the dignity of their Bangsa and the preservation of the Islamic Faith." Throughout this period the Spaniards portrayed the Moros "as pirates, savages and barbaric only because they were steadfast, brave, fierce and courageous in battle."[10]

At the end of the nineteenth century a new force appeared on the scene, the United States. The MNLF claims that "the Bangsa Moro people, lacking in sophistication to understand American expansionism, cordially accepted the presence of the Americans as friends and equals because of the latter's insidious display of goodwill and cordiality." Indicative of their peaceful attitude was the Muslims' refusal to cooperate with General Aguinaldo against the Americans. But the Americans "treacherously" changed policies after their victory in the north and began to interfere in the internal affairs of the Muslim areas. Although some of the Muslim leadership capitulated, others resisted. For ten years, the United States was "locked in armed conflict with the Bangsa Moro people." Then U.S. policy changed again. The MNLF's explanation is that "the mailed first approach was rendered futile in the face of Moro invincibility in battle. And so the much publicized policy of attraction was launched by the colonial government."[11]

The Muslims then entered a new era, which the MNLF describes:

... the American colonial soldiers gained an attitude of cooperation from some Moro leaders. Sultans and Datus accepted monetary annuities and land grants. The irony of it was that the lands parcelled out by the Americans to them were originally Moro lands. Their sons and daughters accepted scholarships to Washington, contributing further to American brainwashing efforts and propaganda balderdash. They forgot the superior ethical basis of Islamic education which had moulded the Moro spirit and character for centuries. The great masses of the Bangsa Moro people were left in the dark but still fiercely yearning to preserve the national homeland. Under this situation, history took its course shifting the character of Moro resistance to a more complex form. Some who were co-opted by the American colonial dispensation, took the path of parliamentary struggle, but others, especially those from among the humble masses, continued the armed defiance against American rule.[12]

The parliamentary efforts were as unsuccessful as the armed defiance. Two parliamentary efforts were made, in 1926 and again in 1935. The first was an attempt by Datu Piang of Cotabato to gain support for the Bacon bill, which sought to separate Mindanao and Sulu from the rest of the Philippines. It failed, the MNLF says, because Congressman Bacon was motivated by "colonial vested interests" who wanted only to exploit Mindanao's resources and because "Quezon, Osmena, Roxas and the other colonial stooges, a vexatious lot, were always in Washington wailing on the walls of the United States Congress and the White House, to beg for Philippine Independence that would incorporate Mindanao and Sulu, no matter how bogus and arbitrary."[13]

The second attempt was significant primarily because of its powerful articulation of Muslim perceptions:

> . . . we want to tell you that the Philippines as it is known to the American people is populated by two different peoples with different religions, practices and traditions. The christian [sic] Filipinos occupy the island of Luzon and the Visayas. The Moros predominate in the islands of Mindanao and Sulu. . . . Should the American people grant the Philippines an independence, the islands of Mindanao and Sulu should not be included in such independence. . . . Our public land should not be given to people other than the Moros. . . . Our practices, laws and the decisions of our Moro leaders should be respected. . . . Our religion should not be curtailed in any way. All our practices which are incidents to our religion of Islam should be respected because these things are what a Muslim desires to live for. . . . Once our religion is no more, our lives are no more.[14]

This attempt also failed, and the Philippine Commonwealth government was inaugurated. The incorporation of Mindanao and Sulu in it, in the view of the MNLF, was "the most monstrous crime not only against the Bangsa Moro people but also against the Filipino people of Visayas and Luzon." The Bangsa Moro people were thus delivered "to a more vicious form of oppression, i.e., to the Christian Filipino oppressive rule, thus setting the Bangsa Moro people and the Filipinos on a collision course."[15]

The Japanese invasion provided an interregnum; Moro resistance reemerged with the establishment of the Philippine Republic after the war. The resistance, as earlier, took two forms, parliamentary efforts to gain independence and isolated instances of armed defiance. Neither was sustained until the Corregidor massacre and the subsequent escalation of fighting in the south, which the MNLF attributed to the actions of the Marcos administration and described as "colossal and heinous crimes." Genocide now joined earlier and continuing manifestations of "Christian Filipino injustice and discrimination" as well as "economic and political aggression," thus no alternative was left to the current revolutionary struggle.[16]

On the basis of these historical assertions and assumptions, the MNLF issued its manifesto and called for the support of the Islamic Foreign

Ministers' Conference. Speaking for "the five-million oppressed Bangsa Moro people, wishing to free ourselves from the terror, oppression, and tyranny of Filipino colonialism which has caused us untold sufferings and miseries by criminally usurping our land, threatening Islam through wholesale destruction and desecration of its places of worship and its Holy Book, and murdering our innocent brothers, sisters and old folks in a genocidal campaign of terrifying magnitude," the MNLF declared the establishment of the free and independent Bangsa Moro Republik in Mindanao, Basilan, Sulu, and Palawan. The republic would have a democratic system of government that tolerated neither exploitation nor oppression, an ideology and legal system based on Islam, an economic system encouraging foreign investment, and a foreign policy committed to world peace and the principle of national self-determination. Filipinos wishing to stay in the "Bangsa Moro national homeland" after independence would be welcome and given equal rights and protection, including property rights and the free exercise of their political, cultural and religious rights—if they renounced their Filipino citizenship and "wholeheartedly" accepted Bangsa Moro citizenship.[17]

The MNLF asked for political, economic, and military aid from the Islamic foreign ministers. Specifically, it wanted formal recognition of the republic, support for the MNLF in the United Nations and in Third World activities, military assistance for the Bangsa Moro army, the channeling of all refugee aid through the MNLF, and the breaking of all diplomatic, economic, and cultural ties with the Philippines. It identified an oil boycott as being of primary significance: The boycott accompanying the Middle East war in 1973 had greatly reduced the Philippines' military operations against Muslims, and the pro-Arab diplomatic initiatives that had resulted in the lifting of that boycott were motivated solely by opportunism.

The Islamic foreign ministers gave the MNLF considerably less than its leaders asked. They did not give formal recognition to, or support for, an independent Muslim state; they did not call for military support for the Bangsa Moro army; and they did not agree to break diplomatic, economic, and cultural ties with the Philippines. However, they condemned as inadequate the socioeconomic measures proposed by the Philippine government as a solution to the Muslims' problems, called on the Philippines to negotiate a political and peaceful solution ". . . to the plight of Filipino Muslims within the framework of the national sovereignty and territorial integrity of the Philippines," and identified the MNLF as an appropriate participant in negotiations. They also appealed to "peace-loving states and religions and international authorities" to use their good offices to insure the safety and liberty of Philippine Muslims.[18]

Thus the Kuala Lumpur meetings gave both the MNLF and the Philippine government clear notice of the intent and extent of Islamic Conference involvement. In subsequent months, while the MNLF consolidated its military organization and extended the scope of its military operations against the rapidly augmented Philippine armed forces, the Islamic Conference continued to take initiatives designed to facilitate a solution to the conflict. The conference's secretary-general made several trips to Manila and succeeded in arranging a meeting between the MNLF leadership and a Philippine delegation in Jedda, Saudi Arabia, in mid-January 1975. After that meeting deadlocked, a four-member committee (from Saudi Arabia, Libya, Somalia, and Senegal), representing the Islamic foreign ministers, prepared a draft agenda for further negotiations. That draft, in turn, was rejected by Muslims whom Marcos had assembled in Zamboanga City. Instead, they endorsed a Marcos plan that the foreign ministers then considered. Not surprisingly, the foreign ministers preferred their committee's agenda and instructed the committee and the secretary-general to arrange negotiations as soon as possible.

That negotiations did not occur immediately was also not surprising because consensus seemed limited to an agreement that "autonomy" was the solution. The MNLF had agreed to give up independence as a goal, substituting in its stead a demand for an internally sovereign, politically "autonomous" Bangsa Moro State that would include all of Mindanao, the Sulu Archipelago, Basilan, and Palawan. This state would have its own security force and exclusive responsibility for maintaining internal order, and it would be loosely associated with the Philippines. The foreign ministers' agenda (which the MNLF supported) provided for Islamic self-government in the territory owned by Muslims before 1944, including that taken from Muslims since then; Christians and non-Christian minorities historically present in Islamic territories would have the status of minorities in a Muslim land. The Marcos plan, in contrast, involved the creation of four "autonomous" regions in the southern Philippines that would be headed by commissioners appointed by the president and directly responsible to him; the appointment (by him) of Muslims to economic and social welfare offices; and the absorption of "sincere" higher-ranking Muslim defectors into the armed forces. There was, in short, agreement on the use of the word *autonomy,* not on its substance.

Negotiations were, however, finally resumed in Tripoli, Libya, in December 1976, after talks between Imelda Marcos and Qaddafi. The preliminary agreement signed on December 23 appeared to indicate that the MNLF, with the help of its Islamic Conference supporters, had achieved most of its objectives. The terms provided for an "autonomy for the Muslims" in thirteen provinces. The "autonomy" was to have Muslim courts as well as a legislative assembly, executive council, and administrative system. In addition there would be special regional security forces; representation in the central government; control over education, finance, and the economic system; and a right to a "reasonable percentage" from the revenues of mines and minerals. The central government was to maintain responsibility for foreign policy and national defense. The role of the MNLF forces in the Philippine armed forces and relationships between structures and policies of the "autonomy" and those of the central government were to be discussed during further talks. In the meantime, there was to be a cease-fire, supervised by a committee representing the Philippine government, the MNLF, and the Islamic Conference's committe of four.[19]

The MNLF's success was short-lived. Negotiations to implement the cease-fire quickly foundered, and Marcos proceeded to hold a plebiscite on critical provisions of the agreement itself. The plebiscite produced the mandate he wanted. Henceforth, the Philippine government "implemented" the agreement as it chose, until in 1980 a spokesperson declared it no longer "in force." The Islamic Conference complained about Philippine bad faith, called on the government to resume negotiations, and occasionally tried to negotiate through its secretary-general. Fighting resumed after the cease-fire collapsed in late 1977, but it eventually subsided. The MNLF's supply of arms decreased markedly after the change in the government of Sabah in 1975 and after a reduction of Libyan aid apparently beginning in 1976. A combination of exhaustion and government policies of attraction encouraged MNLF's troops to defect, and its leadership was factionalized.

Assessment

But what accounts for the MNLF's decline after so rapid an ascent? Why did the combination of ideology, organization, and access to outside resources—elements that originally gained it leadership of the Muslim protest movement and subsequently allowed it to achieve both military and diplomatic success—prove so ineffectual over time? Answers are difficult because the issues are complex and because it is important not to underestimate the MNLF's achievements and its remaining potential. Nevertheless, it seems possible to suggest that there were flaws in the MNLF's ideology and in its organization and that its reliance on outside assistance was a source of weakness as well as strength.

The appeal of the MNLF's ideology was that it articulated an alternative to a social order that Muslims found intolerable. Muslims saw Islam as the essence of their identity and of their way of life, were proud of their history, and felt keenly the loss of their homeland. Many (probably almost all) shared the MNLF's perception of Filipinos as alien and threatening and as contemptuous of their religion and covetous of their land. They opted for separatism as a natural solution.

The problem was that it was an excessively simplistic solution. MNLF writings reflect part of the dilemma. The use of the word *Moro* rather than the word *Muslim* suggests two needs: (1) to place religious identity in space (the homeland) and time (history) and, hence, to give it the legitimacy of nationalism and (2) to include those non-Muslims history had placed in the homeland. Abdurasad Asani, a member of the MNLF's Central Committee, writes in a pamphlet entitled, *Moros—Not Filipinos:*

> ... the fact remains that the Bangsamoro people, honed by their historical and cultural experiences, are nonetheless fortunate to be heirs to distinct social and moral values which characterise them as a nation, proud of its own heritage. ...
>
> Originally, the use of the term *Moro* by the colonialists was meant to perpetuate an image of the Muslim people of Mindanao, Basilan, Sulu and Palawan as savage and treacherous, while they are simply daring and tenacious in the defense of their homeland and faith. But despite its colonial origins the Moro National Liberation Front (MNLF) has cleansed the term of its unpleasant connotation by propagating the more correct view that the tenacity with which the natives conducted their war of resistance against foreign intrusion was a classic exercise in heroism.
>
> The term is not only common to all the indigenous tribes of the region but includes Muslims, Christians and those still adhering to traditional religious values—in a word all those who share common aspiration and political destiny. Hence, the MNLF had adopted *Bangsa* (nation) *Moro* as a national identity and implants it in the consciousness of the masses. Today, it is rooted in the heart of every man and woman and the defense of its integrity has become a national duty.[20]

Asani's own description seems to have an internal contradiction; certainly contradictions appear when one considers other aspects of the MNLF ideology and population statistics. Christians are apparently included among the Bangsa Moro *if* they feel they have "common aspiration and political destiny" with Muslims *and* are willing to accept minority status in an area of "Islamic self-government." Yet, even if one concedes that government figures have consistently understated Muslim numbers, Muslims are clearly a minotiry not simply in the Muslim "homeland" originally claimed by the MNLF—Mindanao, Basilan, Sulu, Palawan (a total of twenty-one provinces)—but also in most of the thirteen provinces specified at Tripoli. Professor Majul, whose pro-Muslim sympathies are strong, says:

> The population of only a few of these provinces—Lanao del Sur, Sulu, and Tawi-Tawi—was almost wholly Muslim, that is, over 90 percent. The population of Basilan and North Cotabato was about 70 percent Muslim. That of Lanao del Norte, Maguindanao, and Sultan Kudarat, however, was less than 50 percent Muslim, and that of Zamboanga del Norte, Zamboanga del Sur, South Cotabato, Davao del Sur, and Palawan less than 20 percent. Of the total population of the thirteen provinces—at least six million—an estimated three million were Muslims, or about 50 percent.[21]

Thus, the MNLF's demand for Muslim domination of the "homeland," as originally defined in its manifesto in Kuala Lumpur or subsequently in the Tripoli negotiations, was unrealistic. Presumably, it could have broadened its ideological base to include non-Muslims also alienated by the Marcos government or reduced its territorial goals; by doing neither, it undermined its achievements.

The MNLF's radicalism was also an issue, partly because it was unclear. Front spokespersons have accused both Christians and Muslims of corruption, abuse of power, and exploitation (particularly land grabbing), and they have rejected the leadership of Muslim sultans as well as of the "Christians" in Manila. There is talk of Islamic socialism, but what it means is not defined. According to Ulangutan, an MNLF commander in Tawi Tawi, who was interviewed in 1974, "Islamic socialism means that everything must conform to the norms, customs and traditions of the Muslims. . . . Socialism comes in specifically in the Islamic practices—not exactly in the economic side. Among Muslims, Islam is a way of life."[22]

Front spokespersons have consistently distinguished themselves from the "Maoists" of the New People's Army (NPA). An early manifesto insisted that the activists were not Communist but "God-fearing people" and demanded freedom to practice Islamic laws and customs without restrictions.[23] Misuari allegedly left the Kabataang Makabayan—a radical student group identified with the NPA—because the Maoists in it were unsympathetic toward Muslims. It was reported in 1975 that a group of Communist insurgents from the north visited Mindanao to arrange a meeting with the MNLF central committee, which they hoped would lead to a military alliance between the two, but the Muslims refused because they felt that the movements were ideologically incompatible and that a link with Communists would weaken relationships with the Islamic world.[24] An MNLF spokesperson interviewed in 1975 was quoted as saying that, although the Front represented an internal social revolution within Moro society, it was not Communist and would have nothing to do with Communists. The Front's leadership has maintained this position, though there is some evidence of at least local cooperation between non-Muslim (specifically NPA) and Muslim resistance groups.

The dilemma of the Front's leadership has been that for ideological and practical reasons they have wanted to emphasize both their Muslim identity and their radicalism. Each of these emphases has attracted particular followers and excluded others. Combining the two has tended more to subtract than to add potential recruits, a tendency Front spokespersons may have tried to counter with vague and inconsistent statements.

Joel de los Santos, in an undated article (apparently written in 1976 or 1977), takes the critique a step farther. In his analysis, the MNLF's problem was less the substance of its ideology than its failure to communicate an ideology. "Only a few MNLF leaders had a high level of ideological commitment and political consciousness," because, he claims, there was an "early emphasis on military training at the expense of political training." He attributes this emphasis to the fact that the MNLF's mass base was provided by the "depredations and dislocations" resulting from the confrontations between Christian armed bands and Muslims and by the heightening of Muslim insecurities caused by the presidential decree ordering the surrender of firearms. With the growing buildup of government forces and the consequent expansion of conflict, there was a natural emphasis on military activities—specifically for preparation for guerrilla warfare. Institutions—such as village and town committees on finance, propaganda, intelligence, and supplies—remained rudimentary, with heavy reliance placed on the personal charisma of local leaders. Loyalty, not ideology, provided the Front's internal cohesion. Because loyalty was prompted by various motives, the links of the local leaders to the MNLF's structure and of the leaders' followers to them had varying degrees of reliability.[25]

Obviously, de los Santos's analysis identifies organizational as well as ideological problems. Formally the MNLF had (and has) parallel political and military structures, topped by a Central Committee of about twenty. The Central Committee regarded itself as setting broad policy outlines and leaving to local units the maintenance of discipline and specific tactical decisions. For reasons de los Santos indicated, it could not do otherwise. The MNLF never managed to bring into its structure all the Muslim groups fighting the government, and it could not control the behavior of many groups nominally fighting along side it. Moreover, some of its early accomplishments—for example, an ethnically balanced central committee (Tausug, Samal, Maguindanaoan, Maranao) and connections between its overseas leadership and its forces in the field—proved difficult to maintain.

Finally, events seem to have demonstrated that the MNLF was excessively reliant on external support. Originally military assistance from Malaysia (particularly Sabah) and later from Libya was significant in subsidizing a level of warfare that would not otherwise have been possible and that put considerable pressure on the Philippine government. The diplomatic support of the Islamic Conference (when coupled with the potential for an oil boycott) was also significant and, undoubtedly, was responsible for securing agreement at Tripoli on terms much more favorable to the MNLF than it could have achieved alone. Yet Islamic support may also have inflated the expectations of the MNLF's leadership and diverted it from developing an institutional base among Muslims and linkages with non-Muslims in the Philippines. Clearly, post-Tripoli, it was Philippine realities, not pan-Islamic ones, that proved dominant. Malaysia had earlier curtailed its military support for the MNLF as its perceived interests changed; Libya later limited its aid. Other Muslim states gave no priority to the achievement of the MNLF's political objectives, even ones they had helped to negotiate.

The Philippine Government, 1977–84

If the Marcos government after 1977 dominated the debate over appropriate political structures and policies for Muslims, it was not simply because of MNLF weaknesses. During the early years of the martial law regime, when the MNLF was successfully challenging both the regime's legitimacy and its control in the south, the government began to develop a series of strategies that provided a basis for its actions in the period following the Tripoli Agreement. In part, the regime's counterattack was ideological, an alternative to the MNLF's efforts at defining its cause as nationalist. Primarily, however, the regime concentrated on devising structures and policies that would attract and/or appease those Muslims at home and abroad sympathetic to the MNLF's critique while consolidating its own control and maintaining the loyalty of both Muslims and Christians who had benefited from the old order.

Assumptions

The MNLF's manifesto was an assertion that the Moros were a distinct nationality, set off by religion, history, and identification with their homeland. They had resisted both Spanish and American colonial efforts but had finally succumbed and had wrongfully been included in the Republic of the Philippines. The Filipino Christian government, in their perspective, was simply a successor to the earlier colonial regimes. It aimed at discrediting Muslims' faith and practices, depriving them of their patrimony, and finally, under Marcos, endangering their very existence. Hence, there was no alternative to a form of separatism, preferably independence—but at least autonomy. Muslims must have control over their own destinies—and specifically over political and military institutions that would protect their religion, land, and lives.

The government, in response, identified the MNLF's view of history as inaccurate, its goals as inappropriate, and its leadership as lacking in integrity. Its version of history was that "the problems in the Southwestern Philippines are the result of several centuries old inequities and misunderstandings caused primarily by the Western colonization of the country." Before the coming of the Spaniards the Malay population of the islands was organized in communities that were separate ("autonomous," in one version) but essentially similar, equal, and peaceful. The coming of the Spaniards began "four centuries of protracted struggle by the Filipinos against colonization [that] bifurcated their historical orientation as a people and . . . left a legacy of social instability in the country." The "Southern Filipinos" started the fight against the Spanish conquistadores and continued it for three hundred years. It was the "Northern revolutionaries," however, "who later succeeded in liberating the entire Philippine Archipelago that resulted in [sic] the declaration of independence on June 12, 1898."[26]

With the coming of the Americans, according to the government's account, roles reversed. Whereas the northern Filipinos continued to fight the Americans to preserve Philippine independence, the southerners signed the Bates Treaty in 1899, thus exchanging sovereignty over Sulu and portions of Mindanao for pensions given to ruling members of the

Sulu sultanate. Later, southern Filipinos opposed the Americans, but inef-
fectually.[27] The Americans then created, in succession, "two regional
autonomous governments" in the south, both aimed at providing gov-
ernance for Muslims and integrating them into the political system. Since
then, the government claimed, "despite recurring inter-ethnic conflicts,
Filipino Muslims have lived peacefully as part and parcel of the Filipino
body politic," with exactly the same constitutional rights as non-Muslims, including guarantees of religious freedom.[28]

The government conceded that tension did break out in "small pockets
of rebellion" in some parts of Mindanao during late 1972 and early 1973.
The government's analysis was that these were caused by the fact that
political warlords and subversive elements had successfully exploited
"ancient grievances," which had been aggravated by land conflicts and
economic opportunism.[29]

Because conditions elsewhere in the country were similar to those in
the south, Marcos declared martial law. In the south, however, according
to the government, rumors spread that martial law had been declared to
convert Muslims forcibly to Christianity; this resulted in Muslim resistance to efforts by the armed forces to collect all guns in civilian hands.[30]
These rumors and other "baseless suspicions" were fomented by a variety
of groups who hoped to gain from disorder:

> Their aims were varied. Some were ambitious politicians who sought the
> secession from the Republic of the islands of Mindanao, Basilan, Sulu,
> Tawi-Tawi and Palawan to coalesce with Sabah in order to form an inde-
> terminate political state. Others were the Communists who sought to divert
> military pressure from the Luzon guerrilla bases. Others were simply ban-
> dits and brigands who took advantage of the general confusion to rob and
> to plunder. Others were adventurist youths. And still others were political
> radicals who manipulated the religious fervor of many Muslim communi-
> ties as one more lever for overthrowing the national government.[31]

The government placed the MNLF among these latter groups. Stripped
of rhetoric and some of its inconsistencies, the government's account was
that the MNLF's membership was recruited from discontented Muslim
students educated at home or abroad, influenced by Maoist ideology, and
trained and armed by foreign powers.[32] Its leadership chose to downplay
its Maoist influences and to seize the banner of Islam for two reasons.
First, an Islamic identification enabled it to emphasize the deeply felt
grievances of Muslims in the Philippines and thus to mobilize them for
its secessionist ends. Second, identifying religion as the cause of its conflict with the government misled Muslims outside the Philippines into
providing support.

In response, the government claimed to have developed a "two-
pronged appraoch of conciliation and development for the Southwestern
Philippines" and a policy of "open diplomacy." Conciliation involved
dialogues with groups engaged in the rebellion to arrive at solutions to

perceived problems and development committed the government "to the provision of economic, social, cultural, and educational facilities and to the expansion of citizen participation in nation-building."[33] Open diplomacy was based on the following premises: that the condition of Filipino Muslims was more advanced than that of Muslim minorities elsewhere, therefore the government had nothing to hide; that the majority of Filipino Muslims were loyal to the government, not to the MNLF; that the MNLF was composed of a handful of young radical rebels, living comfortably in self-exile abroad, who were actually working for the dismemberment of the republic; that the MNLF was in active alliance with the NPA; and, finally, that the Islamic Conference wished to use its good offices to help resolve an internal problem for the benefit of Filipino Muslims.[34]

In short, the government asserted that Muslims—Southern Filipinos, in its argot—shared with other Filipinos a common history and land. They also shared an "intrinsic piousness," which manifested itself in a variety of religions, as well as strong loyalties to ethnolinguistic groupings (eighty-seven in all). The state was defined as secular with the Constitution guaranteeing freedom of religious belief and worship to all citizens. Muslims had suffered in the past, partly because of the malfeasance of their own traditional leaders and politicians, partly because of inadequacies in the political system throughout the country. Martial law was proclaimed to correct such problems, and the Marcos regime was committed to redress any wrongs. According to the government the MNLF's secessionist goals were a threat to national sovereignty and territorial integrity as well as to the welfare and lives of Muslims.

Structures and Policies

The government's outline of its efforts to respond to the needs of Muslims is helpful if one remembers that conciliation and development were accompanied not simply by open diplomacy, but also by a massive expansion of the Philippine armed forces and by the deployment of about seventy percent of them in the south. Their operations there ranged from aerial bombardments and full-scale ground assaults to skirmishes and drunken shootouts. On balance, they probably contributed as much to disorder as to order because their indiscriminate firing and other undisciplined behavior encouraged Muslims to flee their lands (and hence the source of their livelihoods) and/or to join the rebels in the hills. Certainly through most of the 1970s, they constituted the most obvious government presence in the south.

It is, however, true that by 1973 the government was also placing considerable emphasis on conciliation and development programs for the south. The agency primarily responsible for early initiatives was the Presidential Task Force for the Reconstruction and Development of Mindanao, which was chaired by Alejandro Melchor, then Marcos's executive secretary and the regime's top technocrat. The task force had on its staff a number of well-trained young Muslims who shared Melchor's objective of developing an "all out, well-planned program designed to expand all facets of Philippine Muslim participation in the national society."[35] The result was not simply the coordination of the regime's investments of borrowed funds in various activities aimed at economic development in the south, as Marcos's original charge to the task force indicated, but a series of decrees, research projects, and agencies. Among the decrees was a proclamation of Islamic holidays in Muslim areas, provisions for asserting ownership of "ancestral lands," and permission for the resumption of barter trade between Sulu and Sabah. Staff members were involved in a project to develop a Muslim law code. Cotabato, Zamboanga, and Sulu provinces were partitioned, ostensibly to allow greater representation of Muslims. The Philippine Amanah Bank was created. Operating on the Islamic concept of banking following the "no-interest and partnership principles," it was to improve socioeconomic conditions in the economically depressed provinces of Mindanao.[36]

Meanwhile other efforts were underway, some compatible with the task force's activities, others either not coordinated or apparently contradictory. Among other moves, the Department (Ministry) of Education allowed the use of Arabic in schools, and the government took steps to develop a new area for Muslim housing in Manila. But the government also began to consult with, and appoint to office, older, traditional Muslim leaders, some of whom were responsible for the warlordism Melchor regarded as one of the infirmities of the old society.

By 1975, however, the Islamic Foreign Ministers' meeting in Kuala Lumpur and the negotiations with MNLF in Jedda had provided a new focus for government initiatives. Melchor's opening statement at the Jedda meetings stressed that the "New Society" had not been given a chance to institute reforms and development plans because of a lack of peace and order—a lack for which Misuari was blamed—and argued that the logical move was to stop the "senseless enmity" and proceed to implement reconstruction and development. Melchor rejected any form of autonomy, except local administrative autonomy, as incompatible with the Philippine Constitution. Sometime thereafter, Melchor's staff apparently began drafting possible schemes for local and/or regional "autonomous" structures. One of these, a truncated proposal for the creation of four regions in the southern Philippines and for additional appointments of Muslims, was first announced at the "peace talks" held in Zamboanga City in June 1975 and subsequently communicated to the Islamic foreign ministers in Jedda in July. By the time negotiations resumed in Tripoli in December 1976, Marcos had already created two regional offices in areas of heavy Muslim population and appointed commissioners to head them. Western Mindanao (Region 9) included the five provinces of Sulu, Tawi-Tawi, Basilan, Zamboanga del Norte, and Zamboanga del Sur, with headquarters in Zamboanga City. Southern Mindanao (Region 12) included North Cotabato, Maguindanao, Sultan Kudarat, Lanao del Norte, and Lanao del Sur, with headquarters in Cotabato City.

During the meetings in Tripoli, the Philippine position was that these two regions and the ten provinces they included should constitute the "autonomous" area under discussion. The MNLF (and apparently the Islamic Foreign Ministers' team) had proposed twenty-one provinces and a single "autonomy for the Muslims." The agreement on thirteen—with Palawan, Davao del Sur, and South Cotabato added to the Philippines' already constituted regions—and on vocabulary referring to "the autonomy for the Muslims in the Southern Philippines" appeared to be a compromise. Yet, the Philippine government had also insisted on the inclusion of a clause in the preliminary agreement that it would take "all necessary constitutional processes for the implementation of the entire Agreement."[37] According to Philippine documents, it was understood by all parties that "constitutional processes" included a referendum ("to determine various questions including the administrative nature of the government") and elections for public officials.[38] Marcos announced immediately after the preliminary agreement was signed that a plebiscite was "under study," then announced on February 11, 1977, that a referendum would be held on February 21 to get the consent of the people in the thirteen provinces to the territorial scope of the "autonomy"; on February 16 the referendum was postponed until March 17; on March 16 it was postponed until April 17.

Meanwhile, the Tripoli talks had reconvened and deadlocked. The Muslim version of the deadlock was that after the MNLF and the Philippine government had presented their positions, the conference chairman suggested an adjournment for each side to work out a compromise; the MNLF was prepared to do so, the Philippine panel was not. The Philippine government charged that the MNLF was reverting to earlier demands for a separate state and insisted on a referendum, which the MNLF considered unnecessary. Finally Imelda Marcos flew to Tripoli again to work out another compromise. Her efforts produced an exchange of cables between Qaddafi and Marcos on March 18 and 19. Once more, however, the apparent agreement dissolved in claims and counterclaims. Finally, despite objections from Qaddafi, the Islamic Conference's secretary general, and Misauri, the Philippine government held the referendum it wanted, with the questions of its choice. An overwhelming majority of those voting rejected the merger of the thirteen provinces into one region (which had been agreed to at Tripoli) as well as other proposals based on an MNLF draft prepared for negotiations (which someone on the Philippine team had allegedly leaked). Instead, the majority approved a proposal that the administration of the "autonomy" be under the general supervision and control of the Philippine government, with ten provinces clustered in two regions. Representatives from the Islamic Conference, the MNLF, and the Philippine government then met in Manila in an attempt at saving the negotiations; talks ended at the end of April with mutual recriminations.

Thereafter, the Philippine government proceeded to implement the Tripoli Agreement as it chose. By its description, the referendum was followed by: the establishment of the provisional Regional Government in Southern Philippines and an invitation to Misuari to chair it; the promulgation of the Muslim Code as the nucleus of an Islamic judicial system; the strengthening of the Amanah Bank and the Southern Philippine Development Authority as the core of the regional financial and economic system; the establishment of a new university, to strengthen the autonomous educational system; the creation of regional security commands; the addition of the Philippine Pilgrimage Authority to existing Muslim-oriented agencies, to preserve Islam as an integral part of Filipino culture; the reenforcement of the regional commissions as agencies for administration; and the election of members to the regional assemblies and the impending appointment (by Marcos) of members of the regional executive councils.[39]

The government's list was misleading because it suggested a smoothness of implementation and an efficacy of institutions that did not exist. Melchor's task force team on Muslim law had, for example, originally produced a "Proposed Draft of the Administration of Muslim Law Code" on April 4, 1974. The draft raised strong objections from the Philippine judicial heirarchy:

> Instead of introducing progressive new practices, it would serve to institutionalize existing practices. It would answer Muslim demands that their religion and customs be preserved, but it would not serve to "inculcate new habits and attitudes among Muslims." Inclusion of *adat* considerations lessened the possibility that "old customs" would be eliminated. On top of that it created a multiple level judicial hierarchy, the operations of which would be effectively out of the control of the regular judicial bureaucracy.[40]

Consequently, Marcos established a review commission chaired by Professor Cesar Majul, a Muslim, but dominated by non-Muslims. The commission produced a much more conservative code (e.g., it was rooted in Middle Eastern Islam rather than Philippine Muslim customs and it established a compartment within the existing Philippine judicial system rather than a semiautonomous judicial structure). However, this code was ignored from its submission in August 1975 until the Tripoli Agreement apparently encouraged its promulgation in February 1977. Marcos decreed that administrative preparations were to begin immediately and that its provisions were to take effect in forty-five days.[41] As of 1984, administrative preparations continued in the form of training institutes in *sharima* law, but the code was not yet in force.

As for the Amanah Bank, it was "strengthened" because mismanagement and nonpayment of loans had threatened its solvency. Moreover, according to an article in a publication of the Ministry of Muslim Affairs

in 1982, it was not scheduled to start its Islamic (i.e., interest-free) operations until 1983, nine years after the bank's creation.[42] The Southern
Philippines Development Authority, the other agency cited as constitut-
ing the region's financial and economic core, was headed by Imelda
Marcos.

There were also difficulties with the regional governments. In Western
Mindanao (Region 9) the major opposition grouping refused to field candidates in the polls to elect candidates to the regional assembly. In Southern Mindanao (Region 12) the KBL (the government party), the opposition party, and self-identified MNLF candidates (the MNLF boycotted
the election) decided to merge into one party and allow Marcos to choose
the candidates for its regional assembly.[43] Nevertheless, the government
claimed that the election was significant because it implemented the Tripoli Agreement.

There was, however, a more fundamental problem if the issue was
whether or not the government would be said to have implemented the
Tripoli Agreement as it claimed. If one compared the texts of the Tripoli
Agreement with the MNLF's proposed draft of a presidential decree with
Presidential Decree No. 1618 (signed by Marcos on July 25, 1979), it
appeared that the MNLF's draft attempted to institutionalize Muslim
dominance (specifically MNLF dominance) to a degree neither required
by the Tripoli Agreement nor realistic, given population statistics. Nevertheless, it was considerably more in accord with both the letter and spirit
of the Tripoli Agreement than the Government's subsequent version.[44]

The first clauses of the English (for the Philippines) and French (for the
Islamic Conference) versions of the agreement differed markedly: The
English stated agreement on "The establishment of Autonomy in the
Southern Philippines within the realm of the sovereignty and territorial
integrity of the Republic of the Philippines"; the French version of the
same sentence declared agreement on "internal autonomy for the benefit
of Muslims in the Southern Philippines" ("autonomie interne au profit
des muselmans du Sud des Philippines"). Nevertheless, the English version subsequently resembled the French in its reference to "autonomy for
the Muslims," its specific provisions that Muslims shall have the right to
set up their own courts and administrative system in the autonomy, and
its implication that the "authorities of the autonomy" who are to have
the right to establish schools, their own economic and financial system,
and so on are also understood to be Muslims.[45]

There is no doubt that the questions submitted for a referendum were
intended to modify the terms of the Tripoli Agreement as well as to
counter MNLF interpretations of appropriate implementation. Yet Presidential Decree No. 1618 went beyond referendum results to depart in a
fundamental way from the essence of the Tripoli Agreement: Neither the
Muslims nor Islam were mentioned in the entire document, nor was there
the substance of autonomy (if normal usage of the word is adhered to).
Rather, there were provisions for the kind of regional government one

might expect in a secular, centralized state. The regional assemblies consisted of a mixture of members elected from provinces (seventeen) and sectors (four—youth, agricultural workers, nonagricultural workers, and professionals), and those appointed by Marcos (up to five). These assemblies have limited powers, including oversight of the activities of certain national ministries, and the right to initiate certain kinds of programs of their own so long as the programs do not conflict with national plans. Fiscal constraints provided even more stringent limits.[46]

But if the regional insitutions seemed to provide neither for the special representation of Muslim interests nor for autonomy, Marcos did supplement those institutions with a Manila-centered Commission on Islamic Affairs, described in a government publication as "the President's arm for the direct assistance to Muslims in Southern Philippines." In 1981, the commission was given ministry status as the Ministry Affairs and the minister was made a member of the Batasang Pambansa (the National Assembly) and of the presidential cabinet. The functions of the Agency for the Development and Welfare of Muslims were transferred to the ministry, so that is became responsible for handling assistance from the Organization of Islamic Conference. Because the minister (Admiral Romulo Espaldon) and deputy minister (attorney Michael Mastura) also headed the Philippine Amanah Bank, the ministry's influence extended there. Finally, the ministry's mandate was sufficiently broad (or its leadership sufficiently energetic) to allow its involvement in a variety of programs initiated but not yet implemented, for example, the Ancestral Land Decree of 1974, presidential decrees regarding *sharia* law (1974 and 1977), and a presidential letter of instruction (1982) that provided for the development of Muslim community schools and the strengthening of programs in Islamic studies and Arabic.[47]

The government, then, provided structures and policies that deal with many of the issues outlined in Tripoli. In that sense, and in that sense alone, it could be said to have implemented the agreement. Indeed, what it most seemed to have implemented were the proposals it made in Tripoli that were rejected in favor of compromises reflecting Muslim initiatives and interests as Muslims defined them—a point made, at least indirectly, in successive meetings of the Islamic foreign ministers.

The Marcos government was, however, justified in claiming that its moves were supported not simply at home, but also abroad. Its assertion in one of its publications that "Philippine bilateral relations with the 42-member states of the Islamic Conference are good and in most cases, excellent" had some basis in fact.[48] That at least the appearance of good relations existed was the result of a recognized congruence of interest as well as the Philippines' open diplomacy. Certainly, some Islamic states had had reservations over the MNLF's goals and/or ideology and over setting precedents to support interference in the internal affairs of states. Clearly, Indonesia and Malaysia felt they benefited from cooperation with the Philippines on particular objectives and were unwilling to jeopardize ASEAN. Although Middle Eastern states could find other markets for their oil or other sources for their imports of foreign labor, they had established trade and labor exchanges with the Philippines that served their interests. Hence, so long as the Philippines made gestures toward meeting Muslim needs and so long as it refrained from escalating warfare to a point resembling genocide, Islamic states (separately or together) were unlikely to use the forms of leverage they possessed to bring about optimal objectives, such as those they affirmed in yearly meetings.

Assessment

If the Marcos government succeeded in countering the MNLF's assumptions and goals by substituting its own nationalist ideology for that articulated by the MNLF and by institutionalizing (or reinstitutionalizing) its dominance through new structures and policies, it—like the MNLF—had problems of both ideology and organization. Ideological problems were exemplified by a quotation from former President Marcos on the back of a government publication that described "infra-structure development in Muslim Mindanao":

> The challenge before us today is the same challenge that faced all generations before us: that of permanently integrating the nation.
>
> We need to build a nation in which no one will see himself as a Tagalog, Ilocano or Pampango, Tausug, Maranaw or Maguindanao, much more than he sees himself as a Filipino; in which no citizen of the land will identify himself by his religious faith or his ideological persuasion rather than by the common patrimony of nationality which he shares with all Filipinos.[49]

Data from a recent survey of Muslim college students suggested the extent of the challenge, as Marcos posed it; other data called into question its wisdom. The survey, which provided the data for master's thesis for a research intern at the Gowing Memorial Research Center in Marawi City, queried five hundred students about their "self-images and intergroup attitudes."[50] Specifically, it asked them to indicate their citizenship, their nationality, and their preference for "identifying names." The results were startling, both in students' manifestations of alienation from the Philippine/Filipino identifications and in their revelation of differences among Muslim ethnic groups.

Most Maranao, Maguindanaon, and Samal students, for example, listed their "primary citizenship" as "Muslim," but a high percentage of Samal and most Tausug claimed "Bangsa Moro" as their citizenship—undoubtedly both cause and result of the strength of the MNLF in the Sulu Archipelago. The Maranao—the most "integrated" geographically into the Philippines—had the highest percentage identifying as Muslim Filipino (9% of Maranao informants) and Filipino (12%). The totals were 54.6% Muslim, 28.6% Bangsa Moro, 12% ethnic name, 4.2% Muslim Filipino, 3.8% Filipino, and 2.6% not stated.

When asked to indicate whether Filipino (in one question) or Moro (in another) was an appropriate designation for Muslims, a strong majority (89.4%) disagreed that Filipino was accurate. Regarding Bangsa Moro, 43.2% agreed it was accurate, with marked differences among Maguindanaoan (13.6%), Maranao (2.4%), Samal (75.2%), and Tausug (81.6%). On questions asking for identifying names, a majority of students preferred Muslim (58.6%); 31.2% preferred Bangsa Moro; 6.4% preferred an ethnic name; and 3.8% preferred Filipino. Again, however, the totals masked differences among groups, roughly paralleling the findings regarding citizenship identification. Maranao and Maguindanaoan most strongly preferred Muslim (83.2% and 69.6%, respectively), whereas Samal (44.8%) and Tausug (62.4%) had strong preference for Bangsa Moro. Only the Maranao had a significant percentage (12%) identifying as Filipino.

The thesis contained intriguing explanations of the figures, based both on survey data and on interviews, but only the strong identification as Muslim, the comparatively weak identification with ethnic group, and the almost nonexistent (except among Maranao) identification as Filipino deserve emphasis here. Although there was no way of knowing the extent to which the data were reflective of opinion among all Muslims, it seemed reasonable to assume that they were reflective—certainly one would assume that older Muslims would be more traditional (i.e., more religious) in their identifications. In any event, the opinions of an emerging professional class were important. They clearly suggested that the government's goals of subordinating ethnic identifications and eradicating religious identifications are likely to founder. Both the survey findings and the writings of Philippine Muslims would seem to dictate other goals: specifically a definition of Filipino nationality that included both ethnic identification and religion. Certainly, any definition of nationality that forced Muslims in the Philippines to make choices or even to set priorities was destined to lose to Islam.

There was another aspect to the Marcos regime's ideological problems. If divide and rule was not a deliberate tactic, the regime took full advantage of Muslim divisions—ethnic, clan, personalistic, ideological. Clearly, it emphasized and encouraged factionalism among the MNLF's adherents and supporters. In place of the MNLF's ideology it substituted what appeared primarily as a spoils system, with loyalty bought by benefits and cohesion achieved through mutual dependency. But neither the loyalty nor the cohesion so gained was a basis for development, if that could be taken seriously as a goal.

Again as with the MNLF, ideological problems became organizational ones. Without a common sense of purpose, without some loyalty to a greater cause, participants in the regime's projects found more limited goals—personal enrichment through commissions or cuts, political position through publicity. Projects once initiated were not finished; programs were poorly planned and, hence, nonproductive; corruption was rampant. Marawi City had water pipes but no reliable water supply, telephone lines but no functioning phone system. The power from Maria Cristina Falls provided power for plants and for houses around Lake Lanao, but the resultant pollution and the drop in the lake's water level upset the area's ecology and economy. Therefore, Muslims had no money to pay for electricity.

Under the circumstances the Marcos regime's success was dependent on a constant flow of pesos to MNLF defectors, to refugees, and to politicians and their clients. Yet, the regime's delivery capacity was severely curtailed by fluctuating prices for exports, drought, and mismanagement.

Ironically, the regime's chief assets—in the short run—may have come from programs to which it gave little significance. In recent years, the Ministry of Muslim Affairs contributed to the strengthening of a number of institutions that mattered to Muslims and to the development of a cadre of professionally competent and committed Muslims whose potential usefulness would transcend their current assignments. Michael Mastura, while deputy minister of the ministry, talked of communal autonomy in ways reminiscent of post World War II statesmen promoting the Common Market as a step toward European integration. Yet his focus was really a variant of the Islamic resurgence—his goal was to strengthen Muslim institutions and self-help mechanisms and thereby to build a more cohesive and effective Muslim community rather than to expend energies on the apparently futile effort to secure political autonomy for Muslims. Others in or out of the Ministry of Muslim Affairs made similar efforts. Despite the exacerbation of Muslim-Christian relations caused by the fighting and by government programs resented by Christians, there was an impressive amount of Muslim-Christian cooperation in the southern Philippines. Catholics and Protestants, for example, participated in programs designed to educate Christians about Islam, and Christians and Muslims met frequently for dialogues. Research centers and community development programs had Muslim and Christian staff members.

But if these efforts suggested both problems and the possibility of short-term stability, other problems were more acute, and were ultimately responsible for the collapse of the Marcos government. Hence, when Corazon Aquino emerged triumphant in February 1986, she inherited not simply an unresolved debate with the MNLF over appropriate political structures and policies for Muslims. The new government faced a national debate over appropriate political structures and policies for the country, while at the same time it attempted to cope with divisions within its own leadership, a devastated economy, and organized opposition from both the left and Marcos loyalists. The MNLF had splintered, its own internal flaws exacerbated by Marcos's tactics.

Under the circumstances, it was understandable that six months after assuming power the government had not begun the negotiations with Muslims to which it had committed itself. Two Muslims had been appointed to the new Constitutional Commission; others had been appointed to replace officials identified with the Marcos era; but Muslims were quite obviously not being given priority on the national agenda. Mrs. Aquino explained that she was waiting for leaders of different groups in the MNLF to decide who would represent them and whether the Tripoli Agreement was to provide the basis for talks. Other officials commented that the government was taking advantage of the factionalism Marcos had encouraged to deal with other issues it regarded as more pressing.

Meanwhile, Muslims grew increasingly restive. Many were sympathetic initially not only because they opposed Marcos but also because Senator Benigno Aquino, and later his brother Agapito ("Butz"), had sought out Muslim leaders for conversation and had been openly supportive of Muslim demands for increased autonomy. Even the sympathetic, however, were concerned about the role of the Catholic Church and of the military (specifically Defense Minister Enrile and General Ramos) in Mrs. Aquino's victory and subsequently in her government's actions. Delay in the announcement of a specific agenda for dealing with Muslim issues encouraged their skepticism; among the more alienated, it encouraged violence.

For Muslims and the government, then, the Marcos government had left a legacy. If it made Muslims more conscious of their Muslim identities and more assertive of what they believed to be their rights than they had been before, it also left them more divided and perhaps less capable of concerted, effective action. For the government, the costs of conflict and of co-operation were clear. The issue of appropriate political structures and policies for Muslims seemed likely to remain a central feature of Philippine political life.

Notes

1. Numbers are among the controversial "facts." If one assumes that Muslims constitute approximately five percent of the Philippine population, as most sources do, and also assumes that the Philippine population is 52.8 million, one concludes that there are approximately 2.64 million Muslims. However, many sources (including those using the five percent and 52.8 million figures) believe that number is too low.
2. Nur Misuari, "Message of the MNLF Chairman During the 15th Anniversary Celebration," 18 March 1983.
3. Cesar Majul, *The Contemporary Muslim Movement in the Philippines* (Berkeley: Mizan Press, 1985), pp. 42–43.
4. Sali Wali (former MNLF commander), "On the Birth of the MNLF," *From Secession to Autonomy: Self-Government in Southern Philippines"* (Manila: Republic of the Philippines, Ministry of Foreign Affairs, 1980), p. 157.
5. Majul, *op. cit.,* pp. 49–50.
6. *Ibid.,* p. 52.
7. "Proclamation No. 1081: Proclaiming a State of Martial Law in the Philippines," in Isabelo T. Crisotomo, *Marcos the Revolutionary* (Quezon City: J. Kriz Publishing Enterprises, 1973), pp. 240–46.

8. There were two documents prepared by the Office of the Chairman of the MNLF's Central Committee, "The Rise and Fall of Moro Statehood" and "Appeal Letter to the Islamic Foreign Ministers' Conference, Kuala Lumpar, Malaysia (June 21, 1974)."
9. "Rise and Fall," *op. cit.* p. 2.
10. *Ibid.,* pp. 5–6.
11. *Ibid.,* pp. 9–14.
12. *Ibid.,* pp. 14–15.
13. *Ibid.,* p. 15.
14. *Ibid.,* pp. 16–17.
15. *Ibid.,* pp. 17–18.
16. *Ibid.,* pp. 20–40. The text chronicles the escalation of the fighting in the south; provides examples of "Christian" laws, appointments, and actions that evidence discrimination against Muslims; and traces the economic infiltration of the south by "Christian" settlers and corporations.
17. "Appeal Letter," app. 1.
18. *Straits Times,* 26 June 1974.
19. The text of the agreement is found in *From Secession to Autonomy, op. cit.*.
20. Abdurasad Asani, *Moros—Not Filipinos* (Bangsamoro Research Centre), p. 19.
21. Majul, *op. cit.,* p. 74.
22. Frank Gould, "Interview with Commander Ulangutan, a Bangsa Moro commander in Tawi Tawi," April 1974, p. 2.
23. The manifesto was published by the Free Philippine News Service and quoted in *An Asian Theology of Liberation: The Philippines* (IDOC Documentation Project, The Future of Missionary Enterprise, No. 5; New York: IDOC/North America, 1973, p. 63).
24. *Far Eastern Economic Review,* 27 June 1975, p. 21.
25. Joel de los Santos, "Political Movements: The Moro National Liberation Movement," pp. 5–8.
26. *The Southwestern Philippines Question* (Manila: Republic of the Philippines, Department of Foreign Affairs, n.d.), p. 1.
27. *Ibid.*
28. *From Secession to Autonomy, op. cit.,* p. 4.
29. *The Southwestern Philippines Question, pp. cit.,* pp. 1–2.
30. *Ibid.,* p. 2.
31. *Ibid.*
32. *From Secession to Autonomy, op. cit.,* p. 7.
33. *The Southwestern Philippines Question, op. cit.,* p. 3.
34. *From Secession to Autonomy, op. cit.,* p. 11.
35. Alejandro Melchor, "The New Society in the Southern Philippines," *1975 Fookien Times Yearbook,* p. 52.
36. *Salsilah* (Ministry of Muslim Affairs), 3:4 (October–December 1982), p. 23.
37. A longer analysis of Philipine policy during this period is found in Lela G. Noble, "Muslim Separatism in the Philippines, 1972–1981: The Making of a Stalemate," *Asian Survey,* 21:12 (November 1981), pp. 1100–14.
38. *The Southwestern Philippine Question, op. cit.,* pp. 17–18.
39. *Regional Autonomous Governments, Southern Philippines: A Primer* (Manila: Republic of the Philippines, National Council on Multilateral Cooperation for Southern Philippines, 1980), pp. 17–18.
40. G. Carter Bentley, "Islamic Law in Christian Southeast Asia: The Politics of Establishing Shari-a Courts in the Philippines," *Philippine Studies,* 29 (1981), p. 59.
41. *Ibid.,* pp. 62–63.
42. *Salsilah,* 3:4 (October–December 1982), p. 14.
43. *Bulletin Today* (Manila), April 11, 1979.
44. The texts are included as "annexes" in *From Secession to Autonomy, op. cit.*
45. *Ibid.,* pp. 67–75.

46. *Ibid.,* p. 53.
47. There is a very helpful summary of "Development Components of Muslim Affairs" by Faizal U. Hussin in *Salsilah,* 3:4 (October–December 1982), pp. 22–27.
48. *Primer, op. cit.,* p. 18.
49. "Infrastructure Development in Muslim Mindanao" (Manila: Republic of the Philippines, Ministry of Public Works and Highways, 1982).
50. Abdulsiddik A. Abbahil, "The 'Bangsa Moro': Their Self-Image and Inter-Group Ethnic Attitudes," M. A. thesis, University of San Carlos (Cebu City), May 1983.

6

SOVIET CENTRAL ASIA AND CHINA
Integration or Isolation of Muslim Societies

JOHN OBERT VOLL

Many explanations of the modern experience of Muslims are challenged by developments in recent years. In most cases, this involves recognizing the significance of the resurgence of Islam. The old assumption that increasing modernization means a decline in religion's importance needs to be revised, if not discarded. This revision, for most people, involves looking at societies where Muslims are the majority. It ignores a very significant group of Muslims: those who are minorities within their societies. The modern experience of Muslim minorities is an important aspect of modern Islamic history. Even the lives of those Muslims who live in officially antireligious states reflect the continuing vitality of Islam. Because of this, the Muslim communities in the Soviet Union and China provide a valuable starting point for a consideration of the continuing role of Islam in modern societies—as minorities and vis-à-vis Communist systems.

Muslims as Minorities

It is often stated that Islam is not simply a religion but that it represents a whole sense of community and a way of life. It defines both a worldview and a guidance framework for action in all aspects of life. This is related both to the content of the Islamic message and the special historical conditions of the history of the world Muslim community.

Within this very general framework, both Muslim and non-Muslim analysts frequently present descriptions of the modern experience of Muslims in terms that describe the status of minorities as somehow not being acceptable or legitimate for Muslims. That is, this is often the gen-

125

eral position in those presentations that discuss Muslim minorities at all. Frequently, even though Muslim minorities comprise a significant proportion of the total world Muslim population (somewhere between one fifth and one third of the total), they are ignored in discussions of Islam in general or relegated to the periphery of analysis.

The Standard Analysis of Muslim Minority Motivations

Muslim minorities are often ignored because they are not seen as properly living within the Islamic world. The Islamic message defines a whole community and sets standards for human behavior within that context. The life of a Muslim in a society where Muslims are not in the majority and where the political system is not under the control of Muslims would logically seem to be incomplete if not illegitimate. This is the position taken by a number of non-Muslim analysts of Islamic minorities. It is also reflected in the writings of Muslim scholars who take as their model societies where Muslims are a majority.

Most scholars dealing with the Islamic experience and the major teachers who have established the dominant Islamic intellectual positions have, quite naturally, focused attention on those central societies where Muslims are the majority of the population. The ideals of these great Muslim teachers from central Islamic societies create the context of expectations for all Muslims, including those who live as minorities.

These basic teachings and expectations are the product of the experience of Muslims as majorities. This set of ideals might, for convenience, be termed the majoritarian approach to Islam and the creation of legitimate Islamic life. This majoritarian perspective is an important part of much modern analysis. It must be clearly defined when one thinks about the potential roles of the great Muslim minority communities within the contemporary world of Islam. The experience of major Muslim minority communities, like those in the Soviet Union and China, may support a new definition of the obligations of Islam for Muslims who are minorities in their societies. An analysis of the Muslim experiences in China and the Soviet Union may bring about a reinterpretation of the standard majoritarian approach. To see the significance of the Chinese and the Soviet Muslim experience, the current standard ideals need to be defined.

Contemporary Analysis. In specific analytical terms, people looking at the Muslim minorities of the world make a clear assumption that those Muslims would rather be living in a fully Islamic society and also that those Muslims are, in fact, actively working for the creation of such a context. One recent study describes this as an imporant dimension of the modern Islamic experience. The author, Daniel Pipes, calls this drive to create and maintain clearly separate and distinctively Islamic societies autonomism. Pipes identifies autonomism as a significant aspect of Islamic life in Muslim minority communities. He feels that in recent years autonomism may be a more important concern than the desire to implement Islamic law:

> In the large number of countries where Muslims constitute less than a quar-
> ter of the population, autonomist impulses far outweigh legalist ones. . . .
> [L]egalism rarely had much impact in circumstances where the Muslims'
> first concern was either to unburden themselves of kafir [unbeliever's] rule
> or, even more defensively, to safeguard their cultural heritage. (Pipes, 1983,
> 254)

This analysis reflects the common assumption that the first concern of Muslims who are minorities is likely to be the effort to eliminate non-Muslim political control over them. At minimum, it is assumed that there will be a special effort to preserve traditional, Islamically oriented cultural heritages. Although in practice members of Muslim minorities may become socially and culturally assimilated into their non-Muslim larger society, it is believed that, at least from an Islamic perspective, such assimilation is not legitimate, however practical it might be.

This set of assumptions reflects a majoritarian Islamic perspective. It is based on sound historical information because the histories of Muslim minority communities are filled with accounts of revolts against non-Muslim rule and attempts to establish clearly Islamic states or societies. However, such a perspective may miss some of the dimensions of modern Islamic life presented by those Muslims who are neither a majority in their society nor revolting (or hoping for a revolt) against the non-Muslim system of which they are a part. It is this dimension that a consideration of Soviet and Chinese Muslim life helps to explain.

Standard Muslim Position. The line of traditional Muslim analysis of the minority situation also makes the basic assumption of the undesirability of being a part of a minority in a non-Muslim land. The ability to worship God freely in such a context is believed to be limited and always faces the possibility of being denied. "Islam discourages a Muslim to acquiesce willfully to a state of minority if he cannot exercise his right to worship the One True God" (Kettani, 1979, 242). In that situation, the Muslim faces the obligation to emigrate, to engage in holy war *(jihad),* or to keep faith secretly until such time as emigration or holy war is possible.

The concept of emigration is deeply rooted in the symbolism of the faithful and active Muslim. This emigration for the faith, or *hijra,* is seen as reflecting the experience of the prophet Muhammad himself. The *hijra* of the Prophet from Mecca to Medina marks the beginning of the Islamic era. It is the point when the Muslim community made its first transition from being a minority (in Mecca) to the establishment of a Muslim majority community (in Medina).

The call for emigration is part of the call of Islamic reformers over the centuries. It is a major part of the conceptualization of many fundamentalist movements of reform and/or holy war in the past two centuries.

One of the most recent references to this theme is in the name and teachings of the contemporary militant Muslim group in Egypt, *al-Takfir wa al-Hijra* (Excommunication and Emigration). Again, the reference in the title and the ideals of the group is to the necessity for the true believer to emigrate if he or she is living in a land under the control of unbelievers and is unable to alter those conditions of control.

The starting point for the definition of the obligation to emigrate is a Quranic discussion describing the process of judgment after death.

> Those who are still sinning for themselves when the Angels raise them up in death will be asked: "In what conditions were you?" and they will say, "We were among the oppressed of the earth." Then, [the Angels] will say, "Is not the earth of God large enough for you to emigrate in it?" For such as those, Hell is their refuge. . . . He who emigrates in the path of God will find frequent refuge and abundance. (Surah 4:97–100; author's translation)

Muslims in China and the Soviet Union

The history of Muslim communities under Russian and Chinese control contains many movements and events that reflect an understanding of the minority situation in this traditional context. Many of the Muslim communities in the Soviet Union and China became minorities as a result of conquests. Muslims became a part of the Russian empire in significant numbers as early as the sixteenth century when Czar Ivan conquered the old khanate of Kazan. During the following centuries, the gradual Russian expansion into Central Asia brought a growing number of Muslims into the Russian empire, with the last major area to be incorporated being Transoxiana with its great Islamic cities of Bukhara and Samarqand (conquered in the second half of the nineteenth century). Similarly, Chinese expansion into Central Asia brought a number of different Islamic peoples under Chinese imperial control. These peoples, speaking Central Asian languages, are largely concentrated in Sinkiang (Xinjiang) Province or neighboring areas in northwest China.

For these Central Asian peoples, Russian or Chinese control meant a significant alteration of their status. Up until their conquest, they had been clearly part of the Islamic world, ruled by Muslims and living in societies where the majority of the people were Muslims. With the loss of political rule and military control, the traditional alternatives of conquered Muslim groups seemed defined. These Muslims could either emigrate, fight, or run the risk of being absorbed by the conquering peoples and cultures. Assimilation was viewed as apostasy and was usually seen as being as sure an end to Islamic life as massacre or genocide.

Muslim Revolts in China and Russia. One dimension of Muslim minority life in the Soviet Union and China is the continuation of their basic original autonomism. There have been many local and regional revolts led by Muslims that aimed at creating independent or at least autonomous states where Islam was clearly the guiding perspective for the political system as well as for personal life. During the nineteenth century, there were a number of significant Muslim revolts of this kind. For example, in the Russian empire there were the Naqshbandiyyah revolts in the Caucasus region in the middle of the century, there were also a number of revolts among Turkish peoples in Central Asia, reaching a climax with the revolts that spread throughout Turkestan during World War I. In China, the Manchu dynasty, which had been established during the seventeenth century, followed an oppressive policy that aroused many Muslim revolts. Nineteenth-century revolts in Yunnan and Kansu (Gansu) provinces significantly challenged Chinese imperial authority in the areas. For more than a decade, leaders like Ma Hua-lung (d. 1871) were able to maintain control over important Muslim populations. Similarly, in the far west of China, the Muslim leader Yaqub Beg (1820–77) led a revolt that established a state that received at least some international recognition before Chinese imperial control was reestablished.

This tradition of engaging in *jihad* (active effort) in order to insure authentically Islamic rule continued in both the Soviet Union and China after the establishment of their Communist regimes. Perhaps the revolt that was largest in magnitude and most vivid in highlighting the issues is the Basmachi revolt in Turkestan immediately after the establishment of the Bolshevik government in 1917. Because the Basmachi revolt is the one that came closest to success in opposing a major Communist regime, it is worth examining more closely. Initially, most Muslims in Central Asia had supported the overthrow of the czarist regime. Russian suppression of the Turkestan revolts during World War I had been severe and many Muslims believed that the Russian Revolution would mean that the Muslim people would achieve self-rule. However, following the establishment of the Bolshevik government, friction developed in Central Asia that eventually led to a new revolt against central control.

For almost a decade, various movements of opposition to the extension of Communist central control developed. They received support from modern-educated Muslim Central Asians as well as the more traditional groups of tribal leaders and *ulama*. This general cluster of opposition movements came to be called the Basmachi or Freemen's Movement (Olcott, 1981, 352). Although at times there was a regionwide coordination, usually the Basmachi revolt was a scattering of groups that had the same goal of opposition to centralized Russian-Communist control and had some sense of unity based on the common adherence to Islam. There was little long-lasting coordination of efforts. For a brief period of time in 1921–22, especially under the leadership of Enver Pasha (a former leader in the Ottoman empire), the movement achieved a more effective unification, but this did not last long.

The Basmachi movement was finally defeated, but it created an important legacy for the Muslim communities in Soviet Central Asia. Even though there were many different groups in Central Asia with different understandings of Islam, "all elements of Turkestani society were agreed on one, and possible only one, issue: Islam and Turkestan were unquestionably linked. Even if the understanding of what Islam was varied, religion was a fundamental part of the self-identity of Turkestan" (Olcott, 1981, 363–64). Thus, at the beginning of the Muslim experience of being a minority within the Soviet Union, there was a clear linkage, at least in the Central Asian communities, between territorial and national identity and the Islamic faith of the people.

In China, there are also records of various Muslim revolts in the era of the establishment of the Communist government. These are not as well documented as the revolts in the Soviet Union and were not as large in either scope or impact. However, there is a sufficient experience of revolt to establish the existence of this type of activity. The effort to establish an independent Islamic state in Honan (Henan) in 1953 is an example. As in the case of the Basmachi movement, there was an attempt to create a special entity with an Islamic political identity.

Applicability of the Standard Interpretation. These movements fit the pattern predicted by the standard interpretations of the Muslim experience as minority. Muslims in a minority position are supposed to work to establish Islamic political rule or emigrate. They are supposed to try to establish themselves as independent or at least politically separate communities.

It is significant that examples of this typical behavior can be found in the Soviet Union and China. It is satisfying for the analyst, and it helps to confirm an existing standard interpretation. However, the experience of Muslims in China and the Soviet Union goes beyond this basic context. It seems clear that although there have been some small-scale incidents of opposition to the government in Central Asia, there really has been no major large-scale Muslim revolt since the days of the Basmachis. Similarly in China, there have been small movements of opposition, but it does not seem that there has been a provincewide movement of opposition for a couple of decades.

In this context, the standard interpretation would lead us to believe that because of the overwhelming military might of the Soviet and Chinese regimes and because of the difficulty of escape, the alternatives of *hijrah* and *jihad* are not currently viable options and that the more than 40 million Muslims in the Soviet Union and the possibly 20 million in China are silently waiting and biding their time until emigration or revolt are feasible. The sheer magnitude of this assumption calls for new lines of interpretation because the Muslim experience in the Soviet Union has continued for more than half a century, with all of the opportunities for revolt provided by World War II being ignored by most Soviet Muslims.

The Need for Reinterpretation. Sheer survival suggests the need for at least some modification of the standard vision of the Muslim minority experience. At the heart of the Islamic definition of the difficulties of being a minority is the fear that Muslims will end up not being Muslims if they spend too much time as a minority. Either they will be defeated and crushed by the majority or they will be absorbed and converted away from their true faith. The simple fact of the history of Muslim minorities in the Soviet Union and China is that they have neither been crushed out of existence nor assimilated beyond recognition. Reports from the two countries indicate the continued vitality of Islamic faith and practice among millions of people. A general summary of the recent conditions of Muslims in China states, for example: "Persecuted in the early 1970s, the Muslims [in China] became more secure and more willing to stand up for their identity later in the decade" (Pipes, 1983, 258). Many different descriptions of Muslims in the Soviet Union also emphasize the fact that the Muslim communities do not seem to be withering away or crushed out of existence. One might say that without either emigration or *jihad,* the Muslims in the Soviet Union and China seem to be involved in what some have described as an Islamic revival. With less enthusiasm, others might say that there is a continued survival with a remarkable degree of health.

This remarkable degree of health seems to have been unpredictable from a number of perspectives. Ironically, in both standard Islamic views of minority status and orthodox Communist thought regarding religion, these Muslim minorities should be in real trouble by this time in the twentieth century after a number of decades of active atheist rule. However, it is at least possible to suggest that the Muslims have confounded both their atheistic rulers and their majoritarian teachers: It may be possible for Islam to survive authentically as the faith of a minority without *hijra* or *jihad.* This, at least, is the suggestion raised by the Chinese and Soviet Muslim experiences.

Organization for Survival

The Islamic experience does not seem to be developing in the ways that have been predicted for it. Orthodox Communist analysts argue that visible manifestations of religion are simply continuations of the reactionary institutions and attitudes of the past. In this line of analysis, the continued visibility of Islam in the Soviet Union and China is a function of the slowness of the education and development processes in these particular Communist societies. Religion is a continuing residual effect or legacy from the past and its continuation is seen as simply a manifestation of the fact that the creation of a truly Communist society is going to take longer than had originally been anticipated.

Traditional Organizational Requirements. The majoritarian Muslim analysis seems to involve some of the same assumptions found in Communist analysis. The difference is the evaluation of survival. The standard Muslim organizations and institutions are seen as the key. This view is well summarized by a Muslim expert on Muslim affairs in Communist areas, M. Ali Kettani:

> The secret of the Muslim communities which have been able to survive across the centuries and generations lies in one word: *organisation*. Islam cannot survive if individual Muslims believe in it as a personal affair. . . . The implementation by the minority Muslim community of a minimum amount of the *shari'ah* precepts is also necessary if it is to stay in touch with the main body of Islam. Without the establishment of an organisation, a mosque and a school, there is no hope for the survival of Islam in the foreign environment even if there is no oppression from the non-Muslim community (Kettani, 1979, 261).

It is important to note that this same scholar describes the situations of the Muslim communities in the Soviet Union and China in bleak terms. He shows the destruction or closing of mosques, the lack of schools, and the generally hostile policies of the government. Yet, even under these circumstances, he states that in the Soviet Union the Muslims have "established their capacity to survive" and in China "Islam has shown a power of survival hardly paralleled by other Muslim minorities" (Kettani, 1979, 254, 256).

The traditional organizations and institutions of Islamic community have been under attack for decades in the Soviet Union and China. Basic communitywide structures have been destroyed. What is often thought of as the basic minimum for continued healthy survival seems to be weakened: There is no effective implementation of Islamic law, there are no schools where the message of Islam can be taught, and there are very few operating mosques and most of those seem to be under strict government control. Despite this catalog of problems, contemporary observers seem to be in at least some agreement that Islam has not just barely survived in the Soviet Unin and China. It has done more than that.

Muslim Flexibility. It may be that the survival of the Muslim communities in these two countries represents a different kind of process at work. Throughout the history of Islamic communities, one of the striking features of Muslim communal life has been its remarkable adaptability to changing social and historical conditions. In medieval times, the Muslim community survived the splits of civil wars and the transformation of the basic political structures. Initially, the world of Islam was politically united under the leadership of the caliphs or successors to the Prophet. The *ummah* seemed inconceivable without that unity. However, the *ummah* continued not just to survive but to expand even in those very centuries when the caliphate became little more than a token political symbol and eventually was destroyed. The transformation of the basic political order from the caliphate structure to the sultanate structure by the thirteenth century was a major reordering of the community. The community prospered even under the theoretically impossible conditions of not having a single, ruling caliph.

It may be that the conditions of the modern and contemporary world are such that a similar reordering of the Muslim community is again taking place. The standard assumptions of majoritarian Islam may, in fact, not apply to the experiences of Muslim minorities in the context of modern pluralism and contemporary technology. The mission and message of Islam, as sound Muslim thinkers teach us, is never limited to the concepts of human beings in particular ages or places. It is a universally adoptable message whose format, in terms of social or political organization, is not to be limited by the understanding of individual scholars or particular human groupings of Muslims.

The contemporary circumstances of minority Muslims create conditions in which a rethinking of the meaning of the minority experience is being done. One specialist in Muslim minority affairs noted that "certain Muslim communities shall always reside within non-Muslim jurisdictions" and that "there is a crucially significant difference between the struggle for liberation [independence and autonomism] and the struggle to achieve civil and cultural rights within an established and recognised polity" (Abedin, 1980, 20). This expert, Dr. Syed Z. Abedin, stated the task of reconceptualization explicitly:

> How can we live as Muslims in multi-cultural and religiously diverse society? ... We must discover ways to resolve the duality, the twoness that resides in the minority condition.... This is essentially a conceptual challenge. It needs new categories of thought, a fresh understanding of Islam, and a creative capacity for application (Abedin, 1980, 22).

Creative Application or Oppression?

For Muslims in the Soviet Union and China, the critical conceptual issue is whether the contemporary development of structures in the Muslim communities represents a creative capacity for application or simply is a process of destruction and reaction in a context of oppression. The answer is not necessarily obvious. From the perspective of the standard Western analyses and in the viewpoint of most Islamic thinkers, the situation of Muslims in Communist society is primarily a long process of coping with oppression by the best means possible. In these perspectives, it is essentially a long-term waiting game with the ultimate goal being the reestablishment of sovereign, politically independent Muslim communities in the majoritarian model. In the Soviet Union and China, this continues to be represented by the opposition groups in the Basmachi tradition and the sentiments supporting some form of separation or independence.

In a somewhat ironic dimension of the interpretations of the Muslim experiences in the Soviet Union and China, the very broad outlines of the majoritarian Muslim and the anti-Communist Western views seem to agree with the more doctrinaire Communist scholars. Soviet scholars are the ones who have done the most work on this subject and their conclusions also reflect the basic assumption of the incompatibility of Marxist-Leninism and Islam. Manifestations of Islamic beliefs and activities are quite consistently referred to as "religious survivals," and these "survivals" are seen as critical elements that prevent "the participation of believers in the building of communism" (Dzhabbarov, 1979, 79). The importance of Muslim efforts to gain independence or some special, separate status, in other words, receives much attention in Soviet writing, as it does in much of Western and majoritarian Muslim writing on the subject.

The more traditional sentiments and concepts of holy war or emigration may not, however, be the major source of the continuing dynamism of the Islamic message in the Communist context. To understand the continuing strength of Muslim communities in Communist societies, it is helpful to examine what the basic organizations of those communities are. The organizational formats of the Muslim minority communities are much better known in the Soviet Union than are those found in China. As a result, this analysis will focus primarily on the Soviet Central Asian context, citing Chinese experience where the information is available.

In the Soviet Union, there are two types of organization and mode that are most frequently associated with continuing Islamic life. These are the sometimes underground Sufi orders or *tariqahs* and the sense of national identity among the various central Asian peoples. The significance of Islam in these formats is the subject of substantial discussion and disagreement. What follows is one possible interpretation that does not start from many of the assumptions of the doctrinaire Communist analysis or standard Muslim position(s). It attempts, rather, to view the minority Muslim experience in its own framework rather than trying to interpolate conclusions drawn from atheistic doctrines or analysis of the majority situations of Muslim experience. In this way, it may be possible to gain insight into whether the Muslims in China and the Soviet Union are showing a creative capacity or are simply surviving under difficult conditions.

The Sufi Orders

In the early days of the Islamic community, some Muslims paid special attention to lives of piety and devotion. Although these people usually conformed to the prescriptions of Islamic law, they emphasized the meditative and devotional dimensions of Islamic life rather than its legal aspects. By the thirteenth century, distinctive organizations developed within this mode of Islamic life. These groups followed particular devotional paths (or *tariqahs*) that were identified with some great teacher or pious leader. This general Islamic mode is called Sufism and the *tariqahs* are the Sufi orders of Islam.

Tariqahs in Society. The great Sufi orders have performed a variety of functions in the history of Muslim communities throughout the world. They were (and are) important elements in the expansion of Islam in Africa and Southeast Asia. In the great tradition of Islamic communal action without a formal hierarchical church structure, organizations of believers like the *tariqahs* had a freedom of action to adapt to local conditions that was not available, for example, to the great missionary orders in the Christian tradition. The restrictions placed on the Jesuits by the pope in the rites controversy and the ultimate cessation of all Jesuit missionary effort in China in the eighteenth century, for example, are neither conceivable nor possible in the framework of the Islamic community.

Tariqahs have operated as independent social groupings, frequently under the control of no central organization, not even within the *tariqah* itself. The great Sufi orders in the Islamic world developed as active and dynamic traditions of devotional practices and religious groupings. They maintained ties of loyalty and contact among the adherents but there was little centralized organization. For example, the Qadiriyyah Tariqah is historically perhaps the most widespread order in the Islamic world. All Muslims in the devotional tradition of this brotherhood have a special respect for Abd al-Qadir al-Jilani; frequently, his descendents have been special leaders in the *tariqah.* There is also a center of the order in Iraq near the tomb of Abd al-Qadir, which many members of the Qadiriyyah think of as the center of the order. However, this has never meant, in the history of the *tariqah,* that the center of the order has had any ability to direct the activities of any of the regional and local branches spread throughout the Islamic world.

Tariqahs have often been the focus of the activities that make the special adaptations to local conditions in Islamic life. The orders have a special local character and often continue what strict Muslim teachers think of as non-Islamic or pre-Islamic practices in an Islamic garb. Frequently, as a result, the Muslim establishments have opposed the informal, disorganized, or sometimes underground and subversive character of the *tariqah* practices. In a very general comparison, it is interesting to note that the reservations that Muslim political leaders and conservative and strict *ulama* have always had about many *tariqahs* can be seen in the statements of the "official" Soviet *ulama* and the government. This may reflect a reality in which the *tariqahs* in the Soviet Union continue an old function, that of changing Muslim structures and moods to fit the changing local social reality.

Historically, *tariqahs* have been active in a variety of ways. Sometimes they have provided the organization for holy war movements. In the eighteenth century neo-Sufism emerged as a framework for movements of Islamic revival and purification. The Naqshbandiyyah Tariqah in areas conquered by the Russian empire was active in spearheading revolts to maintain or regain Muslim autonomy. Among the most famous of these movements is the nineteenth-century revolt of Shaykh Shamil in the Caucasus region.

The *tariqah* tradition in Islam, however, is not inherently militant or puritanical. In fact, the opposite is more frequently the case. The activist renewalism of neo-Sufism was frequently directed at what were thought to be the compromises accepted by the regular Sufi orders. Political activism is only a small part of the whole picture of the life of believers in a *tariqah* and even in neo-Sufi orders, the episodes of activism are embedded within the broader activities of the order in the ongoing life of the participants.

Tariqahs in Communist Areas. The general reports and descriptions of the activities of the *tariqahs* in Communist lands must be viewed within this broader context. Although there are occasional reports of militant *tariqah* actions of opposition, the general reports seem to indicate a picture not of constant, militant opposition to the regime but rather of continuing quiet devotional activities on the part of believers. One Soviet scholar, for example, notes that in Uzbekistan

> even now one encounters religious wedding ceremonies among the population, baptisms, circumcision, and religious funeral services. Holy places are still venerated and tabibs and mullahs [healers and religious teachers] are still consulted for the treatment of diseases and ailments (Dzabbarov, 1979, 78).

Some of the foremost Western observers of Islam in the Soviet Union paint a similar picture of the basic activities of the *tariqahs* today:

> The activities of the Sufi are usually centered on various "holy places", the tombs of mythical or real men (often Sufi leaders) who died fighting the Russians. These "holy places" serve . . . as meeting places for adepts where they perform the *zikr* [Sufi devotional ritual] and are taught prayers (Bennigsen and Lemercier-Quelquejay, 1979, 47).

The *tariqahs* appear to be an active and important part of Muslim life in the Soviet Union. The extent of their activities and their significance is the subject of much debate. Some analysts see them as an emerging activist alternative to "official" Islam that has the potential of leading major opposition to the Soviet regime (Bennigsen and Lemercier-Qeulquejay, 1979). It is believed that underground organizations based on beliefs other than those of communism will inevitably clash with the Communist state.

Other observers argue that Islamic life in Central Asia "is now unquestionably declining in vitality" (Scott, 1982, 250). Doctrinaire interpretations of the Islamic situation are relatively predictable, with Marxist-Leninist analysts predicting the eventual disappearance of manifestations of religion in general and majoritarian Muslims looking for the eventual, if far-distant, triumph of the message and mission of Islam.

There is a critical assumption behind many of the varying assessments of contemporary Islamic life in Communist countries. This is that Islam and communism are inherently incompatible and, therefore, in the long run, Muslim minority survival in Communist countries is a form of a zero-sum game in which gain by one side is by definition a loss for the other. It may be that this is not the actual social reality even though it may be logically correct. In this issue, the experience of the *tariqahs* in Central Asia may be instructive.

Social Synthesis in Tariqahs. Historically, *tariqahs* have been mediating structures in Islamic communities. They have been vehicles for adjusting the universal message to the local conditions. In the development of ideas and social structures, the *tariqahs* played an important role in creating major Islamic civilizational syntheses. They have not usually been directly involved as a part of an official establishment and have often formed a parallel popular stratum of Muslim religious life. In at least some ways, the *tariqahs* have often been a structural experimentation ground in Islamic societies.

It has been said that the "organization of today's brotherhoods [in the Soviet Union] is a curious blend of the traditional and the new" (Bennigsen and Lemercier-Quelquejay, 1979, 46). These scholars note some special organizational developments among the Soviet *tariqahs*. Among these are a growing role for women in the orders and an increasing participation by younger people, at least some of whom are drawn from the Soviet intelligentsia. However the continued existence of the *tariqahs* may be interpreted, it seems relatively clear that they are not only surviving but that they are developing in sometimes remarkable new forms that seem to be well suited for survival in Communist Central Asian society.

Most Muslims in the Soviet Union are not participants in active movements of opposition to the Communist regime. They appear, in fact, to be participating members of the existing society while they continue to think of themselves as Muslims. Over the years, Soviet Muslims have assured other Muslims that they continue to be Muslims. It may well be that the *tariqahs* are at least as much an affirmation of Muslims being able to live within Communist societies as they are a potential autonomist opposition to those societies. "Soviet Moslems, having repeated to their foreign Moslem brothers for more than twenty years that Islam is able to accommodate itself very well with Communism, have gone on to blend Islam and Communism into an antonishing syncretism" (Carrere d'Encausse, 1981, 280).

If such a new syncretism is emerging, it is not surprising to find Muslims organized in *tariqahs* at the heart of it. *Tariqahs* were the key to the effective blending of local religious customs with Islam in early medieval times. There is a long-standing historic pattern of such blending in Central Asia. In pre-Islamic times, a tradition of religious pluralism developed. Under the historic circumstances of trade, conquest, and religious pluralism, "the boundaries between one set of beliefs and another tended to disappear, with the consequent fusion of theoretically incompatible devotional practices. Syncretism established itself as a permanent characteristic of Central Asian religious life" (Scott, 1982, 234). This syncretistic style continued to characterize at least the popular dimensions of religion in Central Asia after most people became Muslim. One of the chief social vehicles for this mediation among the varying traditions of faith and practice was the *tariqah*.

In this context, it is not surprising that *tariqahs* would continue to form an important dimension in Islamic life in modern times. Following the Communist takeover of the Muslim Central Asian lands, there were critical concerns of survival. Despite military suppression, it soon became clear that physical extermination was not a threat to most Muslim peoples in the Soviet Union. The chief problem, rather, was creating a relationship between communism and Islam in which some form of life and faith that is clearly Islamic could be preserved. Although holy wars and demands for application of Islamic law were possible forms of response, these forms would mean continuing conflict and difficulty. Syncretistic efforts combining Communist and Islamic life might make a more stable and prosperous life possible. It is in this effort that the *tariqahs* may be playing a role. Although some observers note that there is an official effort to eliminate the *tariqahs,* there does not, in recent years, appear to have been a major action to suppress them by force.

The underground Muslim organizations have some secret aspects to them. However, Soviet officials seem to be quite clearly aware of many of the devotional practices involved in popular Islam, such as the visits to tombs. Although such practices are often deplored, the solutions proposed are education rather than arrest. For example, a report from Turkmenistan stated that "more than 300 self-styled Moslem confessors are operating in the republic. They are especially active in the so-called "holy places." Nonworking women are particularly susceptible to this mind-drugging. More women must be drawn into production, public and political life" (CDSP, 35/27, 1983, 9).

Situation in China. There is less evidence readily available for popular Muslim life in China. I would suggest only one possible analogy at this point that may have to be altered on the basis of evidence received later. During the cultural revolution in the 1960s, most of the formal religious organizations were closed or destroyed. Churches and mosques were suppressed and people known to be believers were actively persecuted. However, by the late 1970s, restrictions on religious practices were being lifted. In that context, visitors to China saw a visible increase in public practice of religion. Mosques in the Muslim areas were active.

There were, however, institutional changes that had been brought about by the experience of the cultural revolution. Among Christians, for example, there was a growing practice of having "home churches," which were informal groups that met privately for shared devotions and prayers. As restrictions on institutional religious practices were eased, some Christian leaders noted that many Christians might not return to institutional organizations. Bishop Ting explained that people "enjoy the personal contact and intimate atmosphere of the small in-home gatherings. . . . Many groups simply do not want an ordained minister, and wish to remain self-governing and self-propagating" (Delloff, 1979, 1029).

These "home churches" sound similar in organization to traditional types of Sufi brotherhoods. The lack of centralized organization or hierarchical control may continue to appeal to Chinese Muslims as well as to Chinese Christians. It is possible that such *tariqah*like groupings may be a part of the new Islamic visibility in China. They have not led to holy wars and may represent a survival by accommodation. However, in China the issue of assimilation is older than in the Soviet Union. Chinese Muslims have been under great pressure for centuries to become sinified, and this is an issue that has divided the Muslim communities of China. It is also true, however, that Muslims have survived as identifiably Muslim, even weathering the trauma of the cultural revolution. Adaptation to Chinese Communist life does not seem to have meant the disappearance of Islam.

Islamic Authenticity. The final issue involved in the accommodationism of the *tariqahs* is the degree to which the Muslim life that is reflected in the Muslim communities is authentically Islamic. By the standards of strict traditional Muslim teachers, it might be possible to reject the validity of practices that involve a long-term compromise with, and acceptance of, a non-Muslim (and officially antireligious) political system. Similarly, the Marxist-Leninist would argue that adherence to Islam, in any form, is not full participation in Communist society. However, it is important to ask whether or not the experience of Muslims in China and the Soviet Union can simply be called, by definition, illegitimate. It may be that the modern Muslim experience in these major societies points to the emergence of a tradition of Islam that reflects the experience of minorities.

Thinkers from societies where Muslims are a majority often seem to assume that their style of Islam is the only legitimate form of Muslim social life and they often ignore how many Muslims live as minorities. Two of the five largest Muslim "national" communities are minority communities of less than twenty-five percent of the population of their countries (the Soviet Union and India). In addition, China is possibly the twelfth largest Muslim country in the world. Muslims who are minorities of less than twenty-five percent of their country's population comprise more than one fifth of the world Muslim population. These people maintain Islamic identities in contexts where the success of autonomism is highly unlikely. Most of these view themselves both as "real" Muslims and also as participating citizens of their country. To consign them to a permanent status of illegitimacy within the Islamic world seems a difficult course and not directly within the nonhierarchical traditions of the Islamic community, which has a sense of unity but does not have a formal church structure that defines heresy and dogma for the community as a whole.

The *tariqahs* and other similar informal structures have been a source of Muslim communal strength throughout Islamic history. It would appear, especially in the Soviet Union, that this continues to be the case. The *tariqah* appears to act as a meditating structure, not only providing some support for sentiments of separatism, but also providing a way in which the believing Muslim can participate in an Islamic life while living in a non-Islamic political system and society. Soviet (and possibly Chinese) Muslims add the alternative of synthesis to the more traditional alternatives of *hijra* and *jihad* said to be open to minorities.

Nationalities

A second important organizational format for Muslim life in the Soviet Union and China is the identification of Muslim groups as nations or national minorities. This is a mediating identity that is a compromise between two extremes: no recognition of the existence of the Muslim communities or formal recognition of a religious community. These extremes would be ideologically difficult either for the Communist governments or for the Muslim communities themselves. Muslims would feel uncomfortable, at least, in a political system that gave no recognition to their communities at all. Recognition of the special national character of their communal life gives at least partial recognition to Islam because of the frequently close ties between Islam and the national identities.

For Communist governments to give official recognition to religious communities as legitimate minority groups would run counter to the doctrinaire belief that religion will eventually disappear within Communist society. However, it has been important in the twentieth century for these governments to recognize in some official way the existence of the communities formed by Muslims within their countries. The manner of recognition that emerged was to emphasize the cultural and lingusitic aspects of the life of these communities and identify them as special national communities within Communist society.

Muslim Nationalities in China. In China, this approach to Muslim communities predates the establishment of the Communist regime. Historically, there are two major types of Muslim communities in China. The older derives from groups of merchants and other travelers who came to China as early as the seventh and eighth centuries. Over centuries, these Muslims became increasingly integrated into Chinese society while maintaining a special identity as Muslims. They became

> acculturated through the adoption of Chinese surnames, clothing, and food habits. . . . Gradually Chinese dialects replaced Arabic and Persian not only as a means of communication with the Hans [traditional Chinese of the Middle Kingdom], but among the Muslims as well. As a result of this sinification the Muslims were no longer referred to as "Arabs," "barbarians," or "foreigners," but came to be known as *Hui-hui* or *Hui* (Pillsbury, 1981a, 109). The Hui were often seen as a type of national community within China. The other major type of Muslim communities within China are the Central Asian groups who were brought under Chinese imperial control as a result of the expansion of China in more recent times.

Under the last imperial Chinese dynasty, the various Muslim groups faced active policies of suppression, and there were many uprisings and rebellions. However, the new republican regime established in the early twentieth century opened the way for more direct participation of Muslims in Chinese life without direct oppression. The republican government after 1912, for example, formally identified the Muslims in China as one of the "five great peoples" of China. In this way, the treatment of Muslims as a special community within China predates the establishment of the Communist regime.

The Peoples Republic of China developed a more specified system of recognition. Muslims were not treated as one people. Instead, the particular ethnic groups among the Muslim population were given direct recognition. This was in line with the general policy of recognition of minority groups of all types within China as minority nationalities. Although subject to severe repression during the cultural revolution, the various Muslim nationalities have not disappeared. Instead, the formal recognition of their existence and identity has been insured not simply by the constitutional provisions for freedom of belief, but also through the creation of special autonomous areas for minority nationalities.

There are a number of special areas that are associated with Muslim nationalities. These in some ways reflect the distribution of Muslims within China. The Hui are found throughout China and there are twelve different Hui autonomous areas in eight different provinces. Most of the other special areas are in northwest China, with the largest being the Uygur autonomous region in (Sinkiang) Xinjiang. Although most affairs are in some way under more central control and Han citizens are important even in the various autonomous areas, the system of minority nationalities provides a basic structure of recognition for the Muslim communities. It may be that this provides a vehicle whereby Muslim minority communities can cope with the twoness of minority life.

Although repression is still possible and assimilation is always an important threat, it seems clear that holy war is not a particularly viable option for Chinese Muslims. Major Chinese Muslim rebellions have not created long-lasting Muslim states. Similarly, for most Chinese Muslims, emigration is not a live option. However, despite the absence of the possibilities of either *hijra* or *jihad,* Muslim community life continues in China.

Soviet Muslim Nationalities. The integration of minority communities into a centralized Communist state through a system of nationalities is more clearly and carefully defined in the Soviet Union. From the very beginning of the Communist regime it was recognized that the large, non-Russian groups within the old Russian empire and the new Communist state would have to be integrated in a way that gave at least some meaningful recognition to the special characteristics of the smaller communities.

The whole organization of the state that emerged gave special recognition to the constituent groups. The new revolutionary state was to be a huge union of socialist republics, each with special identities. Although the Russian Soviet Socialist Republic was clearly the largest and most powerful and the Russians were to be seen as elder brothers in the socialist family, the other groups were to be active and separate participants in the Union of Soviet Socialist Republics.

The Muslims in the new state were not seen as a single community and the Central Asian areas were divided up into a number of smaller republics. In each of these, the special traditions of language and local customs were given some encouragement. The encouragement of a sense of a special national character within the framework of the broader socialist union became a solid part of the Soviet Communist ideology, formalized in the writings of major leaders and in the Soviet Constitution. The end result of the teachings and policies regarding nationalities seems quite clear in the 1980s, especially as they relate to the Muslim peoples in the Soviet Union:

> National diversity and intensity of national feelings characterize the Soviet political scene. In this respect the regime's nationality policy constitutes a resounding success—and a no less resounding failure [because a supranational sense of an all-Soviet identity is not emerging in the way that the nationality policy had predicted] (Carrere d'Encausse, 1981, 266).

There are many indications that the multinational character of the Soviet Union continues to be one of its major characteristics. Although there is an emerging Soviet character, this contains components of continuing awareness of nationality that are much stronger than Communist ideology seems to have anticipated originally. The strength of the national awareness varies from group to group within the Soviet Union, but it appears to be very strong among the Muslim peoples. There are indications that the Soviet policies have, in the long run, succeeded in strengthening group identities in the past half century.

From the perspective of the survival of Muslim minorities, there is an important dimension of the nationalities policy. The Muslims are not a recognized nationality in the Soviet Union. In addition, the general category of Turks is also not used as the basis for identifying the particular nationalities. In the definition of the appropriate nationalities, the Communist regime recognized smaller-scale units than either Islam or Turkistan. This ran counter to the aspirations of some of the Muslim-Turk intellectual leaders in the early twentieth century and in the early days of the Communist regime. However, even with the smaller identities, Islam plays an important role in determining the distinctive character of the nation. Thus, the importance of Islam in the Soviet Union has come to be associated with the fortunes of the nationalities whose special identities are in some ways tied to Islam. The most important of these are represented in the separate republics of the contemporary Soviet Union and include Kazakhstan, Kirghizistan, Tajikistan, Turkmenistan, and Uzbekistan.

In recent years, there appears to be a steady increase in the influence and power of the non-Russian nationalities in the Muslim areas. This may be related to the growing educational level of the various national groups in Central Asia and also to developments in population composition. A recent study concludes that in Kazakhstan and Central Asia,

> the indigenous nationalities are increasing their level of educational attainment and increasingly assume a leading role in the economy and the administration of their republics. In part, this process is the indirect result of general economic and social development, modernization, and changing demographic relationships, but it is also linked to deliberate policies both of the native populations themselves and the Soviet authorities (Karklins, 1981, 89).

The growing strength of national identity among the Muslim peoples in the Soviet Union can be, and is, interpreted in a wide variety of ways. Some specialists see the growing national feelings as potential threats to the general Soviet system. One, for example, believes that "national and autonomous strivings . . . [in Kazakhstan and central Asia] are very likely to grow [and that] illustrations of increasing native power in the Muslim republics went beyond cadre selection, education, and demography, and included the growth of native assertiveness and pride (Karklins, 1981, 92).

Other scholars see the emergence of national identities as reflecting the adjustment of non-Russian peoples to the Soviet system. In specific terms, the particular national groupings that have emerged with real strength are smaller groups that have adapted themselves to existence within the Soviet system. They help to prevent the emergence of more threatening, pan-Turkish-type groupings. In this way, it is possible to conclude that the growing sense of nationality

> is being tolerated, even encouraged, today by the Soviet regime as long as it is fragmented and is not in conflict with the principles of economic socialism. . . . [Nationalisms of these smaller groups], while they foster pride in and encourage preservation of ethnic cultures also prevent the homogeneity of Turkish groups and block the ethnic and linguistic unity of various Turkish peoples. This way they will not pose a danger to the security of the Soviet Union. (Basgoz, 1980, 248–49).

Similarly, the official policy of nationalities in China divides the Muslims into separate and sometimes scattered groups. However, the ethnic and cultural identities of the smaller nationalities are closely tied to Islamic traditions in the country. Some scholars argue that even though certain Muslim practices, like recitation of prayers after a meal continue, they "have lost their religious significance. It would be a mistake to consider them the continuation of Muslim practices. People view them as a part of traditional life, an ethnic heritage that may protect them from the onslaught of modern ways" (Basgoz, 1980, 245). Others believe that the continuation of Islamically identified customs represents a clear continuation of the importance of being a Muslim in a Communist society. Practices associated with the major life events—birth, marriage, and death—emphasize the Islamic character of life. For example, in "the USSR, circumcision—even though not one of the obligations of a Moslem—takes on an obvious meaning. It implies that the young Moslem is a member of an overall community, the *Ummah,* which he shares with his brethren and which is the world of Islam" (Carrere d'Encausse, 1981, 225).

Nationality and Islamic Identity. Whether the practices have simply a cultural-ethnic significance or are authentic continuations of Islamic practices, it is clear that these practices have an important significance. They are a major part of the special identity of the various nationalities. They make these nations identifiable as Muslim groups. It is the Islamic practices and beliefs that are permitted when the nationalities' policies are being developed, and it is these same Muslim customs that are attacked when the central governments want to reduce attachment to the national identities. In China, for example, many of the punishments for Muslim officials during the cultural revolution involved having contact with pigs, whereas in the present climate, the non-Muslims living in largely Muslim areas are now very careful not to let pigs forage at large and are cautious in references to the Muslim prohibition against eating pork (Wren, 1983a, 12).

Traditional Muslim scholars have often been suspicious of national feelings and many fundamentalist teachers have argued that Islam and nationalism are incompatible. In these positions, standard Islamic positions and doctrinaire Communist positions are parallel in the assumption that identification with a nation will in some way dilute the universalistic loyalties defined by Islam, on the one hand, or communism, on the other hand. However, in modern history, there have been both Muslim and Communist nationalists who have argued in favor of the compatibility of the universal themes and the national identities.

In this debate, there is usually an assumption that loyalty to the nation is an exclusive loyalty. However, it is clear in actual human experience that Islam often is a factor reenforcing loyalty to a national unit. This results from the very definition of the national unit itself; it usually includes Islamic elements or, at least, elements that people in the nation believe to be Islamic elements. In this sense, it makes little difference if the Islamic elements are seen by some outside observer as being merely social habit or cultural artifact as long as the participants themselves think of the elements as being in some way Islamic.

In China and the Soviet Union, the nationalities do not seem to be direct challenges to the regimes. In the Soviet Union, for example, nationalism

> develops within a special context, that of Soviet ideology and its institutions, so it is futile to interpret it as a movement for national independence. For the moment, belonging to Soviet society is a fact that no one seriously questions. . . . What the national minorities demand in diverse ways is not the destruction of the existing system, but the broadening within this system of their national privileges. (Carrere d'Encausse, 1981, 269).

In this context, the national level of loyalty is a mediating structure of attitudes that helps to make it possible to maintain some type of Islamic identity within the Communist system. As in the case of the *tariqah* organizations, it may be possible that the nationality is a level of loyalty and identity that makes it possible for the Muslim minorities to have an acceptable option other than *hijrah* or *jihad*.

Official Islamic Establishments

In addition to the informal Muslim organizations and the indirectly Islamic nationalities, there is an important third dimension of Islamic minority life in China and the Soviet Union. In both countries, there is some form of an officially organized Muslim establishment. These are often criticized as simply being mouthpieces for government policies. However, the simply but startling fact that these are government-supported Islamic organizations in a political system that is officially atheistic is often overlooked.

The government supported Islamic leaders clearly operate under many restrictions. At the same time, they give at least some visibility to the continued existence of Muslim communities in China and the Soviet Union. The revivals of the Chinese Islamic Association and the reopening of the Chinese Institute of Theology in 1980 represent continuing public presentation of Islam, regardless of how circumscribed the conditions. Similarly, the countrywide religious administration in the Soviet Union gives official visibility to Islam. The four spiritual directorates have staffs, engage in some publication, and are responsible for some educational programs. Although strictly regulated, each of the directorates has enough autonomy that each has some special characteristics that go beyond the different identifications as being affiliated with the Hanafi, Shafi'i, or Shi'i legal traditions. It is possible, as a result, to note that there exist "great differences between the Boards, in particular between the more progressive and modernist Boards of Tashkent and Ufa and the more conservative Causasians" (Bennigsen, 1980, 229).

These Muslim organizations are not directly tied to the officially recognized nationalities. They cross the boundaries of the nationalities and become a different level of Islamic action. The Soviet *muftis* and Chinese leaders have played a role in articulating Muslim ideas in the context of Communist ideology. Muslims whose views are shaped by the experience of societies where Muslims are the majority might not accept the pronouncements of the official Muslim leaders in Communist states, but these statements do represent an expression of explicitly Islamic views from within a Communist regime.

The mediating role of the official establishment is clear. It provides a link between the governing political system and the Muslim communities. This religious establishment is not regime threatening and does not insist on a separatist Islamic program. However, at the same time, it helps to support the continued existence of Muslim communities in a basically non-Muslim society. It provides acceptable ways of articulating Muslim sentiments while remaining within the framework of Communist policies. The existence of this mediation provides the argument from existing institutions that Muslim communities can survive within a Communist society, again, without having to live with only the alternatives of *hijra, jihad,* or hidden, secret belief.

Conclusion

The experience of Muslim minorities living in China and the Soviet Union suggests that it may be useful to rethink older assumptions about Muslim minorities. The simple fact is that these large Muslim minority communities have survived. They have, even more, gone beyond survival. They appear to have grown, not simply gradually withered away.

Certain basic assumptions about Muslim minority life deserve to be reexamined in light of the contemporary Muslim experience in China and the Soviet Union. In particular, the basic assumption of the clear or absolute incompatibility of Islam and communism needs to be reconsidered.

In concrete terms of social and religious life, it appears that mediating structures have emerged that make Muslim minority life in a Communist society possible without resort to the classically defined options of *jihad, hijra,* or secret belief. Public belief and practice appear to be possible within the Soviet Union and China.

The informal devotional groups and *tariqahs,* the nationalities, and the formal official establishments with their govenment-approved mosques and administrations all provide a framework of institutions supporting the continuing life of Muslim communities in the Soviet Union and China. Although, under certain conditions, any of these structures could provide the organization for a movement to establish an Islamic state, this does not, at present, seem to represent their primary function. Rather than acting as a focus for opposition to the existing political system and social order of which the Muslim communities are a part, these structures appear to be performing a significant mediating function. This makes it possible to be, in many significant ways, an individual with those characteristics that—in Communist theory, classical Muslim teaching and much Western analysis—appear to be contradictory and impossible to combine: being a Muslim and being a Communist.

It may be necessary to develop a set of assumptions relating to Muslim life that recognizes more clearly the realities of the Muslim minority condition. In particular, the cases of the Soviet Union and China make it clear that there are large Muslim communities (in fact, the fourth and twelfth largest in the world) that are minorities now and will not gain majority control for the long-term foreseeable future. These communities are living in a context where *jihad* has been tried by parts of the community, but such actions have not been successful. It is difficult to conceive of a Muslim revolt being able to defeat the armed forces of the central governments of either China or the Soviet Union. In addition, it seems quite clear that most Muslims in these two countries do not have a great desire to engage in a *jihad* against their own government.

Similarly, there seems to be remarkably little desire in these communities to emigrate to regions where they could live under the circumstances of being a part of a Muslim majority. It seems clear from many studies that Central Asian Muslims are tied to their homelands and, even with substantial material incentives, have little inclination to move from them.

The Muslim experiences in the Soviet Union and China confirm some of the new conclusions about the emerging Islamic positions regarding minorities. Interpretations and teaching based on the experiences of Muslim majorities often do not directly relate to the needs and experiences of major Muslim minorities. Muslim teachers and other sympathetic observers need to begin the process of reconstructing attitudes and interpretations of the positions of Muslim minorities. Syed Z. Abedin suggests some preliminary lines for this reconstruction: "It needs to be considered that Muslim minorities can preserve their Islamic identity to the extent to which they succeed in providing it with a firm base in, and a direct relevance to, the societies of their residence" (Abedin, 1980, 25).

Muslims in the Soviet Union and China have developed means for establishing the connections of their communities to the broader "societies of their residence." Some of the structures, like the nationalities, are a directly integrated part of the majority definition of the political system as a whole. The nationalities' identities are both vehicles for showing the relevance of Muslim communal life for the society as a whole and structures for maintaining a clearly visible Islamic identity within the society as a whole.

The status of being a minority is usually considered to be a disadvantageous one. There are many groups in societies that have distinctive characteristics but are not generally regarded as minorities. It is only when the majority becomes aware of the distinctive differences of the potential minority group and begins to give negatively differential treatment to the group that there is an awareness that the group is a minority (Kettani, 1980, 90–91). It seems possible that the process may be reversible, at least to some extent. Minority communities can maintain at least some of their special characteristics while becoming a more generally accepted part of the society as a whole. This process sometimes becomes one of assimilation in which the special identify of the group is lost but this is not inevitable.

Mediating structures can provide the links between the minority communities and the society as a whole. This provides ways for integrating minorities without assimilating them in a way that destroys their identity. In the Soviet Union and China, the formal structures, like the official religious establishments and the special recognition of Islamic nationalities, have performed this mediating function. Similarly, unofficial social organizations and groupings, like the Sufi orders, also can provide ways of preserving special identities while being integrated into a broader society.

Adaptations like these require Muslims to express their identity in ways that are different from those in societies where Muslims are the majority. Certain old and standard views, like the obligations of holy war, have to be expressed and manifested in new ways. Some people would see such restatements of Islam as departures from Islam. In the nineteenth century, there were those who felt that the modernizing reforms involved unacceptable departures from Islamic requirements. However, the emergence of a modernist expression of Islam, which combined at least some aspects of Western thought with Islamic ideals, reached a point where by the middle of the twentieth century even most conservative Muslim thinkers accepted the main lines of Islamic modernism.

In the second half of the twentieth century, a similar process may be at work in the intellectual life of Muslim minority communities. This is an important dimension to remember. This paper has primarily concentrated on specific social structures and institutions. These represent the basic practice of daily life and action within the Communist societies as wholes. However, in conclusion, it is useful to note that these are not simply *ad hoc* adjustments to concrete social and political realities. Many Muslims in the Soviet Union and China do not think of the structures of their communities as necessary but evil compromises with a status quo that is too strong to destroy. Many of these Muslims believe that their structures are legitimately Islamic and are willing to say so publically. The Muslim leaders, especially in the official establishments, provide an Islamic articulation and justification for the structures of the Muslim communities in the Soviet Union and China. It would be a mistake simply to charge these spokespersons with being toadies or hypocrites. The explanation of Islamic themes in a Commumist context is a sincere expression of the continuing existence of Muslim communities in China and the Soviet Union.

In both China and the Soviet Union, there is a long tradition of intellectual activity to provide a conceptual foundation for the developing mediating social structures. Before the Russian Revolution, there was an active reformist group that has come to be known as the Jadids. The Jadid Movement was active in education reform and construction, helped to create a basis for Turkish national sentiments, and laid the foundation for an analytically significant school of Islamic modernist thought. The Jadid Movement did not advocate total Muslim separatism nor holy war. It was, instead, a movement for constructive development of Muslim peoples, even within the context of the Russian empire.

Following the Russian Revolution, there were Muslims who were active supporters of communism but who were also clearly Muslim in their identity. They worked to create a synthesis of radical modernist Islamic ideals and Communist ideology. One of the most important figures in this movement was Sultan Galiev, who was purged for nationalist deviationism in the late 1920s. Although both Jadidism and Sultangalievism did not become institutionalized in a permanent manner, they represent early styles of mediating intellectual expressions that provide ideological foundations for the mediating institutions in the Muslim minority communities in the major Communist countries. In the contemporary Soviet Union, the preachers work on defining a progressive Islamic socialism:

> Soviet Moslem sermons pick up this general theme of Islamic-socialist compatibility by finding predictions of the Soviet state in the Koran, by referring to the building of communism as the "great earthly ideal of the Prophet Mohammed," and by proclaiming that the articles of the 1977 constitution of the USSR "correspond fully to the teachings of the holy Koran and the utterance of the Prophet Mohammed" (Larson, 1983, 135).

Although the reasoning and conclusions may not be in accord with standard or fundamentalist interpretations of Islam nor in agreement with what non-Muslim scholars may think, Muslim teachers should be saying in the Soviet Union and China that the adherence of these Muslim preachers both to Islam and to living in Communist societies appears to be sincere.

The special cases of the Muslim communities in the Soviet Union and China may not provide people with firm conclusions about the modern Islamic experience. However, it seems clear that whatever may be the contradictions in terms of logical analysis, in terms of actual life, Muslim minority communities can and are surviving in strong Communist states. They are not disappearing nor are the only viable survival strategies those of *hijra* or *jihad*. Instead, it may be possible to discern the outlines of a nonmajoritarian but permanent style of Muslim community emerging. This is a community with both formal-official structures and informal organizations. These mediate between the Muslim communities and the larger societies, not always in a manner that is free from tension but, apparently, at least in a manner that insures continued, relatively untroubled survival.

References and Sources

Abedin, Syed Z. 1980. "The Study of Muslim Minority Problems: A Conceptual Approach." In *Muslim Communities in Non-Muslim States,* 17–29. London: Islamic Council of Europe.

Basgoz, Ilhan. 1980. "Religion and Ethnic Consciousness Among Turks in the Soviet Union." In *Islam in the Contemporary World,* edited by Cyriac K. Pullapilly. 238–50. Notre Dame, Ind: Cross Roads Books.

Bennigsen, Alexandre. 1980. "Religion and Atheism Among Soviet Muslims." In *Islam in the Contemporary World,* edited by Cyriac K. Pullapilly. 222–37. Notre Dame, Ind: Cross Roads Books.

Bennigsen, Alexandre, and Chantal Lemercier-Quelquejay. 1979. "Muslim Religious Conservatism and Dissent in the USSR." *Studies in Comparative Religion* 13, Nos. 1–2 (Winter–Spring): 40–49.

Carrere d'Encausse, Helene. 1981. *Decline of an Empire: The Soviet Socialist Republic in Revolt.* Harper Colophon edition, trans. by Martin Sokolinsky and Henry A. LaFarge. New York: Harper & Row.

CDSP, 35/27. 1983. "Republics Continue Ideological Campaign." *The Current Digest of the Soviet Press,* 35, No. 27 (3 August): 7–10.

Delloff, Linda Marie. 1979. To Be Truly Chinese. *Christian Century* (24 October): 1028–29.

Dzhabbarov, I. 1979. "Light Against Darkness: Social Progress and Atheism." *Pravda Vostoka* (20 December). Trans. in *USSR Report: Political & Sociological Affairs,* No. 1012 (14 February 1980). Joint Publications Research Service (JPRS) 75139.

Ibn Fudi, Uthman. 1978. *Bayan wujub al-hijra 'ala 'l-'ibad,* ed. and trans. by F. H. El Masri. Khartoum: Khartoum University Press.

Israeli, Raphael. 1980. *Muslims in China: A Study in Cultural Confrontation.* London: Curzon Press.

Karklins, Rasma. 1981. Nationality Power in Soviet Republics: Attitudes and Perceptions. *Studies in Comparative Communism* 14, No. 1 (Spring): 70–93.

Kettani, M. Ali. 1979. "The Muslim Minorities." In *Islamic Perspectives,* edited by Khurshid Ahmad and Zafar Ishaq Ansari, 241–62. London: Islamic Foundations.

Kettani, M. Ali. 1980. "The Problems of Muslim Minorities and their Solutions." In *Muslim Communities in Non-Muslim States,* 91–107. London: Islamic Council of Europe.

Larson, Bryant Leroy. 1983. *The Moslems of Soviet Central Asia: Soviet and Western Perceptions of a Growing Political Problem* (Ph.D. dissertation, University of Minnesota). University Microfilms International, 8318089.

Olcott, Martha B. 1981 "The Basmachi or Freeman's Revolt in Turkestan 1918–24." *Soviet Studies* 33, No. 3 (July): 352–69.

Olcott, Martha B. "Soviet Islam and World Revolution." *World Politics* 34, No. 4 (July): 487–504.

Pillsbury, Barbara L. K. 1981a. Islam: "Even unto China". In *Change and the Muslim World,* edited by Philip H. Stoddard, David C. Cuthell, and Margaret W. Sullivan. 107–14. Syracuse: Syracuse University Press.

Pillsbury, Barbara L. K. 1981b. "Muslim History in China: A 1300-Year Chronology." *Journal, Institute of Muslim Minority Affairs* 3, No. 2 (Winter): 10–29.

Pillsbury, Barbara L. K. 1981c. "The Muslim Population in China: Clarifying the Questions of Size and Ethnicity." *Journal, Institute of Muslim Minority Affairs* 3, No. 2 (Winter): 35–58.

Pipes, Daniel. 1983. *In the Path of God: Islam and Political Power.* New York: Basic Books.

Rahman, Fazlur. 1980. "Evolution of Soviet Policy Toward Muslims in Russia. 1917–1965." *Journal, Institute of Muslim Minority Affairs* 1, No. 2; 2, No. 1 (Winter, 1979; Spring 1980): 28–46.

Scott, Keith. 1982. "Soviet Central Asia: A Religious Limbo." In *Religion and Societies: Asia and the Middle East,* edited by Carlo Caldarola. 231–58. Berlin: Mouton.

Wren, Christopher S. 1983a. "Islam, After Persecutions, Rebounds in China." *New York Times* (15 June).

Wren, Christopher S. 1983b. "China's West Is Challenged by Ethnic Mix." *New York Times* (10 July).

Suggestions for Further Reading

Bennigsen, Alexandre, and Lemercier-Quelquejay, Chantal. *Islam in the Soviet Union.* London: Pall Mall Press, 1967.

Carrere d'Encausse, Helene. *Decline of an Empire: The Soviet Socialist Republics in Revolt.* Trans. Martin Sokolinsky and Henry A. La Farge. New York: Harper & Row, 1981.

Dryer, June Teufel. *China's Forty Millions: Minority Nationalities and National Integration in the People's Republic of China.* Cambridge: Harvard University Press, 1976.

Eberhard, Wolfram. *China's Minorities: Yesterday and Today.* Belmont, Calif. Wadsworth, 1982.

Lubin, Nancy. *Labour and Nationality in Soviet Central Asia: An Uneasy Compromise.* Princeton: Princeton Univesrity Press, 1985.

Muslim Communities in Non-Muslim States. London: Islamic Council of Europe, 1980.

7

INDIA
Muslim Minority Politics
and Society

SYED SHAHABUDDIN AND
THEODORE P. WRIGHT, JR.

The role of Islam, and therefore of Muslims, in public life both potentially and actually differs fundamentally in countries with only a minority
of Muslims in their populations from those with Muslim majorities.
Extremists on both sides, Muslim and non-Muslim, may think that the
minority situation can be changed into a majority one by religious conversion, higher birthrates, or immigration, but the chances of this reversal
happening in India are highly unlikely.

According to the official figures of the Indian census of 1981, which
have just been released, the total population of Muslims in India, excluding Assam, is 75.5 million, still only about 11.35 percent of the whole.
Estimating Assam at about 4.5 million, the total comes to about 80 million, which makes it the third largest Muslim community in the world,
after Indonesia and Pakistan, both Muslim majority countries. Before the
partition of British India in 1947, Muslims formed 24 percent of the population. Partition gave the Muslim majority areas, except Kashmir, to
Pakistan; since the establishment of Bangladesh in 1971, South Asian
Muslims are divided almost equally among the three successor states:
India, Pakistan, and Bangladesh. In India, except for the state of Jammu
and Kashmir and the Union Territory of Lakshadweep (the Laccadives),
Muslims do not form a majority in any of the constituent states or territories of the Union[1] (see Table 7.1).

As for other major states and territories with over 100,000 Muslims, in
Punjab and Orissa they form about one to two percent of the population,
in Haryana four percent, in Manipur and Tripura seven percent, and in
Delhi eight percent.

A country with a Muslim majority can consider a wide range of alter-

Table 7.1 Muslim Population by State

States with Muslim Population over 1 Million	Muslim Population in Millions	Percentage of Total Population of State	Percentage of Total Muslim Population of India
Uttar Pradesh	17.8	15.4	22.2
West Bengal	11.7	21.5	14.7
Bihar	10.0	14.1	12.5
Maharashtra	5.8	9.3	7.3
Kerala	5.4	21.3	6.8
Andhra Pradesh	4.5	8.5	5.73
Assam	4.5	24.03	5.6
Karnataka	4.1	11.1	5.1
Jammu and Kashmir	3.8	64.2	4.8
Gujarat	2.9	8.5	3.6
Madhya Pradesh	2.5	4.8	3.1
Rajasthan	2.5	7.3	3.1
Tamil Nadu	2.5	5.2	3.1
Lakshadweep	0.25	98.0	0.04

Source: 1981 census.

native roles for Islam in public life from the thoroughgoing Islamization of Saudi Arabia or Khomeini's Iran to the complete secularization of Kemalist Turkey. But a Muslim minority has a narrower range of choice, constrained by the preferences of the dominant, non-Muslim majority. Despite six centuries of Muslim rule in large parts of North India, the realistic alternative in the twentieth century for Muslim minorities is between living as a subordinate group in a country regulated by an alien religion or ideology, for example, the Soviet Union, the People's Republic of China, Israel, or South Africa, on the one hand, or in a constitutionally secular and democratic polity like the Western democracies or India. As Wilfred Cantwell Smith perceptively pointed out in 1957, the Constitution of India offers Muslims for the first time in South Asian history the opportunity to share power as legal equals with non-Muslims rather than simply to be the rulers or the ruled.[2]

With the integrity of the Muslim world threatened since 1800 and Islamic traditions reeling under Western political, economic, and cultural pressure, the reaction was sometimes expressed in the idiom of pan-Islamic solidarity. Historically, Muslim Indians were involved, perhaps as no other Muslim community outside the Middle East, in the desperate endeavor to save the Ottoman Empire and the *khilafat* (caliphate) from total disintegration after World War I. Anti-imperialist sentiments were also aroused by the Western effort to create a Jewish homeland in Palestine, by the Italian conquest of Libya, and by the imposition of a French protectorate over North Africa.

After World War II, when the colonial tide receded and Muslim states were reborn one by one, new frontiers arose in the Muslim world, sometimes artificially demarcated along the lines of the division of the spoils of colonialism, but sometimes along historical, geographical and cultural lines of cleavage. Although nursing pan-Islamic sentiments, the Muslim world has been subdivided by following the Western model of nation-state. A new ideology of Islamic nationalism, a cross between pan-Islamism and nationalism, appeared on the scene. Although it may provide a blueprint (inadequate nevertheless) for Muslim majority states, it can have no rational application to Muslim minority areas. Beyond the borders of nation-states, Islam has not served to bring together Muslim states to the point of submergence of their national personalities any more than Christianity or communism has done. As for Muslim minorities, they can safeguard their group interests in a non-Muslim environment within the framework of nation-states, provided that the state does not discriminate among citizens on the basis of religion and respects group identity, granting groups enough autonomy to manage their social and cultural institutions. This is where the Indian experiment, howsoever imperfect, is valuable and relevant. Given a plural and segmented society, Indian nationalism must also learn to compromise with the presence of multiple subnationalisms.

Over the years pan-Islamic organizations, like the World Muslim Congress, the Rabita-al-Alam-al-Islami, and even the intergoverment Organization of Islamic Conferences have made hesitant efforts to enlarge their fields of activity to include Muslim minorities. So far, their involvement has been of a very low order, limited to passing resolutions. Pakistan has often tried to exploit the maltreatment of the Muslim minority in India for its own purposes. India, for its part, has been able to contain Pakistan's efforts in the Arab and Islamic world by taking a pro-Arab position on questions like Palestine. At the First Islamic Conference in Rabat in 1969, Pakistan did succeed in blocking India's participation— even as an observer. But whether out of the inherent weakness of the pan-Islamic linkage or out of Arabocentric concern in the Middle East, the Muslim world has shown minimal interest in the situation of Indian Muslims, notwithstanding their huge numbers.

What solidarity exists is expressed by occasional charitable contributions for religious purposes, such as establishment of *madrasas* or construction of mosques. Even on this account, Hindu chauvinist propaganda about Arab support for conversion of Harijans (Untouchables) to Islam apart, the flow of financial aid, whether from Muslim governments or organizations, institutions or individuals, has not been substantial, no more than a small fraction of the flow of funds from Christian countries to Indian Christians or from overseas Hindus to Hindu institutions. Naturally, therefore, even those groups among Indian Muslims who look toward Muslim states for moral or material support are turning their attention from Islamic solidarity more to self-help, despite the emergence of Qaddafi in Libya and Khomeini in Iran.

Tiny fundamentalist groups that exist among Muslim Indians may continue to look beyond the contemporary nation-states and dream of the unification of the Islamic world or the restoration of the *khilafat*. Yet, objectively speaking, one does not see the possiblity of the emergence of a united Muslim state encompassing most, if not all, of the Muslim majority states that would claim to protect Muslims in Muslim minority areas. One does not even sense the advent of an international Islamic movement at the mass level. Such a movement would involve Muslim minority communities so deeply as to divert them from their continuing concern for meeting the demands of adjustment to their national environment or in resolving immediate local problems.

But the world of Islam, as a whole, has become more conscious of the Islamic heritage and the pressures for Islamization are beginning to be felt, strengthening the desire to go back to the roots. Call it fundamentalism, if you like, but in a sense all believers are fundamentalists. For a Muslim minority like India's, this strengthens its resolve to maintain its identity and survive as a distinct community. But assertion of identity need not imply conflict or confrontation or a desire to serve as the avantgarde of an Islamic conquest, physical or spiritual.

The Constitutional Framework

The founding fathers of the Indian Constitution, a nationalist leadership with a liberal and modern outlook, adopted a secular model for the new Indian state. This, to a certain extent, went against the Hindu sentiment that identified Indian nationalism and the national culture of India with Hinduism and considered India to be, in a special sense, the land of the Hindus because they formed almost eighty-one percent of the population. But the Hindu society itself is not homogeneous; it is divided not only among various linguistic groups, but within the same region by caste and sect. Also, Muslims are not the only religious minority for every religious community and every linguistic group faces a minority situation in one or more states of the Indian Union. In addition, the population complexion shows continuous variations as one goes down from the state to the village level, passing through districts, subdivisions, and blocks. In this sense, India is a land of minorities and needs a national norm to deal with minority situations at various levels of administration.

The Constitution, therefore, provides many safeguards for the protection of minorities. Thus, Article 14 grants equality to all citizens without discrimination on the grounds of religion, language, or caste. Under Article 16, all minorities enjoy equality of opportunity in matters of public employment and underrepresented "backward classes" the possibility of reservations in entry. Under Articles 26, 27, and 28, minorities are free to manage their own religious affairs, the state cannot levy taxes for the promotion of any particular religion nor can there be compulsory attendance at religious worship or religious ceremonies in state-supported educational institutions. The state cannot discriminate against minority-managed institutions in allocation of resources. Under Article 30, all minorities—religious, linguistic, or cultural—have the right to establish and to administer educational institutions of their choice. Articles 345, 347, 350, 350A, and 350B, which relate to rights of linguistic minorities, are also relevant in this context.

The Constitution of India, on the other hand, has a chapter on "Directive Principles of State Policy" in which two articles are objectionable from the point of view of many in the Muslim community. Under Article 44, the state is to endeavor to secure for the citizens a uniform civil code; and under Article 48, the state is to take steps prohibiting the slaughter of cows and calves and other milch and draught cattle. The possiblity of the replacement of the *shariah* (Muslim personal law) by a common civil code, as demanded by a vocal section of Hindu chauvinists as well as a small fraction of secularist Muslims, is looked on by the bulk of the community as a threat to its religious identity, even though it has been done by a Muslim majority country like Turkey. The anticow slaughter principle is regarded as an attempt to use state power to force the cultural ethos of the Hindu majority upon the minority communities, irrespective of the economic consequences to the nation.

Thus, for the most part, the Indian Constitution provides the formal basis for the full and equal participation of Muslims in the country's public life. Moreover, the state does not support Hinduism as a religion. Although it may be argued that in theory the Constitution provides a model for the protection of the rights and interests of religious, linguistic, and cultural minorities, there has been a noticeable gap between the constitutional safeguards and their actual implementation. Indeed, the very objective of minority politics in India would be summed up by many as the closing of this gap between precept and practice so as to secure for minorities full participation in both polity and economy at every level in equality and dignity and at the same time to maintain the minority's identity against the perceived threat of absorption or assimilation into Hindu society.

Goals

The possible goals of a minority, however, range all the way from assimilation or integration to autonomy, secession, or domination.[3] In India, the Muslim minority, except for a few individuals, resists absorption, demands cultural autonomy, and does not aim at domination but rejects secession.

It is often asserted that for a Muslim the world is divisible into two mutually exclusive categories of *dar-al-Islam* (countries where Islam rules) and *dar-al-harb* (countries at war with *dar-al-Islam*). In this view, Islam for its fulfillment requires political power, absolute and unshared, or perpetual confrontation with non-Islam.

During the Indian freedom movement, the *ulama* (Muslim savants)—
who steadfastly espoused the cause of nationalism and, therefore, a
united India—conceived of the future in terms of an independent state
jointly ruled by Hindus and Muslims. They cited the Holy Prophet
Mohammed's pact *(ahad)* with the Jews of Medina after his *hijra* (migration) from Mecca as the model and theological justification for sharing
power with non-Muslims. In their concept, India was to be *dar-al-ahad*
(land of the pact) or *dar-al-aman* (Land of peace), which the Muslim
jurists and political scientists describe as territory in which the Muslims
live peacefully, where their life, honor, and property are safe and where
they are free to perform their religious obligations. Logically, the antith-
esis of *dar-al-Islam* is *dar-al-kufr* (land of unbelief) and that of *dar-al-
harb* is *dar-al-aman.*

But Islam also recognizes the concept of *watan* (homeland) because
everyone is presumed to love his land of birth or domicile. In purely theological terms, therefore, from the Islamic view, India is not *dar-al-Islam,*
but neither is it *dar-al-kufr* nor even *dar-al-harb.* It is *dar-al-ahad, dar-al-
aman,* and *watan.* In any case, if India were perceived as *dar-al-kufr* or
dar-al-harb, the only alternative to *jihad* (armed struggle) would be *hijra*
(migration).

In fact, partition in 1947 did lead to an unprecedent emigration of
Muslims from India to Pakistan as well as of Sikhs and Hindus in the
opposite direction. The exodus was more from North India than from
South India, more from urban than from rural areas (except in the Punjab), more from the ranks of the professional classes and intelligentsia
than from among workers, peasants, and artisans. This outflow of skilled
human resources weakened the economic status of the Muslim community in India, reduced its political role, and disrupted its social structure.
Those who remained were looked on with suspicion and distrust by their
fellow Indians; the credibility of the leader who remained was at a low
ebb. Uncertainty about their future made them wary of investment, and
they were subjected in a rather harsh manner to the operation of evacuee
and enemy property laws. The former landlords and their retainers could
not adjust easily to the abolition of the *zamindari* and *jagirdari* (land-
lord) systems in the north and in native states like Hyderabad. Muslims
found the doors of public and private employment virtually closed to
them. Even the artisans in the traditional centers languished because of
their inability initially to attract state support to replace the loss of aris-
tocratic patronage. Only two classes of Muslims generally remained
untouched by partition: the landholding cultivator in the north and the
trader in the South.[4] Thus, on the whole, the first two or three decades
after partition witnessed the gradual impoverishment of the remaining
Muslim community.

Sporadic emigration, spurred by communal riots and better prospects
in Pakistan, continued until 1971. Then, with the secession of Bangladesh
from Pakistan, disillusionment set in, as Pakistan came to seen not as a

source of strength for Indian Muslims but of weakness because it contin-ued to rankle Hindus and discouraged Muslim efforts to improve their situation in India. Thus, emigration virtually ceased until the Arab oil boom opened a new, if temporary, focus for self-improvement for many Indians of all faiths in the Arabian Gulf.

The Muslim minority in India continues to fear enforced assimilation (Indianization)[5] as well as expulsion and extermination, as advocated by various Hindu militants. Genocide against such a large community (in both absolute and relative terms) would seem to be a practical impossi-bility, whether or not world conscience and Muslim majority states were stirred to do something to prevent it. The Jewish Holocaust in Europe and the Kampuchean case make one hesitant, however, to rule out com-pletely such an attempt. Similarly, expulsion or exodus have their recent precedents in Uganda, Bangladesh, and Afghanistan.

But as between the remaining, less noxious options, assimilation and integration, which do most Indian Muslims want? With the exception of a minuscule but influential segment of secular nationalists who look for-ward to assimilation of all Indians into a modern, nonreligious composite culture, most Muslims fear that such assimilation and integration mean, instead, absorption into Hinduism, and this they resist. The problem is how to preserve their religious and cultural identity without becoming alienated from the political process or without provoking a massive Hindu reaction that may jeopardize the secular democratic order and also the community's physical security.

Hindu revivalism has been an impediment to Muslim goals since the days of the Arya Samaj and the Hindu Mahasabha before independence and the (RSS) since then. Its most powerful political expression since the 1950s has been the Bharatiya Jana Sangh in the north, reborn in 1980 as the Bharatiya Janata party. It equates Indian with Hindu and aims to Indianize the Muslim minority, that is to assimilate it, as Hinduism has done to other religious minorities in the past. Of late, many new variants, such as Virat Hindu Samaj, the Vishwa Hindu Parishad, and Hindu Maha Sangh have appeared.

Strategies

Given the difficulty of keeping a balance between autonomy and integra-tion, between a separate identity and national solidarity, how do Muslims seek to obtain their goals through public life in India? They do enter elec-tions and win seats in national and state legislatures as well as local bod-ies, and they are appointed to cabinets. They also become governors and judges of the Supreme Court and the high courts, though not in propor-tion to their percentage of the population[6] (see Table 7.2). Before inde-pendence, Muslims had enjoyed disproportionately high representation in the legislatures of British India by means of the systems of communal

Table 7.2 Muslim Membership in the Lok Sabha (Lower House of Parliament)[a]

Year	Number of Muslim Members	Percentage of Total Members
1952	36	7.21
1957	24	4.74
1962	32	6.27
1967	29	5.68
1972	27	5.18
1977	32	6.03
1980	46	8.50
1985	41	7.60

Note: [a]The total membership of the lower house (Lok Sabha) is 544. Muslim presence in the less powerful upper house (Rajya Sabha) has always been proportionately higher than in the lower house. In 1980, there were 32 Muslims out of a total of 244 members (i.e., 13%).

Source: Muslim India, April 1983, p. 190.

electorate and reserved seats through proportionate reservation. After independence, these advantages were lost in the framing of the Indian Constitution and Muslims, unlike the Untouchables ("Scheduled Castes") and tribals, had to win representation in legislatures by contesting common constituencies. With rare exceptions in the Muslim majority districts of Kashmir, West Bengal, and Kerala could a Muslim win on the strength of Muslim votes alone or as the nominee of a Muslim political party (see Table 7.3). The new system was designed, in fact, to assure that only "acceptable" Muslim candidates, those with wide appeal to non-Muslims, could win.

Muslim representation is also said to have been reduced by undernumeration in the census, gerrymandering in the delimitation of constituencies, and exclusion of Muslims from the electoral rolls on flimsy grounds

Table 7.3 Districts by State with More than Ten Percent Muslims

Districts: States	More than 50%	20–50%	10–20%	
Andhra Pradesh	—	1	6	
Assam	—	4	1	
Bihar	—	1	11	
Gujarat	—	—	4	
Haryana	—	—	1	
Jammu and Kashmir	6	2	1	
Kerala	1	3	4	
Madhya Pradesh	—	—	7	
Maharashtra	—	—	9	
Karnataka	—	—	10	
Rajasthan	—	1	2	
Uttar Pradesh	—	11	23	
West Bengal	1	6	4	
Total	8	29	84	121

Source: 1971 census.

(including lack of proof of citizenship in border areas like Assam). Burdened with a guilt complex over partition, Muslim participation in the political process began haltingly but has increased with the passage of time. Today, no Muslim group stands, as some did immediately after independence, for nonparticipation in the political process. Even the revivalists Jamaat-i-Islami had to change its line on this in 1967. Most political parties, including those that advocate a Hindu state, project themselves as secular. In order to appear so, they enroll a few Muslim members and include a few even in their leadership.

However, there is widespread dissatisfaction among Muslims with the present political system and the kind of representation it affords them. Generally speaking, Muslim political workers who join a national party receive their party's nomination to contest elections at the municipal, state, or national level are seen as symbols of tokenism among the Muslim electorate, not as legitimate representatives of the Muslim community. They become so dependent on the system that neither within the councils of their party nor in the legislatures do they serve to ventilate effectively the grievances of their fellow Muslims. No wonder that most of those elected are reluctant to identify themselves publicly with the hopes, aspirations, and demands of their Muslim constituents lest they be dubbed communal and be refused party nomination in the future.[7] This is, indeed, ironical, because the fact remains that, with few exceptions, such persons are given party posts and tickets primarily to ensure that the party attract Muslim votes. Rarely has a Muslim candidate won from a constituency with less than twenty percent Muslim votes. Even a stalwart of the National Movement like Maulana Abul Kalam Azad had to seek a safe Muslim constituency. Thus, although the ruling party and the establishment, in their anxiety to buttress their secular credentials, always managed to include some Muslim names, Muslims, in effect, remained underrepresented in the democratic institutions. And so, a communication gap developed between the state and much of the Muslim community, a gap that still remains to be fully bridged. This leads to both the isolation of Muslims from the political mainstream and their alienation from the political system.

For a generation after independence, then, Muslim Indians were too hard-pressed by their circumstances to evolve a strategy for their survival. Many of the Muslim Leaguers had emigrated to Pakistan. And the rank and file were made to feel guilty for their support of partition and their continuing links, both physical and emotional, with Pakistan. Congress Muslims lacked both self-confidence and mass appeal, as they had failed to prevent partition and were likely to be distrusted by ordinary Muslims as agents of the establishment. Thus the generation passed, wallowing in self-pity, lamenting its fate, and leading a double life in which it cursed the power structure for its communalism and partiality when inside its home, yet aligned itself with the same structure when outside, hoping to receive some crumbs and find a place at court. With a few honorable exceptions, Muslim leadership adopted the politics of sycophancy. The Muslim masses were generally advised to keep a low profile and place their trust in the Congress party, which enjoyed a virtual monopoly of power in Indian until 1967.

When the era of Congress-party dominance in politics began to end in that year, Muslims found to their dismay that their identification with one party for so long meant they were taken for granted by that party, ignored, and even distrusted by the others. The Indian Union Muslim League, which survived in Kerala because of a communal balance peculiar to that state, pioneered the strategy of bargaining between two closely matched coalitions, centering on the Congress party and the Communists. So successful was this method that the Muslim League was eventually able to place its leader, the late C. H. Mohammed Koya, in the chief ministership for a time.[8]

In the north, a third strategy was attempted by the Muslim Majlis-e-Mushawarat (Muslim Consultative Committee), founded in 1965.[9] The Majlis brought together a broad spectrum of Muslim leaders: orthodox members of the Jamiat-ul-Ulema, the revivalist Jamaat-i-Islami, and some modernist Muslims both inside and outside the Congress. It proposed to endorse candidates of various parties who agreed with its positions. This strategy failed because it was not seriously applied in the big states of Uttar Pradesh and Bihar and, therefore, did not overcome party loyalty. After the election, the few victorious candidates it had supported backed out under pressure from Hindu majorities within their own parties.

A fourth possible strategy is one of nonparticipation in the political process. This is a measure of desperation and has been largely rejected by the Muslim community, especially where Muslims have been the rulers and have a long tradition of participation in, if not domination of, public life (e.g., North India and Hyderabad). But it has been pursued successfully by various minuscule but prosperous Muslim business communities, like the Bohras, Khojas, Memons, and Navayats on the west coast. They have few demands on government or the political system except to be left alone. In any case, they have too few votes to sway elections.

Political mobilization of the first three types is tempting for a large minority like Indian Muslims living in a democracy where numbers count. The immense influence wielded by the much smaller Jewish minority in the United States on American policy toward the Middle East is often cited without recognizing that the very existence and continuing confrontation between India and Pakistan engenders a hostile Hindu reaction for which there is no analogy in the United States.[10] Besides, the Jews as a minority are much better organized, more affluent, and more intellectually advanced.

Issues

Four of the principal issues that Muslim politicians, press, parties, and pressure groups have agitated for in the public life of India since independence not surprisingly reflect the interests and aspirations of the community's largely North Indian elite who live in the Hindi heartland: share of government employment, control of Aligarh Muslim University, preservation of the Urdu language, and preservation of the Muslim Personal Law. A fifth demand, the prevention of communal (i.e., anti-Muslim) violence ought objectively to be of greater concern to the Muslim masses, who suffer the most from it, than to the elite. Subjectively, however, the uneducated and tradition-bound masses are still more readily mobilizable as Muslims by their elite on emotionally charged symbolic issues than on bread-and-butter questions of economic development, health, and education. Only if one believes that the major problem facing the Muslim community in India is to preserve its identity against the assimilative pressure of Hindu chauvinism can these boundary-maintenance issues be regarded as more important than the physical and economic survival of Muslims as individuals. Muslim assertiveness, which the Hindu majority regards with scant patience and tends to dub as antinational, no doubt contributes to the tense atmosphere in which frequent bloody clashes between the two communities have erupted. So, too, does the demand for sharing the economic pie. Issues relating to identity are typically North Indian in origin and flourish in the milieu of the former Muslim imperium. In coastal South India, the relatively prosperous Muslim communities (referred to earlier), with a history of peaceful conversion by Arab merchants, do not speak Urdu, nor send their children to Aligarh, nor compete for the civil service—they merge culturally with the majority despite their religious orthodoxy.

In West Bengal, the Bengali-speaking Muslims have tended increasingly to support the Marxist parties, primarily because of their relative security from communal riots and minimal restrictions on cow slaughter. Nevertheless, they remain a deprived and backward group.

It is part of the rhetoric of Muslim politics in India that Muslims fell behind Hindus in the adoption of modern education and, therefore, in government employment and in the modern economic occupations. Anil Seal and Paul R. Brass have demonstrated conclusively[11] that this was true for neither education nor civil service at the elite level in North India in the late nineteenth and early twentieth centuries. It is often said, therefore, that the Muslim elite has exploited the real backwardness of the Muslim masses and mobilized their religious sentiments in the game of politics in order to increase their own share of the cake. Playing their own game of divide and rule, the British had accorded to this Muslim elite reservations in civil service as in legislatures.

But these were lost after partition and many of the Muslim beneficiaries opted for Pakistan. Since, then, it is charged that Muslims have been discriminated against in India in both public and private employment. As regards the former, Professor Ghanshyam Shah has concluded[12] that during the last thirty years Muslims have not obtained government jobs in proportion to their percentage of the population[13] (see Table 7.4).

Opinions differ about the causes of this continuing under-representation, whether it is because of their relative backwardness in modern education and their consequent inability to field sufficient eligible candidates, or because of prejudice by Hindu decision-makers against Muslim applicants. To quote Shah again, "There is a widespread complaint, not without foundation, that other things being equal, caste Hindu decision-makers give preference to Hindus or to their own castes over Muslims." Given the anomymity of civil service recruitment procedures except for the oral interview,[14] one suspects that at the higher level the problem is more a lack of qualified Muslim applicants than of discrimination which then becomes a self-fulfilling prophecy as young, educated Muslims become discouraged at the low acceptance rate and cease to apply or to take the examinations. The fact of Muslim underrepresentaiton at the lower levels, clerical and menial, where there is no organized system of recruitment nor is the standard very high testifies to systematic discrimination more clearly.

Job discrimination against Muslims is much easier and more persistent in the private sector, especially by large industrial and commercial enterprises where the Muslim presence is very low indeed except in a few

Table 7.4 Muslim Share of Public Employment

Name of Service	Years/Number of Establishments	Total	Muslims	Percentage
A: All India and Central Services				
Indian Administrative Service	Total in 1981	3,883	116	2.99
Indian Public Service	Total in 1981	1,753	50	2.85
Income Tax I	Intake during 1971–80	881	27	3.06
Railway Traffic and Accounts Services	Intake during 1971–80	415	11	2.65
B: Random Survey of Public Employment				
Central Government Offices	105 offices in 13 states	75,951	3,346	4.41
State Government Offices	876 offices in 13 states	826,669	49,718	6.01
Nationalized Banks	1,317 branches	113,772	2,479	2.18
Public Sector Undertakings (Both Central and State)	168 undertakings in 13 states	476,972	51,755	10.85
Total		1,581,296	107,492	6.60

Source: Muslim India, June 1983, pp. 261–63.

owned by Muslims themselves, like Jeep Batteries, or in sectors where Muslims are still entrenched such as the hides and skins trade in South India.[15] (Table 7.5)

Muslim entrepreneurs have also been handicapped by the prevailing anti-Muslim bias in securing government loans and permits, available on paper, but subject to bureaucratic discretion tempered by bribery. For instance, Muslim industrialists and businessmen are starved of bank credit; their ápplications for licenses, permits, and quotas, which are the key to success in a government-controlled economy, are said to be more likely to gather dust than to be granted. Discrimination in allotment of housing sites or residences in newly developed government colonies is rampant.

Wherever Muslims—because of their traditional concentration and crafts—have achieved a measure of economic progress, such as in Moradabad (brass), Firozabad (glass), Meerut and Aligarh (locks), Mirzapur and Bhadoi (carpets), Bhiwandi (power looms), and Jamshedpur, Ranchi, and Varanasi, their properties, including their stock-in-trade, have been subjected to looting and destruction in frequent communal riots. This dampens both their desire to go out of Muslim slums and to invest in modernization of production units with imports of high technology.

On the economic scene, one should, however, take note also of the recent signs of affluence in some parts of the country, particularly in Kerala, Karnataka, Andhra Pradesh, Gujarat, and Maharashtra, because of the remittances from Indian workers in the Arabian Gulf states. With the exception of Saudi Arabia, none of these states apply any religious preference in hiring, but, although exact figures are not available, it may be fair to say that the proportion of Muslims among the expatriate Indians there may be considerably higher than their proportion in the population of India. So Muslim Indians as a community may be receiving somewhat higher benefits from the job opportunities in the Gulf than non-Muslims are. Remittances have helped their families repair or acquire property, provide education, renovate mosques and run Muslim instititutions. Some surplus is now beginning to be invested in business. It can be

Table 7.5 Muslims Share of Private Sector Employment

Name of Corporation	Executive Cadre (%)	Supervisory Cadre (%)	Worker Cadre (%)
TISCO	4.1	5.60	10.30
Texmaco	nil	0.30	4.40
Mafatlal	nil	1.72	3.53
Calico	0.68	na	10.20
Mahindra and Mahindra	1.48	2.25	5.02
Orkay	3.30	3.00	11.90
J. K. Industries	2.63	2.28	5.41
Indian Explosives	nil	2.73	7.09

Source: Random Survey. Muslim India, from Minorities Commission. January 1984, p. 17.

assumed that the Gulf job market, at least for the unskilled, will dry up soon and that its lasting impact will depend very much on whether the amounts sent home are wisely invested or frittered away in wasteful and conspicuous consumption.[16]

Parenthetically, it should be noted that Kerala is the only state where (through the bargaining skills of the Muslim League discussed earlier) the entire Muslim community has been classified as "backward" and, therefore, entitled to reservations in education and employment under Article 16 (4) of the Constitution to the extent of fifty percent of their share of the population. Because Kerala Muslims are also conspicuous beneficiaries of Gulf employment, it cannot be mere coincidence that communal riots spread to Kerala in the late 1970s. In a scarcity economy, competition and envy quickly spill over into violence.

Many Hindus see yet another connection between Gulf money and the rising profile of Muslim resurgence in India, symbolized by the recent phenomenon of conversions of some Harijans (Untouchables) to Islam in South India.[17] This, it is believed, was largely motivated by the latter's quest for social equality through escape from the Hindu caste system, but it has led to demands by Hindu organizations for a ban on conversion to non-Indian religions and to widespread propaganda that the conversions were part of an international conspiracy to turn India's Hindu majority into a minority. Hindu resentment at polygamy (permitted but rarely practiced by Muslims in India), at the Muslim's allegedly low acceptance rates of family planning, and at illegal infiltration into Assam stem from the same unreasonable fears.[18]

To return to the educational issue, there is no doubt that Muslim enrollment at every level of education (primary, secondary and higher) is lower than their proportion of the population would indicate. This is even true in the areas of relative Muslim concentration. Generally speaking, too, the dropout rate is higher and the educational performance is poorer, which, in turn, limits their access to higher and professional education.[19] From that stems the community's above-mentioned inability to field an adequate number of candidates for those government jobs that are filled by competitive examination. Thus, since independence, the number of Muslims, whether academics, professionals, business executives, or civil servants, has fallen much below their proportion of the population. This has reduced their presence at the decision-making level in government and out, whatever the level of job discrimination that may exist. Certainly educational backwardness is, therefore, a basic reason why such a sizable minority as the Muslim Indians is unable to make a mark in the economic field or in public life. The community has been caught in a vicious circle of poverty and educational backwardness.

But there are other factors as well behind the relative educational backwardness of the Muslim community: the nonavailability of schools in Muslim neighborhoods; the neglect of Urdu, the mother tongue of most Muslims particularly in the Hindi-speaking states; the imposition of San-

skrit, the sacred language of Hinduism, as the second language; the pre-
scription of nonsecular textbooks, which Muslims find offensive; and the
celebration of Hindu religious rites in schools. Finally, Muslims of mod-
est means, especially artisans, are reluctant to deprive themselves of the
fruits of their children's labor or to invest in their education lengthily
when they are convinced that with the doors of government employment
barred to them, any more than an elementary education is a waste.[20]
Female education particularly is neglected by Muslim parents; they tend
to withdraw their daughters from school at puberty. Religiously minded
parents often send their children to religious schools to receive religious
instruction. Hence, large numbers of *maktabs* and *madrasas* have been
opened to provide pre- or extraschool religious instruction. When not
supplemented with modern education, this leaves the children unable to
compete in the modern world.

In the light of all this, the apparent emphasis on establishing Muslim
degree colleges would seem to be a misplaced priority. There is a growing
consciousness that the limited resources of the community should have
been directed to the creation of more facilities: first at the primary, then
at the secondary or vocational level so that Muslim performance at the
high school level could be better both in quality and quantity. This would
then have led to better admissions rates to colleges and professional institutions run by the state. For lack of that, government-aided institutions
of higher education established and administered by Muslims have often
been swamped by non-Muslim students.

Education leads directly to the language issue. Over the years, as a con-
sequence of politicization and communalization of the problem, Urdu
has come to be identified with the Muslim community, yet neither are all
persons who speak Urdu Muslims nor do all Indian Muslims speak Urdu.
In fact, even if for purposes of argument all 23 million people who
declared Urdu as their mother tongue in 1971 were Muslims, that would
mean that only about forty-five percent of Muslims in India use it as their
principal language. The Urdu speakers reside chiefly in the Hindi-major-
ity region of Uttar Pradesh and Bihar as well as in pockets in the states
of Andhra Pradesh, Maharashtra, and Karnataka where the majority languages are Telugu, Marathi, and Kannada, respectively.[21] (see Table 7.6).

Some states with large Muslim concentrations, such as Assam, Bengal,
and Kerala, have very low numbers of Urdu speakers. There, the common language, be it Assamese, Bengali, or Malayalam, bridges the religious divide. Among students of linguistics, there is even a question
whether Hindi and Urdu are separate languages or only two forms of the
same language, written in two different scripts, Devanagari and Persian.
Yet, because of a slow but steady Urduization of the Muslims outside the
Hindi belt, the emergence of Urdu as the medium of Islamization, and
the deliberate attempt to banish Urdu from its birthplace, the language
has become the lingua franca of the Muslim Indian community and a
salient issue even for Muslims for whom it is not the mother tongue.

Table 7.6 Linguistic Diversity of Muslim Indians

	Total Muslim Population (million)	Total Urdu-Speaking Population (million)	Coefficient of Urduization (%)	Main Language
INDIA	61.42	28.61	48	Urdu
Urdu States in Hindi Region				
Bihar	7.59	4.99	65	Urdu
Madhya Pradesh	1.81	0.99	55	Urdu
Rajasthan	1.78	0.65	37	Hindi
Uttar Pradesh	13.68	9.27	67	Urdu
Urdu States in non-Hindi Region				
Andhra Pradesh	3.68	3.30	91	Urdu
Karnataka	3.11	2.64	85	Urdu
Maharashtra	4.23	3.66	87	Urdu
Other States with Muslim Population over 1 Million				
Assam	3.60	—	—	Assamese
Gujarat	2.25	0.53	26	Gujarati
Jammu and Kashmir	3.04	0.01	3	Kashmiri
Kerala	4.16	—	—	Malayalam
Tamil Nadu	2.10	0.76	36	Tamil
West Bengal	9.06	0.95	10	Bengali

Source: Muslim India, January 1984, p. 18.

A major problem for Urdu is that it is the only constitutionally recognized language of India, with the exception of Sindhi, that does not have a homeland—there is no state or Union territory in which it is the language of the majority. Even in Jammu and Kashmir, where Urdu is the official state language, it has been declared as mother tongue by a minuscule proportion of the people; this is bound, in due course, to come into conflict with the legitimate aspirations of Kashmiri and Dogri.

Thus, whereas Urdu has the status of a minority language in all states of the Union, all other national languages outside their home states also have minority status in one or more other states. Theoretically, it should be possible to work out, in a federal union, a national scheme determining the scope for the use of minority languages in education, administration, or the mass media that would apply equally to all languages in minority situations. The Constitution itself lays down, in articles 345, 347, 350, 350A, and 350B, certain norms for fulfilling the aspirations of linguistic minorities, in order to secure the preservation of their cultures. Yet Urdu with no home base of its own and with the burden of political hostility has not been accorded its due place either in education, administration, or the media. So, it has become a major grievance of the Muslim community and repeatedly a major political issue. Implementation of the Gujral Committee Report of 1976 has become a rallying cry for the Urdu-speaking minority.[22]

Slowly, a national consensus is emerging that in addition to the majority language, minority languages should be used for specified official purposes, not only at the state, but also at the district and block levels, which are the effective levels for development and administration if that linguistic minority forms at least ten percent of the population. Second, in education the basic right of every child to be imparted primary education through the medium of his or her mother tongue must be implemented. Third, at the secondary stage, the mother tongue should have primacy and be taught even where it is not the medium of instruction. The choice of a second language should be limited, then, to modern, not classical languages like Sanskirt.

The lack of job prospects for children educated through the medium of Urdu poses a dilemma for the Muslim community. To preserve their cultural identity, their children must learn Urdu; yet, from the point of view of participation in the economy, it is dysfunctional. Comparative study of the ability of other minorities to survive culturally despite loss of their language (e.g., the Irish) might afford a more optimistic prognosis for Muslim Indians.

The fourth Muslim demand is noninterference by the state in the Muslim personal law (marriage, divorce, inheritance) through introduction of a common civil code. This tends to produce a direct confrontation with the modern secular state. Ever since the French Revolution, the secular ideal has been the same set of laws for all citizens. Many Hindus who have sacrificed important aspects of their own religious customs and practices to this legal reform resent the politically expedient exemption of the Muslim minority from, for instance, the prohibition on polygamy or unilateral divorce. Hindu militants charge, unscientifically, that polygamy causes a higher Muslim birthrate. Muslim modernists argue, more persuasively, that polygamy and *purdah* (seclusion of women) inhibit the modernization and progress of the community and that instant divorce destabilizes social life. Orthodox Muslims argue that the divinely ordained *shariah* is an intrinsic part of Islam and that to tamper with the personal law is a violation of freedom of religion. The fact that Turkey abolished *shariah* and that other Muslim majority countries, like Tunisia and even Pakistan, have introduced procedural changes shows that the resistance to social reform originates in the minority situation of Muslim Indians. It is the prospect of assimilation as well as the fear of Parliament with a non-Muslim majority legislating on Islam that makes even many otherwise progressive Indian Muslims hesitant about the fulfillment of this directive of the Constitution. Here, too, comparison with Muslim minorities in other countries might be more fruitful than with Muslim majority polities. One may question whether a common civil code in a multicultural and diverse country like India is a condition precedent either for democracy or secularism.

Finally, security of life and property is the fifth Muslim demand, one of much import to the Muslim masses who suffer most from communal riots. Communal, principally Hindu versus Muslim, riots began in the late nineteenth century under British rule.[23] Social tensions are a symptom, ironically, of modernization and have been accentuated by education, economic development, and political consciousness. Communities in traditional society that were separated by functional and hereditary division of labor come into conflict when modernization and democratization open up competition to all. In a fluid and mobile society, the results of competition, for good or ill, are explained in terms of individuals. But in a transitional or segmented society where individuals are still largely subordinate to, and identify strongly with, family, clan, caste, or religious community, the results of competition are apt to be interpreted in terms of relative group standing. Add to this an economy of scarcity unable to meet soaring ambitions and expectations and the scene is set for group rivalry, unfair competition, and discriminatory practices, which, unmitigated by cross pressures, easily spill over into violence[24] (see Table 7.7).

India and Pakistan were born amid some of the worst mutual slaughter of modern history. The number of riots and casualties declined in the

Table 7.7 Communal Riots, 1960–83

Year	Number of Communal Incidents	Number of Persons Killed	Number of Persons Injured
1960	26	na	na
1961	92		
1962	60		
1963	61		
1964	1170		
1965	676 (173)*		
1966	133	45	
1967	220	251	
1968	346	183	
1969	519	674	
1970	521	298	
1971	321	103	
1972	240	70	1,207
1973	242	72	1,000
1974	248	87	1,206
1975	205	33	962
1976	169	39	794
1977	188	36	1,122
1978	230	110	1,853
1979	304	261	2,876
1980	427	375	2,838
1981	319	196	2,613
1982	474	238	3,025
1983*	404	202	3,478

*Excludes the Assam massacre.

Source: Muslim India, January 1983, p. 37.

1950s during Jawaharlal Nehru's rule but have intermittently risen since his death in 1964, except for an apparent dip during the brief period of the "emergency" in 1975–77. Communal riots, unless government instigated, as in czarist Russia or Nazi Germany, are a phenomenon of democracies in which government is constrained from dealing with them with a strong hand because of electoral considerations. Political parties have been suspected, despite their secular stance, of fomenting communal riots for political gains, for creating or sustaining a fear psychosis in the Muslim community in order to demonstrate to Muslim voters that only a particular individual or party can protect them, or to "punish" the Muslims for not voting for a party's candidates in the preceding election.

The immediate trigger for a riot may be trivial or any one of a number of "historic" reasons: cow slaughter by a Muslim, a Hindu religious procession playing music before a mosque at prayer time, defamation of religious leaders, or abduction of women. The proximate cause is not as important as the underlying suspicion and distrust worsened by economic competition. The fact that communal riots have been concentrated in the cities and towns of North India and the Deccan where Muslims once ruled and have until recently been almost absent from South India and the eastern fringe of the country where there was little or no Muslim rule would seem to indicate that there is some causal relationship in these riot-prone areas. Muslims there retain (to an extent) the former ruling-elite mentality, whereas the Hindus have the chip-on-the-shoulder mentality of former subjects.[25] In these areas, the Muslim minority also often tends to be assertive of its rights; this brings about the retaliatory punishment and the Hindu desire to put them in their place.

Also more and more noticeable is the inability of the national leadership of India to control the local police and the state and party functionaries who, apparently, largely share the communal bias of the Hindu majority. This explains why the Indian army and central paramilitary forces have to be called in to control the riots. The longtime exclusion of Muslims from the police force after Partition makes for direct confrontation between the two communities. The police do not generally concern themselves with the safety of the weaker sections and are seen as a partisan force. Also the communication gap between the various communities, caused by residential segregation and lack of social intercourse, allows negative stereotyping and easy acceptance of rumors.

Many commissions of inquiry about major riots, like those at Ranchi, Ahmedabad, Bhiwandi, and Jamshedpur, have made thorough studies and suggested appropriate steps to prevent or at least curb communal violence. The National Integration Council as well as the National Police Commission have gone into the question and government has issued many guidelines based on their recommendations, yet the graph of communal riots shows a sickening rise during much of the last decade.

Recommendations have included a special multicommunity antiriot force to replace the communally infected state-armed constabularies, imposition of collective fines on disturbed areas, statutory compensation for victims, and special courts. Some of these have even been adopted by government at various levels but not fully or expeditiously enough and therefore have proven ineffective. What seems to be lacking is the political will, such as the finally stopped lynchings of blacks in the southern part of the United States in the 1960s.

Although not among the five demands articulated by Muslim spokesmen, the inadequate and often distorted image of Muslims in the media must contribute to the negative stereotyping referred to. In a democracy, despite the relatively low literacy of the Indian population, the media play an important role in molding public opinion. Muslims are conspicuously underrepresented in the ranks of the national media, both English and Hindi. The Urdu press, with some well-known exceptions (particularly in the Punjab and Delhi), is identified with the Muslim community. On the whole, the Urdu press is anemic and ineffective and serves only the purposes of self-congratulation or lamentation. Moreover, some Urdu papers are closely associated with political parties or ideological groups and therefore have limited appeal. In any case, the Muslim segment of the Urdu press has virtually no readership beyond the Muslim community, and there is no Urdu paper with a nationwide circulation, two or three weeklies apart. In the other regional languages, even when its speakers are largely Muslims, the Muslim point of view is not adequately reflected. Thus the media fail to provide a link between the community and the power structure to bridge the communication gap between the community and the nation as a whole.

Indeed, to a large extent, the media plays the negative role of enlarging the gap through manipulation of news, distortion of facts, and misinterpretation of events. Sometimes, offensive and defamatory writings against Islam, the Holy Prophet, or Islamic history appear. As the government is unable to suppress or punish such malicious writings, these give further impetus to the sense of isolation and alienation in the community and add to the prejudice and distrust of the minority by the majority. The government-controlled radio and television are not free from prejudice and bias and often project Muslims as negative stereotypes. The same is true of films, particularly historical or social ones.[26] To a large extent, the mass media, with the freedom it enjoys in a democratic polity, should be held to share responsibility for maintaining or aggravating intergroup tension and, therefore, impeding reconciliation and harmony. It is not enough and often counterproductive that the press does not refer to Hindus and Muslims by name in reporting riots.

Can this situation be overcome? Can the Muslim community acquire a capacity to project its point of view and to influence the course of events through a press of its own? It is obvious that the Urdu press will not do it because its audience is limited to Urdu-speaking people; nor can newspapers or periodicals in English alone fill the gap. What is needed is Muslim-controlled newspapers and periodicals in English and Hindi as well as in the major national languages: Bengali, Gujerati, Marathi, Telugu, Kannada, Malayalam, and Assamese. In order to make an impact, these papers must have standards matching the best available in those languages. Second, organized efforts must be made for briefing journalists and columnists on the Muslim point of view so that the media as a whole can represent faithfully the Muslim side of the story, even if it leaves the reader free to judge and draw his own conclusions. Third, Muslim youth must be encouraged to take up journalism as a profession.

Conclusions

What emerges chiefly from a study of Islam and public life in India are a number of important distinctions that limit the applicability of any generalizations to other cases, especially to countries in which Muslims are a majority.

First, the Muslim community in India is, and is likely to remain for the foreseeable future, a minority group. Despite a five percent higher rate of increase than the Hindu community and despite the recent conversion to Islam of some Harijans, the reasonable prediction is that Muslims will remain a large community but will represent a relatively small percentage (11 to 12 percent) of the Indian population. Neither is there any possibility for that minority to reclaim its one-time political dominance over the subcontinent. To the contrary, what is less unlikely is that India, Pakistan, and Bangladesh might willingly or unwillingly be reunited; in which case, Muslims would still be no more than a quarter to a third of the population. Or, if the Indian Republic were to fragment (which could happen to Pakistan too), it seems unlikely that any of the components, except Kashmir, would separate or otherwise come under Muslim rule.

Consequently, the *public* role of Islam as a body of doctrine, beliefs, and rituals is bound to be more restricted in India than it is, or potentially can be, in a Muslim-majority country like Pakistan or Iran. That is to say, *nizam-i-Islam* (regulation of polity according to Islam) cannot be achieved in present circumstances in India. Muslim personal law may continue indefinitely as a separate code—despite the explicit injunction of the Indian Constitution—owing to Muslim political pressure. Muslims as voters, Muslim politicians, and Muslim lobbyists will certainly affect this and other policies as long as India remains a professedly secular democracy. One has only to look at Soviet Central Asia to see how little impact a Muslim minority may have on the public life of a totalitarian, non-Muslim state.

Some orthodox *ulama* and revivalist leaders in India may be willing to settle for, or even favor, the transformation of India into a Hindu state—which they claim (incorrectly) it already is in practice—on condition that they should then be allowed, with the sanction of the state, to regulate the affairs of minority Muslims according to the *shariah*. But that bargain, comparable to the *dhimmi* status accorded to non-Muslims in traditional Muslim-ruled states, does not even seem to be the intent of the Hindu groups that are bent on Indianizing the Muslim minority.

The second distinction, a diminishing but still relevant one, is between North India and the coastal south. It is visible in different origins (peaceful conversion vs. conquest), sectarian distribution (more Ismailis), languages (not Urdu but regional languages), occupations (business more than professional), political issues (not civil service entry), party organizations (the Muslim League), state of Hindu-Muslim relations and, consequently, in a lower incidence of communal riots. Unfortunately, the nationalization (and Urduization) of Muslim politics in recent decades has tended to narrow these regional differences in the direction of a spread of northern tension into South India rather than of southern harmony into North India.

A third distinction is among Muslims themselves. Just as there are great variations in condition and outlook between elite and mass, so there are significant differences in viewpoints toward Islam—orthodox, revivalist, modernist, and secularist—that, in part, cut across class and regional lines but that put articulate Muslim leaders on opposite sides of various public issues (e.g., the question of reform of the Muslim personal law).[27] The modernists and secularists may be relatively few in number, but they wield influence disproportionate to their number because of their superior access to the media and their buildup by the national parties and leadership. It is true that, like most minorities, Indian Muslims tend to coalesce in times of crisis when a state of siege mentality develops. But there may be some advantages in diversity of elite viewpoints as well as party affiliations for a minority as it can modify sterotypes and help refute fears and accusations on the part of the majority that the minority is a homogeneous fifth column.

Implicit in much of the foregoing is the difference between Islam and Public Life and Muslims and Public Life.[28] Although Muslims get their identity, both self and other, from a core of common Islamic beliefs and practices, they also share to a greater or lesser extent some attitudes and behavior that are secular rather than Islamic and yet affect the public life of the countries in which they live. For example, one might agree with the modernists that *purdah* (seclusion of women) has no explicit Quranic sanction and, in fact, was borrowed from the Byzantine Greeks or Sassanid Persians. Yet, it is more widespread among Muslims than among other peoples, and it does affect such diverse policy areas as education, family planning, and employment.

Since independence, much of the political energy of the Muslim community in India has been dissipated in dealing with minor but persistent irritations—the ever-simmering threat to physical security or of personal humiliation; offensive articles in periodicals and books; curtailment of religious rites, like Qurbani (ritual slaughter of animals) and Azan (the call to prayers): constraints on construction of mosques and on allotment of land for graveyards; forcible occupation of *wakf (waqf)* properties; motivated criticism of Muslim personal law; persistent discrimination in employment; imposition of Hindu culture and the denial of facilities for learning Urdu or studying through Urdu in government schools; under-enumeration in the census and disenfranchisement in elections; police and administrative harrassment, and the government's demand of loyalty. The main remedial approach has been political, that is case-by-case amelioration through political contacts and the building up of pressure through representations and memoranda. This has given rise to a class of powerbrokers, but it has failed to provide a permanent solution, a stable *modus vivendi,* or an institutional framework.

The political approach is not likely to be abandoned, for the simple reason that there is no viable alternative, but the coming decade may witness an increasing agitational input. Also, the main thrust is shifting from minor irritants to major problems of educational and economic development, from the immediate to the long-term, from the tactical to the strategic. Both these methods for successful handling call for self-reliance as well as a sympathetic milieu. The trouble is that gains always generate pressures for a "due" (proportionate) share of the fruits of development and of public employment. To achieve these goals, Muslims may realize their own political impotence and seek new political alliances with the other relatively deprived sections of the national community. They may demand statutory protection through quota or reservation.

Both the alliance and the demands may, in turn, further exacerbate intercommunal relations unless a national consensus emerges on the rights of minorities and/or demarcates acceptable limits thereto.

In the final analysis, the Muslim community's political goal in India is neither dominance nor separatism. Neither does it look outward for inspiration or support. Its goal is preservation of identity and achievement of equality in a plural society. To the extent that religion continues to define identity, Islam will be a factor in Indian society; and so long as there is de facto discrimination on the basis of religion, Islam shall remain a rallying cry—both for the Hindu and the Muslim communities—and thus a potent factor in the public life of India.

Notes

1. *Muslim India,* 1, no. 1 (January 1983), pp. 3–4.
2. Wilfred Cantwell Smith, *Islam in Modern History* (Princeton: Princeton University Press, 1957), p. 288.
3. Richard A. Schermerhorn, *Comparative Ethnic Relations* (New York: Random House, 1970), pp. 78–85).
4. Imtiaz Ahmad, "Economic and Social Change," in *Muslims in India,* Zafar Imam, ed. (New Delhi: Orient Longman, 1975), pp. 231–55.
5. Balraj Madhok. *Indianisation.* Delhi: Hind Pocket Books, 1970.

6. *Muslim India,* 1. no. 4 (April 1983), p. 190.

7. Theodore P. Wright, Jr., "Effectiveness of Muslim Representation in India," in *South Asian Politics and Religion,* Donald E. Smith, ed. (Princeton: Princeton University Press, 1966), pp. 102–37.

8. Theodore P. Wright, Jr., "The Muslim League in South India Since Independence: A Study in Minority Group Political Strategies," *American Political Science Review,* 60, no. 3 (September 1966), pp. 579–99.

9. Z. Masood Quraishi, "Electoral Strategy of a Minority Pressure Group: The Muslim Majlis-e-Mushawarat," *Asian Survey,* 8, no. 12 (December 1968), pp. 976–87.

10. Theodore P. Wright, Jr., "Ethnic Pressures on Foreign Policy: Indian Muslims and American Jews," *Economic and Political Weekly of India,* 17, no. 40 (October 9, 1982), pp. 1655–60.

11. Anil Seal, *The Emergence of Indian Nationalism* (Cambridge: Cambridge University Press, 1968), chap. 7; Paul R. Brass, *Language, Religion and Politics in North India* (Cambridge: Cambridge University Press, 1974), pp. 138–59.

12. Ghanshyam Shah, unpublished paper presented to International Conference on Ethnic Minorities, Mexico, 1982.

13. *Muslim India,* 1, no. 1 (January 1983), p. 29; 1, no. 6 (June 1983), p. 262; 1, no. 12 (December 1983), pp. 552–54; 2, no. 6 (June 1984), p. 253; 2, no. 10 (October 1984), pp. 470–71.

14. N. C. Saxena in a report for the Minorities Commission—"Public Employment and Educational Backwardness among Muslims in India" (1983)—found that Muslim candidates actually did better on the oral interview than on the written examinations.

15. *Muslim India,* 1, no. 12 (December 1983), p. 546; 2, no. 1 (January 1984), p. 17; 2, no. 5 (May 1984), pp. 228–29; 2, no. 6 (June 1984), p. 279; 2, no. 10 (October 1984), pp. 470–71. See also Theodore P. Wright, Jr., "The New Muslim Businessmen of North India," in *Changing South Asia,* Kenneth Ballhatchet and David Taylor, eds. (Hongkong: Asian Research Service, 1984), pp. 37–46.

16. Theodore P. Wright, Jr., "Indian Muslims and the Middle East, " *Journal of South Asian and Middle Eastern Studies,* 6, no. 1 (Fall 1982), pp. 48–56.

17. George Mathew, "The Politicisation of Religion; Conversions to Islam in Tamil Nadu," *Economic and Political Weekly of India,* 17, no. 25 (June 19, 1982), pp. 1027–34; and no. 26 (June 26, 1982), pp. 1068–72.

18. Theodore P. Wright, Jr., "The Ethnic Numbers Game in South Asia: Hindu-Muslim Conflicts over Family Planning, Conversion, Migration and Census," in *Culture, Ethnicity and Identity,* William C. McCready, ed. (New York: Academic Press, 1983), pp. 405–27.

19. See the reports of A. R. Sherwani in successive issues of *Radiance* (Delhi).

20. Imtiaz Ahmed, "Muslim Educational Backwardness," *Economic and Political Weekly of India,* 16, no. 36 (September 5, 1981).

21. *Muslim India,* 1, no. 12 (December 1983), p. 550.

22. *Muslim India,* 1, no. 5 (May 1983), pp. 225–32, for its recommendations on Urdu.

23. Sarah Jane Moore, *Rioting in North India* (Ann Arbor: University Microfilms International, 1981).

24. *Muslim India,* 1, no. 1 (January 1983), p. 37.

25. Theodore P. Wright, Jr., "Identity Problems of Former Elite Minorities," *Journal of Asian Affairs,* 1, no. 2 (Fall 1976), pp. 58–63.

26. But cinema offers Muslims an alternative career opportunity. See Theodore P. Wright, Jr., "Muslim Mobility in India Through Peripheral Occupations: Sports, Music, Cinema and Smuggling," in *Asie du Sud,* Marc Gaborieau and Alice Thorner, eds. (Paris: Editions du Centre National de la Recherche Scientifique, 1979), pp. 271–78.

27. H.A.R. Gibb, *Mohemmedanism* (Oxford: Oxford University Press, 1949), chap. 10.

28. Theodore P. Wright, Jr., "Islam and Muslims Under Socialism," *Plural Societies,* 8, no. 1 (Spring 1977), pp. 71–81.

Suggestions for Further Reading

Ahmad, Imtiaz, ed. *Caste Among the Muslims.* New Delhi: Manohar, 1973.
————. *Family, Kinship and Marriage Among Muslims in India.* New Delhi: Manohar, 1976.
————. *Modernization and Social Change Among Muslims in India.* New Delhi: Manohar, 1983.
————. *Ritual and Religion Among Muslims in India.* New Delhi: Manohar, 1981.
Engineer, Asgher Ali. *Indian Muslims: A Study of Minority Problems in India.* New Delhi: East India Book Co., 1984.
Gauba, K. L. *Passive Voices.* New Delhi: Sterling, 1973.
Hardy, Peter. *The Muslims of British India.* Cambridge: Cambridge University Press, 1972.
Hollister, John. *The Shia of India.* London: Luzac, 1953.
Husain, S. Abid. *Destiny of Indian Muslims.* New Delhi: Asia, 1965.
Imam, Zafar, ed. *Muslims in India.* New Delhi: Orient Longman, 1975.
Madan, T. N., ed. *Muslim Communities of South Asia, Culture and Society.* New Delhi: Vikas, 1976.
Robinson, Francis. *Separatism Among Indian Muslims.* Cambridge: Cambridge University Press, 1974.
Schermerhorn, R. A. *Ethnic Plurality in India.* Tucson: University of Arizona Press, 1978, chap. 7.
Shakir, Moin. *Muslims in Free India.* New Delhi: Kalamkar Prakashan, 1972.
Smith, Donald E. *India as a Secular State.* Princeton: Princeton University Press, 1964.

8

MALAYSIA
Islam and Multiethnic Polities

FRED R. VON DER MEHDEN

Islam in Malaysia has developed in a religious environment significantly different from those Middle Eastern states where it is the faith of the vast majority of the population. Malaysia is a multiracial, multireligious country in which Islam is dominant politically and culturally but includes among its adherents only a bare majority of the citizenry. The very pluralism of the system has led to a society in which ethnicity and religion have become intimately entwined and in which social policies, politics, and economics are all heavily influenced by communal considerations. This chapter initially describes the character of this diversity and then discusses the role of Islam within the Malay community; the place of that religion in education, government and political activities; and recent efforts to expland the place of Islam in the nation.

Pluralism and Ethnicity

Malaysia is administratively and geographically divided between Peninsula Malaya and the Borneo states of Sabah and Sarawak. The population of the nation as a whole includes approximately forty-five percent Malays,* thirty-five percent Chinese, ten percent Indians, and ten percent others, with the peninsula being approximately fifty percent Malay, thirty-five percent Chinese, ten percent Indian, and five percent others. Several important factors tend to be correlated with this ethnic balance and each tends to reinforce both actual differences and perceptions. Geographically, the Chinese primarily live on the west coast of the peninsula and on Borneo, where they are concentrated in urban areas. The more

---

*In Malaysia, Malays and other indigenous people are called *bumiputra* (son of the soil).

rural Malays are to be found in greater numbers outside the cities on the peninsula, although they are beginning to move into urban settings. The non-Malay indigenous population lives principally on Boreno, whereas the Indians are usually to be found in cities and on plantations on the peninsula.

Historically, the Chinese and, to a lesser extent, the Indians have tended to control local commercial and professional activities, and the Malays have tended to control small-scale agriculture and higher administrative posts. Plantation workers have generally been Indians. This relationship of occupation to race has led to disparities in income between the Chinese and Malays and to efforts by the government to raise the economic conditions of the poorer Malays. Finally, almost all Muslims are Malays. Only a relatively small number of the other groups accept Islam; instead, they maintain the traditions they brought with them from China and India or they follow indigenous beliefs. Thus, with many individual exceptions, ethnicity has historically correlated with geography, occupation, economic status, and religion.

The manner in which Islam came to Malaya† and past colonial policies may help to explain some of these relationships. Although Arab tombstones have been found on neighboring Java from as early as the eleventh century, Islam first arrived in Malaya through the peaceful penetration by Indian and Arab traders, with the first recorded conversion occurring in the early fourteenth century.[1] Then, in 1414, the ruler of Malacca, Muhammad Iskander Shah, was reportedly converted, leading to the spread of Islam through the peninsula. The power of Malacca made the acceptance of the religion politically and economically desirable and conversion of the general population followed through state sponsorship and individual missionary activity. Islam was thus established in a relatively isolated environment insofar as the influence of centers of theological learning in the Middle East is concerned. It was fostered initially by individuals lacking religious sophistication, a condition that lasted into the twentieth century.

The period of British colonialism (from the end of the eighteenth century to the middle of the twentieth) promoted a new environment. While attempting to "protect" the Malay and his religion, the British, as had the Dutch before them, allowed the local sultans to retain responsibility over religion and did not encourage the Malays to enter the modern commercial world. Meanwhile, increased mining and plantation activities demanded heavy manpower commitments and through the years of a gradual influx of Chinese and Indians expanded to a precipitous flow.[2] The non-Malay population of over 500,000 at the turn of the century reached almost 3.5 million at the time of independence in 1957. The reli-

---

†Malaya was the name of the colony and state up to 1963. Then it became Malaysia with the incorporation of Sabah and Sarawak. Singapore was part of Malaysia from 1963 to 1965. The peninsula is also referred to as Malaya.

gious complexion of the society was thus changed by the immigration of Taoist, Confucian, and Buddhist Chinese as well as mostly Hindu Indians. In addition, a small minority of Arabs, Indians, and Pakistanis became influential commercial and religious members of the Muslim population. The result was that by the first census after independence, the Malays, who to all intents and purposes were also Muslims, were but half the total number of people in the new nation.

When Sabah and Sarawak were brought into the Federation in 1963 to form Malaysia, the percentage of Muslims was further diluted. Coastal Malays form only a small percentage of the peoples of the two states, which have a heterogeneous indigenous population that includes sizable Chinese elements. In 1960, Sarawak was only 23.4 percent Muslim and Sabah 37.9 percent.[3] For a period after its incorporation, there were efforts to convert the people of Sabah to Islam under the political leadership of Tun Mustapha and a number of well-publicized conversions took place.[4] However, although the Muslims have dominated the political and cultural life of the nation as a whole and have continued to be the largest religious group, they only now compose slightly over 50 percent of Malaysia's population.

This plural character of Malaysian society permeates politics, economics, and religion in the nation, complicating and intensifying communal relationships. On the one hand, it presents the Islamic activist with a heterogeneous environment, unlike that in the Middle East, which leads to pressure for some form of accommodation. On the other hand, the history of a seemingly ever-increasing non-Muslim population in a modern environment and the resultant challenge to Malay traditions and values have made the Malay-Muslim even more conscious of his ethnoreligious identity and dampened divisions within the community. The perception of Islam as the religion of an endangered indigenous population that has been primarily rural, poor, and noncommercial in its character has also fostered a sense of defensiveness that has been the foundation for Malay-sponsored politics, public policy, and attitudes. This welding of Malay and Islamic identity has been further strengthened by the religious and cultural cohesion of its adherents.

If the plural nature of Malaysia is one major force in explaining the role of Islam, the other force is the interactive relationship between religion and ethnicity to most Malays. According to the Constitution, "Malay means a person who professes the Muslim religion, habitually speaks the Malay language, conforms to Malay customs."[5] As we shall see, this legal definition has important political and economic connotations. At this point, it is important to note the general and sturdy acceptance among Malays of the concept of the identity of Islam with being Malay. Observers over the decades have regularly commented on this relationship. Recently, writing of literary responses, T. S. Chee states, "Religion or the belief in Islam is not the end result of rational analysis, but a symbol of Malayness."[6] S. Siddique wrote that to become a Malay and to become a Muslim are inseparable,[7] and M. Nash said of the rural Malay, "Religion in the context of Kelantan is an interesting cognitive term. For Malays, it is not separable from ethnic identity or cultural heritage. In Kelantan, Malay equals Muslim."[8]

Malay Religious Beliefs

This perception of the unity of ethnicity and religion has a number of important ramifications. Muslims from the Arab world have emphasized the universal elements of Islam, underscoring the concept of the *ummah*. The Malay Muslim, although he takes considerable pride in being part of the world of Islam, also reflects, particularly in the rural setting, a certain parochialism and ethnoreligious nationalism. This parochialism, when combined with the challenges brought about by the non-Muslim communities, has led to an emphasis on particular rather than universal issues and provided obstacles to those seeking to employ religion as a unifying force in Malaysian Muslim society. According to one observer, "Traditional Malay identity was and is defined not so much in terms of universalistic membership in a world religion as it was and is in terms of more specific sorts of contexts and associations—family, *kampong* [village], state, people *(bangsa Malayu)* and perhaps in the past chief and ruler."[9] Thus, the Malay seeking ready models for local solutions is not as likely to find them in the context of issues and actions elsewhere in the Muslim world.

Second, this identification of Islam and Malayness has provided an obstacle to Islamic unity within Malaysia. Although Arabs, Indonesians, Indians, and Pakistanis have been legally and, to a limited degree, socially incorporated into the indigenous *(bumiputra)* community, the more culturally distinct Chinese have had a more difficult time being received into the Malay society.[10] Chinese converts may be publicized in the media, change their names, and live as Muslims; but their ethnic identity continues to provide an obstacle to full acceptance for many Malays.

Third, the interrelationship of Islam and being Malay has led to perceptions among the Malays of an integrated whole that includes lifestyle, values, language, and religion. Attacks on one part are viewed as endangering the whole. Thus, secular education, Western materialism, urbanization, and other aspects of modernization are perceived by many Malays to be challenges to both the religious and ethnic foundations of their society. This correlation of Malay and Muslim provides a powerful tool to Malay politicians who seek to unite the community. Defectors from the party can be charged with weakening a Malay Islamic community that is endangered by nonbelievers. Economic policies to aid the Malays can be described as means of defending and strengthening Islam. The development of Malay as the national language is also perceived as reinforcing the Malay role.

Malay Beliefs and Practices

Prior to analyzing Islam as it relates to political issues, religious law, and education, it is necessary to describe briefly Islam as it has affected the average Malay. Today, as increased urbanization and mobility make it more difficult to define Malay society as a whole, the Malaysian Muslim is no longer almost entirely the product of the traditional rural village. What we wish to present is a modal description of the more central Malay Muslim religious patterns as they are still to be found in a rural population within which even the urban Malay has generally lived his formative years. In doing so, we shall concentrate on only two aspects of a complex environment: basic Islamic tenets and practices and non-Muslim elements.

Malay Muslims are Sunnis, with a complex set of influences derived from Sufi, Hindu, and animistic sources. At the village level, non-Muslim ways interact more with "purer" Islamic beliefs and practices, whereas those educated in the urban areas or with better religious training are more likely to display belief patterns more akin to orthodox Islamic teachings. In general terms, the rural Malay may be described as conservative and ritualistic in religious belief. He is influenced and circumscribed by individual expectations regarding the strong impact of fate and luck on his personal success or failure and community norms within which he is expected to act. These practices and beliefs are important guidelines in defining his place in the world. As one observer noted, "They see Islam or at least certain aspects of Islam as enveloping them in a set of ritual relationships, and as being a major dimension of community life and organization. . . . Along with this there is a set of constraints which reflect an emphasis on social obligation, particularly of a ritual or ceremonial nature."[11]

If we accept the common description of the Malay as oriented toward ritual, we can turn to four of the ritualistic Pillars of Islam: prayer, fasting, pilgrimage, and tithing.[12] (We bypass the first, which relates to belief in the unity of God.) Although this description is brief and provides only a glimpse into Islamic elements of religious belief, it is meant to illustrate basic patterns. Islam calls for prayer five times a day and special services at midday on Friday; in rural Malaysia, these precepts are generally followed, not so much because of the sanctions established by law as to personal belief and peer-group pressure. Although urban Malays are less regular (some would say lax) in their practices, there are signs that more attention is being paid to this pillar among politicians, students, and religious organizations, in part owing to an increasingly religious environment.

Fasting during Ramadan (*Puasa* as the Malays term it), is the most important happening in the Malay religious calendar. The restrictions during the fast are widely followed; legal sanctions and notices in urban hotels and restaurants are generally not the controlling factors as much as individual attitudes and peer-group influences. At the end of the fast,

Hari Raya, the most important Malay celebration of the year takes place. It is a time for special foods, gatherings, and visiting cemeteries and relatives; in urban areas, there are special sales, exchanges of greeting cards, and a crush at airports, train stations, and bus depots as celebrants travel back to their towns and villages.

The *hajj,* the pilgrimage to Mecca, has become considerably more possible to the Malay Muslim since independence, as the government has aided in developing savings for the *hajj,* organizing the trip (now also made available to neighboring Muslim minorities), and seeing to the comfort and safety of pilgrims. The Malay, even more than the Indonesian, has looked on the *hajj* as an important religious act to fulfill during his lifetime; a higher percentage of Malays now make the *hajj* than any other major Muslim country in the region. Given the distance from the traditional centers of Islamic activity, this gives the Malay an opportunity to be part of the wider world of Islam. It also may give social and religious prestige to the returning pilgrim, although the fact that *hajjis* tend to be older and more affluent reinforces a status already present to a degree.[13]

Zakat is a religious tax on agriculture and property, whereas *fitrah* is a personal levy. Traditionally it was an accepted practice in the village and was considered an important part of one's religious obligations. Collected by the local *imam* (leader of the mosque), it is normally used for maintaining and constructing mosques, religious education, and charities. Such levies are no longer unanimously accepted in rural areas; in urban centers, the more atomized community makes collection more difficult. Generally, then, the Malay Muslim has carried out the basic rituals of Islam in a conscientious and orthodox manner.

Although the rural Malay considers himself a Muslim and part of the world brotherhood of Islam, he is also deeply influenced by a set of primarily non-Islamic beliefs, a folk Islam that often combines Islamic elements with animist and Hindu factors.[14] Rites of passage—birth, circumcision, marriage, death—each have their syncretic ceremonies. Magic with its acceptance of special powers, sorcery, amulets, and formulas are mixed with forces derived from a more orthodox religious framework. The rural Malay has also incorporated into his belief system a wide-ranging spirit life that necessitates propitiation through various ceremonies. For example, there are evil spirits of animate and inanimate objects as well as spirits that can inhabit a man's body and influence his actions. Illness can be the result of spells, spirits, and magic, and treatment can be provided through reliance on special magical cures. In rice-growing areas, the rice soul *(semangat padi)* has necessitated particular ways of harvesting and storage. The syncretic nature of many of these acts brings together animist, Hindu, and Islamic elements and can involve local Muslim religious leaders, verses from the Quran, thoughts of God to ward off spirits, and so on.

There has been some decline in these more traditional beliefs and practices as religious leaders have urged the populace to give less emphasis to spirits and magic; the influence of Islamic modernism has challenged these "impure" views and ways; and the process of education, modernization, and urbanization has weakened traditional ties. However, there is no doubt that a substantial portion of the rural population as well as less educated urban migrants retain and accept these beliefs.

Postindependence Issues

We now turn to a description and analysis of Islam as it has related to politics, religious law, and education in Malaysia. Although there have been other arenas in which Islam has been important, these have been the central national issues that have received attention over the years since independence.

Politics

To understand the role of Islam in Malaysian politics, it is necessary to recognize two levels of interaction, that among the country's political parties and that within the Islamic community itself. Malaysian national and state politics cannot be understood outside the communal basis of the society. Since independence the governing elite has recognized the need to maintain a delicate balance between retaining the political dominance of the Malay Muslim in the political arena and placating other communities. Thus the ruling coalition in Kuala Lumpur has always had at its helm the Malay-Muslim United Malay National Organization (UMNO), the party from which all prime ministers, deputy prime ministers, and home ministers have come.[15] Other members of the coalition (originally the Alliance, now called the National Front) have been drawn from largely Chinese- and Indian-based parties. The opposition historically has been composed of dissatisfied socialist-oriented Chinese and Indian elements that have expounded greater rights for non-Malays and for conservative Malays unhappy with the government's multiracial policies. The latter were concentrated in what was first the Pan-Malayan Islamic Party (PMIP), now called PAS.

The issue of religion has thus necessitated a balance that has the leadership of the coalition, on the one hand, espousing a pluralistic society guaranteeing the rights and privileges of all Malaysians and, on the other hand, attempting to assuage its Malay-Muslim constituency. Too heavy-handed Malay-Muslim chauvinist rhetoric and policy endangers the maintenance of the coalition and possibly national stability. At the same time, it is necessary to hold the loyalty of a Malay-Muslim constituency that remains deeply conscious of its ethnoreligious roots and fears the encroachment of other races and cultures. From the early days of independence, parliamentary backbenchers of UMNO, youth organizations, and local traditional leadership have called on their national leaders to increase the role of Islam in Malaysian society and to use the power of the state to advance Islamic goals. Frequently UMNO politicians on the rise have found it desirable to pander to these views in order to attain power. UMNO must also consider its Malay-Muslim opposition, which has long espoused more religiously chauvinistic policies and is able to drain away voters if the government does not appear to be giving sufficient attention to Malay interests.

During the first dozen years, national policy and rhetoric were weighted toward a more pluralistic approach. In its first dozen years after independence, the Alliance leadership fostered pragmatism, even spoke of the need to develop the Protestant work ethic and placated its more religiously oriented constituents with rhetoric more than action.[16] The year 1969 was a watershed for rhetoric and policy as the racial riots of that year led to a shifting of the balance toward a government emphasis on Malay-Muslim goals while not rejecting pluralism. On the economic front, greater attention was given to bringing the Malay into the modern sector. Through subsidies, quotas, and other "affirmative-action" programs, the Malay was encouraged to compete in the marketplace, education, and the factory.

Politically, this increased emphasis on religion, and ethnicity became even more central to Malaysian party politics than was previously the case. UMNO backbenchers and often UMNO youth attempted to push the National Front more actively into the defense of Malay-Islamic interests. As the government sought to meet these pressures, its Islamic opposition found it difficult to compete at the ballot box. This continued inability to increase its political role helped to lead PAS toward an even more narrowly Islamic Malay chauvinist position and finally into a basic change in leadership in which older, more traditional party leaders gave way to younger activists.

Events in contemporary Malaysia have exacerbated differences within the Muslim community itself. On politicoreligious grounds, it is possible to divide Malaysian Muslims into four categories:

1. Radicals
2. Traditionalists
3. Fundamentalists
4. Accommodationists

Radicals. At one end of the spectrum may be found small fringe elements who have demanded basic changes in the relationship between Islam and Malaysian society. They have received considerable publicity because of both the dramatic violence of their acts and the opportunities they gave the government to illustrate the dangers of extremism. Two of the most well-known examples of such actions were the depredation of Hindu temples by a small group of primarily south Indian Muslims and the 1980 attack on a local police station by fifteen white-robed individuals crying, *"Allahu Akbar"*—("Allah is Great").[17] In the latter case, some twenty-six police and civilians were wounded and eight of the attackers killed. The leader of the assault, one Mohammed Nasir, said that the era of Mohammed was over and that he would lead the crusade to rid the country of all evil. Radicals of this sort have received little public support and are condemned by all other major Muslim groups.

Traditionalists. This category includes the bulk of the Malay rural community and provides much of the membership of both UMNO and its Islamic party opposition. These people identify themselves with the synthesis of Islam and Malay ethnicity, and they seek to maintain traditional patterns of life. Although their religious consciousness is infused with animistic beliefs, this does not weaken their vigorous support for a strong role for Islam in Malaysian government and society. Religiously, they also tend to be suspicious of new and foreign influences on Islam. Politically, they tend to be divided between UMNO and PAS. At the local level, contests between these two parties can be based on economic differences within the local Malay community personalities, charges against opponents for being "un-Islamic," and communal issues as each candidate seeks to out-Malay the other.

Fundamentalists. By fundamentalist or revivalist we mean those who actively seek to expand the role of Islam in Malaysian economic, religious, and political life. Employing education, public forums, the printed media, and other nonviolent means, the fundamentalists seek to make Malaysian Muslims more conscious of their faith and to foster an understanding of Islam that goes beyond mere adherence to ritual and practice. In a religious sense, they tend to situate themselves alongside many of the historic basic goals of Islamic modernism.

The most articulate exponent of this position has been Anwar Ibrahim, former head of the Islamic Youth Organization, Angkatan Belia Islam Malaysia (ABIM), and minister of culture, youth, and sports in Dr. Mahathir's cabinet in 1983, later minister of agriculture and now minister of education. His economic and political goals have emphasized equity, pluralism, and social welfare. He has sought a greater role for Islam in the state and a strengthening of the religious consciousness of believers, but not at the expense of non-Muslims.[18] Not all fundamentalists, even within ABIM, accept Ibrahim's pluralist approach, but there are those who want to see non-Muslims educated in, and finally converted to, Islam. Their end goal is the establishment of a totally Islamic society.

The core of the fundamentalist movement in Malaysia comes from educated youth who have come into contact with Western values and material culture during their schooling in Malaysian and foreign universities and have increasingly become part of the country's urban population. Unlike the older and more traditional local leadership of the rural Malays, these young people are more sophisticated in their use of the media, development of modern organization, and ability to employ the technological tools of the West.

Accommodationists. Malay politicians, on reaching national leadership, have publicly espoused what can be called the accommodationist approach. They have emphasized the necessity of a multiracial, mutireligious society in which all elements can freely practice their own religions without government interference. Prior to the 1969 riots, these leaders articulated an almost secularist position in which religious considerations were downplayed in favor of pluralism and pragmatism. Men like the first prime ministers, Tunku Abdul Rahman and Tun Razak, appeared more comfortable in a less sectarian environment (although Tunku became involved in domestic and international Muslim activities after leaving office). While the next two prime ministers, Hussein Onn and Dr. Mahathir still proclaim a multireligious Malaysia, secular rhetoric has given way to a greater emphasis on Islamic values. The accommodationists do not include a large segment of the Islamic community, but they hold key political and bureaucratic offices and are reinforced by the paucity of other alternatives if Malaysia is to remain a peaceful nation. Some fundamentalists, such as Anwar Ibrahim, fall into this group.

It should be noted that secularists, in terms of those declaring that religion should not play a public role in society, are not included as a major force within the Malay community. Although there are nonreligious Malays and secularism has developed, an influential, publicly secular Malay sector simply does not play any important role in political life.

Religious Laws

Historically, Islamic law in Malaysia has been a local rather than a national matter. During the British period, the Malay sultans were accepted as protectors of Malay religion and culture and within their jurisdiction an Islamic court system was established largely limited to civil cases dealing with marriage, divorce, and inheritance. These courts also enforced various regulations regarding prayer, fasting, and so on, although punishment was limited in all cases to a fine of M$10. Those states with a hereditary ruler also had a head *khati (qadi)* (religious magistrate)—as did each district—who was responsible for administering Islamic justice. The British on their part attempted to prohibit proselytizing among Muslims while guaranteeing freedom of belief to other faiths.

With independence came many other changes. However, it is important to recognize that Malaysia has been both a constitutional and federal system. In the first instance, this means that there has been a rule of law and generally religious rules have been codified and operate through a system of courts. Fundamental issues are written into the Constitution. Second, the country is federal, with primary responsibility for religion resting at the state level. Each of the sultans has retained his role as protector of Islam, whereas the states of Malacca and Penang come under the king *(Yang di-Pertuan Agong)*. The Borneo states of Sabah and Sarawak have no official head of religion.

The Constitution of 1957 firmly puts Islam within the state structure while guaranteeing religious freedom to other religions. Its key provisions provide for[19]

1. The establishment of Islam as the religion of the country. "Islam is the religion of the Federation."
2. The sultan as head of the Islamic religion. In every State that has a ruler, he is recognized as the "Head of the Muslim religion in his State."
3. The protection of Muslims from proselytizing. "State law may control or restrict the propagation of any religious doctrine or belief among persons professing the Muslim religion."
4. Freedom of worship for other religions. "Other religions may be practiced in peace and harmony in any part of the Federation. . . . Every religious group has the right (a) to manage its own religious affairs; (b) to establish and maintain institutions for religious and charitable purposes; and (c) to acquire and own property and hold and administer it in accordance with the law."

Each of these constitutional provisions has become the focus of further debate, refinement, and in many cases new laws and interpretations. Regarding the role of Islam in the state: There has been considerable debate as to whether Malaysia should become or already is an Islamic state. Elements within both UMNO and PAS have called for some form of an Islamic state for many years, although there has been a certain vagueness about the meaning of the concept beyond having the government following the precepts of the Quran and *shariah*. Both the new leadership of PAS and spokesmen for ABIM have been somewhat more specific in terms of the structure and goals of such a state, but again this has not been completely spelled out.

The government, under cross pressures from both within and without the United Front, has sought to continue to guarantee religious freedom while at least rhetorically meeting Islamic demands. This has led the prime minister and his deputy to argue that Malaysia already is an Islamic state and Dr. Mahathir has given tacit approval to the vague concept of Islamic rule for the country. However, at this point the strategy appears to be to forestall any move toward a well-defined constitutional amendment creating an Islamic state while political rhetoric and limited actions would increase the perceived role of Islam within the nation.

Role of the Sultans. After independence the role of the states and sultans in protecting Islam was reinforced. Departments of religion were retained or formed in all the states with hereditary rulers and the Islamic courts were able to expand both their jurisdiction and the punishments they could mete out. At the federal level, the Council of Rulers attempted to cooperate on national religious matters.

Two problems arose out of this increased role: A conflict between the sultans and federal authorities over jurisdiction and a lack of uniformity in religious statutes. In the first instance, the federal government has steadily moved into religious issues, engaging itself in areas of conversion, Islamic religious education, international Islamic cooperation, Islamic banking and economics, the *hajj,* and so on. There have also been efforts to become involved in local affairs through the education of Muslim religious leaders and schoolchildren and through support for religious schools and other Islamic institutions. Also, the close association between UMNO and lower level Islamic leaders has long been a fact of political life, leading often to bitter local party conflicts during local and national elections. The sultans have become quite concerned with what they perceive as government efforts to weaken their powers, and there has been increasing tension on several levels. For example, in 1983, the sultans of Perak and Johore proclaimed different periods for the Ramadan than those presented by the federal authorities, leading to both confusion and tension.[20]

Another issue that has disturbed national authorities has been obvious inconsistencies in religious laws and sanctions across states. Although there have been efforts to develop some uniformity over the years, federal officials have privately complained that the unity of Islam and the state has been weakened by the hodgepodge of regulations now in existence. Certainly nowhere in South or Southeast Asia does one find the breadth of rules formulated to assure that Muslims properly follow the precepts of their religion regarding prayer, fasting, morality, and purity of the faith. Historically, Malay Muslims have emphasized the importance of ritual, and these laws reflect this concept of religious obedience. Even the more conservative Indonesian Muslims when discussing the Malaysian situation find these legal strictures on the faithful too demanding; some Malaysian fundamentalists have complained that they detract from a necessary emphasis on more central issues. The provision for Muslim law in the state lists reads:

> Muslim Law and personal and family law of persons professing the Muslim religion, including the Muslim Law relating to succession, testate and intestate, betrothal, marriage, divorce, dower, maintenance, legitimacy, guardianship, gifts, partitions and non-charitable trusts; Muslim Wakfs and the definition and regulation of charitable and religious trusts, the appointment of trustees and the incorporation of persons in respect of Muslim religious and chartitable institutions operating wholly within the state; Malay custom; Zakat, Fitrah and Bait-ul-Mal or similar Muslim revenue; mosques or any Muslim public place of worship, creation and punishment of offences by persons professing the Muslim religion against precepts of that religion, except in regard to matters included in the Federalist; the constitution, orga-

nization and procedure, of Muslim courts, which shall have jurisdiction only over persons professing the Muslim religion and in respect only of any of the matters included in this paragraph, but shall not have jurisdiction in respect of offences except in so far as conferred by federal law: the control of propagating doctrines and beliefs among persons professing the Muslim religion; the determination of matters of Muslim Law and doctrine and Malay custom.[21]

One author collected a representative list of specific state statutes, although these may vary in detail and punishment and may or may not be implemented:

failure to attend Friday prayers at the mosque (M$25);

consumption of intoxicating liquor (M$50);

sale to a Muslim or consumption by a Muslim of any food or drink during daylight during the month of Ramadan (M$50);

any Muslim male found in suspicious proximity with any woman who is not his close relative (three months and M$300) [this is the *khalwat* law that, if strictly enforced, outlaws unchaperoned dating practices];

any female Muslim abetting the offence of khalwat (three months and M$300);

sexual intercourse between husband and wife in a manner forbidden by Islam (M$25 for each party);

willful disobedience by a woman of an order lawfully given by her husband (M$50);

teaching any doctrine of the Muslim religion without written permission of the Malay ruler (1 month and M$100);

propagating religious doctrines other than Islam among persons professing the Muslim religion (1 year and M$3,000);

teaching false doctrine (3 months and M$250);

printing or distributing books or documents repugnant to any lawful Fetwa [official interpretation of doctrine] or contrary to orthodox belief (6 months and M$500);

contempt of religious authorities or officials (1 month and M$100);

contempt of the law of Islam or its tenets (6 months and M$500).[22]

More recently there have also been pronouncements by religious leaders that argue there should be laws against Muslims calling one another infidels over political differences and to have women sit in the back of buses to avoid *khalwat* (close proximity between the sexes) as well as government warnings that "deviant" Muslims could lose their special privileges as *bumiputra* and prohibitions against Muslims working in the gambling casinos at Genting Highlands, outside Kuala Lumpur.

Proselytizing and Freedom of Worship. Every state took advantage of the Constitution by prohibiting efforts to convert Muslims; this in itself has not led to problems. What has been at issue has been the perception of leaders of religions other than Islam that their efforts to propagate their beliefs among non-Muslims have been restricted and that the government has become a vehicle for conversion to Islam of their fellow believers. Certainly, the media has largely been closed to other faiths in terms of religious programs, advertisements, news stories, and so on, and a close watch is held over material that might be detrimental to Muslims. The identity between religion and ethnicity among Malays and the special privileges that come with remaining Muslim would certainly limit conversion and, although legally possible, such rare cases of apostasy have not been recognized by religious authorities.

Also disturbing to other religions are efforts to propagate Islam, arguably the faith of only a bare majority of Malaysians, by way of the media, public forums, official pronouncements, subsidies to Islamic institutions, attempts to make Muslim holy days national celebrations, support of *dakwah* (missionary) organizations in their work to convert non-Muslims, news programs rejoicing at such conversions, and so on. Programs to raise the religious consciousness of Muslims is one thing, but perceptions that there is increasing pressure for the Islamization of the population as a whole have obviously created uneasiness among non-Muslims. These fears were heightened when Islamic courts called for the punishment of non-believers caught in *khalwat* with Muslims, when state governments demanded a ban on non*halal* meat in all hotels and restaurants (later rescinded), or when a deputy within the prime minister's office discussed a morals law with leaders of other faiths, even though he said it would be based on all religions and the government later backed down.[23]

Difficulties in these areas often arise because national political leaders find it necessary to talk to two constituencies: their Muslim base and their multiracial partners. Thus, Musa Hitam, former deputy prime minister, or Anwar Ibrahim, former head of the Islamic Youth Organization, might both support some form of Islamic state before one constituency. Yet, at another time and to another constituency, the former deputy prime minister could also say, "Malaysian leaders are aware that this is a multiracial and multi-religious society. Islamization as in other countries . . . cannot be done."[24] And Ibrahim could also argue that Islamization "is not aimed at mass conversion of Malaysians to Islam. . . . It's a process to inject more spiritual values into our lives."[25] Neither man probably sees any incompatibility in these statements, although their audiences may hear or want to hear differently.

Islamic Education

Prior to independence, education in Malaya was characterized by its considerable variety in mode of instruction and means of support. English, Malay, and vernacular Indian and Chinese languages were all used as the means of instruction, and state and charitable contributions were the bases of school budgets. As one author noted, education for the Malay and Indian was primarily to attain literacy, for the Chinese to maintain ties to China, and for those studying in English to pass the Cambridge Overseas School Certificate examinations.[26] All of this changed after 1957 when the government placed its highest budgetary priority on education as it sought to Malaysianize the educational system through regulation of the curricula and teacher training as well as fostering Malay as the national language.

Until a quarter of a century ago, Malay Muslim education was, with the exception of that available to the aristocracy, not given high priority by the state or national governments and was left to local efforts. The British colonial administration, although prepared to counter illiteracy, did not want to interfere with what it saw as a stable Malay lifestyle. On their part, Malay parents were unsure as to the benefits of furthering the education of their children. The boys were needed on the land and education for females was considered largely unnecessary. The Malay schools that did exist for the average student were generally of a very low quality, and the English-medium schools were usually taught by non-Muslims who appeared to be, at best, unsympathetic to Malay Muslim values. Religious education did not have many of these drawbacks.

Traditionally, the young Malay boy received his initial religious training at the age of seven or eight from a local teacher from whom he learned to chant and memorize the Quran. Further Islamic education, if available and desired, came from local religious schools or individual teachers, with ultimately a very few going abroad for advanced work in the Middle East.[27] Much of the early instruction was by rote with comparatively little understanding of the content or the Arabic language in which it was presented.

With the expansion of education in recent decades, more boys found a greater variety of education available and turned to secular schools or religious institutions, such as the Arab Schools. Here they learned to read and write Arabic and gained a limited elementary education. Or they turned to the Majlis institutions that combined religious and secular training. Most Malays in either a secular or an Islamic system received some instruction in Islam. After independence, if there are fifteen or more Muslims in a school, by law a Muslim religious teacher, supported by the state and federal governments, must be employed. This teaching takes place within school hours and is in Malay.

Islamic education has expanded at the tertiary level as well, with Islamic studies programs at both the University of Malaya and Universiti Kebangsaan. At both of these institutions, a wide range of courses in Arabic as well as Muslim theology, history, law, and so on, is offered to a largely Malay Muslim student body. In 1983, a government-sponsored international Islamic university was opened in Kuala Lumpur that seeks to present a curricula in which Islam permeates all subjects. The language of instruction is English, and it is open to students from all countries and religions.

Thus, what we are seeing in education for the Malay is a complex interaction between expanding secular training and increased government effort to advance Islam in the schools. (Some opponents argue that this

is, in part, in order to take education out of the hands of local religiopolitical PAS teachers.) Elementary education is no longer limited Quranic
instruction for boys, but a primarily secular education for both sexes that
reaches over ninety percent of the schoolage population. In the first six
standards, the children take geography, history, mathematics, science,
civics, physical education, and art from teachers much better trained than
their predecessors. At the tertiary level, Malay Muslims, aided by government quotas and subsidies, are encouraged to enter the sciences, business,
and engineering, formerly the preserve of the Chinese and Indians. At the
same time, "Islamic religious knowledge" is required in the lower standards and religious studies at advanced levels have become broader and
comparatively more sophisticated. This educational policy has not
solved the problem of the often rudimentary rote-learned knowledge of
Islam of the rural student, yet it has engendered disquiet among many
parents that the secular nature of the rest of their children's education
could dilute religious and traditional values.

Contemporary Patterns and Policies

The past decade has seen important real and symbolic changes in the traditional role that Islam played in Malaysian society. It has become far
more obvious in public rhetoric, government policies, and even dress.
Our discussion will address some of these changes, but first it is useful to
assess some of the reasons for this development. Three factors would
appear to be paramount: modernization, international influences, and
domestic politics.

Modernization

The process of modernization, reinforced by government efforts to raise
the economic level of Malays, has brought an increasing number of
Malays into settings where their traditional beliefs and practices have
been challenged. The largely rural Malay coming to the city or experienc-
ing modernization in his own traditional environment has often displayed disgust or antagonism against what he has perceived to be ques-
tionable elements inherent in Western values and activities. It can be
argued that this confrontation with modernization has reinforced the
sense of religious and ethnic identity among the Malays. From time to
time there have been dramatic outbursts against aspects of this new
milieu, such as the individual who threw his television out the window
because of the offensive material broadcast on it.[28] However, television
ownership is rapidly increasing among Malays.

At the elite level, we have also seen an increased sense of religious identity for somewhat similar reasons. Young Malays entering universities in
Malaysia and abroad have been confronted with new ideas and values.

Overseas they have been influenced by other Muslims, often with radical or fundamentalist views. It is from many of these well-educated youth that the intellectual and organizational base for the fundamentalist movement in Malaysia has been formed. The perceived dangers of these "deviate" ideas has obviously made the government nervous; thus efforts have been made to prepare these students to deal with differing Islamic ways of thinking.[29]

International Influences

The past decade has seen a worldwide resurgence of Islam, which has not been ignored in Malaysia. The apparent increased power of Islamic countries since the oil crisis has reinforced pride in their religion among the Malay Muslims. Events in Iran and the Middle East have kindled interest in the new ideas and movements that have swept those areas; and the government has become worried about the possible consequences of the spread of the ideas of the Iranian revolution, Libya's Colonel Qaddafi, and unauthorized international Islamic organizations. With the increased mobility of young Malays, the old, often relatively static, quality of Islam in Malaysia is being infused with concepts from the outside as never before.

Domestic Political Forces

As we have noted, Malaysian politics have always had a communal base and UMNO and PAS have each responded to their Malay and their Muslim constituencies. In a fashion, the contemporary interplay of Islam with the aforementioned domestic and international factors has been circular. As the government has attempted to react to increased demands to defend and develop Islam, it has helped to establish a religious environment in which such religious pressures have had a greater legitimacy and Malay-Muslim expectations of government support have been higher.

There has been a tendency among outside observers and domestic political opponents to describe government actions and rhetoric in this sphere as instrumentalist and manipulative. Although political motives cannot be denied and would be surprising if nonexistent, it would also appear that the general character of the *Weltanschauung* of the Malay elite and community has changed since 1969. The Malay political and bureaucratic leadership no longer lives in the almost totally Chinese and Indian enclave that defined much of urban Malaysia in the past. Malay migration to the cities, their large-scale enrollment in the universities, their domination of the media, and their place in the international world of Islam have all helped to create an atmosphere reinforcing a sense of identity and self-confidence. This, in turn, has been translated into the kind of Malay-Islamic actions and rhetoric that pervades Malay politics today.

There have been numerous examples in recent years of increased government response to these pressures. A regular visitor to Malaysia is struck by the increased time given Islamic subjects on nationally controlled television, the number of women wearing conservative Muslim dress (at one time encouraged in government offices), the greater emphasis on Islamic holidays, constant references to Islamic subjects in the printed media and by politicians, and the proliferation of organizations dealing with Islamic issues and projects. Here we can note three examples of these changes: Malaysia's involvement in the Islamic world, interest in Islamic economics, and the growth of *dakwah* movements.

Malaysia has not simply been the passive recipient of internationally defined ideas and movements. The government has taken advantage of its membership in the wider Islamic community to seek aid for domestic activities, such as the new international Islamic university. It has also attempted to reinforce the perception of its position as defender of the faith and as an important actor in the world of Islam. Malaysia has been a regular participant in a wide variety of international Islamic activities and has hosted numerous such gatherings, Quranic reading contests, and other interactions with the world Islamic community. These are often done with considerable style, such as the international Quranic reading contest that is televised nationally, attended by top UMNO politicians, and held in a large stadium. The government has also involved itself in international Muslim appeals, resolutions, and demands, such as those related to the Soviet Union's occupation of Afghanistan and Israel's activities on the West Bank. There has been some caution in handling such issues so as not to allow nongovernment Islamic groups to take advantage of them to develop their own organizations and goals.

Domestic Economic Issues

Islam and contemporary economic issues interact on two levels: efforts to improve the economic role of the *bumiputra* and recent rhetoric and actions to formulate Islamic economic policies. In the first instance, we return to an earlier discussion of the interplay of religion and ethnicity. Following the 1969 riots, the government of Malaysia set out to develop programs to increase the role of the Malay in the modern economy and to raise his social and economic position in the society. The centerpiece for this effort was the New Economic Policy, which called for the reduction and eventual eradication of poverty and acceleration in restructuring Malaysian society to reduce and eventually eliminate the identification of race with economic function.

To achieve these goals, a multifaceted program was initiated that included efforts to have national racial patterns more accurately reflected in employment and ownership in the modern sector. Thus employers were encouraged to have their work force at all levels reach approximately forty percent *bumiputra,* and strenuous efforts were made to bring ownership in the modern sector by the *bumiputra* from less than two percent in 1970 to thirty percent in 1990.[30] This is not the place to go into detail with regard to the complex set of programs used to implement these goals. Suffice it to state that among them were special subsidies to Malay businesses, training programs for indigenous entrepreneurs, priorities in obtaining contracts, education programs to increase Malay participation in business and modern technological pursuits, the formation of government and quasi-government institutions to aid the expansion of Malay capital, and so on.

The relationship between the betterment of the Malay under the NEP and Islam has not always been clearly articulated by the government, but it has not been lost on many Malay-Muslim politicians. Thus, UMNO tracts have urged the need to develop a more modern, competitive Muslim if Islam is to thrive in the modern world. If Islam is to be defended and develop, the Muslim must be able to compete with the Chinese and the Indians. Politicians have warned that attitudes and habits need to change to reflect more discipline, hard work, and innovation. These policies have been challenged by both the fundamentalists and traditionalists who both argue that this stress on materialism is injurious to Islamic principles or that it is creating class differences among the Malays, thus weakening the unity of the Malay-Islamic community. For some socialist-oriented fundamentalists, the NEP is also viewed as encouraging capitalist tenets and adherents within the Malay society. Certainly the success attained by the NEP at this point has brought more and more Malays into urban settings that challenged their traditional values. Urban attractions, the entrance of Malay women into the factory, and a weakening of ties with the more integrated rural community have all been of concern to those desiring to maintain the integrity of Malay-Islamic life.

A second and quite recent aspect of the interplay of religion and economics has been the attempt to move the state closer to what is perceived to be the tenets of Islam in the economic sphere. For a number of years there has been considerable discussion within UMNO, PAS, ABIM, and Muslim intellectuals of such issues as *zakat,* usury, insurance, lotteries, and banking. For example, when the question arose as to the use of revenues from lotteries to build mosques, a group of theologians were called in to decide the issue. It was agreed that such funds should go into general revenue and then be disbursed for such construction.[31] Until recently, these were issues that usually generated more rhetoric than action. In the past two years, a series of new, and some would argue largely symbolic, moves have been made. In 1982, an Islamic insurance company and Islamic pawnshops were approved. In 1983, the first no-interest Islamic bank was opened in Kuala Lumpur with great fanfare; major Malay politicians publicly deposited money in the new institution. Although there were earlier statements to the effect that a large number of banks would follow, it appears that the government intends moving cautiously. As the prime minister stated,

> There should not be any fear that suddenly there is the intrusion of a very radical system. It is not going to hurt anybody. But it will certainly satisfy a group of Moslems who feel that it is wrong for them to accept interest.[32]

One of the more interesting and, to many establishment politicians, most worrisome new actors has been the *dakwah* movement.[33] Certainly missionary activities in Islam are not new; their organizations have been about for centuries in Southeast Asia. However, in Malaysia today they are taking an active role beyond traditional conversion. At this time, there are two major types: those seeking to convert nonbelievers to Islam and the fundamentalists who seek to combine demands for social and economic change with missionary work among the Muslims themselves. In the first group, the most noteworthy organization has been Perkim, which has received funding from the government and overseas Muslims. Perkim not only has involved itself in proselytizing, but has also sought support for new converts in terms of economic aid as well as helping Muslims among the Indochinese refugees coming to Malaysia.[34]

It is the second type of *dakwah* movement that has led to some negative government reactions. Within this category there are a wide variety of organizations, including radical groups employing violent means to achieve their goals. Dural Arqam is interested in establishing a cooperative, communally oriented system among Muslims in economic, social, educational, and health areas; and the Jaamatul Tabligh is targeted in on Indian Muslims, for example. ABIM has received the most attention, however. Growing from less than 200 members when it was inaugurated in 1971, it now claims 35,000 or more. Under its former charismatic leader Anwar Ibrahim, the organization sought to move the Malay Muslim from his emphasis on ritual to a better understanding of the relationship of Islam to basic economic and social issues facing the nation. Ostensibly apolitical, nonetheless, its leadership has supported an Islamic state and economic and social reform within an Islamic mode, including attaining greater equity for all Malaysians. It has argued that the formation of an Islamic state would strengthen rather than weaken democratic society in Malaysia. These reformist goals, when combined with the strong attraction to the organization and its leadership among young educated Malays, is seen as a political danger by many within UMNO, particularly if ABIM and Anwar Ibrahim join with the opposition PAS. This problem has been partially ameliorated by co-opting Ibrahim into the government, where he has quickly risen to prominence. This has also led to some negative reactions among fundamentalists who feel that the pluralist designs of present UMNO leadership are unacceptable and PAS has made inroads into ABIM's strength on the campuses.

Conclusion

Malaysia remains a pluralist state in which the majority non-Muslim population can practice its own religion freely. But it is a state with a national flag showing the star and crescent, a Constitution that describes Islam as the official religion, a prime minister who gives highest priority to uniting Muslims, a government whose top ministers are all Muslims, and a national ideology, the Rukunegara, that is clarified by a government that claims it is the "sacred duty of a citizen to defend and uphold" a constitution that guarantees a special position to the Malays, the role of the sultans, and the maintenance of Islam as the official religion.[35] Not only is Malaysia a society in which ethnicity and religion have become intimately intertwined, but also one in which communal identification has been historically associated with geography, occupation, and economic position as well as rural-urban lifestyles. Finally, there is both an increasing sense of Malay-Islamic identity and of rapid modernization.

Within this changing and complex environment, several (perhaps inconsistent) patterns have developed. Each one puts added strain on a people attempting to form a nation out of a highly heterogeneous population.

1. There has been a slow weakening of the traditional syncretist practices and beliefs that have characterized village life in the past. Better education, mobility, communications, influence of "purer" Islamic views, and other broadening forces are making inroads into what was once a much more homogeneous belief system. Yet, this very mobility and modernization is helping to increase ethnic and religious identity among many Malays who are being confronted with new lifestyles and values as well as finding themselves in direct competition with the Chinese and Indians who have been the majority population of urban Malaysia. As more Malays leave the village or have modernization thrust upon them, there is likely to be a continued adverse reaction to those attributes of the new environment that are found undesirable.

2. The present prime minister, deputy prime minister, and minister of education all want to see the development of an Islam that looks beyond ritual. When he was deputy prime minister, Dr. Mahathir said,

> Unfortunately, there are still many of us who place more importance on form rather than on substance. Practices required by religion, such as brotherhood, pursuit of knowledge and equipping oneself for defense are unheeded. Priority is given to things like beard, turban, and robe.[36]

About the same time, then Prime Minister Hussein Onn criticized the narrow views of fundamentalist students educated abroad.[37]

Yet, the dilemma the government may find itself in is related to the extent to which the giving up of traditional and politically stable ritual for a more socially involved faith may open Pandora's box: that is, a more fragmented politicized Islam. After all, it was ABIM's "non-political" demands for reform based on Islam that frightened the government when Anwar Ibrahim was its head.

3. The political reality of UMNO/PAS politics necessitates continued support for at least symbolic rhetoric and actions in defense of Islam and the Malays. With PAS always ready to challenge moderate pluralistic policies as un-Islamic or un-Malay, the National Front leadership must maintain its public stance as the protector of Muslim and Malay interests. It is difficult to channel rising fundamentalism and Malay-Islamic identity while assuaging the fears of non-Muslims. However, to this point, the government appears ready to move cautiously toward a deeper commitment to domestic and international Islamic policies. Yet, some of these very policies, such as expanding Malay as the national language and bringing in more Malay-Muslims into the universities may lead to increasing interaction among communal groups. Thus, Malay, Indian, and Chinese youths can now be seen conversing and exchanging views with little apparent tension. In 1980, moderate student organizations won elections at the Universiti Kebangsaan and the University of Malaya, in part, because (as one successful candidate said), "We are not for one group or race, but all Malaysians."[38]

Much depends on whether young Islamic fundamentalists are willing to follow a more pluralistic approach or narrower Islamic goals, the government can channel religious demands, and non-Muslims can see their future in a Malay-dominated Malaysia with a commitment to protect the beliefs and goals of all its peoples.

The basic question for Malaysia remains to be answered: Can there be an increased development of a sense of Islamic identity while still maintaining the delicate communal balance that has made Malaysia the thriving nation it is today?

Notes

1. For the early history of Islam in the area, see G. Coedes, *The Indianized States of Southeast Asia,* Honolulu: East-West Press, 1969; R. Winstedt, *A History of Malay,* London: Luzac, 1934; and J. van Leur, *Indonesian Trade and Society,* The Hague: Van Hoeve, 1955.
2. See T. G. McGee, "Population: A Preliminary Analysis," in Wang Gungwu, *Malaysia,* New York: Praeger, 1964, pp. 67–81; and R. Jackson, *Immigrant Labour and the Development of Malaya, 1786–1920,* Kuala Lumpur: Government Press, 1961.
3. G. Means, "Malaysia: Islam in a Plural Society," in C. Caldarela, ed., *Religion and Societies: Asia and the Middle East,* Boston: Mouton, 1982, p. 482.

4. Tun Mustapha allegedly made active use of the Sabah state and party apparatus to pressure non-Muslims to convert. For a sympathetic view, see Tunku Abdul Rahman, "Mustapha," in *Viewpoints,* Kuala Lumpur: Heinemann, 1978, pp. 142–45.

5. *Malayan Constitutional Documents,* Vol. 1, Kuala Lumpur: Government Press, 1962, p. 124.

6. T. S. Chee, "Literary Responses and the Social Process," *Southeast Asian Journal of Social Science,* 3(1975), p. 87.

7. S. Siddique, "Some Malay Ideas on Modernization, Islam and Adat," M.A. thesis, University of Singapore, 1972, p. 27.

8. M. Nash, "Ethnicity, Centrality and Education in Pasir Mas," in W. Roff, ed., *Kelantan: Religion, Society and Politics in a Malay State,* Kuala Lumpur: Oxford University Press, 1974, p. 253.

9. R. Winzeler, "Malay Religion, Society and Politics in Kelantan," Ph.D. dissertation, University of Chicago, 1970, p. 79.

10. For a discussion of the role of non-Malay Muslims, see J. Nagata, "What Is a Malay? Situational Selection of Ethnic Identity in a Plural Society," *American Ethnologist,* 1(1974), pp. 331–50.

11. Winzeler, *op. cit.,* p. 77.

12. For discussions of traditional Islam, see Roff, *op. cit.,* Winzeler, *op. cit.;* and R. Wilkinson, "Malay Customs and Beliefs," *Journal of the Malayan Branch of the Royal Asiatic Society,* 30(1957). Monographs on Malay Subjects, No. 4.

13. More and more younger educated Malays are taking the *hajj,* although they may not use the title on their return.

14. For analyses of magic in Malay culture, see Winzeler, *op. cit.,* K. Endicott, *An Analysis of Malay Magic,* Oxford: Clarendon Press, 1970; and Wilkinson, *op. cit.*

15. For analyses and descriptions of contemporary political history related to communalism and party politics, see K. J. Ratnam, *Communalism and the Political Process in Malaya,* Kuala Lumpur: University of Malaya Press, 1956; G. Means, *Malaysian Politics,* London: Hodder and Stoughton, 1976; and R. Milne and D. Mauzy, *Politics and Government in Malaysia,* Vancouver: University of British Columbia Press, 1980.

16. Former Prime Minister Tunku Abdul Rahman once stated, "Our country has many races and unless we are prepared to drown every non-Malay, we can never think of an Islamic administration." Quoted in Ratnam, *op. cit.,* p. 122.

17. *Far Eastern Economic Review,* 24, 31 October 1980; and *Asiaweek,* 8 June 1979.

18. Interviews with Anwar Ibrahim, 1979, 1980, and 1983.

19. *Malayan Constitutional Documents, op. cit.,* pp. 27, 31.

20. *Far Eastern Economic Review,* 14 July 1983.

21. Quoted in E. Rosenthal, *Islam in the Modern National State,* Cambridge: Cambridge University Press, 1965, pp. 291–92. Rosenthal provides a description and analysis of constitutional and legal issues centering on Islam in Malaysia.

22. Quoted in Means, "Malaysia: Islam in a Plural Society," *op. cit.,* pp. 471–72.

23. See the *Star,* 12 December 1982, for the morals law controversy.

24. *Star,* 11 February 1983.

25. *New Straits Times,* 27 November 1982.

26. Ministry of Education, Malaysia, *Education in Malaysia,* Kuala Lumpur: Dewan Bahasa dan Pustaka, 1968, p. 6. For a history of education in Malaysia, see F. Wong Hoy Kee and Ee Tiang Hong, *Education in Malaysia,* Kuala Lumpur: Heinemann, 1971.

27. For a description of Muslim education in Kelantan, see Winzeler, *op. cit.,* pp. 123–30, 171–82, and 190–94.

28. I have discussed this in somewhat greater detail in Fred R. von der Mehden, "Islamic Resurgence in Malaysia," in J. Esposito, ed., *Islam and Development,* Syracuse: University of Syracuse Press, 1980, pp. 163–80.

29. For example, Prime Minister Mahathir called for a study of *dakwah* organizations to see which ones were "genuine" and the minister of information warned that, "Youths

especially should keep away from groups known for their deviationist practices," *New Straits Times,* 7 October 1980.

30. See G. Means, "'Special Rights' as a Strategy of Development," *Comparative Politics,* 5 (October 1972), pp. 29–61; Fred R. von der Mehden, "Communalism, Industrial Policy, and Income Distribution in Malaysia," *Asian Survey,* 15 (March 1975), pp. 250–65; D. Snodgrass, *Inequality and Economic Development in Malaysia,* Kuala Lumpur: Oxford University Press, 1980. The recent recession has necessitated a delay in the timetable.

31. See Wang Gungwu, *op. cit.,* p. 185.

32. Quoted in the *Asian Record,* 1982.

33. See S. Siddique, "The Dakwah Movement in Malaysia," forthcoming.

34. See Tunku Adbul Rahman, "Islam and Perkim," in *Viewpoints, op. cit.,* pp. 156–60.

35. See G. Means, "Special Rights' . . . ," *op. cit.,* p. 57.

36. *Asiaweek,* 1 August 1980, p. 23.

37. Even in the 1950s students returning from the Middle East were described as having an "almost unbelievable narrowness of religious feeling and Malay chauvinism." D. Moore, "The United Malay National Organization and the 1959 Malayan Elections," Ph.D dissertation, Berkeley: University of California, 1960.

38. *Asiaweek,* 1 August 1980, p. 25.

Selected Bibliography

Coedes, G. *The Indianized States of Southeast Asia.* Honolulu: East West Press, 1968.

Endicott, K. *An Analysis of Malay Magic.* Oxford: Clarendon Press, 1970.

Jackson, R. *Immigrant Labour and the Development of Malaya, 1786–1920.* Kuala Lumpur: Government Press, 1961.

Means, G. "Malaysia: Islam in a Plural Society," in C. Caldarela, ed., *Religion and Societies: Asia and the Middle East.* Boston: Mouton, 1982.

————. *Malaysian Politics.* London: Hodder and Stoughton, 1976.

————. "The Role of Islam in the Political Development of Malaysia," *Comparative Politics* 2(1969), pp. 264–84.

————. "'Special Rights' as a Strategy for Development: The Case of Malaysia." *Comparative Politics* 5(1972), pp. 29–61.

Milne, R., and Mauzy, D. *Politics and the Government of Malaysia.* Vancouver: University of British Columbia Press, 1980.

Moore, D. "The United Malays National Organization and the 1959 Malayan Elections." Ph.D. dissertation, Berkeley: University of California, 1960.

Nagata, J. *From Peasant Roots to Religious Values: The Reflowering of Malaysian Islam.* Vancouver: University of British Columbia Press, 1985.

Ratnam, K. J. *Communalism and the Political Process in Malaya.* Kuala Lumpur: University of Malaya, 1965.

Roff, W. *The Origins of Malay Nationalism.* New Haven: Yale University Press, 1967.

————, ed. *Kelantan: Religion, Society, and Politics in a Malay State.* Kuala Lumpur: Oxford University Press, 1974.

Rosenthal, E. *Islam in the Modern National State.* Cambridge: Cambridge University Press, 1965.

Snodgrass, D. *Inequality and Economic Development in Malaysia.* Kuala Lumpur: Oxford University Press, 1980.

von der Mehden, F. "Islamic Resurgence in Malaysia," in J. Esposito, *Islam and Development.* Syracuse: Syracuse University Press, 1980.

Wang, G. *Malaysia.* New York: Praeger, 1964.

Winzeler, R. "Modern Religion, Society and Politics in Kelantan." Ph.D. dissertation. University of Chicago, 1970.
Wilkinson, R. "Malay Customs and Beliefs." *Journal of the Malayan Branch of the Royal Asiatic Society.* 30(1957). Monographs on Malay Subjects, No. 4.
Winstedt, R. *A History of Malaya.* London: Luzac, 1934.

9

INDONESIA
Islam and Cultural Pluralism

ANTHONY H. JOHNS

Indonesia is an archipelago nation. It consists of over 1,000 inhabited islands and many more that are uninhabited. Of these, the most widely known are Sumatra, Java, Bali, Borneo, the Moluccas, and the Celebes. These islands enclose a kind of eastern Aegean; they abound in coves and estuaries and furnish numerous potential harbor sites for ships plying the trade routes between the Indian Ocean and the South China Sea.

In 1980, the population of Indonesia was almost 150 million, making it the third largest nation in Asia.[1] This population consists of peoples generally described as being of Malay stock. "Malay Stock" is a term that covers a wide range of ethnic groups, such as the Acehnese, the Bataks, and the Minangkabau of Sumatra; the Javanese and Balinese; and the Makassarese and Torajas of Sulawesi—all distinguished from each other by language, social structure, preferred occupations, and religious traditions. Of these islands, Java is the most densely peopled, being the home of about 80 million people, that is, more than half of the nation's total population. Among the various ethnic groups, at least 250 mutually unintelligible languages are spoken, most of them related. There is, however, a single national language, Bahasa Indonesia, a modern form of Malay. This is the language of public life, education, and modern national culture. Many of the ethnic languages, however, maintain their literary traditions alongside their role in the home and at the village level and in some regions, notably Java, still remain the vehicle for great cultural and artistic traditions, such as the Javanese shadow theater.

Over 130 million Indonesians are Muslims. The remainder of the population are Christians (6 milllion), Hindu Balinese (2.5 million), and smaller groups of adherents of Buddhism, local mystical cults, and primal religions.[2] Indonesia, then, has more Muslims than any other nation in the world.

Nevertheless, there is not one but many Muslim communities in Indonesia. Although all follow the *Shafi'i* school of law, regional loyalties are still vigorous and in some cases primary. The influence of premodern, prenational history in many areas is still strong. Furthermore, from region to region there are great variations between what has been called the scope and focus of Islamic awareness. Responses to Islam include adherence to a fundamentalist scripturalism, the elaboration of complex syncretic theosophies, the absorption of Islamic elements into primal religions, the eclecticism of intellectuals, and combinations of all of these.

In brief, the formula "There is no God but the God" is accepted widely, yet there are great variations in the measure of exclusiveness attached to this profession of faith and to the way in which the legal obligations of the religion, as set out in the law books, are put into practice.

Even so, an Islamic ambience, though often low-key is unmistakable, even to the casual observer, whether from the sound of the call to prayer at dawn in every suburb of Jakarta and other great cities (the purity of the muezzin's voice distorted by loudspeakers) or from the hundreds of smaller mosques and prayer houses scattered throughout the countryside along every main and minor road.

This ambience however is not reflected in the composition of the Indonesian Parliament, a legislative body consisting of both nominated and elected members. The elected members are chosen by universal suffrage and belong to one or another of three parties: Golkar (acronym for Golongan Karya), a coalition of functional groups, such as government employee and businessmen's organizations; the Indonesian Democratic Party (Partia Demokrasi Indonesia [PDI]); and the United Development Party (Partai Persatuan Pembangunan [PPP]). Golkar, the government party, holds a majority of seats, 244 in the current Parliament (1985); the PDI holds 24, and the PPP holds 96. None of these parties has an Islamic title, none campaigns on the basis of its identification with a religion. Equally significant is the fact that in the 1971 general elections, before religion-based political parties were abolished, Muslim parties won less than one third of the seats contested.[3] There is, thus, the paradox that, despite the huge Muslim population, Indonesia is not an Islamic state, Islam is not the state religion, and today there is not even a political party identified by its commitment to an Islamic ideology.

On the other hand, it is not a secular state either. Constitutionally it is a unitary state that embodies and exemplifies a state philosophy called the Pancasila (Five Principles). In the preamble to the Constitution, these are set out as belief in the one Supreme God; a just and civilized humanity; the unity of Indonesia; democracy led by the wisdom of unanimity arising from deliberations among representatives of the people, and social justice for the whole people of Indonesia.

The moral basis of the state, then, resides not in any one religion, but in this state philosophy which all religious traditions are required to recognize as the sole ideological basis of the state. Religious allegiance, therefore, is irrelevant to citizenship. All citizens are citizens of the state in the same way and on the same basis and all religious communities receive the support of the administrative and financial resources of a Ministry of Religion.

The acceptance of religious and cultural pluralism then is a fact of Indonesian public life, and for most Indonesians it is a matter for pride. This pluralism, however, does not indicate indifference on the part of the state to the needs of Islam if its ritual, legal, and social identity is to be maintained. Alongside the state secular educational system, there is a parallel Muslim education system that offers comprehensive training in the Islamic disciplines to ensure the continuing availability of specialists to meet the legal, educational, and spiritual needs of the community. At the tertiary level (in 1979) there were no less than 82 Islamic religious faculties affiliated with 14 Islamic state universities.[4] The graduates of these institutions either find employment in the bureaucracy of religious administration, in Islamic courts, or as teachers and educationalists. A significant number go overseas to study at religious institutions in the Middle East, notably the Azhar in Cairo, but it is becoming increasingly common for such students to seek higher degrees in secular universities in the United States, Canada, and Australia. These state institutions, however, are only part of the story of religious education, for there is a wide range of teaching and devotional institutions scattered throughout the country (*pesantren* in Java, *surau* in Sumatra) that are independent of the government system and rely largely on the initiative and charisma of local teachers and the contributions of local communities.[5]

The state legal system makes provision for the administration of Islamic family law alongside the secular courts that handle civil and criminal matters, Islamic courts being one of the four instruments of the legal system.[6]

The level of personal religious devotion, although it varies from region to region is high. The daily ritual prayers and the Friday congregational prayer are well observed. The fast of Ramadan is widely kept, even by many who are negligent of the daily prayers. This cannot be documented statistically. There are however statistics for the pilgrimage. In 1983–84 there were no less than 49,946 pilgrims. Although this figure represents a decline in the numbers in the two previous years—doubtless due to economic factors and other variables—the figures are impressive: they demonstrate clearly how, despite the distance and costs involved, the rite of the pilgrimage is fully integrated into Indonesian Muslim life.

All in all relations between Islam, the state, and the non-Muslim communities in Indonesia may appear idyllic. In fact, the present position represents a precarious balance of tensions that ultimately derives from a complex dialectic of historical development that can be documented from the thirteenth century.

Historical Background

The relation of the Indonesian past to the present is frequently misunderstood. In part this is because the name Indonesia is misleading. It suggests a homogenous political entity with a long history of relatively stable political frontiers that at a critical period of its history fell under Dutch rule and in August 1945 regained a lost independence. Indonesia is, rather, a new nation, in some respects an artificial and unlikely nation, that has grown out of the diverse world of the East Indian islands in response to two great pressures: Dutch colonial rule and the Japanese occupation.

Islam first made its appearance as a political force in the Indies in the form of port city states at the turn of the thirteenth century. This development followed the establishment of Muslim control of the Indian Ocean trading system. The earliest of these states was Pasai on the east coast of North Sumatra. It was followed by Malacca on the Malay Peninsula in the fifteenth century, Aceh in North Sumatra, Banten and a number of other centers on the north coast of Java in the sixteenth century, and Makassar in the seventeenth century. In the seventeenth century, too, inland Muslim states, such as that of Minangkabau in Central Sumatra and Mataram in Central Java were established.

Such states swiftly became integrated into the system of international trade that linked the eastern Mediterranean Sea, the Indian Ocean, and the China Sea, bringing the Indies into contact with the Chinese fleets of the Sung dynasty, and the Moghul and Ottoman empires. Participation in this system took local peoples as far afield as the Persian Gulf, East Africa, and Constantinople (Istanbul). It likewise provided the economic base for participation in the ritual of the pilgrimage and the means to travel to, and study at, the great centers of Islamic learning.

These city-states were often rivals. They had their own cultural personalities largely determined by the manner of their adaptation to the belief systems and social traditions of the environment in which they developed, a process that often set up tensions between the norms of Islamic jurisprudence as understood by the newcomers and the traditional way of life of the local peoples.

The Dutch East India Company established itself as a political and economic power in the region with the founding of Batavia in 1619. Its enforcement of a monopoly over international trade and skillful intervention in regional quarrels led through the years to an increasing dominance over its client states and eventually to the rule of the Dutch crown over the territories that now comprise Indonesia.

Disagreements between Muslims provided opportunities for the Dutch to serve their own political and economic interests. The Wahhabi-style reform movement launched in Central Sumatra in 1803 by scholars returning from Mecca and the resistance it provoked provided an opportunity for the Dutch to intervene on the side of the status quo. Similar internal rivalries contributed to a Dutch victory in the Java War (1826–30) and later in the long, bitterly fought Aceh War (1873–1910). These wars further illustrate the deep divisions created by the demands of scripturalist Islam. The Dutch could not have fought and won these wars had they not had allies or been requested as allies by Muslim groups fearing and resisting the claims of other Muslims bent on imposing a more rigorous application of Islamic law.

This extension of Dutch rule in the long term had many consequences on the social, cultural, and economic life of the region: in its integration into the economic system of the Western world, in the establishment of Western bureaucratic procedures, in the introduction of Western education, in the printing and distribution of books and newspapers, and in the generation of important, if not large, minorities of Protestant and Catholic Christians, especially in those areas that in the nineteenth century had not yet accepted Islam—for example, the Batak regions of North Sumatra to the east and south of Medan; in parts of Java; in the Lesser Sunda Islands, such as Flores and Sumbawa; and in Central and North Sulawesi.

The Emergence of Religious and Secular Organizations, 1908–45

It was through Western education that the ideas of nineteenth-century European nationalism and the concept of a secular state reached the Indies. These ideas found a fertile environment. From the early 1900s, there began to appear secular and religious associations, organized along Western lines.

From the nationalist point of view, the foundation in 1908 of the Javanese cultural organization, Budi Utomo (Noble Endeavor), is a landmark. It was modern in that it was organized along the lines of a Dutch association. It was also secular. The articles published in its journal were mostly written in Dutch but there were a few in Malay. Thus it was not directed exclusively to the Javanese. It represented a response to Dutch rule by the Western-educated intelligentsia wishing to demonstrate that they also had a culture—one that was a counterpart to that of the Dutch—and that they had a loyalty to, and took pride in, that culture.

Muslim responses to these new ideas continued the dialectic between rigorously scripturalist and accommodationist understandings of Islam.

A Muslim counterpart to Budi Utomo appeared in 1912 with the foundation of the Muhammadiyya. It was directly inspired by the reformist ideas of Muhammad Abduh and Rashid Rida in Cairo. Without argument, it is the most vigorous and stable association ever to appear in the Indies. Like Budi Utomo, it was organized on Western lines. It followed the example and learned from the experience of missionary organizations, founding its own network of schools, teachers' colleges, hospitals, and orphanages by which it both met social needs and spread the reformist message. Today, it is still the most prominent nongovernment educational and social welfare institution in the country, having survived the Japanese occupation, the struggle for independence, and the social upheavals of 1965. One of its secrets for survival has been its skill in distancing itself as an organization from any kind of political activity, whatever the views of its members as individuals.

Another Muslim organization, Sarekat Islam (Islamic Federation) appeared in the same year. It grew out of an organization known as the Islamic Traders Federation, and its goal was to improve facilities and opportunities for indigenous traders. Unlike the Muhammadiyya, it was thoroughly political in orientation. It capitalized on widespread discontent and developed into Indonesia's first mass movement. By 1920, it had a membership of over a million members.

It is characteristic of the continuing dialectic in the thinking of Indonesian Muslims that in 1922 Sarekat Islam broke into two parts: a left wing and an Islamic wing. The left wing became the nucleus of Indonesia's first political party, the Partai Komunis Indonesia (Indonesian Communist Party [PKI]), and the Islamic wing became the first Islamic political party, albeit a minor one, Partai Serikat Islam Indonesia (Indonesian Islamic Federation Party [PSII]).

In 1926, there appeared a Muslim organization of much greater significance, the Nahdatul-Ulama (Revival of the Ulama). It was a response on the part of Muslim traditionalists to the increasing influence of the reformist movement. The traditionalists believed that by its rejection of the authority of the four schools of the law and by direct recourse of every *mujtahid* to the Quran and Sunna, the reformist movement was undermining the traditional authority of the *ulama*. Also, through its passing of the formulations of the traditional schools of law, it was also abandoning the complex system of checks and balances evolved over the centuries that made possible cultural compromise and adaptation. It was a party that was to play a major role in the 1950s and 1960s. Both the PSII and the Nahdatul Ulama (NU) were to maintain an independent political profile from 1948 and 1950, respectively, until 1973, when their political activities were subsumed into the PPP.

It was in the early 1920s that the term *Indonesia* began to establish itself as the indigenous name for the territories of the Dutch East Indies. Perhaps at this stage it seemed a little highbrow, for it was pioneered by an intellectual elite. Certainly, in Batavia at that time, local people asked to define their ethnicity would simply reply "Slam!" ("Islam!") But the terms *Indonesia* and *Indonesian* continued to grow in popularity until, in 1928, the idea and ideal of Indonesia as a modern state was formulated and proclaimed at an all Indies Youth Conference. This was the occasion on which delegates representing some five hundred members of regional organizations made a pledge of loyalty to one fatherland, Indonesia; one language, Bahasa Indonesia; and asserted themselves to be one people, the Indonesian people. The European origin of this concept of nationalism, based on language, land, and people, is plain. The pledge was a decisive public formulation of an Indonesian nationalism. It was secular. It envisaged Indonesia as a nation for all who made their commitment to it, without regard to ethnic origin or religious allegiance.

At this time, the nationalist movement was very much an elitist, Western-educated entity. It developed little during the 1930s. For one thing, it was kept firmly under control by the Dutch government, who did not hesitate to exile nationalist leaders, such as Sukarno, who were politically active. For another, popular loyalties, despite widespread resentment of the Dutch, retained a regional focus. The same was largely true of Muslim perceptions of self-identity.

The concept of an Indonesian nation was, nevertheless, an authentic indigenous response to the Dutch occupation of the archipelago, and the Japanese invasion in 1942 was to provide both the occasion and the means by which this idea was fructified and its potential placed within the nationalist grasp.

Japanese long-term planning was for the emergence of an independent Indonesia, as a younger brother to Japan that would be devoted to the best interests of the Greater East Asia Co-Prosperity Sphere. Toward this goal, the Japanese used all their powers of propaganda. Because it was impractical to teach large numbers of the population Japanese, the occupiers used Bahasa Indonesia as a language of government and indoctrination, thus giving it a distribution, status, and role that it would not have achieved for many years had Dutch rule continued. Thus, although the Japanese did not create the independence movement, let alone the idea of an Indonesian nation, the existence of such a nation was in their interests. Accordingly, they returned Sukarno and other nationalist leaders from exile. Sukarno rapidly assumed a national role as a secular nationalist leader, and the charismatic appeal of his personality and rhetoric ensured that he had no rival.

But the Japanese also envisaged a role for Islam in gaining the kind of popular support they needed, both for forwarding their political policies and for the continuation of the war in Asia and the Pacific. For several years prior to their invasion, they had made a study of Islam and prepared a carefully thought-out Islamic policy. They presented themselves as liberators of Islam, taking care to exploit Muslim anti-Dutch feelings. They used Islamic teachers and the network of Islamic schools as ready-made instruments of mass indoctrination. They cultivated Muslim leaders and, at least tacitly, encouraged Muslim aspirations for an eventual Islamic state of Indonesia.

Even so, although recognizing the potential of Islam as a means of popular manipulation, the Japanese were aware of the potential dangers if such a powerful force were not kept under tight control. Thus, in 1943, they brought together all existing Muslim organizations into a single federation to be known by the acronym Masyumi (Majlis Syura Muslimin Indonesia [Consultative Council of Indonesian Muslims]). This federation was in many ways a two-edged sword: Although it gave the Japanese the central authority they required, it gave to the Muslim groups a unity and national stature that they had not previously enjoyed.[8]

The Struggle for a State Ideology, 1945–73

In early 1945, the Japanese were forced to recognize the possibility that they would lose the war, and they began to set in motion their plans to establish an independent Indonesia. They established a committee of sixty-two members (The Committee of 62) to discuss the ideological basis and structure of the new nation. This committee became the forum in which secular nationalists and Muslim groups confronted each other; thus, the public role of Islam in the state emerged as a major constitutional problem.

At the first meeting of the committee on May 29, 1945, the debate on the nature of the state began. It centered on three issues: whether the state should be unitary or federal; whether the state should be a republic or a monarchy—under this issue was discussed the designation of the head of state (significantly, two members suggested Imam as the title); and the relationship between the state and religion.

One of the first speakers was Mohammad Hatta, a Sumatran and personally devout Muslim who, in August 1945, was to become the first vice president of the republic. He urged that Indonesia should be a unitary state; if so, it necessarily followed that state and religion should be kept separate.

A Javanese member of the committee, Supomo, supported him. He argued:

> Creating an Islamic state in Indonesia would mean we are not creating a unitary state. To create an Islamic state in Indonesia would mean setting up a state that would associate itself with the largest religious group in the state, the Islamic. This would create problems with Christians and other minorities, for although an Islamic state would safeguard the interests of such groups, they would not be able to feel involved in the state. The ideals of an Islamic state are not in accordance with the ideals of a unitary state which we all have so passionately longed for.

He, nevertheless, went on to stress:

> A national unitary state does not mean a state with an a-religious character ... no, this national unitary state is to have a lofty moral base, such as is also advocated by Islam.[9]

It was the tenor of these ideas that led Sukarno on June 1, 1945, to make a speech later described as marking the birth of the Pancasila. In it, he set out the Five Principles stated earlier, but with slightly different wording: belief in one God, nationalism, humanism, social justice, and democracy. These principles had meaning for the adherents of every religious tradition in the nation, but they were not exclusively the monopoly of any one of them.

This, indeed, was Sukarno's purpose. Although Indonesia should not be an Islamic state, it should not be a secular one either. Rather, Indonesia should have a religious state philosophy based on belief in God through which the ideals of every religious denomination could be realized. As such, this state philosophy was fully consistent with the aspirations of the secular nationalists that derived from the youth pledge of 1928, and it was in this light that this philosophy's challenge to the competing ideology of an Islamic state must be understood.

This plea notwithstanding, the proposal of a state based on these five principles as the alternative to an Islamic state—presented with all the force of Sukarno's personality and rhetorical skill—was seen by Muslim groups as an affront, and the atmosphere became dangerously tense. In an attempt to defuse the situation, Sukarno referred the matter to a subcommittee to work out a compromise formula. On June 22, the committee produced a document, later to be known as the Jakarta Charter, which it was hoped would commend wide enough acceptance to serve as a preamble to a constitution. It read:

> The constitution of the Indonesian state which is to exist in the form of the Republic of Indonesia, and to be based upon the sovereignty of the people, is founded on the following principles: Belief in God, "with the obligation for adherents of Islam to practice Islamic law," the principle of righteous and moral humanitarianism; the unity of Indonesia, and democracy led by the mutual deliberations of a representative body which will lead to social justice for the entire people.

For Muslim members of the subcommittee, the crucial phrase was, "with the obligation for adherents of Islam to practice Islamic Law" *("dengan kewajiban menjalankan Syari'at Islam bagi pemeluk-pemeluknya")*. In Bahasa Indonesia, this phrase consists of seven words, and in subsequent discussion was to be referred to simply as "the seven words."

Despite these early hopes, when the document was submitted to the main committee, Christian representatives expressed doubts about the implications these seven words might have for non-Muslim communities. Western-educated Muslims, too, had misgivings. Hoesein Djajadiningrat, a distinguished scholar and the first Indonesian head of the Office for Religious Affairs, objected to these seven words saying, "They may well create fanaticism, because it seems that Muslims will be forced to keep the *shariah*." Other Muslim members of the committee, however, believed that such fears were unfounded, and that to omit them would be unacceptable to the Muslim community.

Discussion became increasingly embittered: Some speakers believed

that "the seven words" went too far in their concession to Muslim ideological pressures, others that they did not go far enough. Sukarno, in an
attempt to retrieve the situation, pleaded with the secular nationalists
that for the sake of the Republic, they accept both "the seven words" and
the provision that the president be a born Indonesian and a Muslim.
Despite misgivings, his plea was given a grudging acceptance.

Sukarno and Hatta jointly proclaimed Indonesian independence on
August 17 in a brief statement that made no reference to Islam. The following day, when a new preparatory committee met to work out in more
detail matters relating to a constitution, the question of "the seven
words" was again discussed. The constitutional position was now seen in
a new light. The highest priority was to safeguard the unity of the nation.
With this in mind, the committee decided that Indonesia could only be
and remain a unitary state if its constitution made no reference to Islam.
Thus, both "the seven words" and the provision that the president be a
Muslim were omitted. True, the expression "belief in God" was
expanded to "belief in the one and only God," but to avoid any identification of the state with Islam, the Arabic word for preamble, *muqad-
dima,* was replaced by *pembukaan* (preface), and at the suggestion of a
representative from Bali, the word *Allah,* in the expression "Grace of
Almighty God," was replaced by *Tuhan.* Within a day of the proclamation of independence, the Jakarta Charter had been abandoned. For the
Muslim groups who had pressed so hard for its inclusion in a constitution, this was a bitter defeat, and in the years following this defeat, "the
Charter" became mythologized as the Islamic keystone of a constitution
that had been treacherously cast aside.

The result among these Muslims was a deep sense of disillusionment
with the new nation, a disillusionment that was within three years to lead
to the outbreak of civil war and the proclamation of a *dar al-Islam*
(domain of Islam) in three provinces. The first outbreak of violence was
in the mountains of West Java. After a series of skirmishes, Kartosuwirjo
as leader of a dissident group of Muslims, on August 7, 1949, proclaimed
an Islamic State of Indonesia (with himself as *Imam*) at war with the
Republic of Indonesia. The justification for his act was that a secular
authority had been set up over Islam. The government of the republic,
by rejecting Islam as the sole foundation of the state, had made itself as
evil an enemy as the Dutch. So far from fighting the Dutch to defend a
non-Islamic republic, Kartosuwirjo and his Islamic army mounted an all-
out attack on the Sukarno/Hatta government. The timing of the revolt
was not accidental. It was launched ten days before the fourth anniversary of the proclamation of the republic, and during a period when the
republican government was militarily hard-pressed as a result of the
Dutch second police action, which had begun on December 17, 1948.
And when the Siliwangi, one of the republic's crack regiments was forced
to withdraw from Central to West Java, the *dar al-Islam* forces caused
them as many, if not more casualties, than did the Dutch. But, and this

is the crucial point in the dialectic of Muslim activism in Indonesia, the West Javanese peasantry largely remained loyal to the republic and regarded the republican troops of the Siliwangi regiment as much their deliverers from Kartosuwirjo's followers as from the Dutch.

Kartosuwirjo's movement gradually disintegrated after the mid-1950s; by the time that he was captured and executed in 1962, his followers were little more than a few bands of terrorists. Early in the 1950s, however, his cause and his charisma exercised a wide appeal.

In 1952, he inspired an Islamic rising in South Sulawese, commissioning Kahar Muzakkar, an army officer, as commander of what was styled the Fourth Division of the Islamic Army of Indonesia, to lead an Islamic rebellion that lasted until 1965.

Even more serious for the republic, in September 1953, an Acehnese leader, Daud Beureu'eh, followed Kartosuwirjo's example and proclaimed an Islamic State in Aceh as part of the Islamic State of Indonesia and headed by Kartosuwirjo, who in 1955 appointed him vice-president. Daud Beureu'eh was to make a negotiated settlement with the central government gaining special status for Aceh in 1962.[10]

Some idea of the thinking and aspirations of these Islamic rebels may be gathered from the text of Daud Beureu'eh's proclamation:

> In the name of Allah we the people of Aceh have made new history, for we wish to set up an Islamic State here on our native soil. . . . For many long years we have been hoping and yearning for a state based on Islam, but . . . it has become increasingly evident . . . that some Indonesian leaders are trying to steer us onto the wrong path. . . . The basic principles of the Republican state do not guarantee freedom of religion, freedom to have a religion in the real sense of the word. . . . [T]he Islamic religion which makes the life of society complete cannot be split up. For us, the mention of principle of Belief in One God [in the Pancasila] is nothing more than a political manoevre. Belief in the One God is for us the very source of social life, and every single one of its directives must apply here on Indonesian soil. It is not possible for only some of these directives to apply while others do not, be this in criminal or civil affairs, in the question of religious worship, or in matters of everyday life. If the Law of God does not apply (in its entirety), this means we are deviating from belief in the One God.[11]

These revolts give some idea of the strength of Muslim aspirations in Indonesia that were frustrated by the abandonment of the Jakarta Charter. Equally, however, they illustrate the strength of commitment of the majority of Indonesians to the concept of the state as it had been proclaimed by Sukarno and Hatta in 1945. These very serious uprisings, which threatened the integrity, not to say existence, of the state, were in the last resort put down by Muslim soldiers under a Muslim president who rejected the concept of a Muslim state. The experience of these rebellions and this bitterness, however, was sufficient to show the secular nationalists that the security and stability of the state required an understanding of the sensitivities of Muslim political ideologues. Although there was no compromise as to the state ideology, it was necessary to exercise great care in the handling of issues that could provide a focus for Muslim reaction; and although political Islam could be domesticated within a political structure, there were matters that needed to be treated with understanding and respect.

Muslim Parties in the Sukarno Period

The proclamation of Indonesian independence in 1945 was soon followed by the establishment of a provisional parliament and the commencement of political activities by a large number of competing parties. Among these parties—some religious, some secular—Masyumi was in a strong position. Late in 1945, it had reconstituted itself as a political organization and its leader, Mohammad Natsir, was for a time prime minister. The Masyumi, however, as has been mentioned, was a federation of Islamic parties and organizations that had been forcibly brought together; each had its own policies and plans for the future. Soon the strains began to show. First, in 1948, the Partai Sarekat Islam withdrew, to campaign in its own right and under its own emblem. Then, as the reformists under Natsir continued their efforts to dominate the federation, the Nahdatul Ulama, the Java-based traditionalist party broke away in 1950, also to campaign under its own emblem. This left the Masyumi to become the political vehicle of the reformist movement, which took over the name virtually by default.

The fact is that the gap between the traditionalists and the reformists was very deep. It was not simply the issue, so often publicly stated, as to whether Indonesia should be an Islamic state based on one or another of the four schools of Muslim Law or based simply on the Quran and the Sunna. It was also a matter of tactics and style. In political terms, this meant on the part of the Nahdatul Ulama a readiness to compromise with the political status quo, to tolerate Sukarno's increasigly radical nationalism and left-wing sympathies, and to participate in successive coalition governments that shared his views. By so doing, of course, they ensured that they were in a position of strength vis-à-vis the reformists. The Masyumi, on the other hand, would not compromise. It refused, on principle, to have any association with a government that included Communist fellow travelers, and it resented Sukarno's broad religious sympathies, his political policies, and his personal lifestyle. In international relations, its policies were pro-Western. It was led by individuals whose personal formation reflected the rationalist emphases of Islam, stressed by Muhammad Abduh, people who attributed Western success to rationalism and techniques of administration that could be taken over by Islamic organizations to ensure their stability and enhance their effectiveness. The party attracted and, indeed, formed a particular type of personality: individuals educated in secular subjects as well as in the principles of religion, many of whom were graduates of Muhammadiyya schools and were enthusiastic, uncomplicated, honest, and hardworking. It is not altogether misleading to call them the Puritans of Islam, for their concern was to realize, in as authentic a manner as possible, the sacred law of Islam.[12]

The Masyumi party, like the Muhammadiyya, had a highly effective public relations machine. It welcomed Western visitors, it created the impression of openness and tolerance, and it had a variety of well-produced brochures and pamphlets. It attracted visiting academics, especially Americans, and insofar as Indonesia was known abroad, it was regarded as a representative of Indonesian Islam, wholesomely anti-Communist and worthy of support. It had, however, its dark side. It was not able to bring itself to condemn without reservation the *dar al-Islam* rebellions, and there were bodies associated with it linked with attempts on Sukarno's life. It is not an exaggeration to say that the reformist ethos tended (and tends) to produce an inflexibility of personality and a fondness for black-and-white judgments that, in a sense, is felt to be "un-Indonesian," especially in Java. The Nahdatul Ulama was then traditionalist in more ways than one, and on the national and international scenes it had a lower profile than the Masyumi.

Nevertheless, the Masyumi, which in the provisional parliament had forty-four seats, was expected to do well and perhaps win an outright majority in the first general elections in 1955. It was a well-known name at the national level and thanks to its umbrella-type role during the Japanese occupation expected to be identified as the Muslim party par excellence. There was general astonishment, then, when the Masyumi won only fifty-seven seats (the same number as the secular Indonesian Nationalist party) and when the underrated Nahdatul 'Ulama,' which in the provisional parliament had had a mere eight seats, won a totally unexpected forty-five seats. This was more than sufficient to exclude the Masyumi from any of the spoils of power when it gave its support to a government headed by the Nationalist party, as did the Communist party and several minor parties. The preelection estimate of the national importance of the Masyumi had been inflated.

Many of the Masyumi leaders were bitter at the results of these elections. The Islamic parties were collectively only a minority in the new Parliament, and their own party had lost its commanding position and right to speak on behalf of Islam in Indonesia. A common reaction was to refer to the Indonesian Nationalist party, taking the initials of its name in Bahasa Indonesia (PNI) as Partai Nafik Indonesia, the Indonesian Hypocritical party, and to attribute the success of the Nahdatul Ulama to the influence of old-fashioned religious teachers over a simpleminded Javanese peasantry.

In view of the electoral shock the party had received, such responses were understandable. But, in effect, the Masyumi was reduced to impotence and frustration. Its already inflexible positions hardened and inevitably led to its removal from the mainstream of Indonesian political life.

As a result of its implacable rejection of Sukarno's policies, his person, and his Communist supporters, the Masyumi found itself progressively more isolated. In desperation, it gave its support (along with the CIA) to the regional revolts that broke out in 1958 that aimed to secure greater regional autonomy in Sumatra and Sulawesi and to replace the Sukarno government (Hatta had resigned as vice president in 1957) with one that would pursue pro-Western and anti-Communist policies. The revolts were crushed, and the Masyumi was banned in 1960.[13]

The Nahdatul Ulama, on the other hand, by its flexibility, continued to remain part of the establishment. The price was high. As Sukarno grew increasingly out of touch with reality, his demands for adulation became more insistent. The Nahdatul Ulama complied with these demands, praising his utterances in a way that was often psychophantic and attributing to him the wisdom of the Prophet Muhammad himself.

The New Order Regime

The attempted Communist coup of 1965 is a watershed in modern Indonesian history. It brought about the fall of Sukarno and in its wake caused terrible bloodshed. The Communist party and its sympathizers were eliminated and General Suharto became president. He assembled a body of technocrats to rebuild the economy and modernize the country, inaugurating what became known as the New Order: a government with the avowed aim of restoring the nation's confidence in itself and ensuring stability, even if authoritarian methods were needed.

Members of the Masyumi had high expectations that their party would be rehabilitated under this New Order. They had been consistent and determined opponents of the Communists for many years. They had suffered considerably, particularly between 1960 and 1965, as a result of denunciations and insults in the government-controlled press and of intimidation and physical violence by left-wing and radical nationalist youth groups. Given all this and the role Muslim irregular paramilitary teams had played in crushing the Communists, it seemed that a new opportunity had come for Islam, as represented by the Masyumi, to have a major role in government, and to ensure for Islam the place that it deserved as the religion of the vast majority of the population, by restoring the "seven words" to the pride of place they deserved in the Constitution.

As early as December 1965, a federation was formed of sixteen organizations that had been associated with the Masyumi. This federation set up a committee to explore ways and means of rehabilitating the party. Before it could submit any proposals however, the government with the army's backing issued a warning that it would take action against any individual or group disloyal either to the Pancasila as state ideology or the Constitution of 1945. It mentioned by name such bodies as the *dar al-Islam* movement, the Islamic Indonesian army, the Indonesian Communist party and the Masyumi! In January 1967, General Suharto refused to consider any representations on behalf of the Masyumi.[14] Suharto himself, though a Muslim, regarded the politically militant understanding of Islam that the Masyumi embraced as a danger to the nation. In his view, the Pancasila was central to Indonesian unity, and he was determined to make the Pancasila state ideology so firmly entrenched that no competing system of ideas could dislodge it. Islam, then, was to have full expression as a religious, cultural, and social complex of ideas and values, but not as a political ideology that could compete with that sponsored by the state.

For many of those associated with the Masyumi, the government backing of the Pancasila was tantamount to according an ideology devised by humans precedence over the divine revelation of Islam. For such as these, the only acceptable state was an Islamic state or, at the very least, a state based on Islam. The denial of the right to campaign for such a state was a denial of democracy. Thus, despite rebuffs, the Masyumi continued the struggle to reestablish its influence, albeit in a different form. In 1967, some of its members took the initiative to establish a new Muslim party, an umbrella-type organization, known as the Indonesian Muslims' Party (Partai Muslimin Indonesia [PMI]).[15]

Relations with the government were not the only cause of tension and frustration among the more radical Muslim groups. In the wake of the terrible trauma of 1965–66, there had been a remarkable growth in the number of conversions to religions other than Islam, especially in Central Java. Hinduism and Buddhism gained new adherents, and the numbers of people turning to mystical Javanese cults and Christianity increased dramatically. In 1931, Christians were 2.8 percent of the population of the Indies; in 1971, they were almost 7.4 percent, an increase not to be explained in terms of natural growth—a significant part of this increase being post-1965. This was most striking in Central Java, where in 1971, Christians amounted to 11.6 percent of the urban population.[16]

These conversions, although from among nominal Muslims and adherents of primal religions aroused resentment, and Islamic magazines denounced the government for policies that, it was alleged, were leading to the Christianization of Indonesia. Plots to Christianize the nation were seen in the most unlikely quarters: the best selling novels of an Indonesian Chinese, Marga T, whose heroes and heroines exemplified Christian virtues, were seen as evidence of one such conspiracy. For the first time in a generation, there were serious outbreaks of violence against Christians, in South Sulawesi and West Java.

These disturbances further served to convince the government of the importance of the Pancasilas the state ideology and of the need to depoliticize expressions of religious belief. It decided to do this as part of a plan to reduce the number of political parties. The general elections of 1971 were contested by nine parties (there had been over forty in the 1955 elections). Of these nine, four were Muslim parties: PMI won 24 seats, Nahdatul Ulama 58, PSII 10, and a small traditionalist party, Partai Tarbia Islam, won 2 seats—in all 94 Muslim political party seats in a chamber of more than 350 seats. In 1973, the government merged these four parties into a single body identified by a name that had nothing to do with religious affiliation, the United Development party (Partai Persatuan Pembangunan [PPP]). At the same time, it merged five minority parties, including the Catholic party, the Protestant party, and the rump of the former Indonesian Nationalist party to form the Indonesian Democratic party (Partai Demokrasi Indonesia [PDI]).[17] Apart from Golkar, only the PPP and the PDI remained. At a single stroke, the number of parties competing for votes at elections was reduced to three and religion ceased to define any political party ideology. As had the PMI, the new federation of Muslim parties, with its secular title, was set the task of working out internal difficulties so complex and personal rivalries within it so deep that its role as an effective political body was limited, and it was eleven years before it was even able to hold its first national conference.

The Struggle For Legal Recognition, 1973–81

Up to this point, the government had succeeded in keeping the initiative in its dealings with the Muslim parties, and its techniques of political manipulation had paid off. Later, in 1973, however it turned its attention to another issue with very different results. It introduced into Parliament a new marriage law. Such a law was urgently needed, in part, because of the great diversity of legal systems and those aspects of the legal systems that dealt with family matters inherited from the precolonial period when Indonesia had been a number of autonomous states and, in part, because of the growing pressure from women's organizations to improve the status of women.

The purpose of the bill was to introduce order and consistency in the system of laws relating to marriage, to establish the state as both the ultimate authority in the administration of such laws and as the arbiter of their legitimacy, to confirm that there were no legal impediments to marriage between Indonesians of whatever religion or ethnic origin by the availability of civil marriage, and to improve the legal position of women by specific regulations relating to divorce, polygamy, and forced marriage.

When the bill, endorsed by the president, was submitted to the Parliament on July 31, 1973, however, it prompted one of the most heated debates in the history of the chamber and generated a massive Muslim reaction. There were widespread angry demonstrations that came to a climax with the occupation of the floor of the chamber by Muslim youths.

Certainly, the government had behaved with grave tactlessness in the way in which the bill had been presented. Neither the Ministry of Religion nor any Muslim leader had been consulted when it was drafted. The crucial objection to it, however, from the standpoint of Islam was that it was a direct encroachment on the right of Muslims to govern their family lives according to divinely revealed laws. As such, it was felt as an affront to Islam that touched grass root sensibilities in a way that manipulation of the political party system had not.

There were several provisions regarded as objectionable, but three were particularly abhorrent. One was that civil registration was necessary for the validity of a Muslim marriage; a second was that Muslims seeking a divorce, and a Muslim male wishing to contract a polygamous marriage, were required to apply for the necessary permission to a civil court; a third was that religious differences were not an obstacle to marriage.

Each of these provisions, in effect, set civil law above the revealed law of Islam in a manner perceived as blasphemous. For a Muslim marriage to be valid, all that was necessary was a contract made in accordance with the *shariah* between the groom and the bride's father or guardian. No human authority had the right to require more. It may be noted that registration of Muslim marriages with Muslim registrars had been a government requirement for many years, but it had never been suggested that this was necessary for a marriage to be valid.

The requirement that applications to divorce or to contract a polygamous marriage be made to a *civil* court was likewise an affront. The rejection of difference of religion as an impediment to marriage and the availability of civil marriage had practical implications that were anathema to Islamic law. It provided a means by which a Muslim woman could opt out of the constraints of Islamic law and marry a non-Muslim man. This facility already existed under the old law and had been upheld by a test case in 1952.

Islamic courts were a symbol of Islamic authority and guarantors of the application of Islamic law. To make them subservient to civil jurisdiction was an offense against God.

It can readily be understood how such provisions, particularly when the atmosphere was filled with rumors of plots of Christianization, could be used to inflame public opinion on the grounds that Islam itself was under threat from a Christianizing, that is, secularizing government.

The government capitulated. It withdrew the bill and resubmitted it a year later, undertaking that the authority of Islamic law in regard to marriage would not be decreased or changed. The bill as finally approved retains some of the elements of the intent of the original version, but in certain respects it enhanced and formalized the public position of Islamic law in Indonesia.[18]

By and large, the Muslim position has been accommodated. No longer is there any question of Islamic law requiring the ratification of civil law. The regulation of marriage, polygamy, forced marriage, and divorce is in the hands of the Islamic courts. The possibility of a Muslim woman marrying a non-Muslim has been removed.

From several standpoints, the bill represents a milestone in the history of Islam in public life in Indonesia. For the first time, a marriage law for Muslim has been codified by the state, a law better able to ensure a measure of consistency in Islamic court decisions than simply "the teaching of the Prophet and the learned scholars of early Islam." Not only this, but to the degree that Islamic law is embodied in this new marriage law, it is part of the positive law of Indonesia.

This confrontation between the government and Islamic militancy was a high point in a dialectic that was to continue throughout the 1970s and has not yet run its course. During these years, *ideology* and *program* emerged as key terms in the compulsory government's indoctrination programs, which provided, with increasing frequency, assurances that the Pancasila was strengthened in its position as the ideological basis of the state. In one sense, the setback over the marriage law was irrelevant to the government's strategy. The Pancasila was not a religion, but since the first *sila* (principle) was belief in the one and only God, it followed that it was part of the state ideology to have a religion—whether Christianity, Islam, or Hindu-Bali was not important. What was crucial was that no one religion should attempt to take over the ideology of the state or be used politically as a solidarity-making device but that all should play their part in realizing the values implicit in the Pancasila.

Meanwhile, the government continued steadily with its policy of distancing the state from any one religious tradition, largely by administrative procedures. Thus, government school holidays were fixed according to the Gregorian calendar and are no longer tied to the occurrence of the fasting month of Ramadan as it moves backward through the solar year. More recently, regulations have been introduced requiring uniformity in school dress, regulations that, in effect, forbid girls to wear to school the distinctive Islamic gown that covers the head and all the body except the face and hands.

Muslim activists and ideologues have responded both by nuanced criticism of the government and by attempts to exert pressure whenever an opportunity arose and it seemed that a point could be made. They made allegations that the government had Christian sympathies, demonstrated by its use of the Pancasila to distance itself from any one religious tradition. This they described as secularism, identified as the twin brother of Christianity, a religion without *shariah!* The government had these sympathies, because, Muslims claimed, there was a higher proportion of Christians in the senior positions in the government bureaucracy and army than was justified by the facts of demography. Another target was corruption and with it the abuse of political power. Islamic periodicals continually mounted attacks on the restrictions on democracy that prevented Islam coming into its rightful inheritance; on the promotion of secularism; on the misuse of public funds, particularly in deals between the army and Chinese businessmen; and against the free rein given to death squads to eliminate criminals outside the due process of law.

In addition, there was pressure applied on single issues for the purposes of point scoring. In December 1978, for example, Muslim pressure resulted in the cancellation of a Christian ecumenical charity function for the unemployed (held for several years in the past) on the grounds that there might be indirect proselytizing of Muslim unemployed benefiting from the gifts distributed. A related issue arose in the Christmas of 1980–81 when the Council of Ulama of Indonesia ruled that Muslims should not take part in Christmas celebrations.

Rethinking and New Options

Not all responses to the government's policies, however, have been negative. There is evidence, even if on a small scale, of vigorous discussion on religious matters as well as attempts to rethink the position of Islam in a pluralistic state, abandoning the triumphalist ambitions of the past.

An illustration of such rethinking is provided by the publication in 1981 of selections from a diary kept by Ahmad Wahib, a devout Muslim student at Gadjah Mada University, Yogyakarta, between 1961–70, who was killed in a motorcycle accident in 1973.[19] It consists in part of his reflections as to how universal Islamic spiritual values are to be freed from outmoded formulations of Islamic belief. He rejects the traditional authority accorded to the *ulama* and the apparatus of *fiqh* by means of which the *ulama* arrive at their juridicoreligious opinions; he condemns their attempts to use the power of the state to impose their human understanding of divine revelation on other human beings. He wholeheartedly welcomes religious pluralism as a fact of life and believes that Muslims, as one spiritual community among many, should trust in the divine guidance promised to the community to help them meet the challenges of the age rather than demand that the government give them rights denied to others. Perceptively, he sees a greater potential for cultural development in the traditionalist Nahdatul Ulama, than in the reformism of the Muhammadiyya/Masyumi, which he sees as anticultural. The diary created considerable interest. It sold ten thousand copies within six months, and quickly generated five hundred pages or more of review and debate.

Wahib's thinking is eclectic. His sources range from the writings of Muhammad Iqbal and the Lahore Ahmadis to Catholic scriptural theology. It would be a mistake to attach too much importance to him as an individual. However, the context in which his ideas were developed is significant. For ten years he was a leading member of the Himpunan Mahasiswa Islam (Islamic University Students Association), a national body with branches all over the country, and he consistently argued his ideas in it until he was forced to resign. He was also a keen member of a closed discussion group in Yogyakarta deeply concerned with religious issues. Before he was killed in Jakarta in 1973, he had spent three years in similar discussion groups there. He is an example of the ferment that is taking place among Muslim students at universities in many parts of Indonesia, where, alongside Muslims whose religious formation is traditional, there are those who have taken part in religious studies programs in Western universities and been trained in the social sciences. It is not possible to quantify this activity, but it is sufficient to be able to demonstrate that it exists.

In the meantime, the government has maintained its pressure on every organization within the state to accept the Pancasila as its sole ideological foundation. It achieved a major success early in 1984 when the Nahdatul Ulama—which alongside its participation in the PPP also retained an individual existence simply as a religious organization—decided to comply with the government's wishes. The government achieved an even greater success in August of the same year when the PPP also passed a resolution recognizing the Pancasila as its sole ideological basis.

The occasion of this resolution was as important as the resolution itself. It was the first national congress of the PPP. Such a national congress is a kind of rite of passage for such an organization. It is the means by which an organization demonstrates its existence, proves its viability, and declares itself ready to make its presence felt amid the constellation of competing social and political movements. It had taken eleven years for the party sufficiently to come to terms with its internal difficulties and rivalries and to reach this point. During the same period, the government alliance of functional groups, Golkar, had held three national congresses and the PDI two national congresses.

The opening of the congress was attended by President Suharto himself, and it passed the resolution in his presence. It meant that the party had formally agreed to accept the function for which it had been created: to channel Islamic political activity into areas approved by the government and serve as an instrument by which Muslims as Muslims could play a role in the creation of programs without being a threat to the state ideology.

The resolution made the congress a national event, and it was reported widely in the media. The national weekly news magazine *Tempo* (a secular publication with the format and style of *Time*) gave it comprehensive coverage. Its report included the reactions of a number of personalities from different age groups and walks of life: directors of religious schools, politicians, academics, a popular singer, and a veteran ideologue of the Sukarno era.[20]

Three schools of thought emerge. The first is that Muslims must accept the government's position, albeit cautiously, and look for new possibilities inherent in the arrangement. For example, two heads of religious institutions—one, *kiyai* (Javanese title for religious teacher) Achmad Siddiq from East Java and the other Abdurrahman Wahid from Jakarta (since 1985 the chairman of the Executive Committee of the NU)—both had penetrating comments to make concerning the new identity of the party now that formally, at least, it no longer had an Islamic identity. Ahmad Siddiq, for example, conceded the value of a party whose membership was not restricted by religious allegiance. Such a party would be able to draw on a greater pool of talent to develop its programs than one with more restrictive membership rules. On the other hand, he pointed out, Indonesians are not yet accustomed to making a choice between parties on the basis of their respective programs. Accordingly, Muslims would see their interests best served by the PPP. No matter how it presented itself, it would continue to bear its Islamic identity.

Abdurrahman Wahid expressed similar concerns. He referred to the legitimate sociohistorical roots of the party, thereby drawing attention to the circumstances of its formation, and he hinted at what the consequences might be were the party to lose the respect it held as the instrument by which Islamic aspirations might be realized and Muslim activists were driven underground.

The PPP members took the same line. Its deputy Secretary General, Mahbub Djunaidi, for example, stressed the need for the party to retain the mass support of the Islamic groupings that had been its former components. He echoed the view of Ahmad Siddiq that the new "open" character of the party could give it an opportunity to attract wide popular support by its intrinsic qualities as a party in addition to its already established role of providing a channel for the realization of Muslim aspirations through the programs it formulated. His fear was that the party's mass appeal in the immediate future would suffer unless it could meet the challenge, as his colleague Ridwan Saidi put it, of establishing the relevance of its pictorial symbol, the *Ka'ba,* to the fact of its having accepted the Pancasila as its ideological basis.

A second school of thought enthusiastically accepts the government position and hopes for a genuine deconfessionalization of Indonesian politics and a movement toward social democracy based on the Pancasila. For example, the veteran nationalist, Roeslan Abdulgani, a close associate of Sukarno, one of the chief ideologues of the former Indonesian Nationalist Party, and a skilled survivor puts rather more strongly a view close to that of the government:

> By accepting the Pancasila, the United Development Party may well lose its Islamic character. . . . But this simply means that the political aspirations of Muslims can flow through whatever channel they wish. I too am a Muslim . . . I used to express my political aspirations through the Indonesian Nationalist Party. . . . Now I do so through the Pancasila. . . . The Darul-Islam [revolts] have created a terrifying image of Islam in Indonesia. The Muslim community has to dispel this bad image. It is very much to be hoped that the young generation of Muslims will play its role in introducing new ideas about Islam.

A third school of thought rejected both the government position and the Islamic party for accepting the policy and thereby betraying the Muslims. The singer, Rhoma Irama, for example, denounced the resolution, declaring that in accepting the Pancasila, the PPP had lost its one sure identity, Islam. Its leaders, he went on, had abandoned God and his Prophet. He described the party henceforth as a transvestite, unsure of what it wanted or where it was going. To continue to support it, he concluded "would be against both my conscience and the religion I believe in: Islam."

There is a symmetry in the spread of reactions to the resolution—in favor, a middle ground, and rejection—that could be misleading, for it is not easy to establish how widely distributed each response is or what measure of active support lies behind it. Those welcoming it were simply elaborating the government position: that Indonesia is a pluralist state and only the Pancasila can ensure that this pluralism continues as a creative element in the national personality. Rhoma Irama's outburst is logically irrefutable in terms of the traditional idea of an Islamic state, with the twin concepts of *dar al-Islam* (domain of Islam) and *dar al-harb* (domain of war). Yet it is significant that he is by profession a singer, not one of the *ulama*. It is the middle ground that is most intriguing, the views of those with a professional relationship to Islam. Their statements are finely nuanced. They recognize the power that the government holds, they concede the good in its intentions, yet they point out the dilemma created by government policy for a party that has no identity but Islam when that identity is taken away. In short, the middle-ground group gives notice that it intends to make use of the traditional device of the *ulama;* to recognize the realities of political power; to compromise judiciously; and, within the areas of activity open to it, to work for a constant deepening of the understanding of Islam in the confidence that time is on Islam's side and that its inherent strength will at length transform the mind of the government.

The government, however, is working on the same principle with all the powers of the state for surveillance and indoctrination behind it. The dialectic between these two polarities has still a long course to run.

Conclusion

Islam in public life in Indonesia may be viewed in terms of three periods in which different aspects of Islamic activity are successively revealed and each is relevant to the understanding of what follows. Around 1912, modern-type Muslim organizations begin to appear on the scene; between 1945–73, Islam is shown primarily as the protagonist in debates and armed struggle relating to ideological issues; between 1973 and 1981 there is the major confrontation on a legal issue represented by the marriage bill, a series of trials of strength on relatively minor issues, and attempts to come to terms with the new political situation resulting from the fusion of four Islamic parties into a non-Islamic program-oriented alignment. The years 1981–84 show shifts and adjustments: on the one hand, by the major victory for the government at the first national congress of the PPP and, on the other hand, by hints that the intellectual challenge is being recognized and that there are ideological alternatives to the traditional formulations of the role of Islam in the state.

The highlighting of particular articulations of Islam in this way is an oversimplification, just as is the reference to the present situation as the outcome of a continuing process of dialectic. Words often carry misleading connotations: *secular nationalist,* for example, should not be misunderstood. The secular nationalists are certainly not secular in the sense that Ataturk was a secularist. Many of them are personally devout Muslims who regularly pray and keep the fast. They believe that Indonesia— the home of such diverse histories, peoples, and cultures—cannot survive as a unitary state if the state is based on one religious confession that has its own diverse local histories, even if that religion is professed by the majority of the population. The Pancasila is the answer to such diversity.

A Pancasila state, with no majorities and minorities, is what was entrusted to the people of Indonesia at the sacral moment of the proclamation of August 1945. To back down would be to renege on the sacrifices of all those, of whatever ethnic or religious group, who had died in the struggle for independence. In the view of the secular nationalists, the Islamic parties, in attempting to take charge of the basis of the state, were betraying the revolution. Their appeal to democracy was simply a tactic to enable them to subvert the Constitution, similar in kind to that of the Communists who in 1955 proposed that the first principle of the Pancasila, belief in one God, should be replaced by freedom of religion. Government policy since 1965, then, has been consistent with the ideals formulated with the proclamation of the state, ideals accepted by the majority of Indonesian Muslims: that an Islamic way of life may adequately be realized through the performance of religious duties and maintenance of the structure of family life and traditional rites of passage by a self-regulating adherence to the relevant provisions of Islamic law with a minimum of interference from the state.

At an official, formal level, the PPP accepts this policy. This does not mean that the heightened sense of Islamic awareness, so noticeable in other areas of the Muslim world, is absent from Indonesia. It is reflected in various ways, none of which need have any direct relevance to political activism, although in some cases it may be a substitute for it and, perhaps, even prepare the ground for it. Observers have commented on an increase in the numbers participating in both daily prayers and Friday congregational prayers at the mosque; the same holds for the observance of the fast of Ramadan. Reference has already been made to the almost 50,000 Indonesians making the pilgrimage in the 1983–84 season. There is a new concern that not only foods, but even cosmetic products should be certified as *halal* (permitted). Women are more likely to wear Islamic dress, hence the concern with the school-uniform regulations. In language, Islamic greetings are becoming fashionable. Twenty years ago, the expression *al-salam alaykum* (Peace be with you) was rarely heard except in religious circles; now, it is common in social intercourse. Writers in Islamic magazines consciously, indeed self-consciously, introduce new Arabic words into the language. Alongside the government supported or subsidized Islamic education system, numerous private schools flourish—some large, some small—based simply on the charisma of a local teacher. Thus, although many of the *ulama* occupy bureaucratic positions in courts, in government offices relating to religious affairs, and as teachers in officially recognized educational institutions, there are large numbers of independent *ulama* not dependent on the system and therefore are outside government control and knowledge. There are numerous formal and informal student groups and discussion clubs at universities, colleges, and technical institutes.

None of these activities are outside the guidelines of the Pancasila, although deep resentment often lies behind outward conformity with the letter of government policy. Muslims tending toward the radical end of the spectrum of discontent view Pancasila as a continuing affront to the Muslim masses of Indonesia. They point to the history of Islamic-inspired risings against Dutch colonial rule and the contribution of Islam to the final struggle for independence. To enshrine the Pancasila as the state ideology in their view is to interfere in the social and religious life of the people by imposing a minority ideology on the majority, who, were they given the opportunity, would declare for Islam. To this appeal for Islam to be given its due as the majority religion, there is added a plea for the recognition of Islam as a charter for social justice, offering a message of hope for the downtrodden and oppressed Muslim masses. In short, the revolutionary rallying cry for the honor of God and the rights of the people may be biding its time.

This wide range of intense spiritual, intellectual, and organizational activity is striking and has led the journalist Jansen to suggest that Indonesia is the state next in line to be the scene of an Islamic revolution.[21] This judgment is a healthy corrective to the widespread, rather patronizing, view that thanks to a damp tropical climate, Islam in Indonesia is more relaxed and tolerant than Islam as understood and practiced in the Middle East. Such a generalization is facile, misleading, and a slur on all who live in equatorial regions! There was nothing relaxed or tolerant in the Islam of Aceh, which sustained a twenty-year war against the Dutch between 1873 and 1910. More recently, there was nothing relaxed or tolerant in the *dar al-Islam* revolts in Aceh, West Java, and South Sulawesi or in the explosion of feelings that led to the occupation of the Parliament by Muslim students in 1973. As elsewhere in the Muslim world, in Indonesia there is vitality, violence, and above all variety.

Nevertheless, there are various reasons why an Iranlike Islamic revolution is unlikely. One is the fact that over sixty percent of the population is concentrated in Java. Although the tens of millions of Javanese peasantry who live by wet-rice cultivation are Muslims, their cultural traditions, through which they perceive Islam, are strongly animist with an Indic religious overlay. This makes it most unlikely that they would ever rise in rebellion under the banner of Islam. Another reason is that the Javanese bureaucratic elite, particularly those with some tangential relation with the court tradition, although by no means rejecting Islam, have long had a rather condescending attitude to the *ulama,* to Muslim activists, and to the exclusive claims made not only by Islam, but by any religion.

A third reason is the system of secular education established during the period of Dutch rule, whether under government or Christian missionary auspices. Especially important were those institutions that catered to the elite and provided some the opportunity to study in Holland. On the one hand, conversions from Islam to Christianity were few. On the other hand, graduates from the system grew up with the view that there was a natural distinction between "church" and state, a distinction that facilitated good government in a religiously plural society. This explains the commitment to secular nationalism of Sukarno and Hatta, and the secular character of the Youth Pledge of 1928. It also explains why, although there was a strong Islamic element in the war for independence, it was the secular nationalists who gave direction to the struggle and defined its goals. The tradition has continued. This is why many Muslims see no need for a nexus between the practice of Islam and the need for an Islamic state.

The fourth reason, and the most important of all, is the fact that the foci of Islamic identification are primarily regional, and each region perceives its Islamic identity in a different way (leaving out of consideration the ideological gulf between the reformists and the traditionalists). The ethnic Javanese of Central Java and the Acehnese are a striking example of such differences in self perception. Even where communities of Muslims share basic attitudes, either they are widely separated by distance or they are kept apart by non-Muslim communities or variant Muslim traditions that serve as shock absorbers. There is no way in which the Javanese can make common cause with the Achehnese by uniting under the banner of Islam to overthrow an "infidel" government in Jakarta. Neither, however, would hesitate to defend Indonesia against an outside enemy. The appeal of nationalism is far greater than the appeal of Islam. The homogeneity of concern and self-perception created by the network of religious teachers throughout Iran that enabled the congeries of various interest groups to unite to overthrow the shah and form an alternative government does not exist in Indonesia.

Nevertheless, there is Islamic extremism in Indonesia: in part, inspired by events outside the country; in part, a response to local conditions and nurtured by a deep sense of frustration. One need only refer to the riot at Tanjung Periok in Jakarta late in 1984, the series of bomb explosions in

Jakarta and Bandung, and the dynamiting of part of the Borobudur, the great Buddhist stupa outside of Yogyakarta in January 1985. Reporting of such events in the Indonesian press is either so nuanced or so bland that it is impossible to be sure whether such acts are the work of fringe groups or of a growing underground movement—or of both simultaneously. Whatever the case, demographic, economic, and political factors suggest that the status quo is here to stay, at least in the medium term. Yet there are many unknowns in the situation. Reference has already been made to the unofficial tier of Muslim schools that are independent of government funding and are inaccessible to foreign researchers. In addition, it is clear that there exist groups that are the counterpart of the Egyptian Jama'at al Islamiyya, the various *jihad* groups associated with it, and the notorious *takfir wa hijra* (declaration of apostasy [on the part of the government] and withdrawal [from an unbelieving community]). The writings of Sayyid Qutb and Mawdudi are available and popular. Undoubtedly, clandestine cells exist, dedicated to a realization of the political ideas in the writings of these authors and their antecedents, cells in which the question as to whether a ruler who is a hypocritical Muslim may be eliminated is discussed, and alongside it the other ideological issues debated in Egypt among the groups involved in the assassination of Sadat. These issues involve basic questions: To bring about an Islamic revolution does one regard the whole of society as corrupt and withdraw from it in order to plan for a total revolution as a long-term goal? Or, in fact, does one decide that society is sound and that the need is simply to replace the ruler and change the laws to Islamic laws? Another basic issue can be set in the terminology of Mawdudi: Is the time one of *istidaf* (weakness) and, therefore, caution? Or is the time ripe for *jihad*, that is, a decisive act of political assassination (as had been attempted on several occasions against Sukarno)?[22]

The final reason is the overall political situation. Only the so-called non-Muslim party, the PPP, represents an organizational focus for an opposition with the potential to command mass support in order to challenge the government both in Parliament and on the streets.

Indonesia still faces many problems. Targets for criticism are easy to find: excessive authoritarianism on the part of government, corruption, bureaucratic inefficiency, and breakdowns in the rule of law. Yet it is important to compare the present situation in Indonesia with that which resulted from the general elections of 1955 when the Dutch parliamentary system was the political model. Then, there were over forty parties competing for seats and there were bitter divisions about the nature of the state.

The present system, for all its shortcomings both intrinsic and those resulting from human failings, has grown out of the experience of Indonesia as a nation that has survived terrible traumas. Since 1965 general elections have been held three times; the number of political parties has been reduced to three; and religion is no longer overtly a political issue.

This is not to deny that the system is still far from democratically responsive or that the government, with its tendency to ideological overkill, may be its own worst enemy in its relations with Islam militants. The great question, however, is whether within this system the PPP can play an effective role in the state in such a way that those Muslims who still see it as the best hope of Islam will feel that their confidence is justified. If it succeeds, then Indonesia will have made a unique contribution to the practice of statecraft in Islam. If it does not, the frustration among its supporters will become a running sore, that may infect the whole of the body politic.

Yet, the responsibility for the outcome is not that of the PPP alone. It rests as much on the quality of leadership of the president and the majority party, Golkar, as on its own responses to the problems it has to face.

Notes

Special thanks are due to the Institute for Advanced Studies of the Hebrew University, where the greater part of this chapter was prepared, for its generous academic hospitality and support. I am particularly indebted to Annette Orrelle who devoted much time and percipience in disentangling a sequence of very untidy drafts to prepare a final manuscript.

1. George Thomas Kurian, *Encyclopaedia of the 3rd World* (London: Mansell Publishing, 1982), s.v. Indonesia.
2. Kurian, *Encyclopaedia*, s.v. Indonesia.
3. *Indonesia Official Handbook 1979* (Jakarta: Department of Information, Republic of Indonesia).
4. *Handbook 1979*, p. 256.
5. Ruth McVey, "Faith as the Outsider: Islam in Indonesian Politics," in James P. Piscatori (ed.), *Islam in the Political Process* (Cambridge: Cambridge University Press, 1983), pp. 40–49; especially see p. 209, where McVey writes: "The schools in their classical form are completely outside state support and control."
6. *Kurian, Encyclopaedia*, s.v. Indonesia.
7. See *Statistik Indonesia/Statistical Yearbook of Indonesia*, s.v. Number of Moslem pilgrims departing to Mecca by province (Biro Pusat Statistik, Jakarta: 1979–83).
8. For a more detailed survey of events in this section, see chaps. 4 and 5 in M. C. Ricklefs, *A History of Modern Indonesia*, Macmillan Asian History Series (London: Macmillan, 1981), pp. 143–200.
9. B. J. Boland, *The Struggle of Islam in Modern Indonesia*, Verhandelingen van het Koninklijk Institut voor Taal-, Land-, en Volkenkunde, No. 59 (The Hague: Martinus Nijhoff, 1971). See chap. 1, especially pp. 18–39. This is the standard account of events during this period.
10. A detailed account of these movements is given in Van Dijk, *Rebellion Under the Banner of Islam*, Verhandelingen van het Koninklijk Institut voor Taal-, Land-, en Volkenkunder, No. 94 (The Hague: Martinus Nijhoff, 1981). See especially chap. 2 (on West Java, pp. 69–81; chap. 4 (on South Sulawesi, pp. 187–194); and chap. 6 (on Aceh, pp. 306–29).
11. H. Feith and L. Castles (eds.), *Indonesian Political Thinking 1945–65* (Ithaca and London: Cornell University Press, 1970), p. 211.
12. This idea is developed in James L. Peacock, *Muslim Puritans: Reformist Psychology in Southeast Asian Islam* (Berkeley: University of California Press, 1978).

13. For a full account of political developments in these years see H. Feith, *The Decline of Constitutional Democracy in Indonesia* (Ithaca, N.Y.: Cornell University Press, 1962), especially chaps. 9, 10.
14. Boland. *Struggle, op. cit.,* p. 151.
15. *Ibid.,* chap. 3, pp. 150–53.
16. Ricklefs. *Modern Indonesia, op. cit.,* p. 273.
17. *Handbook 1979, op. cit.* p. 95.
18. A detailed account of the marriage law affair is given in J. S. Katz and R. S. Katz, "The New Indonesian Marriage Law: A Mirror of Political, Cultural and Legal Systems," *American Journal of Comparative Law,* 23: 4 (Fall, 1975), pp. 653–81.
19. Djohan Effendi and Ismed Natsir (eds.), *Pergolakan Pemikiran Islam Catatan Harian Ahmad Wahib* (Jakarta: LP3 ES, 1981), pp. 97–99.
20. A full report on the Congress, the interviews, and a survey of events since 1973 that lead up to the Congress is given in *Tempo* No. 26, Thn XIV, 25 August 1984, pp. 12–16.
21. G. H. Jansen. *Militant Islam* (London and Sydney: Pan Books [World Affairs], 1979).
22. Mohamed Heikal. *Autumn of Fury: The Assassination of Sadat,* Corgi ed. (Sydney, 1979), pp. 252–59.

10

ASIAN ISLAM
International Linkages and Their
Impact on International Relations

JAMES PISCATORI

The picture that an agitated Muslim world presents to the American and the Westerner generally is perplexing and unfriendly. The memory is still vivid of the few weeks in late 1979 when the taking of the American hostages in Iran, the siege of the Grand Mosque in Saudi Arabia, and the razing of the American embassy in Pakistan made it seem as if some menacing grand conspiracy were under way. Mainly in response to events such as these, a doubly unfortunate image of Islam has gained currency: Islam is returning to a medieval past and it is posing a threat to the West, particularly "satanic" America.

It is a curious combination when one stops to analyze it because rarely today would anyone use the adjectives medieval and threatening in the same breath. On the contrary, the first is generally thought of as putting one out of touch rather than in conflict with the modern world. What is meant, of course, is that Islam is advancing values that are at odds with many of those of Western Christian civilization at the same time as these values are able to work against Western interests. Islam, it is thought, is able to pose these challenges because of the power that comes partly from possessing vast amounts of oil wealth but mostly from the newfound religious and political self-consciousness of many millions of Muslims throughout the world. It is assumed that these Muslims are fostering instability and perhaps revolution in countries ruled by secular, modernizing regimes and, hence, are working against Western interests. Because the Asian Muslim as well as Middle Eastern Muslim countries are strategically located, any weakening of these secular regimes will invite either Soviet or local Communist intrigue.

This perception of tears in the regional fabric fits in with the larger assumption, often held in the West, that Muslims are moving toward greater unity among themselves. The emergence of an Islamic bloc is seen as contrary to Western interests because it would lessen the ability of the West to influence or to pressure Muslim countries. It is assumed that the disposition of mind that leads one to veil women or to apply traditional legal penalties also leads to a commitment to unite all Muslims and even to supersede the current nation-state system. There may or may not be a relationship between the two patterns of thought. But one cannot deny that national borders are proving to be permeable to the chiliastic language of Khomeini or to the antiestablishment violence of such radical groups as the Islamic Jihad Organization. In fact, Muslims in every part of the Muslim world are hearing the message that Islam must accept "neither East nor West" and must reject the blandishments of both superpowers and their respective ideologies.

The question of what Muslims want is a large one and extremely important, but the American and the Westerner also need to look at what is actually happening, to look at the trends and patterns of activity, and then to judge whether we are, indeed, in a threatening or revolutionary era. The obvious first thing to realize is that Islam is not a monolith, neither wishing one wish nor acting in one way. In this chapter, I shall concentrate on the Asian Muslim states. Then, on the basis of these examples, I will look at the extent to which Islam may be said to be a significant international factor today and a stimulus to Muslim economic and political integration.

What constitutes a Muslim state is the obvious first problem. I recognize that there is a large literature and much controversy on what constitutes a proper Islamic state and, hence, my use of the adjective *Muslim,* rather than *Islamic,* is designed to avoid any normative implication and to be simply descriptive. Muslim states are those states where Muslims are in the majority. Yet, even when this definition is accepted, it must be noted that there is considerable variation in their Islamic self-consciousness. The spectrum ranges from Pakistan and Iran, the only two to have proclaimed themselves Islamic states, at one end, to secular Afghanistan and Indonesia at the other end; in between are Bangladesh, Malaysia, and Brunei, where Islam is the "first principle" or "the religion" of the state. Other Asian countries neither have Muslim majorities as do Iran or Bangladesh, nor have extremely small Muslim minorities as do Japan or Vietnam, yet they play an important part in the political consciousness of modern Muslim elites. These states have significant Muslim minorities and include India, the Soviet Union, China, the Philippines, Thailand, and Burma, among others.[1]

In this discussion, I shall look at the general subject in terms of three categories of relationship: (1) the relationship among the Asian Muslim states themselves, and that between them and the states with significant Muslim minorities; (2) the relationship between the Asian Muslim

Table 10.1 Main Sources of Imports of Asian OIC Countries

Importing Countries	Top Three Exporting Countries (in order of precedence)				Share of Total Imports (percentage)			
	1975	1978	1980	1981	1975	1978	1980	1981
Bangladesh	U.S., Canada, W. Germany	Japan, U.S., Canada	Japan, U.S., UK	Saudi Arabia, Japan, UAE	38.0	27.6	36.6	29.6
Indonesia	Japan, U.S., W. Germany	Japan, U.S., W. Germany	Japan, U.S., Saudi Arabia	Japan, U.S., W. Germany	52.6	51.4	51.1	53.3
Iran	U.S., W. Germany, Japan	U.S., W. Germany, Japan	Japan, W. Germany, UK	W. Germany, Japan, Italy	53.5	55.2	36.5	33.4
Malaysia	Japan, U.S., UK	Japan, U.S., Singapore	Japan, U.S., Singapore	Japan, U.S., Singapore	40.8	45.6	49.6	52.1
Maldives	New Zealand, Japan, UK	Japan, Pakistan, India	Japan, India, W. Germany/UK	Singapore, Japan, India	64.3	66.4	58.7	68.1
Pakistan	Japan, U.S., Saudi Arabia	U.S., Japan, Saudi Arabia	U.S., Japan, Saudi Arabia	Saudi Arabia, Japan, U.S.	33.9	33.8	34.0	35.8

Note: Figures on Afghanistan not reported.

Source: Adapted from Journal of Economic Cooperation Among Islamic Countries, No. 16 (July 1983), p. 60; No. 17 (October 1983), pp. 65–67.

(including the minority states) and the non-Asian Muslim states, particularly the Arab states; and (3) the relationship between the Asian Muslim states and the Western states.

Relations Among Asian Muslim States

Economic Cooperation

If ties of sentiment among Asian Muslim and Muslim minority states exist, they do not translate into concrete economic ties. It is perhaps only to be expected that the major trading partners of at least the Asian members of the Organization of the Islamic Conference (OIC) are the industrialized giants. This pattern is particularly true of imports, with the Asian states notably importing from the United States and West Germany. Among Asian regional states, Japan is clearly important: In 1981 it was one of the top three exporting countries to each of the states listed in Table 10.1, and it was one of the top three importing countries from all of these Asian Muslim states, with the exception of Bangladesh (Table 10.2). The only other regional states to have prominence are Singapore, not surprisingly important as an import and export partner of Malaysia, and China, a longtime friend of Pakistan and a top customer for Pakistan's goods (Table 10.2). The Soviet Union falls in the top three export customers only in the case of Bangladesh (Table 10.2), which it has traditionally supported to offset Chinese support of Pakistan, and falls not at all in the listing of important partners. Although I have not looked at the trading pattern of the states with significant Muslim minorities, I doubt that it would reveal a fundamentally different conclusion—that is, there is not significant economic integration.

Institutional Development

Institutional cooperation among Asian Muslim states is somewhat more developed than economic cooperation. Coordination of activities has occurred among Asian youth groups, such as happens elsewhere in the Muslim world under the aegis of the World Assembly of Muslim Youth. This organization, for example, sponsors "International Islamic Youth Training Camps for the Muslim Youth of Asian Countries," whose purpose is to bring together Asian Muslims "from different ethnic groups" to learn about each other's "interests or perhaps problems" and, in doing so, to "help promote and develop genuine understanding among themselves."[2] A periodical publication, *Islamic Vision,* which, although closely tied to the Malaysian youth group, Angkatan Belia Islam Malaysia, reports on the activities of other groups in the Asia-Pacific region. From this one would learn, for example, of the activities of the Assembly of Muslim Youth of Singapore; and, more important, of how Muslim youth in one Asian country interact with those in other Asian countries.

Table 10.2 Main Export Customers of Asian OIC Countries

Exporting Countries	Top Three Importing Countries (in order of precedence)				Share of Total Exports (percentage)			
	1975	1978	1980	1981	1975	1978	1980	1981
Bangladesh	U.S., USSR, Mozambique	U.S., Pakistan, USSR	UK, U.S., USSR	U.S., Singapore, Mozambique	29.0	32.6	32.1	24.8
Indonesia	Japan, U.S., Singapore	Japan, U.S., Singapore	Japan, U.S., Singapore	Japan, U.S., Australia	79.3	75.3	81.3	83.1
Iran	Japan, U.S., Netherlands	U.S., Japan, W. Germany	U.S., Japan, W. Germany, Brazil	Japan, Bahamas, Spain	44.6	45.1	46.9	42.9
Malaysia	Singapore, U.S., Japan	Japan, U.S., Singapore	Japan, Singapore, U.S.	Singapore, Japan, U.S.	50.7	56.4	58.2	56.2
Maldives	Japan, Sri Lanka, Pakistan	Japan, Mauritius, Denmark	Mauritius, Japan, Switzerland	Japan, Sri Lanka, Malaysia	97.2	81.8	72.9	65.4
Pakistan	Hong Kong, Japan, Saudi Arabia	Japan, Hong Kong, UK	China (PRC), Japan, Iran	China (PRC), Japan, U.S.	24.3	25.2	23.9	39.0

Note: Figures on Afghanistan not reported.

Source: Adapted from Journal of Economic Cooperation Among Islamic Countries, No. 15 (April 1983), p. 55; No. 17 (October 1983), pp. 62–64.

This interaction occurs in such programs as the training program in *dakwah* (Ar. *dakwah,* "call" to Islam) that the Pakistani government runs for Muslim students in Pakistan coming from ASEAN countries.

More noteworthy is a second type of institutional development. In November 1980, delegates from sixteen Asian states met in Kuala Lumpur to launch a new regional coordinating body, the Regional Islamic Da'wah Council of Southeast Asian and the Pacific (RISEAP). The Malaysian and Saudi governments are the main financial supporters, and, as one might expect of an organization with such patronage, it is specifically not intended "to interfere with the political" situation of the regional states. Rather, its purpose, according to its secretary-general, Tunku Abdul Rahman, is "to help Muslims to help themselves." In practical terms, this means the establishment of an Islamic training center, the publication of a regular magazine called *Al-Nahdah (The Renaissance)* that reports on various regional activities and events, and the production of books on Islam in the thirteen languages used in the area. Over sixty groups are now members of RISEAP, and Tunku Abdul Rahman seems to have found in this population a platform for urging better treatment of Muslim minorities in Asia. He has made not only relatively ordinary trips in this regard, such as to Australia in 1981, but also more noteworthy ones, such as to China in 1982, where he offered assistance to the China Islamic Association. In December 1984 the General Assembly of RISEAP endorsed the resolutions of the OIC Conference on Muslim Minorities, which was held in Perth in September 1984, and specifically endorsed the idea that *zakat* revenues should be used to improve the status of minorities. It also called upon the governments of Australia and New Zealand to show as much generosity to Afghan refugees as they have to refugees from Southeast Asia.

I would not want to argue that RISEAP has the potential to make great changes in the status of Muslims in the area. It is too diffuse and too self-consciously apolitical for that. But it is the first attempt at the linkage of *dakwah* groups anywhere in the Muslim world, and the bringing together on a regular basis of Muslims in the same general region is bound to enhance their knowledge of each other and to create a greater sense of community. It is a way of making the abstract notion of Islamic fraternity, the *umma,* take on more concrete significance. Yet, even as Muslims gain a greater sense of community, they may also more clearly see what concerted action can do—and this, despite the avowed apoliticism, is a political perception. Very definite political ideas could well creep in, especially given that member groups, such as the Muhammadiyya of Indonesia, which are supposedly nonpolitical, have very definite political ideas and the desire to spread them; and given that states less conservative than Malaysia and Saudi Arabia might occasionally provide funds and thus influence the organization. Both the Burmese and Thai governments have recently recognized the potential political importance—and menace—of RISEAP. In 1982, the Burmese government denied an entry

visa to Tunku Abdul Rahman, who wanted to attend an Islamic conference, presumably out of the fear that his visit would encourage Burma's
dissident Muslims. In 1983, the Thai government banned a RISEAP
meeting in Bangkok because, it charged, Libya was behind the meeting
as it was behind the separatist movement of southern Thailand.

Whether or not the Libyan regime, in fact, sees value in trying to use
RISEAP, in at least one instance it is clear that some Muslim governments rate secular regional organizations higher than specifically Islamic
ones. This is the case in the reaction of the Malaysian and Indonesian
governments to the Muslim minority problem of the southern Philippines and, to a lesser extent, of southern Thailand. Both these governments have consistently tried to keep the minority question from the top
of the agenda of the OIC for fear of antagonizing the Philippines and
Thailand, fellow members of ASEAN. Indonesia and Malaysia plainly
want to preserve good working relations with their ASEAN partners, even
at the cost of failing to seem assertively Islamic, as they might have if
they had encouraged the OIC to take definite action in support of the
Filipino and Thai Muslims. They have even been acting against an
Islamic consensus.

The Islamic community's concern over the Filipino Muslims in particular has been growing since the early 1970s when armed clashes between
the army and the Moro National Liberation Front (MNLF) occurred with
some regularity and when martial law was declared. Libya was especially
strong in its support of the Muslims and condemnation of the Marcos
regime. For example, at the fourth Islamic Foreign Ministers' Conference, which was held in Banghazi in 1973, there was a considerable effort
by Libya to put the Filipino matter at the top of the agenda. Indonesia
tried to prevent it being considered at all, however, arguing that it was an
internal concern of a sovereign state and therefore beyond the legitimate
interest of the OIC. Malaysia countered a Libyan draft resolution, which
was very critical of the Filipino government and called for the suspension
of diplomatic relations, with its own draft centered on the idea that the
problem was fundamentally a Filipino one, not an international or even
Islamic one, and that the OIC's proper role was to encourage communication between the protagonists. After rather intense debate, the ministers
adopted a compromise resolution that could not have been displeasing to
Malaysia and Indonesia. In addition to setting up a committee of four
states to discuss the problem with the Filipino government, it called on
Malaysia and Indonesia to use their good offices through their common
membership in ASEAN. The resolution conceded that the "problem is
full of complications, the more so as it concerns the internal affairs of an
independent sovereign state."[3]

At the fifth Islamic Foreign Ministers' Conference in Kuala Lumpur in
1974, Indonesia continued to exert a moderating influence, arguing that
any call for a "just solution" be "within the framework of the national
sovereignty and territorial integrity of the Philippines."[4] However, the

trend toward greater support of the Muslim rebels and impatience with Manila was quickly establishing itself. At this 1974 meeting, the ministers specifically mentioned the MNLF for the first time; in 1977, in an "exceptional measure," they admitted it as an observer and called on member states to support it "by all ways and means"; in 1978, they invited members to extend their "moral and material support" to it; in 1980, they called on Muslim states to "exert the appropriate economic, social, and political pressure" on the Filipino government to induce it to abide by the Tripoli Agreement of 1976, which had set out the basis for regional autonomy. In recent meetings, the ministers have reaffirmed their support for the Tripoli Agreement but have refused to be drawn into the internal fighting within the MNLF that has been acute since 1977. More important, they have refused to back the change of strategy of Nur Misauri, leader of the MNLF, who now advocates full-scale independence for the Muslims rather than the autonomy most Muslim states advocate. An indication that OIC members do not wish to go further is the fact that although a special committee was set up to look at the question during the sixteenth Foreign Minister's Conference in Fez in January 1986, no report was issued or resolution passed.

The point here is that Malaysia and Indonesia have been instrumental in keeping the OIC from a complete break with the Philippine government, which would have helped to isolate it internationally. There is no doubt, though, that the consensus of the OIC has shifted toward greater criticism of the Philippines. The OIC became more openly critical of the Marcos regime than it was in the early and mid-1970s, and it is no longer inclined to accept that the problem is purely an internal affair. But as the refusal to support Misauri's call for independence shows, the OIC is still firmly behind the idea of preserving the territorial integrity of the Philippines. This position must be considered a victory for Malaysia and Indonesia, both of which have an obvious self-interest in defeating the idea that minorities have a right to secede from multiethnic and multireligious states.

However, the preeminent concern of both countries has been to preserve good working relations with an ASEAN partner, and thus to preserve ASEAN itself, from which they feel they derive the substantial benefit of subregional stability in an unstable region. According to former Deputy Prime Minister Datak Musa Hitam, Malaysia's commitment to ASEAN is paramount, and its commitment to the OIC is secondary (with the Non-Aligned Movement and the Commonwealth coming third and fourth).[5] It is not surprising that this is so when one bears in mind the not very distant past of hostility between Malaysia and the Philippines over rival claims to the island of Sabah. It is also not surprising that the Malaysian government will not help the Muslim rebels in southern Thailand when one bears in mind that it needs the cooperation of the Thai government to control the Communist insurgents in the north of Malaysia. The Indonesian government shares a similar perception of the need to ensure ASEAN harmony above all. The era of Indonesia's confrontation with Malaysia (1961–66) is never far from the consciousness of the elites, and the general fear of Communist penetration of the region guarantees that Jakarta will not wish to do anything that might weaken its anti-Communist neighbors. This concern, along with the fear of being considered an "Islamic State" with all the unacceptable ramifications that such a designation would have in domestic politics for the secular elite, accounts for Indonesia's decision not to apply for full membership in the OIC but rather to accept associate membership.

Foreign Policy

As the discussion so far indicates, to nongovernmental groups, institutional Islam seems sometimes to have a life of its own, yet, to governments, it seems to be of secondary interest. As a foreign policy matter, Islam is often a concern to Asian governments. But it is a subsidiary, and perhaps complicating, but rarely by itself a determining, factor in the clash of national interests. There is no question, of course, that genuine outrage at the plight of the Afghan *mujahidin* accounts for the condemnation of the Soviet Union by the governments of the Muslim states, but this outrage has not led them to break diplomatic relations. Nor has this outrage prevented them from working toward an accommodation with Soviet interests similar to the one sought by the Pakistani government.

That Islam does not very often determine foreign policy is best shown in such a highly ideological state as revolutionary Iran. Until recently, despite what one might have expected from an assertively Islamic regime, the relationship with the Soviet Union was lukewarm. Although the Ayatoullah from the beginning had called for a foreign policy of equal antagonism toward both superpowers and in spite of the strong reaction against the Soviet invasion of Afghanistan, Iran's trade with the Soviet bloc increased as relations with the Western states deteriorated during the American hostage crisis. Moreover, the Soviet-backed Tudeh party was free to operate until early 1983.[6] In recognition of the rather unexpected toleration they received, the Soviets moderated their initial attacks on the Shi'ite *ulama;* at the time of the 26th Party Congress in February 1981, Brezhnev deemed it prudent to make a relatively generous concession: "The main thing is what aims are pursued by the forces proclaiming various slogans. The banner of Islam may lead into the struggle for liberation. This is borne out by history, including very recent history."[7] The reversal of fortunes since 1983 has had nothing to do with Islam, but has been due to the Iranian government's belief that it is stable enough to act against the Tudeh and that the Soviets have moved from a kind of neutrality in the Gulf war to active support of Iraq, with which they have a Treaty of Friendship and Cooperation.[8]

Yet, it must be said that Iranian Islamic ideology probably determines Iranian foreign policy in the case of exporting the revolution. The media are full of reports of "Islamic terrorism," and although the term is certainly objectionable, as "Catholic terrorism" would be when talking of the activities of the Irish Republican Army, there is no doubt that the Islamic revolution of Iran has been for export. The Iranian regime distanced itself from a number of terrorist acts in 1985, such as the attack on the Kuwaiti *amir* in May and the hijacking of the TWA airplane in June, but major figures have consistently argued the need to spread the message of Ayatoullah Khomeini and to have others follow the example of a successful revolt against Westernized regimes.

Very little hard information is available, but it is widely believed that the Islamic Jihad Organization, which has taken responsibility for terrorist acts in Lebanon, Kuwait, and other places in the Middle East, is not one single group but rather a convenient label for a number of groups whose main inspiration, if not also source of funding, is Iran. The Jihad name surfaced in Jakarta in March 1984 in connection with threats made to the British, American, French, and Italian embassies that promised: "From now on, neither you nor your wives and children will find peace on Muslim soil."[9] Malaysia has also been worried about the activities of the Iranian embassy in Kuala Lumpur, which had distributed revolutionary leaflets and could, the government fears, be encouraging dissent among the growing number of activist Muslims there.

The Philippine government has also been worried about the Iranian factor in its domestic politics. It was reported in August 1983 that Tehran had sent a hit team to eliminate opponents of the Ayatoullah among the five hundred to nine hundred Iranian students in the Philippines and in December 1983 that a bomb wrapped in Iranian newspapers was defused outside the American embassy in Manila. A pro-Khomeini group also claimed to have distributed more than 5 million pamphlets calling for revolution: "We have succeeded in effectively provoking the Filipino masses—Moslems and Christians alike—to take overt action against the corrupt regime of prostitutes and dictators."[10] Even more worrisome for the government is the belief of many that Iran has displaced Libya as the main financial backer of the MNLF.

Iranian activism, however, is probably the exception that proves the rule and, in general, rather than determining policy by itself, Islam tends to play three other roles: confirming the national interest, contradicting the national interest, and facilitating the implementation of policy. In saying this, though, I may seem to imply that Islam is a monolith and that it is an independent variable, able to take action on its own, to play roles. But this is not always the case, or even often the case. More exactly, the role of Islam varies according to those who use its name, and, although there are values that are generally perceived and shared, specific interpretations of these values might sometimes differ among Muslims.

First, Islam may add to or confirm considerations of *realpolitik.* This tendency is clearly seen in Pakistan's dispute with India over Kashmir. There is no doubt that Pakistanis genuinely feel an affinity with the Muslims of the Kashmir valley and are aggrieved by what they view as the historical injustice of a Hindu ruler calling upon the Indians to preserve his throne against the wishes of his Muslim subjects. The majority of the Indian state of Jammu and Kashmir, who are Muslim, ought to have their say, the Pakistanis insist. Their concern about the plight of Muslims in the Indian federation can only have intensified since the bloody Assam riots in 1983. But other, more practical, considerations also explain the Pakistanis' insistence. They look upon Kashmir as of vital strategic importance because it is located in an area of relatively greater Indian vulnerability than elsewhere along their common border. Indeed, in the Indo-Pakistani wars of 1965 and 1971, which were fought in part over this issue, the only major successes for Pakistan occurred along the Kashmiri frontier. Moreover, since the Soviet invasion of Afghanistan, as indeed before, it cannot have been lost on the government in Islamabad that only a thin strip of Afghanistan separates Pakistan from the Soviet Union. Although control of the whole of Kashmir would obviously not eliminate this strip, it would enhance Pakistan's security in a very unsettled region and, more concretely, deprive India, which has close relations with the Soviet Union, of about 3.5 million people and of a forward staging post for its troops. It would also extend the border with China, with which Pakistan has close relations. The skeptic will say that these geostrategic considerations are the only ones that count in Islamabad, but I think it would be wrong to deny that Islam is also a consideration, though admittedly not necessarily an equal consideration.

Second, Islam may provide a reason for *not* doing what the national leaders were intending to do, and, although this may not cause them to alter their conduct, it may embarrass them. This tendency is seen, for instance, in the dilemma that the Malaysian and Indonesian governments face in their policy toward the Filipino and Thai Muslims. The sense of community that all Muslims share and the engrained sense of obligation to come to the aid of maltreated coreligionists stand in powerful contrast with the official hands-off approach. As Peter Gowing wrote, "The fact is, there is a common feeling of solidarity among the Muslims of the Malay world where, after all, Islam is the predominant religion."[11] This contrast between popular opinion and government policy is particularly strong in Malaysia, and it could account, in part, for the fact that the government there cannot afford to be seen as insensitive to demands for greater Islamization at home.

Third, Islam could be important in the implementation of policy rather than in its formulation, as in the first and second points, because it can be used to legitimate. One can point to the rather remarkable proposal by the government of Brunei to settle by reference to Islamic law *(fiqh)* the long-standing dispute with Malaysia over the Limbang district in Sarawak. Brunei sees the issue as vital because the loss of Limbang has meant the effective partition of the country into two unconnected zones. There is a historical argument that Limbang had been an integral part of Brunei until 1890, when British imperialism caused the division. But the government seems to feel that invoking *fiqh* is a more attractive defense. Thus, in its view, Malaysia as a Muslim state is bound to give up the territory because it is stolen property. The reference to Islamic law here is not designed to influence the opinion of Muslims within Brunei—they do not need to be convinced of the merits of the sultanate's case—but rather to influence the opinion of Muslim activists within Malaysia, who just might then lobby for Islamic justice to be done.

A better example of how governments use Islam as a legitimating— and, indeed, delegitimating—force in international relations is found in the rivalry between the Soviet Union and China. Both countries aim propaganda blasts at each other's significant Muslim minorities in order to convince them of how badly they are treated at home. It is in each state's interest to engage in this kind of activity because Muslim dissension would turn the attention of its rival inward and probably also induce the diversion of scarce resources to efforts at pacification of the Muslims. The stakes seem all the higher when one realizes where the Muslims are located in each country: The Soviet Muslims inhabit the soft underbelly of the Central Asian republics, what neighboring Khomeini refers to as his *cordon sanitaire;* the Chinese Muslims are located in areas bordering the Soviet Union, particularly the uranium-rich Xinjiang (Sinkiang) province, which also borders on Mongolia, Afghanistan, Pakistan, and India.

The Soviets have accused the Chinese government of moving non-Muslim, Han people en masse into these border areas in order to make them more dependable and to militarize them, and, in the process, the Soviets charge, perpetuating Mao's "great-Han, chauvinistic policy" that is harmful to the indigenous, often largely Muslim, people. The Chinese government is, indeed, worried about the stability of its border regions and vividly remembers that in 1962 some sixty thousand Kazakhs from Xinjiang crossed into Soviet Kazakhstan. It is reported that China currently keeps three hundred thousand troops in Xinjiang. It certainly sees the hand of Soviet intrigue there, denouncing "Soviet revisionists" for trying to initiate rebellion and warning of the "danger that Xinjiang faces from Soviet revisionist social-imperialism."[12] Taking the offensive, Beijing accuses the Soviet regime of trying to suppress the identity of its own Muslims. Moreover, Beijing is clearly trying to enhance its own legitimacy in the eyes of the Muslims in Asia and elsewhere by its repeated denunciation of the Soviet invasion of Afghanistan as "criminal," and by suggesting that this invasion is but the thin edge of the wedge for the Muslim world: "The Soviet Union has not halted since its military occupation of Afghanistan, and during the past twelve months and more, the Islamic countries have suffered a great deal from intensified Soviet infiltration and expansion, particularly in the Gulf and Red Sea areas, and through the continuously enhanced Soviet military forces in the Indian Ocean and the Pacific."[13] I shall say more about this competition for legitimacy later on.

Relations Between Asian Muslim States and Other Muslim States

This second category covers the relations between the Asian Muslim states and the rest of the Muslim world. In practical terms, the relationship of the Asian Muslims with the Arab states is what matters. Islamic theory suggests that a community of interests as well as of spirit exists between them, and certainly the public rhetoric of leaders and the media and the talk of ordinary Muslims are full of references to Islamic brotherhood. There is some reality to this fraternal sentiment, but there are also real differences between Asian and non-Asian Muslims. These differences are revealed in several ways.

First, despite the increasingly pronounced activity among Muslim states, particularly within the OIC system (i.e., the OIC itself and its many affiliated organizations, such as the Islamic Chamber of Commerce and the Islamic Broadcasting Organization), little economic integration has occurred among member states. Specifically, there has been little economic integration between the Asian member states and the non-Asian member states of the OIC. Whereas not all statistics on these countries can be viewed as entirely reliable, what figures we do have clearly show that trade between the Asian Muslim countries and the non-Asian Muslim countries is insubstantial. Table 10.3 shows, for instance, that, of the countries listed, Pakistan has the highest level of economic integration with other Muslim states, with perhaps thirty (or more) percent of its 1981 exports going to OIC member states and about thirty-five percent of its imports coming from member states. Bangladesh and Afghanistan (the latter with regard to exports only) are next, with Iran and Indonesia coming at the bottom of the list. Indonesia, for example, is reported to have only one percent of its exports going to OIC states and under two percent of its imports coming from these states. However, it must be noted that the Islamic statistical office based in Ankara reports a figure of nine percent for the 1982 imports. It is also to be noted that, although the trend is generally upward over the years reported, the movement is certainly not dramatic. Take the case of Malaysia. Whereas its export figure for 1970 was about two percent, it was only about four percent for 1981, and its import figure for 1970 was eight percent, which was roughly the same as in 1981. These trends are only to be expected, though, because these countries (as the developing countries generally) are dependent on the industrialized countries for the bulk of their trade.

Political integration has also been minimal between the Asian Muslim and other Muslim states. The one significant exception is the fact that the

Table 10.3 Flow of Trade of Asian OIC Countries with Member Countries

Country	Exports to Member Countries (percentage)						Imports from Member Countries (percentage)					
	1970	1973	1978	1979	1980	1981	1970	1973	1978	1979	1980	1981
Afghanistan	9.0	16.9	21.5	16.4	14.3	24.6	3.4	5.0	6.6	7.2	5.9	6.4
Bangladesh	—	6.0	21.2	17.8	18.4	21.3	—	4.3	11.8	12.0	13.6	25.9
			(20.0)[a]		(20.0)	(25.0)			(15.0)		(18.0)	(26.0)
Indonesia	3.3	1.1	1.3	1.2	0.9	1.0	2.1	3.6	4.5	6.0	7.8	1.8
			(1.0)		(1.0)	(1.0)			(5.0)		(8.0)	(9.0)
Iran	ng[b]	ng	ng	ng	ng	ng	ng	ng	ng	ng	ng	ng
			(3.0)		(3.0)	(6.0)			(2.0)		(7.0)	(7.0)
Malaysia	2.3	2.0	2.9	3.3	3.4	4.3	8.0	5.3	6.9	8.4	9.2	8.2
			(3.0)		(4.0)	(4.0)			(8.0)		(9.0)	(9.0)
Maldives	—	—	7.7	9.1	3.6	19.7	—	—	17.7	7.6	1.6	0.0
			(—)		(4.0)	(20.0)			(—)		(2.0)	(1.0)
Pakistan	11.1	19.9	29.1	27.4	25.8	29.9	5.9	10.9	18.9	22.9	35.0	35.1
			(36.0)		(32.0)	(36.0)			(18.0)		(34.0)	(34.0)

[a]The Islamic Development Bank (see Source) says that its figures are derived from the International Monetary Fund's *Direction of Trade Statistics Yearbook, 1982,* but its percentages do not always seem to be derived from what is actually reported in the *Yearbook.* For example, my calculation of Afghanistan's exports to the OIC countries listed in the *Yearbook* for 1978 as a percentage of its total exports is 14.2 percent, not 21.5 percent. The figures in parentheses are an alternative view, derived from the *Journal of Economic Cooperation Among Islamic Countries,* No. 10 (January 1982), p. 73; and No. 14 (January 1983), p. 67. Obviously, however, all figures must be viewed as inexact.

[b]ng equals not given.

Source: Adapted from Islamic Development Bank, *Seventh Annual Report, 1402 AH 1981–1982),* p. 28.

Palestinian issue has clearly become an Islamic issue. Over time, almost all Muslims everywhere have come to accept that the question of self-determination for the Palestinian people cannot be separated from the liberation of Jerusalem, the third holiest city of Islam. Strong feelings along these lines can be found in Indonesian society, but the government's pro-American conservatism has kept it from active support of the Palestinian Liberation Organization (PLO). By way of contrast, the Mahathir government in Malaysia, which has been developing broad and warm contacts with the Arab Gulf states, has moved to a position of more open support of the PLO. The PLO was allowed to open an office in Kuala Lumpur in 1981, and in July 1984 Yassir Arafat paid an official visit during which he was received by the king and spoke to a rally of fifteen thousand people. The prime minister has said that the government's only motivation is to help see justice done, but these moves must also be seen as useful signals to the Arab states that Malaysia is diplomatically cooperative and to its own people that it is moving in tandem with their increasing Islamic self-assertiveness.

The Palestinian exception apart, national leaders pursue their own national interests regardless of opinion elsewhere in the Muslim world. This fact means that the OIC has not become a powerful, independent political actor. But to say this is not to make a damning indictment because international organizations, such as the OIC, the Arab League, or the Organization of African Unity, can do no more than the member states will let them do. The reality of any international organization is that it survives as long as it is useful to its members. Utility most of the time derives from the organization's ability to contribute to the long-term goal of regional stability, but often the organization is useful to a member because it advances its own foreign policy.

Pakistan, for example, has found the OIC useful in its more or less constant diplomatic competition with India. It was able to prevent India's admission to the organization in the first place and, since then, has been able to find a sympathetic hearing at OIC meetings. The Indian nuclear explosion of May 1974 prompted the Pakistanis to try to secure a resolution that, if it did not forthrightly condemn India, did specifically name it, and thereby implied that it was posing a threat to regional and world peace. Senegal tried to avoid the singling out of India, but Pakistan, although unable to secure a clause calling on India to accept nuclear inspection by the United Nations, was successful in having only India named and thus put again in the dock of the court of world opinion. That Pakistan was successful is partly due to that amorphous yet palpable thing, Islamic solidarity, and partly to the enormous sympathy that Pakistan won, particularly in the Arab world, as a result of India's role in the dissolution of a sovereign state in the 1971 Indo-Pakistani war. It is no wonder, then, that Pakistan regards the OIC as its most important commitment—all the more so, it must be added, because its commitment to CENTO (Central Treaty Organization) and SEATO (Southeast Asia

Treaty Organization) has evaporated. As a result, owing to the Arab majority in the OIC, Pakistan now primarily looks to the Arab world for diplomatic support.

Outside of the OIC, relations between the Asian Muslim states (and those with significant Muslim minorities) and other Muslim states are often complicated when the Islamic element is especially evident. For example, the Indian government, under domestic pressure, has been critical of Arab governments for pouring money into the country for the purpose of inducing the conversion of *harijans,* Mahatma Gandhi's word for the untouchables. After voicing concern about mass conversions in 1981, India said it would not ban foreign money from coming into the country's Islamic organizations but would amend the Foreign Contribution (Regulations) Act so that it could regulate the inflow. However, the Assam riots in 1983 prompted the government to prevent such organizations as the All India Muslim Majlis-Mushawarat, Jamaat-e-Islami, and Jamaat-e-Ahl-Hadis from receiving foreign money. When Mrs. Gandhi charged in the Indian Parliament that the violence was due to such foreign money, no one could have missed the implication that it was Arab money. For their part, many Arab Muslim states have been severely critical of the Indian government for failing to prevent the riots and generally for failing to protect the Muslim minority.

Another example of how contention over an Islamic issue sours relations between an Asian Muslim state and a non-Asian one involves the Iranian-Saudi dispute over the nature of the *hajj* (pilgrimage) to Mecca. This dispute must be seen as part of the general tension in the region created by the Iranian Revolution, but the issue of the pilgrimage has taken on particular significance. The Iranians believe that the pilgrimage is an opportune occasion to advance their views of Islam and thus their political views, whereas the Saudis, who are apprehensive about the events across the Gulf, insist that the pilgrimage must not be turned into a political rally with the unfortunate demonstration effect that it could create within Saudi Arabia. It is no mean problem from the Saudi perspective, given the approximately one hundred thousand Iranians who make the pilgrimage and the fact that the Iranian regime consistently condemns the Saudi dynasty as corrupt and un-Islamic. The Saudis, however, cannot even appear to try to exclude Iranian pilgrims lest that undermine their primary claim to legitimacy—being the protectors and guarantors of safe and open holy cities. But they have expelled some pilgrims who attempted to carry weapons into the sanctuary area or to distribute pamphlets, and they have tried to enlist the support of other Muslim states in condemning what Khomeini's followers have done during the pilgrimage. As the Kuwaiti newspaper *al-Anba'* said, "Allah ordered the *hajj* to be a framework for cohesion among Muslims, not an arena for conflict and differences, and what Khomeini seeks is unacceptable to Allah and His Prophet."[14] There would be bad relations between the Gulf countries and Iran in any event, but the pilgrimage issue is important because it affects something all Muslims everywhere feel strongly about and because it represents a challenge to the legitimacy formula of the regime that prides itself on administering the *hajj* for the rest of the Muslim world.

The Afghanistan invasion is the most notable instance of the souring of relations. It is seen as an Islamic issue because of the nature of the regime that the Soviets are trying to prop up and because the guerrillas have self-consciously called themselves *mujahidin,* fighters in a *jihad* against the godless Soviets. The OIC, in an extraordinary session of the Foreign Ministers' Conference in Islamabad in January 1980, condemned the Soviet invasion and suspended Afghanistan's membership. But few concrete actions, including the suspension of diplomatic relations with the Soviet government, have taken place since then. Humanitarian aid has been given to the refugees in Pakistan, certainly, and some money and arms have been channeled to the *mujahidin,* but notably absent is the willingness to be seen as militantly anti-Soviet. At the Islamabad meeting, for instance, the ministers passed a balancing resolution that condemned American "pressure" and "threats of punitive action" against Iran.[15] Indeed, some Afghans are embittered by the lack of concrete help:

> [The] Russian invasion . . . at a time when all Muslim countries enjoyed . . . advanced military facilities for defence and for waging Jehad, made it incumbent on all Muslim countries of the world to have mobilized Jehad against the Red heathen army. . . . [T]hey should have taken [their] share in the Jehad against the great common enemy of Islam by helping their Afghan Muslim brethren in accordance with the valuable tenets of the Holy Quran. But unfortunately, not even a sound has been heard from most of these leaders. Contrarily some of them even continued their economic and social co-operation totally for the benefit of the Russians.[16]

Despite what these Afghans expect, it is obvious that there are political limits to Islamic outrage in the Muslim, particularly the wealthy Muslim, states.

But the Soviets have felt defensive, and they, like the Chinese, with one eye on their domestic Muslim situation, have tried to convince Muslims throughout the world, especially in the Arab world, that, after all, they are not so objectionable. The most effective way to convince them of this, they believe, is to allow contacts between foreign Muslims and some of their own, albeit carefully vetted, Muslims. The Muslim Religious Board for Central Asia and Kazakhstan publishes a journal, *Muslims of the Soviet East* (in Persian, Arabic, Uzbek, English, and French) that is designed to show that the Soviet Union's enlightened policy toward its own Muslims is of a piece with its enlightened policy in international relations. Unsubtle language is used to condemn Israel and its American patron, but such bombast also makes the more subtle point that if we Russians seem to be bad because of Afghanistan, the other side is even worse: "[The] mufti, as well as all those who were present at the mosque, prayed before Almighty Allah that He may reprimand Israeli Zionists and their protectors in [the] USA who are conducting criminal actions against all the Muslims and those of Palestine in particular."[17]

China, without the burden of Afghanistan, is more effective in the use of Islam in its relations with the Arab states. The China Islamic Association has been important in this respect not only because it arranges for foreign Muslims to visit China in order to see for themselves that Islam is not proscribed, but also because it sends its own delegations to the Arab world, which often meet political leaders there. Its chairman, Burhan Shahidi (Pao Erhan), for instance, met King Sa'ud of Saudi Arabia and King Husayn of Jordan in 1956, and, shortly after he met the Yemeni crown prince and his brother in Cairo, diplomatic relations were established between Yemen and the People's Republic of China (PRC). The association had also been instrumental in securing the recognition of Egypt and Syria. More recently, a delegation from the association visited Libya and Saudi Arabia, prompting one Soviet commentator to conclude that it might lead to the establishment of diplomatic relations between Saudi Arabia and the PRC.[18] This event has not occurred, but such visits do provide an informal channel of communication. What is important is that the regime in Beijing believes that the use of Islam can help to legitimate it in the eyes of the Arab regimes, and the record shows that it has had some success at it.

Although the economic and political integration of the Asian and non-Asian Muslim states is not high, contacts are growing between them. The point about Soviet and Chinese delegations visiting the Arab countries is evidence of this, but so are two other points. First, the Gulf states give considerable amounts of aid to some of the Asian Muslim and Muslim-minority states. Pakistan is a major recipient of aid, particularly from Saudi Arabia. Twenty-five percent of Saudi aid in 1976, for example, went to Pakistan and, roughly speaking about $100 million a year in Saudi aid went there until the decline in oil revenues in 1981–82. Saudi aid continues at a reduced level. Kuwait gave about $50 million and Qatar about $15 million in 1980 and 1981, and the United Arab Emirates (UAE) has given about $30 million a year.[19] Part of these funds are outright grants and part loans. The Kuwait Fund for Arab Development, which had been originally set up to help only Arab states, has since 1975 been generous to several Asian states. Twenty-eight percent of its total loans have gone to Asian states, and this figure represents over sixty percent of its non-Arab loans (see Table 10.4). Eleven Arab/OPEC institutions also make concessional disbursements. Looking at their total for 1981, one can see that Bangladesh received 7.9 percent, India 1.4 percent, and Pakistan 1.2 percent. This is not small, as it might seem, because only one country, the Sudan, received more than Bangladesh, and because the aggregate disbursements for the three countries came to more than US$70 million.

Table 10.4 Loans of Kuwait To Asian Countries Fund
for Arab Economic Development[a]

	April 1975–June 1980 (in thousand Kuwait dinars)
Afghanistan	8,845
Bangladesh	15,450
India	24,400
Indonesia	13,800
Malaysia	15,400
Maldives	3,000
Nepal	7,000
Pakistan	25,300
Philippines	3,500
Sri Lanka	8,070
Thailand	13,000
Vietnam	2,900
Total	140,665
Total Loans for Non-Arab Countries	230,045
Total Loans Worldwide	500,399
Loans to Asian Countries as Percentage of Total Non-Arab Loans	61.1%
Loans to Asian Countries as Percentage of Total Loans Worldwide	28.1%

[a]The Kuwait Fund changed its charter in 1974 to allow loans to non-Arab countries. The first such loans were signed in the 1975–76 fiscal year.

Source: Adapted from Kuwaiti Ministry of Planning, Central Statistical Office, *Annual Statistical Abstract,* Vol. 13 (1976), p. 200; Vol. 18 (1981), pp. 296–98.

Second, the Arab states are host to large numbers of Asian migrant workers. Although the number of foreign workers generally will decline as oil revenues decline and as more of the indigenous population enters the work force, there will remain a need for unskilled and semiskilled foreign laborers for the foreseeable future. A great many of these will come from Asia. Recently, Asians have constituted the vast majority of migrant workers in Bahrain, Oman, Qatar, and the UAE (see Table 10.5). Malaysians, for example, have found lucrative jobs in the Gulf, particularly working on infrastructural development in Saudi Arabia. Because a shortage of manpower has existed in the oil-based economies generally, migrant workers have been important to their maintenance; this, in turn, has meant that the Asians in some Arab countries have been nearly indispensable. The benefits to the Asian countries have been obvious. They have disposed of large numbers of people who would be unemployed—drains on the social and economic system and potential recruits to political oppositional movements—and they have received considerable money in remittances—in the early 1980s $2.2 billion a year in the case of Pakistan, eighty-five percent of which came from the workers in the Arab countries.[20] It has been estimated that in 1980 there were some

Table 10.5 Asian Migrant Workers in Major Labor-Importing
OIC Countries (in thousands)

Host Country	Indian Workers		Pakistani Workers		Other Asian Workers		Asian Workers as Percentage of Total Migrant Workers	
	1975	1980	1975	1980	1975	1980	1975	1980
Bahrain	8.9	11.0	6.7	10.0	3.0	10.0	63.5	68.9
Iraq	5.0	25.0	5.0	30.0	40.0	30.0	75.9	21.3
Jordan	—	0.5	—	5.0	—	8.0	—	22.5
Kuwait	21.5	25.0	11.1	16.0	30.1	45.0	30.1	30.7
Libya	0.5	6.0	4.5	50.0	0.5	10.0	1.7	16.5
Oman	26.0	30.0	32.5	40.0	0.6	4.0	83.6	82.2
Qatar	16.0	25.0	16.0	25.0	6.0	25.0	71.7	78.9
Saudi Arabia	15.0	80.0	15.0	110.0	18.0	180.0	6.2	26.4
UAE	61.5	80.0	100.0	120.0	23.0	43.5	73.4	73.8

Source: Adapted from *Journal of Economic Cooperation Among Islamic Countries*,
No. 14 (January 1983), p. 4.

120,000 Filipino workers in Saudi Arabia who earned between $250 and
$2000 a month and helped to provide the $700 million the Philippines
had in invisible receipts from Saudi Arabia.

It is not clear at all, however, whether either of these developments
suggests an emerging economic and political integration of the Asian and
non-Asian Muslim states, despite the lack of substantial trade and political coordination that I have described. The aid and the migrant workers'
patterns suggest Asian dependence on the Arabs. But when it comes to
aid, there is really mutual dependence: The making of a loan ties the
banker to the fortunes of the borrower and creates a kind of need for each
other once the loan is made. But is there any political influence to be
derived from the lending, or the granting, in the first place? It is hard to
say, as it is hard to say when talking about Western aid to any Third
World country. Many believe that President Marcos made concessions to
Muslim demands out of fear that Saudi Arabia would cut off aid if he did
not do this. In November 1980, the Saudis did terminate a contract to
supply ten thousand barrels of oil per day specifically because of the Philippine government's policy toward its southern Muslims. In addition,
there is no doubt that the Pakistanis, recipients of a great deal of aid,
follow Saudi policy lines closely. But it is impossible to say in both cases
if the aid, or the denial thereof, is the cause, and, in any event, the example of stubbornly independent India suggests that there are times when
aid and political influence seem almost not correlated at all.

There has been a dramatic increase in the amount of Arab-sponsored
dakwah [Arabic, *da'wah*] activities in Asia. Saudi Arabia has been partic-

ularly active as a patron, establishing mosques, training centers for Islamic officials, and institutes for the study of the Arabic language and the Quran. It funds these activities through direct government grants and also through the intermediaries of the Muslim World League and the Supreme World Council for Mosques, both based in Mecca and virtually appendages of the Saudi government. For example, in 1981 the league organized a training program for a thousand *imams* (mosque prayer leaders) in Indonesia and the Saudi government set up an Arabic language institute in Jakarta in conjunction with the Indonesian Ministry of Religious Affairs. In 1982, the Supreme World Council of Mosques devoted half of its budget of $29 million to the maintenance of mosques in Southeast Asia. In 1983, the Saudi government promised to provide $2.4 million for the transmission of a radio program, "Voice of Islam," to Southeast Asia in cooperation with the Malaysian government.

The Libyan Islamic Call Society is more active in Africa, but it, too, is involved in Asia. For example, it encourages and arranges visits of academics to Libya from such countries as Malaysia, sends teachers of Islam abroad, and offers scholarships to worthy students to study in Tripoli, as was the case in early 1984 with students from Sri Lanka. In addition, the Islamic Solidarity Fund of the OIC regularly contributes to the development of Islamic studies and provides for "humanitarian" aid to such groups as the MNLF, which was given a grant of $100,000 in 1983.

The result is that Muslims in the poorer areas of the Muslim world are increasingly beneficiaries of the sense of fraternal obligation that the richer Muslim states tend to feel. It is true that these wealthy states probably look upon *dakwah* aid as a way of maximizing their international influence, but they also see it as part of their Islamic duty. Moreover, there is no doubt that the beneficiaries feel increasingly part of the larger Islamic community, the *umma*. Yet, at the same time, this sentiment may have a negative effect on their loyalty to their own states. As the *Mindanao Cross* editorialized after an Arab delegation's visit to the southern Philippines in 1972: "The visit proved that the religious ties of the Muslims in Mindanao with other Muslim countries are as strong if not stronger than their allegiance to their government."[21]

A linkage of ideas between the Arab and Asian Muslim worlds has also developed. The works of the Pakistani writer, Abul A'la Mawdudi, and the Indian writer, Abul Hasan Ali Nadvi, are now widely known in the Arab countries and elsewhere among the Asian countries. Sayyid Qutb's *Ma'alim fi'l-tariq (Signposts on the Road)* has been translated into Thai and is also available to Soviet Muslims. Moreover, the library of the religious board in Tashkent is fairly well stocked with newspapers and periodicals from other parts of the Muslim world, and Arabic newspapers often carry lengthy pieces on the status of Muslim minorities in the Asian countries. This familiarization with writers from, and events in, faraway places is partly due to modern telecommunications and publishing and the resultant ease of dissemination. It is also due to the fact that the rich Arab countries, as we have seen, are funding the establishment of educational and language institutes throughout Asia that help to introduce young Muslims to major works of Arab writers and often also give them the ability to read them in the original Arabic.

But perhaps another reason why ideas are so shared now is that the greater ease of making the *hajj* brings together a vast number of people from all parts of the Muslim world in one place at one time in a highly charged, emotional atmosphere. In 1982, almost thirty-five percent and in 1984 over forty percent of the total number of pilgrims came from Asian countries (see Table 10.6). It is to be noted, however, that although the Saudi government has done a great deal to improve the conditions of the pilgrimage and has corrected many of the injustices perpetrated by the local guides and hoteliers, economic conditions still govern the ability of Asian Muslims to make the journey. For example, a study of the Thai

Table 10.6 Pilgrims from Asian Countries

Country	1979	1980	1981	1982	1983	1984
Afghanistan	990	4,386	2,356	4,206	9,033	5,388
Bangladesh	7,435	10,522	11,296	12,258	24,508	22,188
Brunei	398	3	421	1,947	1,911	1,895
Burma	10	74	156	167	148	201
Cambodia	—	3	55	—	—	—
China (PRC)	—	—	—	—	—	60
Hong Kong	—	1	6	5	3	2
India	24,863	21,881	26,280	26,229	30,896	32,563
Indonesia	43,723	74,741	69,002	57,478	54,904	40,928
Iran	74,963	10,539	75,391	89,503	103,044	154,958
Japan	7	10	—	—	—	—
Malaysia	9,511	14,846	22,704	25,277	25,013	24,749
Maldives	46	144	13	278	354	476
Nepal	29	—	25	28	6	59
Pakistan	74,296	78,624	69,343	72,844	85,019	91,872
Philippines	1,699	1,836	1,851	1,955	2,630	2,526
Singapore	1,838	2,490	3,103	2,328	2,998	2,947
South Korea	42	2	3	10	2	—
Sri Lanka	594	520	728	836	715	999
Taiwan	86	123	73	114	252	832
Thailand	1,906	2,978	2,753	1,888	2,273	2,610
USSR	28	26	26	20	19	14
Vietnam	1	—	—	—	—	—
TOTAL	242,415	223,749	285,579	297,371	343,728	385,267
Total Number of Pilgrims Worldwide	862,520	812,892	879,368	853,555	1,005,060	919,671
Asian Pilgrims as Percentage of Worldwide Total	28.1%	27.5%	32.5%	34.8%	34.2%	41.2%

Source: Adapted from Saudi Ministry of Interior, The Directorate General of Passports, *Pilgrims Statistics for A.H. 1403–1983 AC,* pp. 4–5, 28–29; and *Pilgrims Statistics for A.H. 1404–1984 AC,* pp. 10, 13, 26. The 1984 figures will probably be subject to slight revision as the complete statistics are reviewed by the Saudi government.

hajjis shows that the fluctuating cost of fuel and hence airfares, the rate of inflation, and the price of rubber, the major local commodity, are all relevant factors affecting the Thai's decision to travel to Mecca, and this explains why there was a major decline in their numbers between 1975 and 1978.

The language barrier is another problem, but the level of education has generally so risen that growing numbers of *hajjis,* especially the younger ones, are able to communicate with Muslims from all over the world in French, and perhaps Arabic, or, more likely, English. Many Muslim leaders might prefer communication to be more difficult because these young Muslims could be introduced not only to Muslim Brotherhood ideas but also to those of the Islamic revolution in Iran. And, indeed, it must be pointed out that even though the numbers of *hajjis* are increasing, making the pilgrimage is increasingly organized by national bureaucracies, such as LUTH (Lembaga Urusan dan Tabong Haji) in Malaysia. This means that individuals often go to Mecca in "packaged tours," staying with their fellow citizens during the ceremonies and returning with them as a group. The contact with foreign Muslims, therefore, may not be as great as we tend to think in terms of this rite of ingathering.

Relations Between Asian Muslim States and Western States

Islam is indirectly relevant to the international relations between Asian Muslim and Western states. It mainly affects people's attitudes, and, in this way, it can sometimes impinge on policy.

Muslim Attitudes

Take, first, the attitudes of Muslims who have come into contact with the West. For some Muslims, this contact provides a positive experience because it offers an opportunity to organize themselves into Islamic organizations. They may be denied this opportunity at home, but, even if they have it there, the Western experience, usually at university, has an important advantage. It allows them to interact with Muslims from many parts of the world and to read Islamic literature of all kinds that might be unavailable at home. The Federation of the Students' Islamic Societies (FOSIS) in Britain is particularly active and has had a notable impact on Malaysian students. In the view of one writer, it has instilled "a sense of Islamic consciousness" in them: "FOSIS' Annual Conferences and Winter Gatherings [draws] hundreds of students to such places as Stanswick and Manchester where they [are] able to 'enhance [their] spiritual understanding of Islam' through readings and discussions."[22] Parallel experiences in other Western countries can be found.

But the contact with Western societies can also prove to be a negative experience for Muslims. For example, students subjected to racist attack are not likely to forget or forgive it. It could be that just such a consideration would weigh heavily on their minds one day if they were to become important decision makers. The experience is more likely, though, to be less dramatic. For many, the moral and social climate of Western countries will simply confirm their inclination to regard the West as decadent and to try to revise Western models of politics and development for application to their own countries.

There is another way in which Muslim attitudes can be affected negatively by exposure to the West and Western organizations. This occurs when there is a feeling that Christian missionary work is a front for Western imperialism or, at least, that it is expanding to the detriment of Islam. This sentiment is often heard in Malaysia and especially in Indonesia, where at least one unpleasant incident occurred in which Muslims burned a new church in Aceh, a strongly conservative Muslim area of Indonesia. Public uproar was heard in 1978 when a Kuwaiti newspaper charged that Mrs. Suharto had become a convert and that her conversion was only the beginning of a Christianization drive. Others charged that Adam Malik, the former vice president, and many high military officials were perpetuating a Christian conspiracy to make secularism the official ideology of the state precisely in order to rob Islam of the central political role that its size would command in Indonesia. In response to attitudes such as these, the government issued a decree in August 1978 requiring foreign funding to be channeled through the Ministry of Religious Affairs and declaring that "the employment of foreigners in developing and propagating religion is limited."[23] The government issued a further decree in January 1979 that put severe restrictions on the mobility and freedom of action of groups seeking to proselytize among those already professing a religion.

To give some idea of the sensitivity of the issue, let me note that Islamic groups have assumed that these restrictions are directed against them and their *dakwah* activities. Thus the decrees have had little impact on assuaging anti-Christian sentiment, and this fact only redounds to the disadvantage of the Indonesian government, which, with its official secularism, is seen by many as tolerant of Christianity or, worse, encouraging Christianization and, at any rate, as firmly pro-Western.

Western Attitudes

With regard to the other side of the relationship, Western attitudes toward Muslims, there are also positive and negative experiences. Among the positive ones, one can say that the small Muslim community in Australia[24] helps to make Australians generally, and thus the government, more aware of the plight of their coreligionists in the Asian countries to the north. The effect on policy, however, is not demonstrable.

If we consider Japan broadly part of the West, a kind of anti-Orientalism has also emerged among Japanese intellectuals that is analogous to that which has come to dominate the discussions among Western intellectuals in the past few years. The writings of Anwar Abdel Malek and Edward Said on Orientalism have produced disquiet and even guilt in Western scholarly circles, but they and others have helped to advance the new orthodoxy of Islamic studies. The argument runs that Islam has been misunderstood, having been filtered through cultural prisms that made it seem inflexible and militant, and thus greater efforts must be expended to show Islam for what it is—adaptable and tolerant.

The Japanese, never far behind Western trends, are making the same types of arguments as those heard in the West: (1) Westerners think of Islam as inferior: "[T]he average Japanese supposes Islam to be the religion of devout nomads, and an irrational obstacle to modernization"; (2) this way of thinking is due to cultural bias: "[T]he Japanese perception of Islam is strongly colored by prejudice. . . . It is seen as representing an anti-modernist, obscurantist way of thought and as totally alien to Japanese culture"; (3) Western scholars have not helped much to improve the understanding of Islam: "Shumei Okawa, a rightwing thinker who played an important role in Japanese Islamic studies during the 1930s and 40s, started his study not from contact with the realities of life and thought among Asian peoples, but by trying to apply to Asia the ideal types he had formed in his own mind." Moreover, "Islamic studies in Japan are handicapped in a number of ways"—that is, no university has a department of Islamic studies, only one university has a department of Arabic, and the Japan Association for Islamic Studies has no money— "and these handicaps must be quickly overcome."[25]

A Japanese twist to these arguments emerges, however. It is that the Japanese view of Islam was derived from the Western one; therefore, what might be required is to go back to basics. Indeed, it is said, Japanese have an advantage in spite of themselves in the legacy of their historical lack of proximity to the Muslim world:

> Europe has been in direct contact with the Islamic world; it has competed with Islam and attempted to build its own history by dominating it. Consciously or unconsciously, Europeans have been unable to throw off their colonialist mentality in their understanding of Islam. It will be difficult for them to break out of their habit of dealing, from an ethnocentric viewpoint, only with that part of Islam that has been absorbed by Europe. But we Japanese have the comparative advantage of greater distance and are in a position to examine and evaluate from the perspective of world history. We can do this fairly and without prejudice, without forcing our own position on anyone.[26]

Much of this argument must be seen as self-serving when Japan's pre-World-War II and wartime Islamic strategy is taken into account. Rather than a distant and benignly uninterested Japan, there emerges from the historical record a Japan actively concerned to use and to impose on Islam for Japan's own imperial interests. By the early 1930s, the government was convinced of the value of supporting its own association with Islam in order to win and to influence Muslim friends in the region and beyond in the Middle East. To this end, the Society for Islamic Culture gained official sanction and financial support, published abroad, and widely distributed copies of the Quran; mosques were built in Kobe and Tokyo; Asian students were granted scholarships to study in Japan; and legations were established in Kabul and Tehran as well as in Ankara, Cairo, Baghdad, Beirut, and Jerusalem. More covertly, the Japanese tried to make inroads among both the Soviet and the Chinese Muslim populations in order to destabilize both countries. The famous Muslim trials of 1929, 1935, and 1939 established the Japanese role in instigating several ultimately unsuccessful revolts in the Soviet Union, and the Japanese supported first Abdul Kerim and then P'u-Kuang, both unworthy of this confidence, as leaders of the Muslim revolt of Xinjiang (Sinkiang). During the war, the Japanese argued that they were the liberators of Islam and thus hoped thereby not only to pacify their new Muslim subjects in the Dutch Indies, Malaya, Burma, and the Philippines, but also to encourage the anti-British nationalist movement in India. The Japanese foreign minister declared in the Diet in 1943, "Japan is ready to consecrate all efforts in order to free these victims of Anglo-American tyranny and to support with energy the Muslim's political and cultural aspirations."[27]

We have already seen how states with Muslim minorities of some magnitude, such as the Soviet Union and China, are able to use Islam as an instrument of diplomacy, but the Japanese case is remarkable for the same ability to use Islam without the benefit of a significant number of Muslims at home. According to one wartime American report, this was mostly due to the singular commitment of key figures in the elite to the advancement of Japan's sphere of influence, even if it meant converting to Islam themselves and holding out the hope of an Islamic Japan to Muslims abroad. Shintoism, the report maintained, would have presented no obstacle to such flirtations with Islam, even conversion. In any event, it was clear from the so-called Muslim Pact of the early years of this century that the promoters of Islam were above all patriots who saw Islam as a means to the realization of a greater Asian Japan. One of the adherents of the Muslim Pact, Tsuyoshi Inukai, became prime minister, and later the general policy came to have the support of such individuals as General Senjuro Hayashi, prewar minister of war and prime minister (and head of the Japanese Islamic Association, Dai Nippon Kaikyo Kyokai); General Sadao Araki, minister of education during the war and a confidant of Prime Minister Tojo; and General Iwane Matsui, once commander-in-chief of Japan's Central China army. The report concluded: "Small wonder, therefore, that with this kind of backing at the top Japan could count for the execution of this policy on a faithful and self-denying band of lieutenants, happy to devote their lives to the cause with the ecstatic abandon of a dervish."[28]

Whether or not such a happy band of devoted men actually existed, Japan was somewhat successful in attracting support from Muslim groups abroad. More important, it was largely successful in governing Muslim societies under occupation. This success was partly due to the relief of the locals at having their European governors removed. It was also due to the cleverness of the Japanese in what is now Indonesia, for example, in recognizing the utility of the *ulama* and in cultivating both these religious scholars and the more modern-educated intelligentsia in preference to the *priyayi* (Javanese adminstrative class) whom the Dutch had favored and everyone else despised. But the Japanese were not able entirely to restrain the heavy hand. They tried, for instance, to Nipponize Indonesia, insisting that people bow in the direction of the divine emperor's palace, to forbid the reading of the Quran and the teaching of Arabic, and to control the curricula and personnel of private Islamic schools.

Perhaps because of the partial recognition of this background rather than, as the earlier quotation suggests, no recognition of it, contemporary Japanese intellectuals are intent on contributing to the critical self-examination—what can only be called the *mea culpa*ism—among Orientalists today. In this manner, they are contributing to the significant change in the non-Muslims' perception of Islam that one can now begin to detect, and this intellectual lead must be seen as a positive experience.

Other contact between Westerners and Muslims, however, is often negative. For example, Western public opinion often turns against the presence of a minority in economically difficult times. This turn of public opinion is what has occurred in Europe with the rise of racism and resentment toward the guest-workers. It does not follow that such negative public attitudes translate into antagonistic state relations. They most often do not, but as Algerian President Chadli's visit to Paris in November 1983 suggests, the matter of how one's nationals are treated is never far below the surface of diplomacy and can affect the quality of communication between governments. Moreover, a government might take advantage of negative public attitudes to adopt a restrictive immigration or educational policy that, in turn, would harm a state-to-state relationship. There is no question that the British government's policy of raising tuition for foreign students, for example, produced outrage in Malaysia, from where many thousands of students go to Britain for higher studies, and prompted the Mahathir government to formulate a "buy British last" policy.

There might also be a negative effect from the failure of Western statesmen to take the Muslim countries on their own terms. It is not surprising that whatever interest these statesmen show in Asian Islam, it comes mainly from concern over the stability of such pro-Western regimes as

Indonesia, Thailand, and the Philippines, which, in varying degrees, face Muslim political agitation. Western leaders would not want these regimes undermined because they are strategically situated in an area where the Chinese, the Vietnamese, and the Soviets are all active (though in different ways and degrees) and supportive of local Communist groups. In the case of Indonesia, added concern stems from the possible loss of the presently secure supply line of oil—yet location, not oil as in the Middle East, primarily accounts for Western interest.

It is incumbent on statesmen and diplomats to think in terms of the worst; thus their thinking of Islam as a destabilizing factor is only to be expected. To *assume* that the worst will happen, however, might very well mean missing the fact that reality is somewhat different. Certainly a major block in Western perception in the past occurred when Westerners assumed that Islam was monolithic and monolithically anti-Western. But some evidence exists that the monolith might now have been replaced by a division of the world into good Islam and bad Islam. Good Islam is on "our" side, or at least tame; bad Islam is on "their" side, or at best destabilizing. Islam in Afghanistan is good, as it is in Pakistan; it is bad in Iran, as it seems to be in Indonesia and Thailand. Afghan Muslim fighters are said to be "freedom fighters" and to constitute a brave "resistance movement," but Thai or Filipino Muslims are "separatists" or "extremists." This kind of thinking could well lead Western decision makers to conclude that any attack or criticism of a pro-Western regime by an Islamic opposition means that the opposition is intent on working against Western interests.

Muslims themselves would find such logic amusing because many, if not most, of them envision their demands in terms of the promotion of social justice through Islamization rather than the rejection of the West itself or assistance lent to the West's political enemies. Some Muslims do speak of Westoxification *(gharbzadegi),* but such rhetoric is a direct response to both the overwhelming and often egregiously indiscreet physical and cultural presence of Westerners within Muslim societies and to the fact that Western money and arms have propped up what are seen as secularizing, even anti-Islamic, regimes such as that of the shah. For all of Khomeini's hyperbolic vitriol against the United States, the core of his reaction is based on what he saw as a simple and unjust lack of symmetry in the American-Iranian relationship during the time of the shah: "American cooks, mechanics, technical and administrative officials together with their families . . . enjoy legal immunity, but the *'ulama* of Islam, the preachers and servants of Islam, are . . . banished or imprisoned."[29] In this sense, anti-Westernism among some Muslim activists, although obviously emotionally based, does not necessarily mean that future cooperation, even amity, with Western states is unthinkable, unless, of course, Western decision makers by their own ideological predisposition lock themselves into a self-fulfilling prophecy.

Conclusion

The picture that emerges from these three categories of relationship is mixed. On the one hand, little concrete integration appears to exist among the Muslim states. There is clearly minimal economic integration. On the political level, Islam is either irrelevant, perhaps indirectly relevant—as it is in the relationship of Muslims with non-Muslim states generally—and thereby fails to stimulate greater Islamic cohesion because of the contrast with the non-Muslim world; or, on the other hand, Islam is a tool of individual foreign policymakers who use it to advance their own national interests rather than those of the general Islamic community. This last point is borne out by the national differences of attitude toward the Islamic revolution in Iran, the minority problem in the Philippines and in Thailand, and the role that the OIC was meant to play. With regard to the OIC, Pakistan, for instance, has wanted to develop it further, whereas Indonesia has remained largely aloof. But it must also be said that Pakistani enthusiasm has a great deal to do with its view of the OIC as a convenient foil to India's domination of the Non-Aligned Movement. By playing the Islamic card, a state such as China or the Soviet Union might be more successful than a state such as India in advancing its diplomatic goals. But, in any event, playing the Islamic card adds little to the idea of tangible political cooperation among Muslim states and is scarcely what Muslim visionaries have in mind when they talk of activity consistent with the idea of an Islamic commonwealth.

On the other hand, the picture shows that some substance is being added, almost imperceptibly and certainly gradually, to the idea of the *umma* (Islamic community). The spiritual longing for unity, not unlike the Welshman's *Hiraeth* (longing for the Celtic valleys), has always been important to individual Muslims, but in our era it has taken on a measure of institutional coherence. The OIC is certainly not paving the way to a federal or confederal union, but it is no more inept as an interstate institution than any other international organization—all of which, after all, are the instruments of their members. Moreover, it serves as a useful forum for discussion from which an international diplomatic consensus—a contemporary type of *ijma*—occasionally emerges, such as on Palestine and to some extent on Afghanistan. It may also help to reconcile members at odds with each other, as it did with Pakistan and Bangladesh. To this we must add the contribution it makes through the Islamic Solidarity Fund of supplementing the generosity of individual Arab states and encouraging *dakwah* activities, such as international Quran recitation competitions, and institutions such as RISEAP. These activities have done much to make Muslims more aware of each other and to familiarize them with the major intellectual currents of Islam today. Sometimes these ideas clash with each other, but even the debates that ensure from such clashes have helped to convince a great many Muslims for the first time in centuries that this is all part of healthy family life.

I recognize that, given the natural tendency of outsiders to see differences more clearly than similarities and disagreements more clearly than consensus, I run the risk of being seen to say that this second point counts for little. I do not mean that, however: I mean that there is a sense that Muslims have kin in every Muslim country and Muslim minority and that this sense of kinship is discernibly more pronounced today and growing. Moreover, it is understandable why greater cohesion has not taken place. European imperial intervention and the imposition of national institutions and ideologies, as well as the inevitable weaknesses of developing economies, have assured political divisions and skewed the direction of economic relations. Neoconservative opinion in the West tends to underrate these factors. Yet, it would be unrealistic to leave the impression that trade patterns will significantly change in the foreseeable future and that national differences will abate as the Islamic community becomes more defined and visible. The reality is that the world economic structure is weighted, to a considerable extent, against the developing Asian Muslim states and also that, as the Iran-Iraq War unmistakably shows, Islam has been nationalized. Muslims will be happy to acknowledge this first point, no doubt, but hardly the second.

The picture, then, is a mixed one, and, becuase of this, there is a danger for the social scientist, the involved Muslim, and the Westerner who are looking at it. The first may be tempted to conclude that Islamic solidarity is more symbolic than real, the second that an Islamic culture is emerging and gradually undermining the culture of nationalism, and the last that the unity that Muslims say is evolving is a challenge to the norms of the interstate system and, in particular, a threat to the West. The situation today seems to require of each a willingness to look at the whole. The social scientist should see the possibility of transnational forces undercutting, or reshaping, the institution of the nation-state. The Muslim should see the possibility that familiarity breeds contempt rather than greater harmony, perhaps leaving *hajjis* and migrant workers disliking their spiritual brothers when observed at close range; and he should see that existing in each country of the Muslim world is a powerful apparatus of state socialization that has successfully promoted national identities for half a century now or longer. For his part, the Westerner would do well to recognize that there is indeed an enormous reservoir of good will that Muslims can draw upon to increase their cooperation, but that, as this cooperation in fact occurs, there is no reason to assume that it will put them out of bounds of the prevailing interstate system or even that it will automatically mean ill will for the West.

Notes

1. There is the obvious difficulty of establishing what is "significant." Using aggregate population figures—if they can be found and are fairly reliable (which is most often not the

case)—does not put the minority in the context of the total population. Using a certain percentage of the population as a threshold figure is arbitrary. Common sense must be relied on.

2. The quotation is from the comments of the program organizer, Sayyid Faiyazuddin Ahmad, reported in *Islamic Vision*, 1, no. 1 (January 1980), p. 4.

3. For the text of Resolution 4/4 see OIC, *Declarations and Resolutions of Heads of State and Ministers of Foreign Affairs Conferences, 1969–1981*, p. 48.

4. Text of Resolution 18/5-P in *Declarations and Resolutions*, p. 100.

5. Interview, Datauk Musa Hitam, Kuala Lumpur, 26 November 1981.

6. In July 1981, a three-year agreement for the military training of the Iranians in the USSR was signed and Iranian-Soviet trade reached a volume of US$1.1 billion in 1981. See Shahram Chubin, "The Soviet Union and Iran," *Foreign Affairs* 61 (Spring 1983), 934, 937. In 1978, 5.5 percent of Iranian trade was with the Soviet bloc, whereas in 1982, it rose to 15 percent. On the clampdown on the Tudeh, see the *Times* [London], 9 February 1983, and for a Soviet reaction, see *New Times* (May 1983), p. 10. In May the Iranians also expelled eighteen Soviet diplomats: *Gulf Times*, 5–6 May 1983.

7. "Report of the Central Committee of the CPSU to the 26th Congress of the Communist Party of the Soviet Union and the Immediate Tasks of the Party in Home and Foreign Policy," in *Documents and Resolutions, the 26th Congress of the Communist Party of the Soviet Union* (Moscow: Novosti Press Agency Publishing House, 1981), p. 18. On the earlier attacks, see Hans Braker, "The Implications of the Islamic Question for Soviet Domestic and Foreign Policy," *Central Asian Survey*, 2 (July 1983), pp. 123–24.

8. In the early part of the war, the Soviets seemed to favor Iran, perhaps in recognition of the Tudeh's cooperation with the regime and perhaps out of a hope that Saddam Husayn would be toppled and replaced by a more compliant pro-Moscow leader. But the position began to change toward favoring Iraq in late 1982 when the Soviets undertook to supply arms on a large scale. See *Daily Telegraph*, 11 January 1983.

9. The *Times* [London], 24 March 1984; quotation in *International Herald Tribune*, 31 March–1 April 1984.

10. *International Herald Tribune*, 31 March–1 April 1984.

11. Peter Gowing, "Religion and Regional Cooperation: The Mindanao Problem and ASEAN," *Journal of Institute of Muslim Minority Affairs*, 4, nos. 1–2 (1982), p. 19.

12. Quoted from New China News Agency, 14 October 1975, in Raphael Israeli, "The Muslim Minority in the People's Republic of China," *Asian Survey*, 21 (August 1981), p. 910.

13. *Xinhua News Agency*, 30 January 1981; *Beijing Review* (29 March 1982), p. 9.

14. *Al-Anba'*, 18 August 1983.

15. Resolution 3/EOS in *Declarations and Resolutions*, p. 537.

16. *Mirror of Jehad* (publication of Jamiat-i-Islami, Afghanistan), 1, no. 4 (July/August 1982), pp. 8–9.

17. *Muslims of the Soviet East*, no. 3 (1982/1402 A.H.), p. 2.

18. L. Andreyev, "China's Middle East Policy," *International Affairs* (Moscow), no. 10 (October 1980), p. 52. A Muslim World League official from Saudi Arabia visited China in June 1981: *Xinhua News Agency*, 10 June 1981.

19. Interview with director, Middle East-1, Ministry of Foreign Affairs, Islamabad, 4 May 1982.

20. *Ibid.* I should point out, though, that a drawback—for both, considering the nature of the *hudud* penalties—is the crime that may result from the presence of foreign workers. Saudi Arabia claims that any increase in crime in the kingdom is due to these workers to whom it applies the traditional penalties. For example, a Filipino had his right hand cut off for theft in December 1982: *Arab News*, 24 December 1982.

21. *The Mindanao Cross*, 8 July 1972, quoted in Michael Mastura, "The Philippines State and 'Secularized' Muslim Concepts: Aspects and Problems," in *On the Codification of Muslim Customary (Adat) and Qur'anic Laws* (Manila, Muslim Information Center, 1976), p. 229.

22. Mohamad Abu Baker, "Islamic Revivalism and the Political Process in Malaysia," *Asian Survey,* 21 (October 1981), 1042–43.
23. Article 3 (1) of Decree No. 77 (1978) of Minister of Religious Affairs, in Ahmad von Denffer, *Indonesia: Government Decrees on Mission and Subsequent Developments,* Situation Report No. 2 (Leicester: Islamic Foundation, 1979).
24. The Australian Department of Immigration and Ethnic Affairs estimates that in 1981 there were 76,792 Muslims in Australia, but Muslim groups put the figure at 300,000. Most independent observers would accept that the number is roughly 100,000 today. See *Australian Foreign Affairs Record* (June 1983), p. 230; *The Bulletin* (1 November 1983), p. 29.
25. Yuzo Itagaki, "Perception of Different Cultures: The Islamic Civilization and Japan," in *The Islamic World and Japan: In Pursuit of Mutual Understanding* (Tokyo, Japan Foundation, 1981); quotations (in order) pp. 146, 143, 145.
26. *Ibid.,* p. 141. Quotation in Shuntaro Ito, "Islamic Civilization as Seen from Japan: A Non-Western View," in *The Islamic World and Japan,* p. 138. Also, generally see *Dialogue on Middle East and Japan: Symposium on Cultural Exchange* (Tokyo: Japan Foundation, 1977).
27. Quoted in Secret Docment No. 890, "Japanese Infiltration Among the Muslims Throughout the World," Office of Strategic Services, 15 May 1943, U.S. National Archives, Washington, D.C., p. 11.
28. *Ibid.,* p. 13.
29. Speech of 27 October 1964, precipitating his exile; reproduced in *Islam and Revolution: Writings and Declarations of Imam Khomeini,* trans. by Hamid Algar (Berkeley: Mizan Press, 1981), p. 186.

The Peoples of Islam

Muslim communities and individuals can be found in almost every country. A few countries may not appear on this chart owing to the small size of their Muslim communities. In some cases, also, the census data is highly uncertain.

Country	Total Population (000's)	% Muslim	Muslim Population (000's)
Afghanistan[1]	15,500	99%	15,345
Albania	3,000	70%	2,100
Algeria	22,200	99%	21,798
Bahrain	400	99%	396
Bangladesh	101,500	89%	90,335
Benin	4,000	16%	640
Bhutan	1,400	5%	70
Brunei	200	64%	128
Bulgaria	8,900	11%	1,014
Burkina Faso (Upper Volta)	7,000	44%	3,080
Burma	37,000	4%	1,480
Cameroon	9,600	22%	2,112
Central African Republic	2,622	8%	210
Chad	5,000	51%	2,550
China (PRC)[2]	1,042,000	1.44%	15,000
Comoros	424	99%	420
Cyprus	700	18.5%	130
Djibouti	300	90%	270
Egypt	48,000	91%	43,680
Ethiopia	36,000	35%	12,600
Fiji	700	8%	56
Gambia	650	87%	565
Ghana	14,500	15%	2,175
Greece	9,900	2.5%	250
Guinea	5,700	69%	3,933
Guinea-Bissau	850	38%	323
Guyana	800	9%	72
India	750,000	12%	90,000
Indonesia	165,000	85%	140,250
Iran	43,000	98%	42,140
Iraq	15,000	95%	14,250
Israel[3]	4,200	12.5%	525
Ivory Coast	9,500	25%	2,375
Jordan	2,900	93%	2,700
Kampuchea	6,200	2.4%	149
Kenya	20,000	6%	1,200
Kuwait	1,475	95%	1,416
Lebanon	3,000	57%	1,710
Liberia	2,200	21%	462
Libya	3,600	98%	3,528
Madagascar	10,000	2%	200
Malawi	7,100	16%	1,136
Malaysia	15,700	49%	7,693
Maldive Islands	200	100%	200
Mali	7,700	80%	6,160
Mauritania	1,900	100%	1,900

Country	Total Population (000's)	% Muslim	Muslim Population (000's)
Mauritius	1,000	17%	170
Mongolia	1,900	9.5%	180
Morocco	23,000	99%	22,770
Mozambique	13,800	13%	1,794
Nepal	17,000	5%	850
Niger	6,400	87.4%	5,593
Nigeria	89,000	45%	40,050
Oman	1,000	100%	1,000
Pakistan[4]	95,000	97%	92,150
Panama	2,000	4.5%	95
Philippines	56,000	5.6%	3,136
Qatar	280	96%	270
Reunion	500	2.4%	12
Rwanda	6,000	8.6%	516
Saudi Arabia	9,000	99%	8,910
Senegal	6,500	91%	5,915
Sierra Leone	3,600	40%	1,440
Singapore	2,600	18%	468
Somalia	5,000	99%	4,950
Soviet Union	277,000	18%	49,860
Sri Lanka	16,000	8%	1,280
Sudan	21,700	72%	15,624
Surinam	400	14%	57
Syria	10,200	88%	8,976
Tanzania	21,500	30%	6,450
Thailand	52,000	4%	2,080
Togo	2,900	16%	464
Trinidad & Tobago	1,200	6.5%	78
Tunisia	7,100	99%	7,029
Turkey	50,000	99%	49,500
Uganda	14,700	6.6%	970
United Arab Emirates	1,000	90%	900
U.S.A.[2]	238,900	0.6-1.2%	1,500-3,000
Yemen (North)	6,066	100%	6,066
Yemen (South)	2,200	100%	2,200
Yugoslavia	23,000	16%	3,700

Footnotes:
[1]Estimated 2.5 million Afghan refugees are included in Pakistan, not Afghanistan.
[2]Countries with less than 2% Muslim population have not been listed except for China and the U.S.A., which were included because their total populations are large enough so that their Muslim populations are numerically significant.
[3]Does not include Muslim populations of West Bank and Gaza, estimated at total of 1,100,000.
[4]Estimated 2 million expatriate Pakistan workers are included elsewhere, esp. in the Gulf countries, not in Pakistan figure.
Other Notes:
(1) The data listed above are for mid-1985.
(2) Figures for the Gulf states include workers as well as citizens.
(3) Sources include the Population Reference Bureau, the IBRD, the State Dept., other published and unpublished materials, and previous studies by AIIA. The principal source for Muslim populations was the second edition of *Muslim Peoples, A World Ethnographic Survey*, by Richard V. Weekes. (Greenwood Press, Westport, Conn., 1984).

GLOSSARY

ahl al-kitab—"People of the Book"; Jews, Christians, and others who have received revelation from God.

ashura—the "tenth" of the Muslim month of Muharram when Shi'i Muslims commemorate the martyrdom of Imam Husaynat Karbala.

ayatollah—"sign of God," title of a high-ranking Shi'i religious leader.

baya—oath of allegiance.

bida—innovation; deviation from Islamic tradition.

caliph—for Sunni Muslims, successor of Muhammad as leader of the Islamic community.

dar al-harb—"abode of war"; non-Islamic territory.

dar al-Islam—"abode of peace"; Islamic territory, that is, where Islamic law is in force.

dawah (dakwah)—"call to Islam," propagation of faith; more broadly, social welfare and missionary activities.

dhimmi—"protected" or covenanted people; non-Muslim citizen who is subject to poll tax *(jizya)*.

faqih (pl. *fuqaha*)—legal expert; jurisprudent.

fatwa—formal legal opinion or decision of a *mufti*.

fiqh—Islamic jurisprudence, religious laws.

hadd (pl. *hudud*)—"limits"; Quranically prescribed penalty or punishment for theft, adultery, fornication, false witness, and drinking intoxicants.

hadith—narrative report of the Prophet Muhammad's actions and sayings.

hajj—pilgrimage to Mecca.

hakimiyya—sovereignty of God.

halal—permitted, legal.

harijan—"children of God," term used by Mahatma Gandhi for the untouchables or outcasts of India.

harram—prohibited, unlawful.

hijra—emigration (flight) of Muhammad from Mecca to Medina in A.D. 622 where he established the rule of a Muslim community/state.

ibadat—"worship"; regulations in Islamic law governing religious observances.

ijma—consensus, or agreement of the community, which is the source of Islamic law.

ijtihad—independent analysis or interpretation of Islamic law.

imam—"leader," prayer leader. In Shi'i Islam refers to successor of the Prophet Muhammad, descended from Ali, who governs as a divinely inspired religio-political leader of the Islamic community.

imam jumah—Friday mosque prayer leader.

islah—reform.

islam—submission to will of God.

jahiliyyah—period of ignorance, that is pre-Islamic Arabia.

jamaat—party, society.

jihad—"strive, effort, struggle" to follow Islam. Includes defense of the faith, armed struggle, or holy war.

jizya—poll tax on *dhimmi* (non-Muslims).

kafir—nonbeliever, infidel.

khalifah—"successor"; *caliph* in Sunni Islam.

kharaj—land tax.

khati—see *quadi*.

khalirat—close proximity between the sexes in a manner unacceptable to Islamic law.

khums—"⅕"; tax, one fifth of annual income paid directly to religious authorities in Shiah Islam.

madrasa—religious school, seminary.

mahdi—divinely guided leader who is to come in the future to establish God's rule on earth, a socially just society.

majlis-i-shura—originally consultative body that selected *caliph;* now used for advisory council or parliament.

maktabi—of or pertaining to Khomeini's ideological line.

marja-i-taqlid—"source of emulation"; supreme authority on law in Shi'a Islam whose interpretation should be followed. Title is conferred by the people on the most distinguished clergymen of the period.

millat—"community"; nation.

muamalat—human relationships; Islamic laws (e.g., civil, criminal, family) governing social relations.

mudaraba—profit/loss sharing in economic transactions, used in Islamic banking.

mufti—specialist on Islamic law, competent to deliver a *fatwa,* that is, legal interpretation/brief.

mujaddid—one who brings about renewal *(tajdid)* of Islam.

mujahid (pl. *mujahidin*)—soldier of God.

mujtahid—one who exercises *ijtihad,* that is, interprets Islam.

mullah—local religious leader or preacher.

nizam—system, for example, *nizam-i-Islam,* Islamic system of government.

purdah—seclusion of women.

qadi—judge who administers shariah law.

qadhf—false accusation of adultery.

qiyas—juristic reasoning by analogy, source of Islamic law.

riba—usury; bank interest.

salaf—pious ancestors, early Islamic community.

salat—official prayer or worship observed five times daily.

shahadah—confession or profession of faith: "There is no god but Allah and Muhammad is His Prophet/Messenger."

shahid—martyr ("witness" to faith).

shariah—Islamic law.

shirk—idolatry or associationism.

sufi—a follower of sufism, Islamic mysticism.

shura—consultation.

sunnah—normative practice or exemplary behavior of Muhammad.

tajdid—revival; renewal.

taqlid—unquestioned imitation or following of tradition.

tawhid—unity of God (radical monotheism), absolute sovereignty over the universe.

taziyah—a passion play in Shi'a Islam that reenacts the tragedy at Karbala, the martyrdom of Husayn and his forces.

ulama—(learned) religious scholars or experts.

ummah—the Muslim community.

ushr—religious tax on agricultural land.

usul al-fiqh—principles of Islamic jurisprudence, the sources of Islamic law (Quran, Sunnah of Prophet, consensus [*ijma*], analogical reasoning [*qiyas*]).

vilayat-i-faqih—guardianship or government by the religious authority, legal expert.

waqf—endowment of property for religious purposes, such as building of mosques, schools, hospitals.

zakat—annual alms tax or tithe of 2.5% levied on wealth.

zina—adultery.

zulm—oppression; sin.

SELECTED BIBLIOGRAPHY

Abrahamian, Ervand. *Iran Between Two Revolutions*. Princeton: Princeton University Press, 1982.

Ahmad, Aijaz. "400 Year War—Moro Struggle in the Philippines," *Southeast Asia Chronicle*, No. 82 (February 1982).

Ahmad, Aziz. *Islamic Modernism in India and Pakistan, 1857–1964*. Oxford: Oxford University Press, 1967.

Ajami, Fouad. *The Arab Predicament*. New York: Cambridge University Press, 1982.

Akhavi, Sharough, *Religion and Politics in Contemporary Iran*. Albany: SUNY Press, 1980.

Akiner, Shirin. *Islamic Peoples of the Soviet Union*. London: Kegan Paul, 1983.

Algar, Hamid (tr.). *Islam and Revolution: Writings and Declarations of Imam Khomeini*. Berkeley: Mizan Press, 1981.

Arjomand, Said Amir, ed. *From Nationalism to Revolutionary Islam*. Albany: SUNY Press, 1984.

Ayoob, Mohammed, ed. *The Politics of Islamic Reassertion*. New York: St. Martin's, 1981.

Azari, Farah, ed. *Women of Iran*. London: Ithaca Press, 1983.

Bakhash, Shaul. *The Reign of the Ayatollahs*. New York: Basic Books, 1984.

Banuazizi, Ali, and Weiner, Myron, eds. *The State, Religion, and Ethnic Politics: Afghanistan, Iran and Pakistan*. Syracuse: Syracuse University Press, 1986.

Behbehani, Hashim, S. H. *China's Foreign Policy in the Arab World, 1955–75*. London and Boston: Kegan Paul International, 1981.

Benard, Cheryl, and Khalilzad, Zalmay. *"The Government of God": Iran's Islamic Republic*. New York: Columbia University Press, 1984.

Benda, Harry J. *Continuity and Change in Southeast Asia*. New Haven: Yale University Southeast Asian Studies, 1972.

————. *The Crescent and the Rising Sun: Indonesian Islam Under the Japanese Occupation 1942–1945*. The Hague and Bandung: W. van Hoeve Ltd., 1958.

Bennigsen, Alexandre, and Lemercier-Quelquejay, Chantal. *Islam in the Soviet Union*. London: Pall Mall Press, 1967.

Carrere d'Encausse, Helene. *Decline of an Empire: The Soviet Socialist Republics in Revolt*. Trans. Martin Sokolinsky and Henry A. LaFarge. New York: Harper & Row, 1981.

Chelkowski, Peter J., ed. *Taziyeh: Ritual and Drama in Iran*. New York: New York University Press, 1979.

Dawisha, Adeed, ed. *Islam in Foreign Policy*. Cambridge and New York: Cambridge University Press, 1983.

Donohue, John, J., and Esposito, John L., eds. *Islam in Transition: Muslim Perspectives*. New York: Oxford University Press, 1982.

Dreyer, June Teufel. *China's Forty Millions: Minority Nationalities and National Integration in the People's Republic of China.* Cambridge: Harvard University Press, 1976.

Eberhard, Wolfram. *China's Minorities: Yesterday and Today.* Belmont, Calif.: Wadsworth, 1982.

Enayat, Hamid. *Modern Islamic Political Thought.* Austin: University of Texas Press, 1982.

Endicott, K. *An Analysis of Malay Magic.* Oxford: Clarendon Press, 1970.

Esposito, John L., ed. *Islam and Development.* Syracuse: Syracuse University Press, 1982.

————. *Islam and Politics.* Syracuse: Syracuse University Press, 1984.

————., ed. *Voices of Resurgent Islam.* New York: Oxford University Press, 1983.

Fischer, Michael M. J. *Iran: From Religious Discourse to Revolution.* Cambridge: Harvard University Press, 1980.

Gellner, Ernest. *Muslim Society.* New York: Cambridge University Press, 1981.

George, T. J. S. *Revolt in Mindanao: The Rise of Islam in Philippine Politics.* Kuala Lumpur: Oxford University Press, 1980.

Gowing, Peter Gordon. *Muslim Filipinos—Heritage and Horizon.* Quezon City: New Day Publishers, 1979.

Gowing, Peter Gordon, and McAmis, Robert, eds. *The Muslim Filipinos.* Manila: Solidaridad Publishing House, 1974.

Haddad, Yvonne Y. *Contemporary Islam and the Challenge of History.* Albany: State University of New York Press, 1982.

————., ed. *The Islamic Impact.* Syracuse: Syracuse University Press, 1984.

Hassan, Mohammad Kamal. *Contemporary Muslim Religio-Political Thought in Indonesia: The Response to "New Order Modernization."* Kuala Lumpur: Dewan Bahasa dan Pustaka, 1980.

Hooker, M. B., ed. *Islam in South-East Asia.* Leiden: E. J. Brill, 1983.

Ibrahim, Ahmad, ed. *Readings on Islam in Southeast Asia.* Institute for Southeast Asian Studies. Forthcoming.

Israeli, R. *The Crescent in the East Islam in Asia Minor.* London and Dublin: Curzon Press Ltd.; and Atlantic Highlands, N.J.: Humanities Press Inc., 1982.

Israeli, Raphael, and Johns, Anthony H., eds. *Islam in Asia,* Vol. 3, *Southeast and East Asia.* Jerusalem: Magnes Press, Hebrew University, 1984.

Johns, A. H. "Islam in Southeast Asia, Reflections and New Directions," *Indonesia* (Cornell) No. 19, 21–52.

Keddie, Nikki R. *Iran: Religion, Politics and Society.* London: Frank Cass, 1980.

————. *Roots of Revolution: An Interpretive History of Modern Iran.* New Haven: Yale University Press, 1981.

Keddie, Nikki R., and Beck, Lois, eds. *Women in the Muslim World.* Cambridge: Harvard University Press, 1978.

Keddie, Nikki R., and Bovine, M., eds. *Modern Iran.* Albany: SUNY Press, 1981.

Keddie, Nikki R., and Cole, Juan, R. I. *Shiism and Social Protest.* New Haven, Yale University Press, 1986.

Lambton, Ann K. S. *State and Government in Medieval Islam.* Oxford: Oxford University Press, 1981.

Lubin, Nancy. *Labour and Nationality in Soviet Central Asia: An Uneasy Compromise.* Princeton: Princeton University Press, 1985.

Majul, Cesar A. *Muslims in the Philippines.* Quezon City: University of the Philippines Press for the Asian Center, 1973.

Mastura, Michael O. *Muslim Filipino Experience: A Collection of Essays.* Manila: Ministry of Muslim Affairs, 1984.

Means, G. Malaysia: "Islam in a Plural Society," in C. Caldarela, ed., *Religion and Societies: Asia and the Middle East.* Boston: Mouton, 1982.

————. *Malaysian Politics.* London: Hodder and Stoughton, 1976.

————. "The Role of Islam in the Political Development of Malaysia," *Comparative Politics* 2 (1969), 264–84.

————. "Special Rights as a Strategy for Development: The Case of Malaysia," *Comparative Politics* 5 (1972), 29–61.

Milne, R., and Mauzy, D. *Politics and the Government of Malaysia.* Vancouver: University of British Columbia Press, 1980.

Momen, Moojan. *Shi'ite Islam.* New Haven: Yale University Press, 1985.

Mortimer, Edward. *Faith and Power.* New York: Random House, 1982.

Mottahedeh, Roy. *The Mantle of the Prophet.* New York: Simon & Schuster, 1985.

Muslim Communities in Non-Muslim States. London: Islamic Council of Europe, 1980.

Nagata, J. *From Peasant Roots to Religious Values: The Reflowering of Malaysian Islam.* Vancouver: University of British Columbia Press, 1985.

Nashat, Guity, ed. *Women and Revolution in Iran.* Boulder, Col.: Westview Press, 1983.

Noble, Lela Garner. "Ethnicity and Philippine-Malaysian Relations," *Asian Survey,* 15/S (May 1975), 453–72.

Noble, Lela Garner, and Suhkre, Astri, "Muslims in the Philippines and Thailand," in Suhkre and Noble, eds., *Ethnic Conflict in International Relations.* New York: Praeger, 1977.

Noer, Deliar. *The Modernist Muslim Movement in Indonesia.* Singapore: Oxford University Press, 1973.

Piscatori, James, ed. *Islam in the Political Process.* Cambridge and New York: Cambridge University Press, 1983; reprinted 1984.

————. *Islam in a World of Nation States.* Cambridge: Cambridge University Press, 1986.

Poole, Fred, and Vanzi, Max. *Revolution in the Philippines: The United States in a Hall of Cracked Mirrors.* New York: McGraw-Hill, 1984.

Rahman, Fazlur. *Islam,* 2nd ed. Chicago: University of Chicago Press, 1979.

————. *Islam and Modernity.* Chicago: University of Chicago Press, 1982.

Ratnam, K. J. *Communalism and the Political Process in Malaya.* Kuala Lumpur: University of Malaya, 1965.

Roff, W. *The Origins of Malay Nationalism.* New Haven: Yale University Press, 1967.

Rosenthal, E. *Islam in the Modern National State.* Cambridge: Cambridge University Press, 1965.

Smith, Jane, ed. *Women in Contemporary Muslim Societies.* Lewisburg, Pa.: Bucknell University Press, 1980.

Snodgrass, D. *Inequality and Economic Development in Malaysia.* Kuala Lumpur: Oxford, 1980.

Steinberg, David Joel. *The Philippines: A Singular and Plural Place.* Boulder, Col.: Westview Press, 1982.

————, ed. *In Search of Southeast Asia: A Modern History.* New York: Praeger, 1976.

Suryadinata, Leo. *Political Parties and the 1982 General Election in Indonesia.* Singapore: Institute for Southeast Asian Studies, 1982.

Tabataba'i, Muhammad H. *Shi'ite Islam,* 2nd ed. Albany: SUNY Press, 1979.

Tan, Samuel K. *The Filipino Muslim Armed Struggle, 1900–1972.* Manila: Filipinas Foundation, Inc., 1977.

Voll, John Obert. *Islam, Continuity and Change in the Modern World.* Boulder, Col.: Westview Press, 1982.

von der Mehden, F. "Islamic Resurgence in Malaysia," in J. Esposito, *Islam and Development.* Syracuse: Syracuse University Press, 1980.

Wang, C. *Malaysia.* New York: Praeger, 1964.

Weiss, Anita, ed. *Islamic Reassertion in Pakistan.* Syracuse: Syracuse University Press, 1986.

Winzeler, R. "Modern Religion, Society and Politics in Kelantan." Ph.D. dissertation. Chicago: University of Chicago, 1970.

Wright, Robin. *Sacred Rage.* New York: Simon & Schuster, 1985.

CONTRIBUTORS

SHAHROUGH AKHAVI is Professor, Department of Government and International Studies, University of South Carolina, in Columbia. Among his publications are *Religion and Politics in Contemporary Iran: Clergy-State Relations in the Pahlavi Period* (1980: State University of New York Press, Albany); "Clerical Politics in Iran Since 1979" in *The Iranian Revolution and the Islamic Republic: New Assessment,* Nikki Keddie and Eric Hoogland, eds. (1982: The Middle East Institute); and numerous articles for such publications as *Comparative Studies in Society and History, Iranian Studies,* and the *Middle East Journal.*

JOHN L. ESPOSITO is Professor, Department of Religious Studies, College of the Holy Cross in Worcester, Massachusetts. His publications include *Islam and Politics* (1984: Syracuse University Press); *Voices of Resurgent Islam* (1983: Oxford University Press); *Women in Muslim Family Law* (1982: Syracuse University Press); with John J. Donahue, *Islam in Transition* (1982: Oxford University Press), and *Islam and Development* (1982: Syracuse University Press).

KEMAL A. FARUKI, Barrister-at-Law, is a member of the Karachi Bar and Advocate of the Supreme Court of Pakistan. He was, until 1980, Professor of Islamic Jurisprudence, S. M. Government Law College, University of Karachi. He has authored six books on Islamic law and constitutional matters, including *Islamic Jurisprudence* (1962, rev. ed. 1975), *The Constitutional and Legal Role of the Umma* (1979), and *Islam Today and Tomorrow* (1974).

ASHRAF GHANI is Assistant Professor, Department of Anthropology, Johns Hopkins University. His published articles include "Islam and State-Building in a Tribal Society: Afghanistan 1880–1901" in *Modern Asian Studies* (1978) and "Afghanistan's Sorrow and Pity" in *Natural History* (1980). Ashraf Ghani is currently completing *Production and Domination: Afghanistan 1747–1901,* to be published by Columbia University Press.

ANTHONY H. JOHNS is currently head of the Southeast Asia Centre, Faculty of Asian Studies, A.N.U. He has worked for considerable periods in Egypt and Indonesia, and in 1985 was a Fellow of the Institute for Advanced Studies, the Hebrew University of Jerusalem. His academic interests are Quranic exegesis, with special reference to the work of Fakhr Al-Bin-Razi, and Islamic intellectual life and culture in Southeast Asia.

DAVID D. NEWSOM is Associate Dean of the School of Foreign Service and Director of the Institute for the Study of Diplomacy at Georgetown University. Ambassador Newsom began his career as a journalist and then joined the Foreign Service, having a variety of postings abroad and in Washington. He was Ambassador to Libya (1965–69), Assistant Secretary for African Affairs (1969–74), Ambassador to Indonesia (1974–77), Ambassador to the

Philippines (1977–78), and Under Secretary of State for Political Affairs (1978–81).

LELA GARNER NOBLE is Professor of Political Science and Associate Academic Vice President for Faculty Affairs, San Jose State University. She is the author of *Philippine Policy Toward Sabah: A Claim to Independence* (1977: University of Arizona Press); and co-editor with Astri Suhrke of *Ethnic Conflict and International Relations* (1977: Praeger). She has written numerous articles on Islam in the Philippines, including "Muslim Separatism in the Philippines, 1972–1981: The Making of a Stalemate" in *Asian Survey* (1981).

JAMES P. PISCATORI is a Fellow, Department of International Relations at Australian National University and was formerly with the Royal Institute of International Affairs in London. Professor Piscatori is the editor of *Islam in the Political Process* (1983: Cambridge University Press) and author of *Islam in a World of Nation States* (forthcoming, 1986: Cambridge University Press). He has contributed to a number of books, including "The Roles of Islam in Saudi Arabia's Political Development" in *Islam and Development,* John Esposito, ed. (1980: Syracuse University Press) and "Islamic Values and National Interest: The Foreign Policy of Saudi Arabia" in *Islam in Foreign Policy,* A. Dawisha, ed. (1983: Cambridge University Press).

SYED SHAHABUDDIN is editor of *Muslim India* and since 1984 has been President of the All India Muslim Majlis-e-Mushawarat (the apex body of Muslim organizations in India). He is also General Secretary of the Janata Party and was a member of the Rajya Sabha (Upper House of the Indian Parliament) until 1984.

JOHN OBERT VOLL is Professor of History and Coordinator of Religious Studies at the University of New Hampshire where he first joined the faculty in 1965. Professor Voll is the author of *Historical Dictionary of the Sudan* (1978: Scarecrow Press); *Islam: Continuity and Change in the Modern World* (1982: Westview); and *The Sudan: A Profile in Unity and Diversity* (1985: Westview).

FRED R. VON DER MEHDEN is Albert Thomas Professor of Political Science at Rice University in Houston, Texas. His books include *Religion and Nationalism in Southeast Asia* (1963: University of Wisconsin Press); *Politics of the Developing Nations* (1964, rev. 1969: Prentice-Hall); *Issues of Political Development* (1967, rev. 1974: Prentice-Hall); and *Comparative Political Violence* (1973: Prentice-Hall).

THEODORE P. WRIGHT, JR., is Professor of Political Science at the Graduate School of Public Affairs, State University of New York at Albany. His more than thirty articles have appeared in numerous American and Indian journals; they include "Indian Muslim Refugees in the Politics of Pakistan" in *Journal of Commonwealth and Comparative Politics* (1974); and "Muslims and the 1977 Indian Elections: A Watershed?" in *South Asian Politics and Religion,* Donald E. Smith, ed. (1966: Princeton University Press); and "Identity of Muslims in Modern India: The Socio-Political Aspect" in *Muslim Identity in India* (1977: Kalamazoo, Michigan).